# DUNGEON MASTER'S GUIDE®

## ROLEPLAYING GAME CORE RULES

James Wyatt

# CREDITS

**D&D® 4th Edition Design Team**
Rob Heinsoo, Andy Collins, James Wyatt

**D&D 4th Edition Final Development Strike Team**
Bill Slavicsek, Mike Mearls, James Wyatt

*Dungeon Master's Guide* **Design**
James Wyatt

*Dungeon Master's Guide* **Development**
Andy Collins, Mike Mearls, Stephen Radney-MacFarland,
Peter Schaefer, Stephen Schubert

*Dungeon Master's Guide* **Editing**
Michele Carter, Jennifer Clarke Wilkes, Julia Martin

*Dungeon Master's Guide* **Managing Editing**
Kim Mohan

**Additional Design and Development**
Richard Baker, Greg Bilsland, Logan Bonner, Bart Carroll,
Michele Carter, Jennifer Clarke Wilkes, Bruce R. Cordell,
Jeremy Crawford, Jesse Decker, Michael Donais, Robert
Gutschera, Gwendolyn F. M. Kestrel, Peter Lee, Julia Martin,
Kim Mohan, David Noonan, Christopher Perkins,
Matthew Sernett, Chris Sims, Ed Stark, Rodney Thompson,
Rob Watkins, Steve Winter, Chris Youngs

**Director of R&D, Roleplaying Games/Book Publishing**
Bill Slavicsek

**D&D Story Design and Development Manager**
Christopher Perkins

**D&D System Design and Development Manager**
Andy Collins

**D&D Senior Art Director**
Stacy Longstreet

**Cover Illustration**
Wayne Reynolds (front), Brian Hagan (back)

*Special Thanks to Brandon Daggerhart, keeper of Shadowfell*

**Graphic Designers**
Keven Smith, Leon Cortez, Emi Tanji

**Additional Graphic Design**
Karin Powell, Mari Kolkowski, Shauna Wolf Narciso,
Ryan Sansaver

**Concept Artists**
Rob Alexander, Dave Allsop, Christopher Burdett,
Adam Gillespie, Lars Grant-West, David Griffith, Lee Moyer,
William O'Connor

**Interior Illustrations**
Rob Alexander, Steve Argyle, Wayne England, Jason
Engle, David Griffith, Espen Grundetjern, Brian Hagan,
Ralph Horsley, Howard Lyon, Lee Moyer, William O'Connor,
Wayne Reynolds, Dan Scott, Ron Spears, Chris Stevens,
Anne Stokes, Eva Widermann

**Cartography**
Mike Schley

**D&D Brand Team**
Liz Schuh, Scott Rouse, Sara Girard, Kierin Chase,
Martin Durham, Linae Foster

**Publishing Production Specialists**
Angelika Lokotz, Erin Dorries, Moriah Scholz,
Christopher Tardiff

**Prepress Manager**
Jefferson Dunlap

**Imaging Technicians**
Travis Adams, Bob Jordan, Sven Bolen

**Production Manager**
Cynda Callaway

**Building on the Design of Previous Editions by**
E. Gary Gygax, Dave Arneson (1st Edition and earlier);
David "Zeb" Cook (2nd Edition); Jonathan Tweet, Monte Cook,
Skip Williams, Richard Baker, Peter Adkison (3rd Edition)

*Dedicated to the memory of E. Gary Gygax*

620-21750720-001 EN
9 8 7 6 5 4 3 2 1
First Printing: June 2008
ISBN: 978-0-7869-4880-2

**U.S., CANADA, ASIA, PACIFIC,
& LATIN AMERICA**
Wizards of the Coast, Inc.
P.O. Box 707
Renton WA 98057-0707
+1-800-324-6496

**EUROPEAN HEADQUARTERS**
Hasbro UK Ltd
Caswell Way
Newport, Gwent NP9 0YH
GREAT BRITAIN
Please keep this address for your records

**WIZARDS OF THE COAST, BELGIUM**
't Hofveld 6D
1702 Groot-Bijgaarden
Belgium
+32 2 467 3360

VISIT OUR WEBSITE AT WWW.WIZARDS.COM/DND

# CONTENTS

# CHAPTER 1

# How to Be a DM

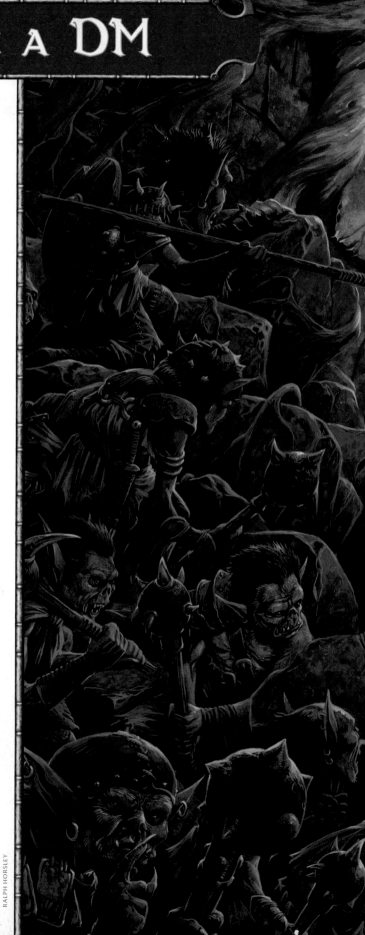

MOST GAMES have a winner and a loser, but the DUNGEONS & DRAGONS Roleplaying Game is fundamentally a cooperative game. The Dungeon Master (DM) plays the roles of the antagonists in the adventure, but the DM isn't playing against the player characters (PCs). Although the DM represents all the PCs' opponents and adversaries–monsters, nonplayer characters (NPCs), traps, and the like–he or she doesn't want the player characters to fail any more than the other players do. The players all cooperate to achieve success for their characters. The DM's goal is to make success taste its sweetest by presenting challenges that are just hard enough that the other players have to work to overcome them, but not so hard that they leave all the characters dead.

At the table, having fun is the most important goal–more important than the characters' success in an adventure. It's just as vital for everyone at the table to cooperate toward making the game fun for everyone as it is for the player characters to cooperate within the adventure.

This chapter includes the following sections.

✦ **The Gaming Group:** Here you learn what components you need to play the D&D game.

✦ **The Players:** Understand your players, help them to assemble as a successful party of player characters, and run a game they want to play.

✦ **The Dungeon Master:** Understand the role of a DM in the game and what kind of game you want to make.

✦ **Table Rules:** Consider table rules you should agree on–guidelines for you and the players' behavior during the game.

RALPH HORSLEY

What do you need to play the D&D game? The heart of a gaming group is the players, who roleplay their characters in adventures set forth by the Dungeon Master. Every player contributes to the fun of the game and helps bring the fantasy world to life. Beyond players, to play the D&D game you need space to play, rulebooks, and supplies such as dice, paper, pencils, a battle grid, and miniatures. Your game can be as simple as that, or you can add items for your convenience (character sheets, snacks) or to enhance the game with digital components (check out www.dndinsider.com).

## PLAYERS

D&D players fill two distinct roles in a D&D game: characters and Dungeon Master. These roles aren't mutually exclusive, and a player can roleplay a character today and run an adventure for the characters tomorrow. Although everyone who plays the game is technically a player, we usually refer to players as those who run the player characters.

D&D is a game of the imagination, all about fantastic worlds and creatures, magic, and adventure. You find a comfortable place where you can spread out your books and maps and dice, and you get together with your friends to experience a group story. It's like a fantastic action movie, and your characters are the stars. The story unfolds as your characters make decisions and take actions—what happens next is up to you!

**Six People in a Group:** The rules of the game assume that you're playing in a group of six people: the DM and five other players.

**More or Fewer than Six:** Playing with four or six other players is easy with minor adjustments. Groups that are smaller or larger require you to alter some of the rules in this book to account for the difference.

With only two or three characters in a party, you don't have the different **roles** covered (see "Covering the Character Roles" on page 10, and "Character Role" on page 15 of the *Player's Handbook)*, and it's

harder to get through combat encounters even if the encounter is scaled down for your smaller group. With more than six characters, the group gets unwieldy and tends to split into subgroups. We give you some tips and tricks for managing a large group in "Group Size" in Chapter 2 (page 31), but if your group gets too large, you might want to split into two or more groups that play at different times.

## THE DUNGEON MASTER

One player has a special role in a D&D game. The Dungeon Master controls the pace of the story and referees the action along the way. You can't play a game of D&D without a DM.

**What Does the DM Do?:** The Dungeon Master has many hats to wear in the course of a game session. The DM is the rules moderator, the narrator, a player of many different characters, and the primary creator of the game's world, the campaign, and the adventure.

**Who Should Be the DM?:** Who should be the Dungeon Master for your gaming group? Whoever wants to be! The person who has the most drive to pull a group together and start up a game often ends up being the DM by default, but that doesn't have to be the case.

**Dungeon Masters Can Partner, Trade Off, or Change:** The role of Dungeon Master doesn't have to be a singular, ongoing, campaign-long appointment. Many successful gaming groups switch DMs from time to time. Either they take turns running campaigns, switching DM duty every few months, or they take turns running adventures and switch every few weeks.

## SUPPLIES

What do you need to play D&D?

### WHAT YOU NEED TO PLAY
+ A place to play
+ Rulebooks
+ Dice
+ Paper and pencils
+ Battle grid or *D&D Dungeon Tiles*
+ Dungeon Master's Screen
+ *D&D Miniatures*

### USEFUL ADDITIONS
+ Character sheets
+ Snacks
+ Laptop computer, PDA, smart phone, or digital camera
+ *D&D Insider*

---

### TIPS FROM THE PROS

In my years of playing D&D, I've played in college classrooms, in a school and a public library, in my parents' basement and in their dining room, sprawled out on couches and crammed in at too-small tables, at my house and at many different friends' houses, and in company meeting rooms. White boards (and the blackboard in that classroom) are quite useful. In general, I prefer a more private spot where we can celebrate an important critical hit with appropriate volume.

—James Wyatt

**A Place to Play:** The bare minimum of space you need to play D&D is room for everyone in your group to sit. Most likely, you also want a table for everyone to sit around. A table holds your battle grid and miniature figures, gives you a place to roll dice and write on character sheets, and holds piles of books and papers. You can pull chairs around a dining table or sit in recliners and easy chairs around a coffee table within reach. It's possible to run a game without a table for the battle grid, but combat runs more easily if everyone can see where everything is.

**Rulebooks:** As DM, you need a copy of all the rulebooks you're going to use to play. At a minimum, that should be a copy of the *Player's Handbook*, the *Dungeon Master's Guide*, and the *Monster Manual*. Your players each need the *Player's Handbook*, since every character's broad assortment of powers, feats, and items means the game runs more smoothly if all the players bring their own copies of the *Player's Handbook* to the table.

**Dice:** You need a full assortment of dice. It's helpful to have at least three of each kind. (That might seem to be a lot, but when you have to roll 4d12 + 10 fire damage for the ancient red dragon's breath weapon, you'll be glad you have more than one d12.) A lot of powers use multiple d6s, d8s, and d10s. Each player at the table should also have a set of polyhedral dice, since most players get very attached to their dice.

**Paper and Pencils:** Everyone should have easy access to a pencil and paper. During every round of combat, you need to keep track of hit points, attack penalties and defense bonuses, use of powers, spent action points, the consequences of conditions, and other information. You and your players need to take notes about what has happened in the adventure, and players need to make note of experience points (XP) and treasure their characters acquire.

**Battle Grid:** A battle grid is very important for running combat encounters, for reasons outlined in the *Player's Handbook*. D&D Dungeon Tiles, a vinyl wet-erase mat with a printed grid, a gridded whiteboard, a cutting mat, or large sheets of gridded paper—any of these can serve as a battle grid. The grid should be marked in 1-inch squares. Ideally, it should measure at least 8 inches by 10 inches, and preferably 11 inches by 17 inches or larger.

**Dungeon Master's Screen:** This accessory puts a lot of important information in one place—right in front of you—and also provides you with a way to keep players from seeing the dice rolls you make and the notes you refer to during play.

**Miniatures:** You need something to place on the battle grid to mark the position of each character and creature in an encounter. *D&D Miniatures* are ideal. These prepainted plastic figures are three-dimensional representations of the actual people and monsters involved in the battle.

**Character Sheets:** All the players need some way to record important information about their characters. You can use plain paper, but a character sheet photocopied from the one printed in the back of the *Player's Handbook* is more helpful—or use the D&D *Character Sheets* product. Some players put their powers on index cards instead of their character sheets to make it easier to keep track of which ones they've used.

**Snacks:** Snacks are not a necessary component of a D&D game, but they can be an important one. Food and beverages at the table help keep everyone's energy up. If you start your game sessions in the evening after work or school, you might want to eat dinner before you play. You can get all the socializing out of the way while you eat, and hunker down for some serious die-rolling once everyone is finished.

**Computers, PDAs, Smart Phones, and Digital Cameras:** If you own a laptop computer, a personal digital assistant (PDA), or a smart phone, you can use it to keep notes and track items instead of paper and pencils. Players can use their computers to store and update copies of their character sheet in a number of file formats, and you can keep notes about your campaign and encounters you've built. You can also use a digital camera as an easy way to keep track of a fight that you have to stop in the middle of. You just look at the picture to replicate the positions of the player characters and monsters to resume the battle. You could also snap pictures of the game in progress to post in your blog or website to share with members of the group or their friends.

**D&D Insider:** Finally, you can enhance your game with a subscription to *D&D Insider* (D&DI)—www.dndinsider.com—an online supplement to the pen-and-paper game. D&DI gives you a ready source of adventures, new rules options to try out, and an array of online tools to make your game go more smoothly. You can use D&DI to play D&D over the Internet, bringing friends scattered across the country or the world back together around a virtual gaming table.

# FUN!

The last essential component of a D&D game is fun. It's not the DM's job to entertain the players and make sure they have fun. *Every person playing the game is responsible for the fun of the game.* Everyone speeds the game along, heightens the drama, helps set how much roleplaying the group is comfortable with, and brings the game world to life with their imaginations. Everyone should treat each other with respect and consideration, too—personal squabbles and fights among the characters get in the way of the fun.

Different people have different ideas of what's fun about D&D. Remember that the "right way" to play D&D is the way that you and your players agree on and enjoy. If everyone comes to the table prepared to contribute to the game, everyone has fun.

Everybody plays D&D to have fun, but different people get their enjoyment from different aspects of the game. If you're preparing and running a game for a group of players, understanding player motivations—what they enjoy about the game and what makes them happiest when they play—helps you build a harmonious group of players and a fun game for all.

## PLAYER MOTIVATIONS

Most players enjoy many aspects of the game at different times. For convenience, we define the primary player motivations as types of players: actors, explorers, instigators, power gamers, slayers, storytellers, thinkers, and watchers.

### ACTOR

The actor likes to pretend to be her character. She emphasizes character development that has nothing to do with numbers and powers, trying to make her character seem to be a real person in the fantasy world. She enjoys interacting with the rest of the group, with characters and monsters in the game world, and with the fantasy world in general by speaking "in character" and describing her character's actions in the first person.

The actor values narrative game elements over mechanical ones. Unlike the storyteller, she values her character's personality and motivations over other story elements.

#### AN ACTOR . . .

+ Provides PC background, emphasizing personality.
+ Plays according to her character's motivations.
+ Prefers scenes where she can portray her character.
+ Often prefers social encounters to fights.

#### ENGAGE THE ACTOR BY . . .

+ Facilitating her PC's personality and background development.
+ Providing roleplaying encounters.
+ Emphasizing her character's personality at times.
+ Recruiting her to help create narrative campaign elements.

#### BE SURE THAT THE ACTOR DOESN'T . . .

+ Bore the other players by talking to everyone and everything.
+ Justify disruptive actions as being "in character."

### EXPLORER

An explorer loves to see new places in the fantasy world and to meet the residents of such places, fair and foul. All the explorer needs is the promise of an interesting locale or different culture, and off he goes to see that place.

The explorer wants to experience the wonders the game world has to offer. He also wants to know that there's more out there to find. He presses for details: proper names of characters and places, descriptions of the environment, and some idea of what's over the next hill. He's sometimes interested in the adventure plot and his character's motivations. (The explorer is close kin to both the actor and the storyteller.) The wonder of new discoveries is what is key to keeping the explorer happy.

#### AN EXPLORER . . .

+ Seeks out new experiences in the game's setting.
+ Likes learning hidden facts and locating lost items and places.
+ Enjoys atmosphere as much as combat and story.
+ Advances the plot by being willing to move ever on.

#### ENGAGE THE EXPLORER BY . . .

+ Including encounter elements that call for exploration.
+ Rewarding curiosity and willingness to explore.
+ Providing rich descriptions, and using cool maps and props.
+ Recruiting him to map for the party.

#### BE SURE THAT THE EXPLORER DOESN'T . . .

+ Use knowledge of the game world to his own advantage.
+ Bore the other players or exhaust you with his thirst for detail.

### INSTIGATOR

An instigator enjoys making things happen. She has no patience for careful planning or deliberation. She'll open an obviously trapped chest "just to see what happens." She provokes authority figures and opens dungeon doors to bring more monsters into an already difficult fight. The instigator loves the vicarious thrill of taking enormous risks and sometimes just making bad choices.

The instigator can be disruptive, but she can also be a lot of fun for the other players. Things rarely grind to a halt with an instigator in the group, and the stories that get retold after the game session often revolve around whatever crazy thing the instigator did this week.

#### AN INSTIGATOR . . .

+ Likes to make things happen.
+ Takes crazy risks and makes deliberately bad choices.
+ Thrives in combat and dislikes having nothing to do.
+ Takes decisive action when things grind to a halt.

#### ENGAGE THE INSTIGATOR BY . . .

+ Including objects and encounters that invite experimentation.

- Letting her actions put the characters in a tight spot but not kill them all.
- Including encounters with nonplayer characters who are as feisty as she is.

## BE SURE THAT THE INSTIGATOR DOESN'T . . .
- Get the rest of the group killed.
- Attack the other PCs or their allies.

# POWER GAMER

A power gamer thrives on gaining levels and loves the cool abilities that come with those levels. He defeats monsters to take their stuff and use that stuff against future enemies. The story and roleplaying are secondary to action and awesome abilities and magic items.

Most players have a little power gamer in them. A couple of the core elements of fun in the D&D game are the accumulation of power and the use of that power to accomplish astonishing deeds. Nothing is wrong with enjoying that in the game.

## A POWER GAMER . . .
- Optimizes character attributes for combat performance.
- Pores over supplements for better character options.
- Spends less time on story and roleplaying elements.
- Prefers combat to other kinds of encounters.

## ENGAGE THE POWER GAMER BY . . .
- Stressing story element rewards, such as quest XP.
- Using a desired magic item as an adventure hook.
- Facilitating access to new options and powers.
- Including encounters that emphasize his PC's attributes.

## BE SURE THAT THE POWER GAMER DOESN'T . . .
- Become a lot more powerful than the other characters.
- Try to take more than his share of treasure.
- Treat the other characters as his lackeys.

# SLAYER

The slayer is like the power gamer, but she is even easier to please. She emphasizes kicking the tar out of monsters. Maybe she does so to let off a little steam in a safe way, or she likes the joy of feeling superior. Perhaps it's the pleasure of having the power to mete out punishment to villains.

D&D combat is thrilling. Few other aspects of the game put a character in such apparent jeopardy. Beating the bad guys is a clear success. Most players enjoy these D&D elements, but the slayer seeks them foremost.

## A SLAYER . . .
- Optimizes like a power gamer.
- Might pick simple options to get into the action quicker.
- Spends less time on story and roleplaying elements.
- Wants to fight monsters and take bold action all the time.

## ENGAGE THE SLAYER BY . . .
- Springing an unexpected battle when the slayer looks bored.
- Making some battles simple and others more complex.
- Vividly describing the havoc the slayer wreaks with powers.
- Recruiting her to track initiative during combat.

## BE SURE THAT THE SLAYER DOESN'T . . .
- Ruin adventures by killing monsters the characters should talk to.
- Rush past social and skill challenge encounters to the next fight.

# STORYTELLER

The storyteller is a player who prefers the narrative of the game to individual character motivations and personality. This player sees the game as an ongoing chronicle of events in the fantasy world, and he wants to see where the tale goes.

For the storyteller, the rules are there to support the game's ongoing story. He believes that when the rules get in the way, the narrative should win. Compromise for the sake of the story is more important than individual character motivations.

## A STORYTELLER . . .
- Often provides an extensive background for his PC.
- Works hard to make sure his character fits the story.
- Likes dramatic scenes and recurring characters.
- Prefers adventures that include at least some plot.

## ENGAGE THE STORYTELLER BY . . .
- Facilitating his PCs background development.
- Using his background to help define adventures and nonplayer characters.
- Including at least a little plot in every adventure.
- Recruiting him to record important events and encounters.

## BE SURE THAT THE STORYTELLER DOESN'T . . .
- Insist on making his character the center of the story.
- Dictate other characters' actions to fit his idea of the story.

# THINKER

A thinker likes to make careful choices, reflecting on challenges and the best way to overcome them. She also enjoys herself most when her planning results in success with minimal risk and use of resources.

Solving a challenge in a creative way is more important to the thinker than character power or roleplaying issues. In fact, the thinker might prefer sound tactics to acting in character or straightforward, brute force battle.

## A THINKER . . .
- Engages any challenge as a puzzle to be solved.
- Chooses her actions carefully for the best possible result.
- Is happy to win without action, drama, or tension.
- Prefers time to consider options over bold action.

## ENGAGE THE THINKER BY . . .

+ Including encounters that require problem-solving skills.
+ Rewarding planning and tactics with in-game benefits.
+ Occasionally allowing a smart plan to cause a one-sided win.
+ Recruiting her to help come up with quests.

## BE SURE THAT THE THINKER DOESN'T . . .

+ Constantly tell the other players what to do.
+ Grind the game to a halt when considering tactical options.

## WATCHER

A watcher is a casual player who comes to the game because he wants to be part of the social event. A watcher might be shy or just really laid back. He wants to participate, but he doesn't really care if he's deeply immersed, and he doesn't want to be assertive or too involved in the details of the game, rules, or story. He enjoys the game by being part of a social circle.

## A WATCHER . . .

+ Shows up to be a part of the group.
+ Helps calm disputes by not being as attached to the game.
+ Often fills a hole in the PC group, facilitating the fun.

## ENGAGE THE WATCHER BY . . .

+ Never forcing him to be more involved than he wants.
+ Accepting that he's fine with his watcher status.
+ Prompting him when he needs it.

## BE SURE THAT THE WATCHER DOESN'T . . .

+ Distract the other players with TV, a video game, or surfing the Internet.
+ Disappear from the table at crucial moments.

# BUILDING A PARTY

Assembling an adventuring party is more than bringing together a bunch of players and the characters they create. Building a party lets the players to be involved in the creation of the campaign's story and in details about the world. It's also the first time when players learn the importance of cooperation.

## COVERING THE CHARACTER ROLES

The *Player's Handbook* discusses the four character roles: controller, defender, leader, and striker (see page 16 of the *Player's Handbook*). When players are making new characters, they should discuss their preferences in roles, and agree on how to cover all the roles in the characters they create to allow for a good balance of abilities in the party. Otherwise, you might end up with a party of five strikers.

What happens if the party doesn't cover all the roles?

**No Defender:** Without a defender, the party's controller is particularly vulnerable, and the strikers might have to sacrifice some mobility. The leader can take on some of the defender's role. Enemy soldiers are more successful at controlling the battlefield, and enemy brutes become particularly dangerous to the characters.

**No Leader:** When a party doesn't have a leader, it's less effective overall, and healing during combat is both more difficult and less effective. A paladin can help cover the leader's absence, providing both limited healing and boosts to the rest of the party. Healing potions can give the characters more access to their healing surges during combat. Enemy controllers and leaders have more influence on the battle.

**No Striker:** The absence of a striker is perhaps the easiest to cover. The defender and controller might need to find ways to increase their damage output to bring monsters down faster. Enemy brutes, with their high hit points, and artillery positioned in hard-to-reach places, become a greater threat to the characters.

**No Controller:** Not having a controller can free the defender up to move around more, since at that point the defender lacks a soft ally to protect. However, as with a striker, a missing controller means that monsters last longer. Large groups of monsters, and minions in particular, survive much longer in the absence of a controller who can damage multiple creatures with a single attack.

## PARTY BACKGROUND

At the start of a new campaign, work with the players to fit them into the world and the story you have in mind. Set some parameters for them. You might tell them you're starting the game in the town of Fallcrest, for example, and you want them all to have grown up in that town. Or you could ask each player to give you a reason his character has come to Fallcrest from somewhere else. Then ask the players to talk about how their characters know each other, to establish some relationships among them at the beginning of the game.

Those starting relationships can take any form the players desire. Perhaps two characters are siblings, or they've been friendly rivals since childhood. One character might have saved another's life. Two characters might have served in the town militia before or worked as caravan guards together. Perhaps all the characters were born in a different town that was destroyed when they were young children, forcing their families to flee to another town.

---

## TIPS FROM THE PROS

The story in the *Player's Handbook* about the dragonborn paladin Donaar, who carries a piece of the shell he hatched from as a reminder of his heritage, came from exactly this sort of player background creation. The player, reading the then-current description of dragonborn, exclaimed, "I hatched? Can I carry a piece of my eggshell with me?" Thus was born an interesting cultural detail about dragonborn in that game world.

—*James Wyatt*

Relationships between characters can also mirror real-life relationships between players. If two players are related, for example, they might decide that their characters are related as well, or that their characters are childhood friends.

Encourage each player to forge connections to at least two other characters. These connections create a network of relationships that gives the characters a good reason (in the game world) to work together as an adventuring party. These relationships also give them plenty of material to work with in roleplaying and give you hooks for future adventures.

## CAMPAIGN DETAILS

When you work with the players to create connections between their characters, you're also inviting them to share in the process of building the campaign world. If players come up with the idea that their characters worked as mercenaries together, for example, they can help you create details about the missions they undertook and what led them to pursue an adventuring career instead.

Each player can also help you fill in details about the different races of the game, their place in your world, and their cultural traits. If the player with a dragonborn paladin of Erathis (god of civilization) wants to be an exile from a distant city-state where dragonborn still appear in great numbers, you can run with that idea. Visiting the city of the dragonborn can be an exciting part of a future adventure. What's the role of Erathis's church in the city? Is Erathis a prominent deity there, or was the character's devotion to Erathis the reason for her exile?

Of course, you probably have some ideas of your own about the world of your campaign. Shaping those details is a job you can share with your players, but

you can also take as much control over it as you want to. You might decide that tieflings in your world are both extremely rare and severely mistrusted. If you do, though, make sure to let the players know that before anyone makes up a tiefling character. If you know that the forest near your campaign's starting area burned to the ground ten years ago, driving the elves who lived there into the human lands, tell your players.

If some details of the story are still vague in your mind, though, your players can help fill them in. Who destroyed the elf forest? If it's not important to your plans for the campaign, let the player with an elf character help you think of ideas. If a player does make a tiefling character, maybe he can help you explain why tieflings are so feared, or create a clan of tiefling merchants who have earned the grudging respect of their human neighbors, or create an underground network of tieflings who help each other in the face of hatred and prejudice.

## USING CHARACTER BACKGROUNDS

If your players create detailed backgrounds for their characters and their group, reward their efforts. Use their backgrounds to craft quests and adventures. Invent situations where their backgrounds are useful. Let the character who was raised by a blacksmith charm some important information out of the baroness's blacksmith—or notice an important fact how a metal lock was forged. Give the characters important information they know because of their past history, such as the location of a particular shrine or magical location that appears in the lore of their original homeland.

One small warning: Make sure you make every character's background useful or important from time to time. Don't let a whole campaign revolve around one character's story.

A competitive sport has referees. It needs them. Someone impartial involved in the game needs to make sure everyone's playing by the rules.

The role of the Dungeon Master has a little in common with that of a referee. If you imagined that all the monsters in an encounter were controlled by one player and all the adventurers by another player, they might need a referee to make sure that both sides were playing by the rules and to resolve disputes. D&D isn't a head-to-head competition in that way, but the DM does act simultaneously as the player controlling all the monsters and as the referee.

Being a referee means that the DM stands as a mediator between the rules and the players. A player tells the DM what he wants to do, and the DM responds by telling the character what kind of check to make and mentally setting the target number. If a player tells the DM he wants his character to swing his greataxe at an orc, the DM says, "Make an attack roll," while looking up the orc's Armor Class.

That's such a simple example that most players take it for granted and don't wait for the DM to ask for the attack roll. But if the player tells you that he wants his character to knock over a brazier full of hot coals into the orc's face, you (as the DM) have to make some snap judgments. How hard is it to knock over the heavy, solid metal brazier? "Make a Strength check," you might respond, while mentally setting the DC at 15. If the Strength check is successful, you have to figure out how a face full of hot coals affects the orc, and might decide it deals 1d6 points of fire damage and gives the orc a –2 penalty to attack rolls for a round.

Sometimes this role mediating the rules means that a DM has to enforce the rules on the players. If a player tells you, "I want to charge up here and attack the orc," you might have to say, "No, you can't charge to there, it's too far." Then the player takes this new information and comes up with a different plan.

---

## TIPS FROM THE PROS

When I started working at Wizards of the Coast, it took a long time before I felt comfortable running a game for any of my coworkers, even though I used to always DM for my friends back home. They all knew the rules better than I did, and I didn't want to get caught in a stupid mistake. Eventually, I got over that. When I'm not sure of a rule, I ask my players what they think. If I make a mistake, my players point it out respectfully, and I reconsider my decision. From my perspective, the DM is the person who prepares adventures, plans a campaign, and runs the monsters and NPCs. I don't want to be a referee or judge, and my players don't expect me to.

*—James Wyatt*

---

Remember, though: Being the DM doesn't mean you have to know all the rules. If a player tries something you don't know how to adjudicate, ask the opinion of the players as a group. It might take a few minutes, but it's usually possible to hash out an answer that seems fair.

Some DMs fear that asking their players' opinions will undermine their authority and give rise to claims that they are being unfair. On the contrary, most players like it when the DM asks their opinions, and they're more likely to feel that the results are fair when they can give their opinions.

## DM STYLE

What's the right way to DM? That depends on your DMing style and the motivations of your players. Consider your players' tastes, your style, table rules (see page 14), the type of game you want to run, and your campaign. Then take a little time to describe to the players how you want the game to go. Let them give you input. It's their game, too. Lay that groundwork early, so your players can make informed choices and help you maintain the type of game you want to run.

| DM Style Considerations | | |
|---|---|---|
| Gritty | . . . or . . . | Cinematic |
| Medieval fantasy | . . . or . . . | Anachronistic |
| Silly | . . . or . . . | Serious |
| Lighthearted | . . . or . . . | Intense |
| Bold | . . . or . . . | Cautious |
| Preplanned | . . . or . . . | Improvised |
| General | . . . or . . . | Thematic |
| Morally ambiguous | . . . or . . . | Heroic |

The considerations listed above are a set of extremes. Are you big on realism and gritty consequences, or are you more focused on making the game seem like an action movie? Do you want the game to maintain a sense of medieval fantasy, or can you tolerate some incursions of the modern world and modern thinking (anachronism)? Do you want to maintain a serious tone, or is humor your goal? Even if you are serious, is the action lighthearted or intense? Is bold action key, or do the players need to be thoughtful and be cautious? Do you have a hard time improvising, or are you great at winging it? Is the game full of varied D&D elements, or does it center on a specific theme such as horror? Is it for all ages, or does it involve mature themes? Are you comfortable with a moral ambiguity, such as allowing the characters to explore if the end justifies the means, or are you happier with straightforward heroic principles, such as justice, sacrifice, and helping the downtrodden?

Many D&D games lean more toward the right-hand side of the above list, but most find a balance between the extremes. However, since the right-hand side qualities are what D&D players expect in a game, so it's up to you to set a different tone if that's what you're after.

# KINDS OF GAMES

Several key decisions define the kind of game that you and your players have. Many D&D games are single-DM, ongoing campaigns, in which the DM orchestrates a series of adventures that link together to form an epic story arc. But successful D&D games can have multiple DMs, be episodic rather than having a campaign arc, and can even be one-shot games or convention events. These game models have different strengths and weaknesses.

**Single DM:** One player serves as DM for every session. That person is the mastermind behind every adventure. The DM plans the campaign's overarching plots and maintains continuity.

## A SINGLE DM IS GREAT BECAUSE . . .

✦ Everyone arrives at the game knowing who's doing what.

## THE WEAKNESSES OF A SINGLE DM ARE . . .

✦ One person does a lot of work.
✦ If the DM can't play, no one can.

**Multiple DMs:** Different players take the DM role for different sessions. Two or three players might pass the job around, everyone in the group might take a turn, or two people might collaborate to DM. In a campaign, the DMs work together to maintain some continuity from session to session and make sure that adventures advance the larger story. Every player has a character, but when it's your turn to DM, your character sits out for that adventure. Your character still gains levels along with the other characters, though.

## MULTIPLE DMS ARE GREAT BECAUSE . . .

✦ Adventure preparation gets spread around.
✦ You all feel like part of a group together.
✦ Other DMs can cover absences or burnout.
✦ The DMs also get to play characters of their own.

## THE WEAKNESSES OF MULTIPLE DMS ARE . . .

✦ Continuity sometimes gets shaky.
✦ Characters move in and out of the group, and sometimes their absence is hard to explain in the story.
✦ Adventures might feel disconnected.

**Campaign:** A campaign is a connected series of adventures. These connected adventures share a sense of a larger purpose or a recurring theme (or themes). The adventures might feature returning villains, grand conspiracies, or a single mastermind who's ultimately behind every adventure of the campaign.

## A CAMPAIGN GAME IS GREAT BECAUSE . . .

✦ The campaign feels like a great fantasy epic.
✦ The things you do in one adventure matter in the next.

## THE WEAKNESS OF A CAMPAIGN GAME IS . . .

✦ If the DM burns out, the story doesn't have a conclusion.

**Episodic:** An episodic game is like a television show where each week's episode is its own self-contained story. The game might be built on a premise that explains its nature: the player characters are adventurers-for-hire, perhaps, or explorers venturing into the unknown and facing a string of unrelated dangers. They might even be archeologists, venturing into one ancient ruin after another in search of ancient artifacts. An episodic game can still have story, even if it has no overarching plot.

## AN EPISODIC GAME IS GREAT BECAUSE . . .

✦ Adventures don't need to fit in to a larger story.
✦ It can be easier to use published adventures.

## THE WEAKNESS OF AN EPISODIC GAME IS . . .

✦ Disconnected adventures can start to feel purposeless.

**Ongoing Games:** An ongoing game is simply one where you get together with the same group of people at a recurring time period. Whether you play weekly, monthly, or once a year when your old gaming buddies converge from across the country, an ongoing group has a sense of continuity about it, even if it's an episodic game.

## AN ONGOING GAME IS GREAT BECAUSE . . .

✦ You know the people you're gaming with.
✦ Familiarity breeds cooperation.
✦ You find a play style you like and can stick with it.

## THE WEAKNESS OF AN ONGOING GAME IS . . .

✦ You're not exposed to new ideas or different play styles.

**One-Shot Games and Convention Events:** Any situation where you sit down to play with people you don't normally game with falls in this category, whether it is an event at your local gaming store, or a local or nationwide gaming convention. Usually, the DM provides characters or tells the players to bring characters of a specific level. The group plays for a single session, or all the way through an adventure, and then the game's over.

Established groups can do one-shots as well. A short adventure, perhaps one with a different tone than the usual style of the group, can clear the palate between two longer campaigns or provide a fun game when the regular DM can't play.

## A ONE-SHOT GAME IS GREAT BECAUSE . . .

✦ You get to try something different.
✦ You might meet new players.
✦ You'll get new ideas for your regular game.

## THE WEAKNESSES OF A ONE-SHOT GAME ARE . . .

✦ You might not know the people you're gaming with.
✦ The game or the people in it might not be to your taste.

While setting up a D&D game, every gaming group needs to set some table rules—rules that outline everyone's responsibilities to keep the game fun. Some table rules deal with the conflict between the needs of the game and the realities of life, such as when players are gone and can't play their characters. Others are about coming to agreement on special situations, such as how cocked die results are treated.

**Respect:** Be there, and be on time. Don't let disagreements escalate into loud arguments. Don't bring personal conflicts to the gaming table. Don't hurl insults across the table. Don't touch other players' dice, if they're sensitive about it. Don't petulantly hurl dice across the table.

**Distractions:** If you run a casual, light-hearted game, it might be fine to have players wandering away from the table and back. Most groups, though, have come together to play D&D—so play D&D. Turn off the television, ban the portable video games, and get a babysitter if you have to. By reducing distractions you have an easier time getting in character, enjoying the story, and focusing on playing the game.

**Food:** Come to a consensus about food for your session. Should players eat before arriving, or do you eat together? Does one player want to play host? Do you all chip in for pizza or take-out? Who brings snacks and drinks?

**Character Names:** Agree on some ground rules for naming characters. In a group consisting of Sithis, Travok, Anastrianna, and Kairon, the human fighter named Bob II sticks out. Especially when he's identical to Bob I, who was killed by kobolds. If everyone takes a light-hearted approach to names, that's fine. If the group would rather take the characters and their names a little more seriously, urge Bob's player to come up with a better name.

Player character names should match each other in flavor or concept, but they should also match the flavor of your campaign world. So should the names you make up—nonplayer characters' names and place names. Travok and Kairon don't want to visit Gumdrop Island or talk to the enchanter Tim.

**Missing Players:** How are you going to deal with the characters of missing players? Consider these options:

✦ *Have another player run the missing player's character.* Don't do this without the permission of the missing player. The player running the extra character should make an effort to keep the character alive and use resources wisely.

✦ *Run the character yourself.* Having the DM run the missing character is extra workload for you, but it can work. You need to play the character reasonably, as the missing player would.

✦ *Decide the character's not there.* You might be able to provide a good reason for the character to miss the adventure, perhaps by having her linger in town. Make sure you leave a way for the character to rejoin the party when the player returns, though.

✦ *Have the character fade into the background.* This solution requires everyone to step out of the game world a bit and suspend disbelief, but it's the easiest solution. It amounts to hand-waving. You act as if the character's not there, but don't try to come up with any in-game explanation for his absence. Monsters don't attack him, and he returns the favor. When the player returns, he picks up where the party left off as if he was never gone.

**Multiple Characters:** Most of the time, one player runs one character in the D&D game. The game plays best that way. Each player has enough mental bandwidth to keep track of the things his character can do and play effectively. But if your group is small, you might want one or more players to take on the roles of two characters.

Don't force a reluctant player to take on two characters, and don't show favoritism by allowing only one player to do it. You might make one character the mentor or employer of the other, so the player has a good reason to focus on primarily on roleplaying just one character. Otherwise, a player can end up awkwardly talking to himself in character (in conversations between the two characters he plays) or avoiding roleplaying altogether.

Another situation in which multiple characters can be a good idea is in a game with a high rate of character death. If your group is willing to play such a game, you might have each player keep one or two additional characters on hand, ready to jump in whenever the current character dies. Each time the main character gains a level, the backup characters do as well. Just make sure your players understand the nature of the game and your guidelines for these backup characters.

**Table Talk:** It's a good idea to set some expectations about how players talk at the table.

✦ Make it clear who's speaking—the character, or the player (out of character).

✦ Can players offer advice if their characters aren't present or are unconscious?

✦ Can players give other players information such as how many hit points they have left?

✦ Can players take back what they've just said their character does?

**Being Ready:** Every round of combat is an exercise in patience. The players all want to take their turns. If a player isn't ready when his turn comes up, the others can get impatient. Encourage your players to consider their actions before their turn, and let them know that if they take too long to make a decision, you'll assume that the character delays. (Be more forgiving to newer players, and urge the other players to do the same.)

**Rolling Dice:** Establish some basic expectations about how players roll dice. Rolling "in full view of everyone" is a good starting point. If you see players roll their attacks or damage and scoop the dice up before anyone else can see, you might nudge that player to be a little less cagey.

What about strange die rolls? When a die falls on the floor, do you count it or reroll it? When it lands cocked against a book, do you pull the book away and see where it lands, or reroll it?

What about you, the DM? Do you make your die rolls where the players can see, or hide them behind your *Dungeon Master's Screen* with your adventure notes? It's up to you, but consider:

✦ *If you roll where players can see, they know that you're playing fair.* You're not going to fudge the dice either in their favor or against them.

✦ *Rolling behind a screen keeps the players guessing about the strength of the opposition.* When the monster is hitting all the time, is it of much higher level than the players, or is the DM just rolling a string of high numbers?

✦ *Rolling behind the screen lets you fudge if you want to.* If two critical hits in a row would kill a character, you might want to change the second critical hit to a normal hit, or even a miss. Don't do it too often, though, and don't let on that you're doing it, or the other players feel as though they don't face any real risk—or worse, that you're playing favorites.

✦ *You need to make some rolls behind the screen no matter what.* If a player thinks there might be something invisible in the room and rolls a Perception check, roll a die behind the screen. If you didn't roll a die at all, the player would know there's nothing hiding. If you rolled in front of your screen, the player would have some idea how hidden the opponent was, and be able to make an educated guess about whether something is there. Rolling behind the screen preserves the mystery.

Sometimes you need to make a roll for a player character, because the player shouldn't know how good the check result is. If the character suspects the baroness might be charmed and wants to make an Insight check, you should make the roll behind the screen. If the player rolled it herself and got a high roll, but she didn't sense anything amiss, she'd be confident that the baroness wasn't charmed. If she made a low roll, a negative answer wouldn't mean much. A hidden die roll allows some uncertainty.

**Rolling Attacks and Damage:** Players are often used to rolling first their attack roll and then their damage roll. If players make attack rolls and damage rolls at the same time, things move a little faster around the table than if they wait to roll damage after you've told them that the attack hits.

You might find it helpful if your players tell you how much damage an attack did, wait until you've recorded the damage, and then tell you any additional conditions and effects of the attack—like stunning or knocking prone.

When making area or close attacks, which use a single damage roll but a separate attack roll for each creature in the area (see page 271 of the *Player's Handbook*), it's helpful to roll damage first. Once you've established how much damage the effect deals on a hit (and on a miss), you can run through attack rolls against the creatures one at a time.

**Rules Discussions:** Set a policy on rules discussions at the table. Some groups don't mind putting the game on hold while they hash out different interpretations of the rules. Others prefer to let the DM make a call and get on with things. If you do gloss over a rules issue in play, make a note of it (a good task to delegate to a player) and get back to it later at a more natural stopping point.

**Metagame Thinking:** Players get the best enjoyment when they preserve the willing suspension of disbelief. A roleplaying game's premise is that it is an experience of fictional people in a fictional world.

Metagame thinking means thinking about the game *as a game*. It's like a character in a movie knowing he's in a movie and acting accordingly. "This dragon must be a few levels higher than we are," a player might say. "The DM wouldn't throw such a tough monster at us!" Or you might hear, "The read aloud text spent a lot of time on that door—let's search it again!"

Discourage this by giving players a gentle verbal reminder: "But what do your *characters* think?" Or, you could curb metagame thinking by asking for Perception checks when there's nothing to see, or setting up an encounter that is much higher level than the characters are. Just make sure to give them a way to avoid it or retreat.

# CHAPTER 2

# RUNNING THE GAME

WHAT A Dungeon Master does is commonly called "running the game." That's a bit of a loaded phrase, since it suggests that the DM is in charge, an absolute authority, and responsible for the rest of the players. This chapter is not about just the DM's job, but everyone's responsibility for keeping the game moving smoothly.

This chapter includes the following sections.

✦ **Preparing and Getting Started:** Learn how much time you need to invest to prepare and how to prepare effectively, and how to kick off your game session.

✦ **Modes of the Game:** The D&D game unfolds in different modes—setup, exploration, conversation, encounter, and passing time. Understand what you need to run the game in each mode.

✦ **Narration:** A big part of the DM's job is letting the players know what's going on. Give the players the information they need and keep it lively.

✦ **Pacing:** Keep the rhythm of action and anticipation going in your game.

✦ **Props:** Bring your game to life with props and handouts.

✦ **Dispensing Information:** Give the characters the information they need to make smart choices.

✦ **Improvising:** Learn to wing it—and have fun!

✦ **Ending a Session:** What's the best time to end a game session?

✦ **Troubleshooting:** How to deal with some of the most common problems that come up in the game.

✦ **Teaching the Game:** How to introduce new players to the D&D game.

HOWARD LYON

The more you prepare before your game, the more smoothly the game will go—to a certain point. To avoid being either under- or overprepared, keep in mind the one-hour rule of thumb and prioritize the tasks of preparation within the time you have available.

# THE ONE-HOUR RULE OF THUMB

Any game session has 15 to 30 minutes of easing into the game and 15 to 30 minutes of wrapup time. Most groups get through about one encounter in an hour of play. So if you play one encounter, it usually takes about two hours for a game session. If you play two encounters, it takes about three hours.

# PREPARATION TIME

These guidelines assume that you're running a straightforward, dungeon-based adventure. Many of the same principles apply when you run more interaction-focused or investigation-heavy adventures.

## ONE-HOUR PREPARATION

If you spend one hour each week preparing for your game:

+ Select a published adventure to run.

+ Flip through the adventure. Keeping in mind the length of time you're going to play in a game session, figure out how likely it is that your players will play each encounter. Prioritize them as: definite, possible, or unlikely.

+ Carefully read each encounter you marked as "definite." Review the monsters in the encounter, including their special abilities and tactical information. Create some tactical notes if you have to. Note any special rules that apply to the terrain in the encounter.

+ Consider how each of these definite encounters relates to the particular motivations of your players. If you have one or more players who are left in the lurch by the encounters you have planned, think about elements you can add to the encounter to hook those players in. For example, if the night's encounters don't give your actor player a chance to roleplay, find a way to inject some negotiation into the start of an encounter.

+ For an encounter that focuses more on interaction, make notes about the relevant NPCs in the encounter—their motivations and goals. Pick a quirk for each important NPC to help the character stand out in the players' minds, focusing on something that's easy to play.

## TWO-HOUR PREPARATION

Add:

+ Carefully review each "possible" encounter and any monsters used in them. If you're creating an adventure of your own, prepare a few more encounters and build some more options into the map, creating more possible encounters.

+ Devote any time you have left to creating improvisational aids (see page 28).

## THREE-HOUR PREPARATION

Add:

+ Skim each of the "unlikely" encounters.

+ Create a new encounter designed to appeal specifically to one particular player, or alter an existing encounter to relate specifically to his or her character's goals and hooks. Over the course of several sessions, make sure you spread that attention out over all your players.

+ Instead of or as well as additional encounters, create one or two minor **quests** (see page 102) that tie into the adventure, including either existing encounters or the new encounters you create.

## FOUR-HOUR PREPARATION

With four hours to spend, you can take the time to craft an adventure of your own that's not quite so rushed. Build in elements designed to appeal to each player. Design a major quest to lead the characters on the adventure, a handful of minor quests to spice things up, and at least two or three definite encounters and a like number of possible encounters. Make notes about the encounters you'll design next week.

# NO TIME TO PREPARE!

Sometimes you have no time to get ready for your game. Check out the sections on "Improvising" (page 28), "Random Dungeons" (page 190), and "Random Encounters" (page 193) for ideas on what to do.

## CREATING AN ADVENTURE IN ONE HOUR

If you don't want to use a published adventure, it's possible to create an adventure with no more than one hour of preparation. Choose a dungeon map. Section off an area that contains a limited number of potential encounters. (That railroads your players somewhat, but they'll forgive you if it means the difference between playing this week or not.) Use the sample encounter groups in the *Monster Manual*, as well as the sample traps and hazards in this book.

Don't expect to show up at the appointed time and start rolling dice at the top of the hour.

**Settle In:** D&D is a social activity, and taking a while to get settled and socialize is a time-honored ritual. Don't try to fight it. A game group works better together when the people in it have had time to talk, joke, and catch up before jumping into the dungeon. If that time coincides with a meal, so much the better—neither conversation nor dinner plates will get in the way of the game once you get in gear.

Over time, many game groups develop a signal to indicate when it's time to begin play in earnest. One player might say, "Game on!", everyone might put their dice on the table, or the DM might set up the Dungeon Master's screen.

**Recap:** Just as many television series do, it's a great idea to start each game session with a recap of what happened the week before. This time helps players get back into the story and the mindset of the game. It also helps any players who missed the previous session catch up with what's been going on.

You can give this recap, but the recap is a great task to delegate. When a player (or the group) summarizes the events of the last adventure, you get a glimpse into the players' minds. Actor or storyteller players shine here. They might even decide to talk in or write the recap in character. Listening to a player's recap lets you see what the players remember and what they think is important, shows you their understanding of the story, and can even give you ideas for future plot twists.

**Listen:** The recap is one of the most important opportunities you have to listen to your players and get a sense of their experience of the game. Be sure to pay attention to each player's contribution to the recap. Even a snide comment or joke can tell you a lot about what your players are getting out of the game.

## DELEGATING

You shouldn't be afraid to delegate some of the job of running the game to your players. If there are parts of the game you find burdensome, assign them to players who enjoy them. If you don't want to break your narrative stride by looking up a rule, designate another player to be the rulebook reference expert. If you don't like tracking initiative, have another player do it for you. Players can make the DM's life easier in a lot of little ways, from never making you pay for pizza to helping to flesh out the background of the campaign world. You have enough to do—delegate what you can.

When a group of players shares the responsibilities of running the game, everyone has more fun. Best of all, the players feel as though it's their game, not just yours.

---

### CHRONICLING A GAME

Game groups often enjoy saving their recaps and forming them into a chronicle of the ongoing sessions or campaign.

**Low Tech:** You can write the recap on sheets of paper, noting the date of each recap. Some chroniclers like to pick out a special notebook or buy a nice blank book in which to write the game recaps.

**High Tech:** Chroniclers who have computers sometimes type the recap into a text processing program and keep it in an ongoing file, emailing it to others in the group. Other creative and technically savvy folks create Web sites for their game groups, set up blogs to post each recap on, or set up message boards for the game group and post on them.

*D&D Insider* allows you to chronicle your campaign through the Web, too.

**Outtakes:** The story of your game sessions is the driving plot of a chronicle. However, funny things that players say during a game session often spark the memory of the events—the emotional context—as much as describing the encounters. Include a few fun things that the players and their characters said in the recap at the end. They can often provide hooks in the players' minds when the neutral facts have faded from their memories.

WILLIAM O'CONNOR

Over the course of a session of D&D, the game shifts in and out of five basic modes—setup, exploration, conversation, encounter, and passing time. The five modes are also five different kinds of tasks or activities the characters engage in during their adventures.

Part of the job of running the game as DM is figuring out what mode the game is in based on what the player characters are doing. The shifts are generally smooth and organic, and you might not even notice the change from one to another unless you're paying attention.

Your role as DM is different depending on which mode the game is in. You interact with the players according to the mode the game is in. You provide the scene, describe and play the NPCs and monsters, and dispense any information the PCs need or gain. You ultimately determine the group's success or failure based on the players' choices, the difficulty of the situation, and the luck of the dice.

## SETUP

The game is in setup mode when you're telling the players what they need to know about the adventure and they're gearing up for the first encounter of the gaming session. The characters might be buying supplies or working out plans. You might be reading a short introductory paragraph about the adventure, perhaps summarizing events that have brought them to where they stand at the start of the adventure.

Setup can evolve into conversation, particularly if the players have questions about the quest they're beginning. For example, they want to ask more about the bandits that have been raiding merchant caravans. These questions could even evolve directly into a skill challenge if they believe that whoever is sending their characters on this adventure is deceiving them or withholding information, or if they try to negotiate the reward they've been offered.

Setup also naturally evolves into exploration. If you give the players a summary of events that have brought them to the entrance of a dungeon, your next words might be "What do you do?" That question is a hallmark of the beginning of exploration mode.

## EXPLORATION

In exploration mode, the characters move through the adventure setting, making decisions about their course and perhaps searching for traps, treasure, or clues. The game spends a lot of game time in exploration mode. It's what usually fills the space between encounters. It usually ends when an encounter begins.

Follow these steps to run the game in exploration mode.

1. **Describe the environment.** Outline the options available to the characters by telling them where they are and what's around them. When you detail the dungeon room the PCs are in, mention all the doors, chests, shafts, and other things the PCs might want to interact with. Don't explicitly outline options. (Don't say: "You can either go through the door, search the chest, or look down the shaft.") That's putting unnecessary limitations on the PCs' actions. Your job is to describe the environment and to let the PCs decide what they want to do with it.

2. **Listen.** Once you're done describing the area, the players tell you what their characters want to do. Some groups might need prompting. Ask them, "What do you do?" Your job here is to listen to what the players want to do and identify how to resolve their actions. You can and should ask for more information if you need it.

   Sometimes the players give you a group answer: "We go through the door." Other times, individual players want to do specific things, such as searching a chest. The players don't need to take turns, but you need to make sure to listen to every player and resolve everyone's actions.

   Some tasks involve a skill check or an ability check, such as a Thievery check to pick the lock on a chest, a Strength check to force open a door, or a Perception check to find hidden clues. Characters can perform other tasks without any check at all: move a lever, take up a position near the entrance to watch for danger, or walk down the left fork of a passage.

3. **Narrate the results of the characters' actions.** Describing the results often leads to another decision point immediately or after time passes. "Behind the door is a passage stretching off to the left and right" gives the characters an immediate decision point. "The sloping hall leads you hundreds of feet down into the earth before finally ending in a door" sets up a decision point after some time. Whenever you reach another decision point, you're back to step 1.

   A character's actions can also lead right into an encounter. "When you look down the well, a gigantic tentacle snakes up from its depths and starts coiling around you!" leads straight to a combat encounter. "When you move the lever, a block of stone slams down across the entrance, stirring up a cloud of dust. With a horrible grinding sound, the walls begin to move slowly inward." That description leads to a skill challenge.

# CONVERSATION

In conversation, the PCs are exploring the information inside an NPC's head, rather than exploring a dungeon room. It's not a social skill challenge, with specific goals and a real chance of failure. The PCs just ask questions, and the NPC responds. Sometimes a check is involved–usually Bluff, Diplomacy, Intimidate, Insight, or Perception. Often the characters and NPCs trade questions and answers until the PCs have the information they need to make a decision and carry it out.

Conversation mode ends in one of two ways: The conversation ends and the PCs move on their way, lapsing back into exploration mode. Or, the conversation escalates into a social skill challenge or a combat encounter.

# ENCOUNTER

Encounters are the exciting part of the D&D game. They have tension and urgency about them and a chance of failure. They involve lots of die-rolling (often in the form of attack rolls) and strategic thinking. They give almost every kind of player something to enjoy.

The rules of the game are most important in encounters. The rules are all about determining whether you succeed or fail at the tasks you attempt– and thus whether you successfully complete the encounter.

# PASSING TIME

The game has a rhythm and flow, and the action in the game is interspersed with lulls. These lulls are like the places where a movie fades to black and comes up again with the understanding that some time has passed. Don't give these situations any more time than the movies do. When a rest period passes uneventfully, tell the players that and move on. Don't make the players spend time discussing which character cooks what for dinner (unless the kind of group you are playing with finds this useful for building characters). Gloss over the mundane, unexciting details and get back to the heroic action as quickly as possible.

At times, the players discuss the events of the game or spend time laying their plans. You don't need to be involved in those discussions at all unless they have questions you need to answer. Learn to recognize the times when it's fine to sit down, rest your voice, or replenish your snacks. Give yourself a breather, and then get back into the action as soon as everyone's ready.

Just like the narrator of a novel, a play, or a movie, you serve the essential function of telling the players what is going on in the game world. The game relies on your descriptions and players' imaginations to set the scene. Using a few time-honored techniques of effective narration helps paint a vivid picture in each player's mind and bring the game to life.

## LEAD BY EXAMPLE

When you roleplay and narrate with enthusiasm, you add energy to the game and draw the players out. Encourage them to follow your lead and to describe their actions in the same vivid way. Then incorporate their narration into your accounts of their successes and failures.

## BREVITY

Don't describe everything. Most players' eyes start to glaze over after about two sentences of descriptive text. Give just enough information to excite and inform the players, then let them react or ask for specific details.

- ✦ **Don't overdescribe.** Anything you describe in intricate detail sounds important, and players sometimes waste a lot of time trying to figure out why insignificant things matter.
- ✦ **Don't omit important details**. Make sure the players know about important terrain features before the fighting starts—if their characters can see or perceive them.
- ✦ **Don't give only the most important information all the time.** If you do that, you encourage metagame thinking. The players quickly realize that anything you take the time to describe must be important. Remain brief, but add touches of atmosphere and enticement in your narration.

## ATMOSPHERE

Describe a setting's features and sensory impressions: emotional overtones, lighting, temperature, texture, and odor. A rich environment has plenty of innocuous but interesting sensations that alert explorers pick up on. Little details are important, such as a lingering smell of ash or tiny beetles scurrying along the dungeon floor. Small anomalies—a tiny flower blossoming in the otherwise desolate and gloomy graveyard—help establish the overall atmosphere of a place.

## CINEMATIC STYLE

It's a cliché, but it's also an important rule of narration: "Show, don't tell." Imagine how the environment would look and sound in a good movie, do your best to describe it that way, then add details of smells and texture that a movie can't communicate. Don't tell the players that there's a pool of bubbling acid nearby, show it to them with a vivid description. Think about how acid might smell, talk about a cloud of noxious vapor hovering above the pool, and describe what the pool bubbling sounds like.

**Your Only Limit Is Your Imagination:** Your imagination is the only boundary in your description. You aren't limited by a special effects budget. Describe amazing vistas, terrifying monsters, dastardly villains, and bone-crunching fight scenes. Your enthusiasm and liveliness are contagious, and they energize the whole game.

**Portraying Rules Situations:** It's easy to fall into the rut of describing events merely in terms of the applicable rules. Although it's important that the players understand what's going on in such terms, the D&D game can be at its dullest if everyone talks in "gamespeak." You know you've fallen into this trap when the table chatter is: "That's 26 against AC," "You hit, now roll damage," "31 points," and "Now we're to initiative count 13."

Instead, use such statistics, along with your knowledge of the scene, to help your narration. If 26 is barely a hit, but the 31 points of damage is a bad wound for the enemy, say: "You swing wildly, and the dragonborn brings his shield up just a second too late. Arrgh! Your blade catches him along the jaw, drawing a deep gash. He staggers!"

## ENTICEMENT

Your narration helps players find the fun, enticing them to explore details of the environment that lead to encounters or important information. Anything you describe with extra, subtle details draws the players' attention. Give them just enough to invite further exploration, but don't describe the equivalent of a flashing neon sign reading, "This way to adventure!"

If the players come to a decision point where the options seem indistinguishable, you can use little sensory details to distinguish the options. Should the characters take the left fork or the right? Perhaps the left fork smells of ash, while the faint sound of lapping water emerges from the right. Unless the players know they're specifically looking for fire or water, these details don't steer them, but they make the choice of one option over the other seem less arbitrary.

# REALISM

Your narration of the fantastic world of the game needs to seem real–not as a simulation of the real world, but as if the game world were a real place with coherent, logical rules. Actions should have logical consequences, and the things the PCs do should have an impact on the world. The people and creatures of the world should behave with consistency in ways that players can understand.

Sometimes realism is a matter of very small details. If two wooden doors appear to be exactly the same, but one requires a DC 16 Strength check to break through and the other one requires a DC 20 check, the world feels arbitrary and inconsistent. It's fine for one door to be harder to break down, but your description should give cues about why one door is so much sturdier than the other, whether it has adamantine reinforcements or a noticeable aura of magic sealing it shut. That makes the game world seem realistic.

# ROLEPLAYING

You don't just set the scene for adventure, you also take on the roles of villains, monsters, and other people and creatures that the heroes encounter in their travels. Putting a little effort into portraying these people and creatures has a big payoff in fun.

**Portraying Monsters:** When a monster is involved, it's usually easy for the players to imagine its actions, especially when you're using representative miniatures and the creature is a simple beast. Appropriate sounds and vocalizations are entertaining, as are descriptions of how a monster reacts to the environment and the PC actions. For example, a wolf snarls at its enemy, savages a downed foe, and whimpers when wounded. If your wolves (even your dire wolves) do that, your game comes alive.

**Portraying NPCs:** Nonplayer characters, including humanoids and magical beasts, are people of some sort. They have abilities and quirks that make them unique and memorable to the players. Use these to help you roleplay. Consider how the NPC's intelligence, goals, and quirks play into the scene at hand. Don't be afraid to act in character and even use a unique voice for the NPC. Keep track of the way you have important NPCs act so you can maintain consistency if the same character appears again. The "Cast of Characters" section (page 116) of Chapter 6 helps you determine some aspects of important NPCs.

Even when an NPC isn't very detailed, use the racial or monster description to help you along. For instance, orcs that shout fearsome battle cries and that roar and hurl insults in battle are more fun to fight than those who act like silent axe-wielding bags of hit points.

# SUSPENSE

Part of the reason players keep coming back to the table is that they want to see what happens next. Will their characters succeed? How will they accomplish the great task set before them, and at what cost? That's suspense.

Suspense exists in the game when the players can see how they want things to turn out, but they don't know for sure how to make it happen. It's excitement mixed with a little bit of worry. When you use narration to create such dramatic tension, you keep players focused and excited about the game. Then they drive the game forward to see what's going to happen next.

**Small Doses:** During an encounter or a series of encounters, add small elements of uncertainty in your descriptions that lead to a payoff within a reasonable amount of time.

For example, the PCs could notice a sickly sweet smell in the ancient tomb. When they encounter guardian mummies, the smell becomes overpowering–it's the odor of the spices and oils used to embalm the mummies.

When they smell the odor next, it sets them on edge, but here you throw them a curveball: They find embalmed but inanimate corpses in the next room, spicing up a scene of pure exploration. Just before the climactic encounter, the smell rises up again–wafting from under the door where the mummy lord awaits them. The players are rewarded if they remain cautious and prepare for a fight with a mummy.

Use a controlled hand about throwing too many curveballs like the harmless corpses. If you use such narrative tricks too often, you dilute the impact of the suspense you're trying to create. Also, make sure that your narrative details point to something useful within a reasonable amount of time. If the characters spend hours wondering what the smell is, they end up bewildered, not in a state of suspense.

**Big Picture:** Suspense builds as the players learn more about the adventure situation and what they have to do to accomplish their goals. With each bit of new information, the original situation takes on new facets. It might change entirely when the players uncover a dramatic twist. The players and the characters have to adapt, maybe even change their goals as the truth unfolds. The unfolding of layered events and information builds suspense within an adventure or even within the whole story arc of a campaign.

Pacing is all about ebb and flow—a rhythm of action and anticipation, of building tension and climactic excitement. Just like in a movie or play, a book, or a video game, pacing is what keeps the game exciting, interesting, and fun. Glossing over mundane details is an important element of good pacing as you run the game, but respect the need to punctuate running excitement with natural breaks, and set up your game sessions for good stopping points—including judiciously setting up cliffhangers for optimal suspense.

**Building Anticipation:** When the game is in exploration mode, the pacing is relaxed. That doesn't mean exploration mode should be boring. It should be a period of building tension. Exploring a dungeon shouldn't be a matter of walking casually down hallways and throwing open doors, but an experience of brooding menace building to the action of an encounter.

In exploration mode, build tension. Use a lower tone of voice, avoid dramatic action, and stay in your seat. Take your time with your narration, indulge in a little extra description, and create the sense that danger could erupt suddenly from around the next corner or behind the next door. See if you can get the players leaning forward in their seats to see what happens next. If you've got them hooked, it's even more startling when you jump to your feet and describe the sudden attack of a horrible monster.

**Finding the Fun:** Don't make players search for the fun in exploration mode. When the players can't find an option that leads to action, the dramatic tension dissipates, and the game becomes a slog or a stalemate. Make sure that you give the players enough clues (or ways to find clues) to solve puzzles and overcome obstacles.

**Climactic Action:** When exploration turns to encounter, shift from building anticipation to pulse-pounding action. Communicate the excitement and danger of the encounter with your voice and body language. Get to your feet, talk faster and a little louder, gesture broadly, and pour as much energy as you can muster into your narration.

In the middle of an encounter, don't let the action grind to a halt. Be prepared: Know the rules that are likely to come up during the session, or flag the relevant pages in your books. Don't let the game get bogged down in rules discussions. Put questions on hold until the end of the encounter. Speed through the initiative order, spurring your players to take their turns as quickly as they can. Be ready when your turn comes up as well!

**Taking Breaks:** At the end of an encounter, the tension you've been building dissipates until you start building it up again. If you or your players need a break, take one at this natural point of pause. Use the restroom, eat or get fresh drinks, let the players (and yourself) catch their breath. Then start building the tension again toward the next encounter.

**Wrap-Ups and Cliffhangers:** As you progress through a session, keep an eye on the clock. You should have an idea of when the session's going to end, and you should make sure that the game comes to a good stopping point around that time.

You can't end every session with a cliffhanger, and you probably shouldn't. Let a session end when an adventure comes to a natural end or resting spot. But try to leave the players with something to look forward to, some clear idea of what they're going to be doing next, to keep some dramatic tension lingering from session to session.

The best place to stop the game is when the players want more—a cliffhanger moment. The characters throw open a door and see the villain they've been pursuing, but they don't get to roll initiative until next week. They open a treasure chest and find a tome that holds a startling revelation, but the session ends before they can do anything in response.

Think about the times a television show has faded to black with "To be continued" on the screen, making you yell back at the screen in protest. That's how you want your game session to end—with the players eager to find out what happens next.

*Example of a handout*

WAYNE ENGLAND

Some players can get deeply immersed in the game purely by listening to your evocative description and imagining the scene in their heads. For the rest of us, there are props. Props are concrete. They give players something they can see, read, and handle, helping them to engage and participate in the game. Use every prop you can to enhance immersion and fun, but keep the narration lively just the same.

### DEPICTING COMBAT ENCOUNTERS
✦ Battle maps
✦ Miniatures

### HANDOUTS
✦ Illustrations
✦ Maps
✦ Notes
✦ Objects

### ATMOSPHERE
✦ Music
✦ Other atmospheric elements

**Items to Depict Combat Encounters:** Battle maps and miniatures are perhaps the most fundamental props. They confirm that everyone around the table imagines the same number of combatants arrayed around the encounter area in the same locations. They also help players imagine the monsters they're fighting—including the size of those monsters. (When you put a Gargantuan dragon down on the table, encourage your players to look at it from the level of their characters' eyes. It's a very different perspective from what even a scale drawing gives.)

A battle map drawn with colored markers on a wet-erase vinyl mat isn't the most evocative prop in the world, but it does help the players understand what's in the room and where. Printed maps (such as in D&D adventures and *D&D Miniatures* products) and *D&D Dungeon Tiles* are even better. They show professional artistic representations of common and fantastic dungeon features.

*D&D Miniatures* portray the monsters of the D&D game as no other miniatures can, and they include a helpful prop for your own use—a card that summarizes the monster's statistics and abilities for easy reference. You can also use other miniatures or plastic toys at an appropriate scale. Unusual figures can even spark ideas for new monsters. (Some of the classic monsters of the D&D game were born in exactly that way.)

**Handouts:** Props can be just as important and evocative outside combat. Handouts often depict some element of the game world. Well-done illustrations are worth a thousand words of narration, and they're easy for players to refer back to. Published D&D adventures include illustrations you can use as handouts to give your players. For adventures of your own creation, look for fantasy art that sparks your imagination. Check the Wizards of the Coast Web sites (www.wizards.com and www.dndinsider.com), fantasy calendars and book covers, photographs of incredible real-world landscapes, or screen shots from computer games.

Maps are great reference during an adventure, and can spark adventures all on their own. It's a time-honored ritual of the game for players to draw their own maps of dungeons as they explore them. You can also let the players find a map in the course of the adventure. Such a map might be a classic treasure map with the location of buried gold marked on it—but without any mention of the horrible monsters that guard it. It could be the record of a past explorer who made it into the depths of a dungeon but didn't quite make it back out.

Any time the characters find something written down—a coded message in the dead assassin's pouch, an incriminating letter from the baroness to the hobgoblin warchief, or a riddle carved into a stone door—think about giving it to the players as a handout. You can use a special computer font and print it out on parchment paper, or scrawl it on notebook paper if you're in a hurry. If the players will want to refer back to the text again, having a handout available saves everyone a lot of trouble.

Don't stop at printed handouts such as art, maps, and letters. Try coins (foreign currency or plastic coins work well), unusual dice or playing cards, statuettes or figurines, or any strange knickknacks you find. Antique and secondhand stores are great places to find this sort of thing. Look for anything that sparks your imagination.

**Atmosphere:** Finally, don't neglect the impact of background music. The right music works with your narration to create an atmosphere. Try playing orchestral music, world music, and movie soundtracks.

Depending on your game, you can create atmosphere by lighting candles, burning incense, draping gauzy fabric over lamps, or using spooky sound effects. Whatever works for you and your players is great. Just remember to use sensible safety precautions, and keep in mind that players need to be able to see their character sheets and their dice and hear the conversation.

As Dungeon Master, one of your important tasks is figuring out exactly how much information to give to the players and when. Sometimes you just describe the scene, giving the players all the information. At other times, you tell the players only what their characters can detect using their skills, their knowledge, and the use of divination rituals. When you're creating an adventure, be sure to note the appropriate DCs for skill checks.

## The Information Imperative

If there's information the PCs absolutely must have in order to continue the adventure, give it to them. Don't make them have a chance to miss the information by failing a skill check or not talking to the right person or just not looking in the right place. The players should be able to uncover important information by using skills and investigation, but for crucial information, you need a foolproof method to get it into the players' hands. Tell them.

## Passive Skill Checks

Passive skill checks are a great tool to help you know how much to tell the players about an object, situation, or scene right away. Without bringing the game to a halt by asking for skill checks, you can keep the momentum and suspense building. It's a great idea to use passive checks regularly, saving active checks (the checks that players request when they want to use skills actively) for when the PCs want to learn more based on the cues you give them.

**Make a List:** To make using passive skill checks easy, keep a note of each character's passive skill check modifiers (10 + skill check bonus) for Perception, Insight, Arcana, Dungeoneering, History, Nature, and Religion.

**Perception:** Passive Perception checks help you set the scene. They tell you right away how much of the details of a room or encounter area the characters notice. Very alert characters can instantly pick up on significant details and hidden creatures or objects that would go unnoticed by others without a more thorough search.

✦ Make sure you give enough cues at lower Perception DCs to encourage PCs to make a more rigorous search of important features.

✦ Don't rely too heavily on passive Perception checks. Make sure you give the PCs information they need to find the fun in your adventure, regardless of their Perception modifiers.

**Insight:** Passive Insight checks provide information from social and emotional intuition and awareness that can serve a character in social encounters. You often use the result of a passive Insight check in social interactions as the DC for the Bluff check of a nonplayer character. (In other words, as an opposed check, Insight vs. Bluff.) If the NPC's Bluff check result is lower than any character's passive Insight check result, that character should get a sense that the NPC isn't being straightforward.

When you give the player this information, make sure to mention that the Insight skill is the reason behind the knowledge. This lets the player feel good about the choice to take training in Insight (if he has done so) and suggests that the player might want to make an active Insight check to learn more.

**Knowledge:** You can use passive knowledge checks to let characters gain some basic information about their surroundings and the creatures they encounter, based on past experience and education. Use passive checks for characters in the situations noted here.

✦ **Arcana:** Magic, the elements, the Elemental Chaos, the Feywild, the Shadowfell, the Far Realm, elemental, fey, or shadow monsters

✦ **Dungeoneering:** Underground environments and terrain, navigating underground, stonework, fungi, subterranean animals, and aberrant creatures

✦ **History:** The history of a region, the chronological record, arts, literature, geography, warfare, nations, historical figures, laws, royalty and other leaders, legends, customs, traditions

✦ **Nature:** Natural environments, navigating through wilderness, the outdoors, terrain, climate, weather, plants, seasons, natural creatures, handling a natural beast, foraging

✦ **Religion:** Gods, holy symbols, religious ceremonies, clergy, divine effects, theology, the Astral Sea and divine dominions, immortal and undead creatures

## Informing Players

All the information the players need to make their choices comes from you. Therefore, within the rules of the game and the limits of PC knowledge, Insight, and Perception, tell players everything they need to know. You don't have to reveal all aspects of a situation or hazard in one go. You should, however, give enough information that the players know what's up and have an idea what to do—and what not to do.

**"Gotcha!" Abilities:** Pay attention to monster abilities that change the basic rules and tactics of combat, and give players the cues they need to recognize them. Describe the ability as it might appear in the game world, and then describe it in game terms to make it clear.

For example, if the characters are fighting a pit fiend, whose aura of fire deals fire damage to creatures within 5 squares, you might tell the players (before their characters come in range), "The heat emanating from the devil is intense even at this distance. You know that getting within five squares of it is going to burn you."

**Game States, Conditions, and Effects:** Since PC abilities can sometimes hinge on a game state, condition, or effect that affects their opponent, make it clear to the players how their enemies are doing. Be descriptive, considering the source of the condition, but also be explicit.

The most important combat state is bloodied, which is a gauge for the players on how the fight is going as well as a cue to use certain powers. Tell them when an enemy is under any condition, is bloodied, or under an effect and tell them when it ends. Further, if an adversary heals, the PCs should notice, and the players should be told—especially if the monster is no longer bloodied.

For example, when a monster gets bloodied by lightning damage, you might say, "Lightning courses over its body, forcing it to stagger backward, opening small wounds and burning its skin. It's bloodied." When the characters' troll opponent regenerates, say, "Recent cuts knit together before your eyes. It's regenerating!" If a creature is dazed due to a fear-inducing power, you could say, "Its eyes bulge wide, and it starts to shake. It's dazed."

**Hazards, Traps, and Obstacles:** Be sure to include any important setting details the players need to know. If the PCs can sense a hazard or obstacle, you should emphasize that element. It's better for the game if the PCs sense hints of impending danger. Tell the players how dangerous something looks, or tell them the PCs aren't sure how dangerous something is, and more investigation might be required. A little prompting can go a long way. Further, knowing that something might be dangerous actually builds tension and fun. A hazard that springs out of nowhere has none of that appeal.

For example, if a weak floor might collapse under the PCs, you might describe the floor as cracked or sagging slightly. A trap could leave behind signs from its past victims or the times it was tripped and missed. Rubble from a cave-in might let air through, hinting that the PCs might be able to get through, whereas rubble that slowly lets water through lets the players know that removing the debris is a bad idea. Crackling lightning on an unattended weapon might mean the weapon is dangerous (some sort of trap), but it could just mean the item is magical.

**Magic Items:** Speaking of magic items, when the characters get over their fear of the lightning-charged magic sword and pick it up, tell them what it is and what it does after they've examined it over the course of a short rest (see page 263 of the *Player's Handbook*). It's not fun to make characters guess what a magic item is or try to use a magic item without knowing its capabilities. You can make an exception for really special items, including artifacts. Even then, tell the player at least any numerical bonus the item gives. You don't want to hear, "I hit AC 31 . . . plus whatever this sword's bonus is," for hours or weeks on end.

## PAYING ATTENTION

Make sure you look around the table occasionally to see if the game is going well. If everyone seems to be having fun, relax and just keep going. If the fun is waning, ask the players what they want or need to bring it back, and take their opinions seriously. Refer to "Player Motivations" (page 8) and "Troubleshooting" (page 30)—especially "Balancing Player Tastes" (page 32)—if you run into problems.

## RITUALS

While you're disseminating information, think about how rituals might give some advantage to the PCs. Divination and scrying rituals can allow characters, especially epic-level characters, to bypass obstacles to information as easily as they can bypass physical obstacles at those levels. Design your adventures accordingly, paying careful attention to the ritual descriptions in the *Player's Handbook*. Don't give the characters less than they're entitled to, but don't let them short-circuit your whole adventure by using rituals, either. For instance, the Observe Creature ritual requires the caster to be extremely specific when describing the ritual's intended target. If allowing the ritual to succeed would throw a monkey wrench into your plans for the adventure, you'd be within your rights to rule that the ritual failed to locate the intended target because the caster's description wasn't specific enough. Also, remember that high-level villains have access to the same rituals that the characters do, including wards they can use to protect themselves from scrying attempts.

No matter how carefully you prepare for a gaming session, eventually the players do something unexpected, and you have to wing it. Relax. A lot of DMs feel a lot of anxiety about being caught unprepared, and they overprepare as a result, creating tons of material they never have a chance to use.

With a little bit of focused preparation, some familiarity with basic improvisation techniques, and a lot of flexibility, you can handle any curve ball your players throw at you. You might even be surprised to realize that the game is better than it would have been if it had stuck to your original script.

## IMPROVISATIONAL AIDS

When you have some extra time in your game preparation, spend it preparing some tools you can use to help you improvise when the need arises. Assemble lists of names for use in the future, design a variety of modular encounters, collect a packet of mini-dungeons, and keep your campaign lists up to date.

**Lists of Names:** The names in Chapter 3 of the *Player's Handbook* are a good starting point of lists of names. Time you spend putting together such lists (organized by at least gender and race) pays off when you have to create an NPC on the spur of the moment. You can use baby-naming books or search the Internet for multiple resources for fantasy-flavored names.

**Encounters for Every Taste:** Keeping the particular tastes and motivations of your players in mind, design modular encounters crafted to appeal to their interests. Put together groups of monsters or thugs who could kick in the door and attack at a moment's notice,

and the slayers in your group are happy. For straightforward combat encounters, use the encounter groups in the *Monster Manual* as a starting point. The sample skill challenges in Chapter 5: Noncombat Encounters can also provide a foundation for similar encounters that are more customized to your campaign. Once you've designed them, you can use these encounters to keep things moving when the players make an unexpected decision or pick a surprising route, or to make sure that all your players are staying interested in the game.

**Mini-Dungeons:** Keep a small supply of encounter area maps on hand—not just little dungeons (a ruined mill house with its cellars, a jailhouse, or a cave behind a waterfall), but also unusual wilderness and urban areas. Combined with the encounters you design, these maps can provide a whole session of adventure if things go awry or you just run out of time to prepare one week.

Don't forget that you can carve up larger published adventures into their component encounters and loot them. Or rotate an older encounter map to a different orientation and change the names in a pinch. *D&D Insider* provides many short dungeons and encounters you can also use in short notice.

**Campaign Lists:** Keep track of what's going on in your campaign. Keep the story of the adventure and the whole campaign in mind, and keep a list of things that can happen to drive the story forward. If the PCs decide to wander off to an unexpected place and you end up using one of your prepared maps and some random encounters, pull something off your campaign list to tie the whole excursion into the broader story. This one element tied to the ongoing story makes the players think you had the whole thing planned from the start, no matter how random the encounters seemed!

## SAYING YES

One of the cornerstones of improvisational theater technique is called "Yes, and . . ." It's based on the idea that an actor takes whatever the other actor gives and builds on that.

That's your job as well. As often as possible, take what the players give you and build on it. If they do something unexpected, run with it. Take it and weave it back into your story without railroading them into a fixed plotline.

For example, your characters are searching for a lich who has been sending wave after wave of minions at them. One of the players asks if the town they are in has a guild of wizards or some other place where wizards might gather. The reasoning goes that such a place would have records or histories that mention

---

### TIPS FROM THE PROS

Something amazing happened one time I was playing D&D with my 9-year-old son. When we finished an encounter, my son took over. He decided that he was going to search around one of the statues in the room, that he was going to get hit by a trap (an arrow would shoot out at the statue), and that he'd find a treasure there.

Hey, wait a minute. I thought I was the DM!

That was my first reaction. But I bit my tongue. I rolled damage for the trap, and I let him have his treasure. (I determined what it was—I wasn't about to relinquish *that* much control.)

He never enjoyed the game more.

I learned the most important lesson about D&D that day. I remembered that this is a game about imagination, about coming together to tell a story as a group. I learned that the players have a right to participate in telling that story—after all, they're playing the protagonists!

—*James Wyatt*

this lich's activities in the past, when the lich was still a living wizard. That wasn't a possibility you'd anticipated, and you don't have anything prepared for it.

Many DMs, at this point, would say, "No, there's no wizards' guild here."

What a loss! The players end up frustrated, trying to come up with some other course of action. Even worse, you've set limits to your own campaign. You've decided that this particular town has no association of wizards, which could serve as a great adventure hook later in your campaign.

When you say yes, you open more possibilities. Imagine you say there *is* a wizards' guild. You can select wizards' names from your prepared lists. You could pull together a skill challenge encounter you have half-prepared and set it up as the encounter that the PCs need to overcome in order to gain access to the wizards' records. You could use a mini-dungeon map to depict the wizards' library if the PCs decide to sneak in, and then scrape together an encounter with a golem or some other guardian. Take a look at your campaign lists, think about what would help the PCs find the lich, and tell the players they find that information after much digging through the wizards' records.

Instead of cutting off possibilities, you've made your campaign richer, and instead of frustrating your players, you've rewarded them for thinking in creative and unexpected ways. Make a note of the things you just invented about this wizards' cabal (adding them to your campaign lists), and use the cabal again later in your campaign. Everyone's happy!

# ENDING

As we discussed under Pacing (page 24), two great times to end a game session are at a natural rest point after a climactic encounter or at a cliffhanger. Whichever ending you choose, make sure you leave a little time at the end of the session to wrap things up.

The end of a session is a casual time, a return to the social energy of the session's start. Listen to your players during this time, even if you have other things occupying your attention, like handing out experience points or treasure. The things the players say or do at the end of the session are the best feedback you receive from your players, as well as a great source of ideas for your preparation.

At the end of a session, players will tell you what they most enjoyed, whether the challenges and rewards felt appropriate, what they think the villain is up to, and where they plan to go next. They won't usually tell you all this directly, but they'll reveal it as they talk about the night's adventuring at the end of the session.

Use this information to say yes to your players, as we just discussed under Improvising. Prepare for the players to do what they discussed they would do at the end of the session. Maybe their thoughts about the villain's plans are better than your ideas were, or their notions can add an extra dimension to what you already have sketched out. Listen, and make your next plans accordingly, and your players will feel as though they are a part of the story.

Sometimes your game group, your adventure, or your campaign runs into problems. Remember that gamers play to have fun, and the people are human beings before they are gamers. They have real-life needs and motivations that can affect the game. The best things you can do are remain calm, be fair, and listen and respond to what the players have to say when there are problems.

## CHARACTER DEATH

Adventures involve risk by definition. With every encounter, the characters can fail. In the case of a combat encounter, one cost of failure is the chance of death—of a single character or an entire group.

Players get attached to their characters. That's natural. A character represents an investment of a lot of time at the table, and a big emotional investment as well. The biggest problem resulting from character death is hard feelings.

The best way to avoid hard feelings connected to character death is to be fair and to make sure the players know you're being fair. Rolling dice in front of them helps that perception. The players know that you're not cheating in the monsters' favor, or singling out a single character for punishment. (See "Rolling Dice," page 15, for the benefits and pitfalls of rolling dice in the open.)

Don't ever punish a character for a player's behavior or some personal grudge. That's probably the quickest way to undermine your players' trust in you as DM and as a fair arbiter of the rules. Let characters face the consequences of their stupid actions, but make sure you give enough cues for the players to recognize stupid actions and to give the players every opportunity to take back rash decisions.

Your players also have to know that you're fair in designing encounters and are not stacking the odds against them from the beginning. It's fine to throw tough encounters at them and sometimes to let them face monsters they can't beat. But it's not fair if the players have no way to know they can't win the fight or have no way to escape. Scare them, but don't trap them.

When a character does die, it's usually up to the players as a group to decide what happens. Some players are perfectly happy to roll up a new character, especially when they're eager to try out new options. Don't penalize a new character in the group. The new member should start at the same level as the rest of the party and have similar gear.

You might want to discourage players from bringing a clone of the dead character in as a "new" character, adding "II" to the character's name or altering it slightly, but otherwise leaving the character unchanged. It's obviously artificial and interferes with the players' sense of the fantasy world as a believable and coherent place. On the other hand, copying a character might be fine depending on the style and seriousness of your game, and it does keep the game moving forward with no delay.

If the characters have gained at least a few levels, the death of a character is the loss of a significant investment of time and energy. Fortunately, dead characters can be brought back to life. The most common way is through the Raise Dead ritual described in the *Player's Handbook* (page 311). Usually, a dead character means that the party has to take at least 8 hours to use the Raise Dead ritual and rest afterward.

By epic level, many characters can return from death in the middle of combat by a variety of means (epic destiny abilities, potions, and so on). At that point, death can be little more than a speed bump, but the consequences of failure can be much worse than death.

## FIXING YOUR MISTAKES

It's going to happen sometimes: You make mistakes. That doesn't make you a bad Dungeon Master. It means you're human. What matters most is how you deal with those mistakes.

### BAD RULES CALL

You do not have to have a perfect mastery of the rules, and you should be open to at least some discussion of the right way to apply a rule in any situation. But you also want to keep the game moving, which means that at some point you have to cut off discussion. When you do, tell one of the players to make a note of the issue and how you resolved it, and reopen the discussion at the end of the encounter or the end of the session.

If you realize you made a mistake, admit it. If you don't admit it, you'll start to lose your players' trust. Then, if you need to, make it up to the players. If your mistake had a significant effect on the outcome of the encounter, do what it takes to correct for your mistake. You can give the characters a little more experience or a little more treasure, or you can resolve the issue within the context of the adventure. Maybe that goblin didn't escape to warn the ogres after all.

### ENCOUNTER TOO HARD

It can be hard to judge ahead of time just how tough an encounter is. Throwing a 13th-level monster at a 9th-level party is often fine, but if the creature has regeneration that negates all the damage the characters do to it, they will be hard pressed to survive that fight.

If you see the characters obviously overwhelmed in an encounter, you can:

✦ give the characters an escape route;

✦ make intentionally bad choices for the monsters;

✦ "forget" to roll to see if monsters recharge their powers;

✦ come up with a story reason for the monsters to leave the fight; or

✦ let the monsters win, but leave the characters alive for some reason.

If you let the characters beat an encounter that was too hard for them, don't give them full experience for that encounter because it wasn't as challenging as its level indicates. Reduce the XP award by about a level's worth.

## HARD ENCOUNTER TOO EASY

Usually, this isn't a problem. If the adventure assumes that the encounter is hard (for example, you need the villain to escape but the players figure out a way to prevent that), you can step up the difficulty as you go. Bring in reinforcements. Give the villain a new capability the players didn't know about.

## CHARACTERS GET TOO POWERFUL

Characters can become too powerful if you give out too much treasure, or if you create special effects that are more powerful than you intended. For example, the characters might vanquish a villain they weren't intended to defeat and acquire his magic sword, which is six levels above their level. Or, you could place a magic fountain in your adventure and decide that drinking from it gives a character an extra encounter power that deals way too much damage for the characters' level.

✦ **In-Game Fix:** Figure out ways to remove items from the players' possession. Perhaps the villain's sword has a mind of its own and the means to travel by flight or teleportation. Retrieving it could become a quest that occupies the characters until they're high enough level to wield it without unbalancing the game. The power granted by the magic fountain could turn out to have a limited number of total uses. Once they're spent, the magic fades.

✦ **Out-of-Game Fix:** Talk to your players, explain that you made a mistake, and ask them to voluntarily relinquish the overpowered items or powers. Mature players recognize that the game is more fun when challenges are meaningful, and they help you deal with the problem.

## GROUP SIZE

This book provides rules and guidelines for running a group of four to six player characters. If your group varies from that size, you have some specific issues to deal with.

## SCALING

The general encounter-building rules scale easily to larger or smaller parties. If you have only three player characters, use three monsters of their level as the baseline encounter. If you have seven, use seven monsters. You should still try for a balance among the different monster roles (see page 54).

## SMALLER THAN FOUR

Small groups can't cover the four basic character roles. If you have only three player characters, you can do without a controller or a striker at the cost of a little damage output. It's hard to play an effective game with only two player characters, but you can do it. A striker with a leader is probably the best. It pairs high damage output with a tough character who can keep the pair alive. If you're running a game for only a single player character, a defender or leader is best—staying alive is the most important consideration. See "Building a Party," page 10, for more information on character roles and how to adjust for missing roles.

## LARGER THAN SIX

The biggest problems with large groups are maintaining order at the table and keeping combat moving. Outside of combat, have the players designate a party leader, who is then the only person who tells you what the group is doing. It's too difficult to listen to six people who are all trying to tell you what they do at the same time. In combat, keep the players on their toes. Make sure you have a solid way of tracking initiative (see page 38), and force characters to delay if their players take too long to decide on their actions.

With a particularly large group, make sure that your encounters take place in areas big enough to hold all the characters and all the monsters while leaving room for movement and tactical positioning. An area about 10 squares by 16 squares is a good minimum for parties of seven or more characters.

## DESIGN ADVENTURES FOR SIZE

Adventure design is also important. Don't send a large group on quests that require infiltration, scouting, or negotiation. Large groups do better in military-style situations and straightforward fights against similarly large groups of monsters. Small groups, on the other hand, are ideal for quests that require stealth or subtlety, especially if the players build their characters with that in mind. Adventures focused on espionage, intrigue, or interaction can be very effective with a small group.

# PROBLEM PLAYERS

Sometimes the problem at your game table is not your game, but your players. We can't tell you how to deal with every kind of problem between friends. A few situations are unique to the game environment, though, and we do have some advice on handling those. Because these issues are really problems with players, to solve the solutions you need to address most of these issues outside the game.

## SETTING EXPECTATIONS

Most player problems occur because you and your players have different expectations for the game. You want different things out of it or enjoy different aspects of it. Often, you can keep the game going smoothly by being clear about your expectations before problems arise and by making sure you understand your players' expectations. Take their opinions and desires seriously, and make sure they take yours just as seriously. Ideally, you'll find a style of play that everyone enjoys.

## OUT-OF-CONTROL PLAYERS

People often play D&D because it lets them, through their characters, do things they can't do in real life—fight monsters, cast spells, defeat evil so that good can triumph. Some people play because D&D lets them run wild, wreaking havoc in towns and going on what amounts to crime sprees or betraying their allies. What they want in the game has nothing to do with heroic adventure, but with using the game rules to act out antisocial fantasies.

---

## TIPS FROM THE PROS

If I'm running a demo game of D&D, and I don't know the people around the table that well, I rely on an easy way of handling initiative order. It's quick and dirty, and isn't good for nonbeginner players, but it is useful when you want to clear brain space for other DMing tasks.

I have all the players roll initiative at the beginning of combat. Whoever rolls highest goes first, of course. However, after that, I assign initiative sequentially from that player's left, which is clockwise. Monsters all go when I come up in seating order around the table. This works like a charm in demonstration games, but when more advanced players begin to delay or hold their actions, this little trick runs off the tracks.

Keep it in your back pocket for when you want to run a game for your younger relatives, your chums at school, or other friends who are interested in how D&D works. Otherwise, use the rules.

—*Bruce Cordell*

---

Talk to your players, reopening the conversation about the kind of game you want to play. If it's just one player causing the trouble, it's perfectly appropriate to issue an ultimatum: If an out-of-control player wants to continue playing with the group, he has to stop being disruptive and play as part of a team.

## PRIMA DONNA PLAYERS

Some players feel that the game should center on them, even if they'd never say it in those words. They hog the spotlight, tell other players what their characters should do, claim the best magic items for themselves, and verbally bully the other players. Away from the game, point out that the player's behavior is spoiling the fun for everyone else and ask him to tone it down, or if necessary, ask the player to leave the group.

## RULES LAWYERS

You don't have to be a rules expert to be the DM, but that doesn't mean one other player should assume that role. A rules lawyer is a player who argues against the DM's decisions by referencing the rules. You should welcome players who know the rules. They help when you're stuck or you make mistakes. But even helpful rules lawyers become a problem if they correct you continually or give you rules advice that's just wrong. Much worse are players who can't stand negative results, and who comb the rules for loopholes and misinterpretations that their characters can exploit.

A table rule about holding rules discussions until the end of the game is enough to dissuade some rules lawyers. Stay open to minor corrections, though, as long as they're not too frequent.

If the game grinds to a halt while a rules lawyer tries to find a specific rule or reference, invite the player to take as long as he wants to search for it while you and the rest of the players continue the game. The rules lawyer's character essentially steps out of the game for as long as it takes. Monsters don't attack him, and he delays indefinitely. This solution makes the other players happy, because they get to keep playing D&D instead of letting one player stop the game.

## BALANCING PLAYER TASTES

Plenty of gaming groups share very similar tastes and motivations. Whole groups made up of actors or slayers aren't uncommon. It's easy to run these groups, as long as your tastes are similar. It's more difficult to please players in the same group who have very different tastes.

You can avoid problems by first identifying the motivations of each player in the group, and then varying the encounter mix in your adventures. The discussion of player motivations on page 8 suggests ways to please every player. Don't try to put a group of actors through a run-of-the-mill dungeon crawl, and don't expect a group of slayers to negotiate their way through the intricacies of royal politics. If you spend some of your preparation time reviewing the adventures you're planning to run with player motivations in mind, and then designing additional encounters or encounter elements to make sure something has something they fun among the encounter mix, you avoid most problems stemming from differing player taste.

Other problems arise when players assume that their particular style of play is superior to others, and they lose patience with encounters aimed at other players. This attitude surfaces most often with actors who look down their noses at slayers and power gamers. Deal with this issue by reminding the offending player (away from the table) that you have a group to please, not just one player, and that the slayers are patiently enduring the roleplaying-intensive encounters. The actors should extend the same courtesy to the slayers in the group.

In game, though, you can also design single encounters that appeal to multiple player motivations. Imagine a fight pitting the player characters against a small army of orcs, making the slayers happy. A young dragon wanders into the middle of the fight. Suddenly the fight can swing one of two ways: The dragon could help the orcs against the party or help the party against the orcs. It's up to the actor in the group, set off in his own small roleplaying encounter, to persuade the dragon to help the party. Everyone's happy!

DAVID GRIFFITH

# TEACHING THE GAME

When siblings, spouses, new friends, or children of existing players join the game, you face the happy task of teaching a new player how to play D&D. Teaching new players isn't just your job. It's something the group can share.

**What Is D&D?:** The first, most important, and possibly hardest part of teaching a new player the game is explaining what the game is. A lot of people are familiar with the concept of a roleplaying game from past experience or computer gaming, but people also have some weird misconceptions about how you play the D&D game. Chapter 1 of the *Player's Handbook* covers the basics.

**The Core Mechanic:** Explain the core mechanic of the game: Make a check and compare it to a defense. Make sure the new player can recognize a d20, and then explain that a check means rolling the d20 and adding some number. That's the core mechanic in a nutshell.

**What You Can Do in the Game:** Explain that the character can try anything the player can imagine, and it's up to you to determine whether it works. Explain the three main types of actions in combat: standard (the important thing), move (getting around), and minor (the things you do so you can do other things). Make sure the player understands trading down (using a move action instead of a standard action, for example).

**Reading a Character Sheet:** Highlight the key information on the character sheet. (You might want to use a highlighter to mark these spots.) Explain these concepts:

✦ **Class and level** describe your role in the group and how powerful you are.

✦ **Hit points** are how much damage you can take. **Healing surges** are how many times you can be healed in a day, and how much you heal at a time.

✦ **Defenses (AC, Fortitude, Reflex, Will)** are the target numbers that the monsters try to hit when they roll an attack against you.

✦ **Speed** is how many squares you can move with one action.

✦ **Initiative** is what you use to determine who goes first in combat.

✦ **Powers** are the attacks and other special things you can do in and out of combat.

**Mentoring:** Finally, make sure one more experienced player at the table has the job of helping the new player, particularly in combat.

Then start playing! The best way to learn is by playing.

# CHAPTER 3

# COMBAT ENCOUNTERS

**STRIPPED TO** the very basics, the D&D game is a series of encounters. Encounters are where the game happens—where the capabilities of the characters are put to the test and success or failure hang in the balance. An encounter is a single scene in an ongoing drama, when the player characters come up against something that impedes their progress. This chapter talks you through running combat encounters, whether they're encounters from a published adventure or encounters you've designed yourself.

This chapter includes the following sections.

✦ **Combat Fundamentals:** How to run a combat as the DM: preparation, monster readiness, surprise, rolling and tracking initiative, tips on running the combat (including tracking individual monsters, conditions, and effects), and how to wrap up an encounter.

✦ **Additional Rules:** Rules for actions not covered by the rules, cover, forced movement, aquatic combat, mounted combat, flying, disease, and poison.

RON SPEARS

Whether you're running a pitched battle, a tense negotiation, a pulse-pounding attempt to scale a cliff, or a dangerous run down a trap-filled passage, don't forget everything you learned in the last chapter. It's never just a combat encounter—it's a life-or-death struggle between heroic adventurers and horrific monsters. It's not just the exchange of numbers and the strategy of moving pieces around on a board—it's a test of the adventurers' skill and mettle against terrible odds. Keep the pace fast, the narration vivid, and the players enthralled!

Below is a quick summary of how to run a combat encounter. The rest of this section gives you the tools you need to follow these steps.

✦ Come prepared with all the information you need

✦ Determine monster readiness and surprise

✦ Set up the encounter

✦ Roll initiative!

✦ Run combat

✦ Wrap things up

## COME PREPARED

Before a combat encounter begins, you should have some information at hand. If you're running a published adventure, most of this information is provided for you. Otherwise, figure it out as you're creating the encounter.

✦ The player characters' passive Perception checks (see the description of the Perception skill in the *Player's Handbook*).

✦ A map and a description of the area where the encounter takes place. This description might take the form of a brief bit of narration you can read to your players to set the scene. It should also include details they might notice, depending on the group's passive Perception.

✦ Statistics for the opponents in the encounter. The statistics should include passive Perception checks for the opponents.

## MONSTER READINESS

Monsters and NPCs aren't always ready for trouble at a moment's notice. The dragon might be sleeping, and the goblins might be playing cards when they should be watching the entrance for intruders. As the player characters approach an encounter, decide how ready the monsters are for the encounter. Choose one of these states: asleep, distracted, ready, or alert.

**Asleep:** The monster (or group of monsters) isn't awake and is only marginally aware of its surroundings. Asleep monsters take a –5 penalty to their Perception checks.

A monster that's asleep doesn't have any prepared defenses and is surprised when it wakes up. At the start of its next turn, it's ready if there's an obvious danger present or distracted if there's no obvious threat nearby.

**Distracted:** The monsters are doing something that occupies their attention or simply daydreaming. Distracted monsters take a –2 penalty to their Perception checks.

**Ready:** Monsters have their weapons with them, but they are not necessarily in hand. They're idly waiting—not poised to engage a specific danger, but prepared in general terms to face danger. Most of the monsters the PCs meet are in the ready state unless the PCs are particularly sneaky. Ready monsters get no bonus or penalty to their Perception checks.

**Alert:** The monsters have perceived a possible threat and made themselves ready to face it. They have weapons at the ready, and they've moved to the best positions to engage a straightforward attack from a likely source. They prepare any available defenses, possibly including powers that enhance their combat abilities. They roll active Perception checks each round. If no threat materializes after 10 minutes, most monsters revert back to the ready state.

## SURPRISE

Determining surprise is usually pretty straightforward: If one side notices the other side without being noticed in return, it has the advantage of surprise.

In many situations, surprise is extremely unlikely. Two groups traveling an open road or blundering through a forest notice each other, with no need for Perception checks of any kind. Neither group surprises the other.

Surprise can happen when characters or creatures are actively hiding: Characters try to sneak past the giants guarding the outskirts of the enemy encampment. Kobolds hide along a well-traveled road, hoping to ambush travelers. A fey panther stalks through the forest, looking for prey. If one group is actively trying to avoid detection, it might achieve surprise.

In this case, the group member with the lowest Stealth check modifier rolls a check. (Use this as a simplification to save time, rather than having each character or monster roll a check.) Any group member that's at least 10 squares away from the rest of the group can roll a separate check. Compare the check result to the passive Perception checks of the creatures that might notice the hiding group, or the active checks from alert creatures. Creatures that fail to notice the sneaking characters are surprised if the group members attack.

**Blocked Vision:** Objects or circumstances that block vision can contribute to an attempt to achieve surprise. The characters approach a dungeon door. Thick fog swirls around the moors, eerily lit by a full moon overhead. The PCs, shrouded in invisibility, try to get the drop on the ancient dragon.

Blocked vision provides some degree of concealment, which is one way that characters or creatures can attempt to actively hide. Characters wandering through fog or making their way down a dungeon corridor toward an open archway are also effectively invisible to other creatures, but they might not be actively hiding.

Beyond the lowest character levels, surprise is rare without some attempt at stealth. Creatures that want to achieve surprise in heavy fog or similar conditions must make an effort to be quiet and stay out of sight, making Stealth checks.

A dungeon door not only blocks sight but also muffles sound, making it easier for characters to get close to their opponents without being detected. The characters can move right up to the door without being noticed, assuming they're at least reasonably quiet. They can listen at the door, making an active Perception check to hear what's beyond, and barge in ready for a fight.

The PCs can't be surprised when they open a dungeon door prepared for a fight. They can listen at the door to get some idea of what they'll be facing, but the monsters won't get the jump on them. It's a different matter if the monsters in the room are actively hiding, so the characters burst in and don't see a threat until the monsters spring their ambush.

Refer to the Listening Through a Door table, below, for Perception DCs if the characters actively listen at the door. Then answer these two questions to determine if the PCs can gain surprise over the monsters.

✦ *Do the monsters hear the PCs approach?* If the PCs are moving at normal speed through the dungeon and making no attempt at stealth, monsters in a room behind a door hear them with a DC 25 Perception check (active or passive). If the PCs are quiet, the PCs make a Stealth check with a +5 bonus (to account for the muffling effect of the door) to set the monsters' Perception DC.

If the monsters hear them, the monsters can't be surprised.

✦ *Do the PCs give their presence away?* If the characters set off a trap on the door, trigger an alarm in place outside the room, or have to try more than once to break the door down, the monsters know they're coming and can't be surprised.

## LISTENING THROUGH A DOOR

| Perception DC* | Sounds the PCs Hear |
|---|---|
| Monsters' Stealth check + 5 | Monsters moving quietly around the room |
| 5 | Battle in progress, or agitated or dramatic conversation** |
| 15 | Normal conversation or ritual casting** |
| 15 | Doors opening or closing (and similar sounds) |
| 25 | Quiet conversation, whispers* |
| 35 | Battle preparations (weapons being drawn, and so on) |

\* Add 2 to the DC if the characters are more than 10 squares away.

\*\* If you succeed by 5 or more, and you know the language being spoken, you can understand what the creatures are saying.

# Roll Initiative!

Whether it's the moment negotiations with the duke break down or the instant the goblins spring their ambush, rolling initiative marks the real start of a combat encounter.

Initiative is usually a simple Dexterity check (one-half level + Dexterity modifier + other modifiers). Every monster statistics block in the *Monster Manual* or a published adventure includes the creature's initiative check modifier, but it's easy enough to figure it out for a character on the fly.

Each player character rolls initiative separately, of course, but don't give the monsters the same attention. Roll once for each distinct kind of monster in the encounter. For example, in an encounter with one orc Eye of Gruumsh, two orc berserkers, two orc raiders, and three orc warriors, make one initiative roll for each of the four kinds of orcs. So as you run through the initiative order, all the orc warriors act at once, all the orc raiders go together, and so on.

Individual monsters can delay and ready actions just like other monsters, so it's possible you'll end up with the two orc raiders acting at different times by the time the encounter is over. Monsters can also ready within their turn without shifting their place in the initiative order. For example, the orc raiders can both move into a flanking position and then both attack with combat advantage. Technically, the first

one to move would have to ready its attack until the other one moved into position, but it all works out the same in the end.

## Tracking Initiative

Different DMs use different methods to track initiative order in combat. Use the one that works best for you and your players. The two key factors about tracking combat order are how you handle readying and delaying, and if the players can see the initiative order.

**Combat Cards:** One effective method of tracking initiative and other details of combat is with index cards. Each character gets a card, and each group of identical monsters gets a card. When the players tell you their initiative check results, write the numbers on their PC combat cards and arrange them in order with the highest result on top, then insert the monsters' cards. Then move through the stack, starting at the top. After each character acts, move his or her card to the back of the stack.

If a character readies an action, it's a good idea to shift the position of the card—turn it so it sticks out from the stack, for example. Then when the character takes the readied action, pull the card and insert it into the stack in the correct new place (either before or after the creature that triggered the action). If a character delays, you can do the same thing. Alternatively (particularly if you have a large group), you can hand

the combat card to the player and give him or her the responsibility of telling you when he or she is jumping back into the action.

The players don't have much knowledge of the order of play when you use combat cards. They don't know where the monsters fall into the order until they act, which some DMs enjoy. On the other hand, they often forget when their turn is coming up. It can be helpful, when you call out the name of the character whose turn it is, to also mention who's next so that player can start thinking ahead.

Example combat cards, one for PCs and one for monsters, can be found on page 220.

**Visible List:** You can use a white board to track initiative. As the players tell you their initiative check results, write them on the white board in order (highest results on top), leaving room between each name. You can either write the monster results on the list at the same time or add them to the list on each monster's first turn.

When a character readies an action, make a mark next to that character's name in the order. When the character takes the readied action, erase the character from his or her old position on the list and add him or her back in at the new position. If a character delays, you can do the same thing, or you can erase the character from the list and let the player tell you when he or she is jumping back in.

As a further improvement, use magnets that you can attach to the white board with characters' and monsters' names written on them. Moving these elements around is even easier than erasing and rewriting.

A visible list lets everyone see the order of play as you go. Players know when their turns are coming up, and they can start planning their actions in advance. On the down side, a visible list involves erasing and rewriting, which can slow down the action in complicated battles.

A variation on the visible list is having one of the players keep track of initiative, either on a white board or on a piece of paper the other players can see. This method reduces your mental processing load, freeing you up to think about the rest of what's going on at the table. On the other hand, it can be hard for you to remember when the monsters' turns are coming up!

**List Behind the Screen:** You can also keep track of initiative on a list the players can't see: either your own private white board or a piece of scratch paper. Some argue that this combines the worst features of the other two methods: Players have no visibility into the order, and it involves erasing and rewriting. However, some DMs feel that it keeps control of the battle where it belongs—solidly in the DM's hands.

WILLIAM O'CONNOR

# Running Combat

Chapter 9 of the *Player's Handbook* tells you everything you need to know about the mechanics of combat. Here are some tips to help you keep things moving smoothly.

## Describing the Circumstances

"Dispensing Information" (page 26) discusses the information you should give your players that is most important in combat encounters: Avoid unfairly hitting them with "Gotcha!" abilities, be sure to communicate conditions and states, and alert them to possible dangers and hazards in their environment.

## Monsters and Fallen Characters

Don't hit people when they're down. When a character falls unconscious, monsters turn their attention to enemies who are still up and fighting. Monsters don't usually intentionally deal damage to fallen foes.

Some monsters are interested only in eating, and might drag a fallen character away from the combat to enjoy a peaceful meal. Usually these creatures are lurker monsters that are attached to other encounters, such as a lone cavern choker. Dragging a character away is slow going (unless the monster is very strong), so the other characters should always have a chance to rescue their fallen allies.

## Legitimate Targets

When a power has an effect that occurs upon hitting a target—or reducing a target to 0 hit points—the power functions only when the target in question is a meaningful threat. Characters can gain no benefit from carrying a sack of rats in hopes of healing their allies by hitting the rats.

When a power's effect involves a character's allies, use common sense when determining how many allies can be affected. D&D is a game about adventuring parties fighting groups of monsters, not the clash of armies. A warlord's power might, read strictly, be able to give a hundred "allies" a free basic attack, but that doesn't mean that warlord characters should assemble armies to march before them into the dungeon. In general, a power's effect should be limited to a squad-sized group—the size of your player character group plus perhaps one or two friendly NPCs—not hired soldiers or lantern-bearers.

## Tracking Individual Monsters

Tracking individual, identical monsters once they start taking damage or using rechargeable powers strains your brain's processing power. One way to help differentiate monsters of the same kind is to use different miniatures for each individual. On a piece of scratch paper, you can track hit points and power use for each monster next to a brief description of the miniature you're using for it. You can also tag the miniatures with small stickers of different shapes or colors.

You can also just note which character each monster is currently attacking. If you know that the worg attacking Rieta has 14 hit points left, then if Rieta attacks—or the wizard attacks "the one that's on Rieta"—you know where to mark off the resulting damage.

One way to keep rechargeable powers simple is to initially have all the monsters use the same rechargeable power for the first time in the same round. For example, in the second round of combat, when they're all in good positions, all the hell hounds use their breath weapons. Then each time an individual hell hound acts, roll to see if its breath weapon recharges, and use it if it does. When a hell hound is taking an action other than using its breath weapon, you know that its breath weapon is not charged. All you need think about is the recharge roll at the start of each creature's turn.

The simplest way doesn't always work, of course. Smart monsters don't always use rechargeable powers as soon as they recharge, for example, and monsters with more than one rechargeable power complicate things. In these cases, track limited powers the same way you track hit points.

## Tracking Conditions and Effects

Keeping track of conditions can get tricky. For monsters, use the same techniques discussed above. Note conditions and effects on combat cards or wherever you track initiative.

The players should remember any conditions in place on their characters. However, they could forget, since they have little incentive to remember hampering conditions, though they might honestly try. Mark character conditions on combat cards or a white board. You might also try keeping a supply of index cards marked with conditions (and the effects of those conditions) and handing the cards to players as the conditions come up. Having a bright pink index card on top of his or her character sheet helps even the most absent-minded player remember a condition, and remember to roll a save to get rid of it.

Players should also remember which monsters they've marked as special targets (such as with a paladin's *divine challenge* or a fighter's *reign of terror*). Place cardboard or magnetic counters by the miniatures of designated targets to help everyone remember what effects are in place. Similar tokens can also remind the players which monsters are bloodied—and help you remember the same thing about characters.

## What the Bad Guys Do

Monsters and even nonplayer characters don't have the same breadth of options in combat that player characters do. Often one power builds on the effect of another. Don't hold onto monsters or NPCs' best powers. If you do, often they die before getting a chance to use them. Start with the big guns.

**Basic Tactics:** The *Monster Manual* suggests basic tactics for the monsters in its pages. Your first guide to a monster's behavior in combat, though, is its role. Artillery monsters avoid melee and favor their ranged attacks. Skirmishers move a lot and avoid the front line. Soldiers and brutes engage the party's defenders and leaders. Controllers position themselves to make best use of their abilities.

**Smart Monsters:** Smart monsters act differently in combat than dumb ones do. Look at the monster's Intelligence score to help you decide what it does. Smart creatures plan their actions and choose the best course of action. A vampire might focus its attacks on the cleric who keeps hitting it with radiant damage. Less intelligent creatures don't plan, they react. A wolf turns to bite the last opponent that hurt it or the nearest enemy.

# AFTER AN ENCOUNTER

When an encounter is over, you need to address lasting consequences, scouring the room, rest, and encounter rewards.

**Encounter Consequences:** Encounters don't occur in a vacuum. What happens in one encounter impacts future encounters—and the adventure.

Did any of the PCs' opponents escape? If so, you need to determine what the fleeing foes do. Most intelligent creatures look for safe refuge or reinforcements. The same monsters, healed and ready for more action, might be waiting in another room, along with more powerful allies.

Did the PCs kill an NPC that's important to the adventure's plot? Make note of how that character's death affects the ongoing plot.

**Searching the Room:** PCs use Perception checks to find anything of interest in the room, such as treasure chests, secret doors, or a holy symbol of Zehir hidden on the body of the supposedly good priest of Pelor they just captured. The PCs scour the room, rolling a lot of Perception checks. Unless the characters are under a time constraint, assume that they're going to roll a 20 eventually, and use the best possible Perception check result for the party. (Effectively, this result equals the best passive Perception check +10.) Assume the characters spend a minute or two searching, and move on to tell them what they find.

A published adventure tells you what there is to be found in a room and how hard it is to find. For your own adventures, use the Difficulty Class and Damage by Level table on page 42, with these guidelines:

## SEARCH THE ROOM DCS

| Perception DC | What the PCs Might Find |
|---|---|
| Easy | Anything valuable in a chest full of junk |
| Moderate | A valuable item tucked away in an unlikely place |
| Moderate | A secret latch or compartment |
| Hard | An average secret door |

**Resting Up:** When combat has ended, PCs can quickly restore their strength with a short rest, or take an extended rest to get back to full health, fully refresh their powers, and reset their action points (see "Rest and Recovery" on page 263 in the *Player's Handbook*).

**Encounter Rewards:** Typical encounter rewards are experience points (XP), action points tied to milestones, and treasure. Chapter 7 discusses each kind of reward in detail.

*Experience Points:* You can give characters XP at the end of every encounter, or wait until they take an extended rest, or wait until the end of the game session. Simply divide the XP total for the encounter by the number of characters present.

*Action Points:* If the characters have reached a milestone, give them 1 action point.

*Quest Rewards:* If the players have completed a major quest or minor quest, tell them so, and give them XP for completing it after their next extended rest, or at the end of the game session.

*Treasure:* The PCs might also find treasure, either in the form of wealth or as magic items they can use. The players can decide among themselves how to divide the treasure they find.

## WHEN IS AN ENCOUNTER OVER?

Typically, encounters are separated by a short rest and some amount of travel time, even if it's as little as crossing the room to open the next door. An encounter ends when the monsters are dead or have fled and the characters take a short rest to regain hit points and encounter powers. The next encounter begins when the characters engage new opponents.

Effects that last "until the end of the encounter" actually last about 5 minutes. That means they never carry over from one encounter to another, as long as those encounters are separated by a short rest. If characters use them outside combat, or plow through multiple encounters without taking a short rest, they enjoy the effect for a full 5 minutes.

What if characters don't take a short rest? Sometimes they feel as though they can't—they have to get to the high priest's chamber before the assassin strikes! Sometimes they just choose not to, perhaps because they hope to enjoy the benefit of an effect that lasts until the encounter ends. In any event, starting a new encounter without the benefit of a short rest after the last one makes the new encounter more challenging.

If you're designing encounters in which you expect characters to move from one to the next without a rest, treat the two events as a single encounter. If the characters surprise you by running on to a new encounter without resting, it might be worth scaling back the new encounter a bit.

# ADDITIONAL RULES

A few combat situations come up rarely enough that the rules for them intentionally aren't covered in the *Player's Handbook*—in particular, mounted combat and combat underwater.

## ACTIONS THE RULES DON'T COVER

Your presence as the Dungeon Master is what makes D&D such a great game. You make it possible for the players to try anything they can imagine. That means it's your job to resolve unusual actions when the players try them.

**Use the "DM's Best Friend":** This simple guideline helps you adjudicate any unusual situation: An especially favorable circumstance gives a +2 bonus to a check or an attack roll (or it gives combat advantage). A particularly unfavorable circumstance gives a –2 penalty.

**Cast the Action as a Check:** If a character tries an action that might fail, use a check to resolve it. To do that, you need to know what kind of check it is and what the DC is.

*Attacks:* If the action is essentially an attack, use an attack roll. It might involve a weapon and target AC, or it might just be a Strength or Dexterity check against any defense. For an attack, use the appropriate defense of the target. Use an opposed check for anything that involves a contest between two creatures.

*Other Checks:* If the action is related to a skill (Acrobatics and Athletics cover a lot of the stunts characters try in combat), use that check. If it is not an obvious skill or attack roll, use an ability check. Consult the Difficulty Class and Damage by Level table below, and set the DC according to whether you think the task should be easy, hard, or somewhere in between. A quick rule of thumb is to start with a DC of 10 (easy), 15 (moderate), or 20 (hard) and add one-half the character's level.

**Setting Improvised Damage:** Sometimes you need to set damage for something not covered in the rules—a character stumbles into the campfire or falls into a vat of acid, for example. Choose a column on the Difficulty Class and Damage table based on the severity of the effect. Use a normal damage expression for something that might make an attack round after round, or something that's relatively minor. These numbers are comparable to a monster's at-will attack. Use a limited damage expression, comparable to a monster's special powers, for one-time damaging effects or massive damage.

**Example:** Shiera the 8th-level rogue wants to try the classic swashbuckling move of swinging on a chandelier and kicking an ogre in the chest on her way down to the ground, hoping to push the ogre into the brazier of burning coals behind it. An Acrobatics check seems reasonable.

This sort of action is exactly the kind of thinking you want to encourage, so you pick an easy DC: The table says DC 15, but it's a skill check, so make it DC 20. If she makes that check, she gets a hold on the chandelier and swings to the ogre.

Then comes the kicking. She's more interested in the push than in dealing any damage with the kick itself, so have her make a Strength attack against the ogre's Fortitude. If she pulls it off, let her push the ogre 1 square and into the brazier, and find an appropriate damage number.

Use a normal damage expression from the table, because once the characters see this trick work they'll try anything they can to keep pushing the ogres into the brazier. You can safely use the high value, though—2d8 + 5 fire damage. If Shiera had used a 7th-level encounter power and Sneak Attack, she might have dealt 4d6 (plus her Dexterity modifier), so you're not giving away too much with this damage.

**DIFFICULTY CLASS AND DAMAGE BY LEVEL**

| | Difficulty Class (DC) Values | | | Normal Damage Expressions | | | Limited Damage Expressions | | |
|---|---|---|---|---|---|---|---|---|---|
| Level | Easy | Moderate | Hard | Low | Medium | High | Low | Medium | High |
| 1st–3rd | 10 | 15 | 20 | 1d6 + 3 | 1d10 + 3 | 2d6 + 3 | 3d6 + 3 | 2d10 + 3 | 3d8 + 3 |
| 4th–6th | 13 | 17 | 21 | 1d6 + 4 | 1d10 + 4 | 2d8 + 4 | 3d6 + 4 | 3d8 + 4 | 3d10 + 4 |
| 7th–9th | 15 | 19 | 23 | 1d8 + 5 | 2d6 + 5 | 2d8 + 5 | 3d8 + 5 | 3d10 + 5 | 4d8 + 5 |
| 10th–12th | 17 | 21 | 25 | 1d8 + 5 | 2d6 + 5 | 3d6 + 5 | 3d8 + 5 | 4d8 + 5 | 4d10 + 5 |
| 13th–15th | 18 | 22 | 26 | 1d10 + 6 | 2d8 + 6 | 3d6 + 6 | 3d10 + 6 | 4d8 + 6 | 4d10 + 6 |
| 16th–18th | 20 | 24 | 28 | 1d10 + 7 | 2d8 + 7 | 3d8 + 7 | 3d10 + 6 | 4d10 + 7 | 4d12 + 7 |
| 19th–21st | 22 | 26 | 30 | 2d6 + 7 | 3d6 + 8 | 3d8 + 7 | 4d8 + 7 | 4d10 + 7 | 4d12 + 7 |
| 22nd–24th | 23 | 27 | 31 | 2d6 + 8 | 3d6 + 8 | 4d6 + 8 | 4d8 + 8 | 4d12 + 8 | 5d10 + 8 |
| 25th–27th | 24 | 28 | 32 | 2d8 + 9 | 3d8 + 9 | 4d6 + 9 | 4d10 + 9 | 5d10 + 9 | 5d12 + 9 |
| 28th–30th | 25 | 29 | 33 | 2d8 + 10 | 3d8 + 10 | 4d8 + 10 | 4d10 + 9 | 5d10 + 9 | 5d12 + 9 |

For skill checks: Increase DCs by 5

For attacks with weapons or against AC: Increase DCs by 2

# COVER

The rules in the *Player's Handbook* for determining cover are straightforward. A creature that's around a corner from the attacker, or protected by terrain, has cover. A significant terrain advantage gives superior cover. Most of the time, those rules are the only rules you need.

As the referee, you decide based on common sense whether a creature has cover against an attack. If you want rules that can let you determine cover more precisely, you can use these. They're the same rules that appear in the *D&D Miniatures* game. In D&D, though, we recommend that you make a quick decision about cover and move on to the fun.

## MELEE ATTACKS

Cover in melee comes up most often when the target is in a square at the corner of the attacker's space and a wall or other solid obstacle fills one of the squares between them. If the target of the attack occupies the same square as a pillar or tree, that terrain also grants cover. If the attacker is trying to jab the target between the bars of a portcullis, the target has superior cover.

### DETERMINING COVER FOR MELEE ATTACKS

✦ **Defender's Burden:** The target of a melee attack has to prove that it has cover. That proof consists of a line between the attacker and the defender that is blocked by a solid object.

✦ **Corner to Corner:** The defender has cover if an imaginary line from a corner of the attacker's space to a corner of the defender's space is blocked.

✦ **Getting Technical:** If you need to be extremely precise, choose a square the attacker occupies and a square the defender occupies. Draw an imaginary line from *every* corner of the attacker's space to *every* corner of the defender's space. If even one line is obstructed, the defender has cover. (A line that runs parallel right along a wall isn't blocked.)

✦ **Superior Cover:** Only specific terrain features (such as grates and arrow slits) grant superior cover from melee attacks.

## RANGED ATTACKS

Cover comes up a lot more often for ranged attacks, simply because it's harder for the attacker to move into a position with a clear shot. In melee, a character can usually shift 1 square to avoid attacking around a corner and negate most cover. A ranged attacker might have to move halfway across the battlefield to get a clear shot at a target taking cover around a corner. In addition to shooting a creature partially protected by a corner, an important situation to remember for ranged cover is the presence of other enemies (potential targets) between the attacker and the target.

### DETERMINING COVER FOR RANGED ATTACKS

✦ **Attacker's Burden:** For ranged attacks, the attacker has to prove that he has a clear shot. That proof consists of one corner in his space that has clear lines to every corner of the target's space.

✦ **Choose a Corner:** The attacker chooses *one* corner of a square he occupies, and draws imaginary lines from that corner to every corner of *any one* square the defender occupies. If none of those lines are blocked by a solid object or an enemy creature, the attacker has a clear shot. The defender doesn't have cover. (A line that runs parallel right along a wall isn't blocked.)

✦ **Cover:** If you can't find a clear shot, the target has cover. No matter which corner in your space you choose, one or two lines from that corner to every corner in the defender's space are blocked.

✦ **Superior Cover:** The defender has superior cover if no matter which corner in your space you choose and no matter which square of the target's space you choose, three or four lines are blocked. If four lines are blocked from every corner, you can't target the defender.

## CLOSE AND AREA ATTACKS

Close and area attacks work very much like ranged attacks except that you care about the origin square of the effect, not the creature that creates it. A tree between a creature and the center of a fireball helps protect that creature from the blast, not a tree between the creature and the wizard casting the spell.

Also unlike ranged attacks, creatures don't provide cover. An orc in a fireball doesn't get any protection from the other orc standing between it and the center of the fireball.

### DETERMINING COVER FOR CLOSE AND AREA ATTACKS

✦ **Like Ranged Attacks:** You determine cover for these attacks in the same way as for ranged attacks, with two exceptions:

✦ *Origin, Not Attacker:* Treat the origin square of the effect as the attacker's square.

✦ *Creatures Aren't Cover:* Creatures don't provide cover against close and area attacks.

# Forced Movement and Terrain

Many creatures have ways to move others around on the field of battle. "Pull, Push, and Slide" on page 285 of the *Player's Handbook* discusses the general rules for forced movement. One extra wrinkle that might come up in your game is how forced movement interacts with various kinds of terrain.

## FORCED MOVEMENT AND TERRAIN

✦ **Difficult Terrain:** Forced movement isn't hindered by difficult terrain.

✦ **Blocking Terrain:** Forced movement can't move a creature through blocking terrain (page 61). Every square along the path must be a space the creature could normally occupy.

✦ **Challenging Terrain:** Forced movement can make some powers more effective or hinder them, depending on the specific challenging terrain (page 61). The DM can require the target of forced movement to make a check as if it were moving voluntarily across the terrain, with the same consequence for failure.

✦ **Hindering Terrain:** Forced movement can force targets into hindering terrain (page 61). Targets forced into hindering terrain receive a saving throw immediately before entering the unsafe square they are forced into. Success leaves the target prone at the edge of the square before entering the unsafe square.

  If the power that forced the target to move allows the creature that used the power to follow the target into the square that the target would have left, the creature can't enter the square where the target has fallen prone.

  If forced movement pushes a Large or larger creature over an edge, the creature doesn't fall until its entire space is over the edge. On the creature's next turn, it must either move to a space it can occupy or use a move action to squeeze into the smaller space at the edge of the precipice.

  A DM can allow a power that pushes a target more than 1 square to carry the target completely over hindering terrain.

Using forced movement to pull, push, or slide a creature onto ice, or into a pit, or into a cloud of daggers is a clever tactic.

Challenging terrain can make forced movement powers more effective, but it can also hinder them, depending on the specific terrain. For example, if a white dragon pushes a character over slick ice, you could tell the character to make an Acrobatics check

or fall prone. On the flip side, if a shambling mound pushes a character through thick mud, which might require an Athletics check to move through at the cost of paying an extra square of movement, you might let the character use the mud to slow his or her movement, reducing the distance he or she is pushed by 1 square.

Targets of forced movement in hindering terrain (pits, precipices, fire) can avoid plunging into a pit or over the edge of a cliff or being pushed into a raging fire. The creature makes a saving throw rolled immediately before entering the unsafe square, with success leaving the creature prone at the edge of the precipice. If the power used to move the creature would allow the character using the power to follow the target into the square it leaves, the character can't enter the square where the creature has fallen prone. For example, a fighter who bull rushes an orc off a cliff can't move into the square of the prone orc when the orc catches itself at the edge.

At your option, you can allow a power that pushes the target more than 1 square to carry the target over hindering terrain in the way. You might imagine a titan with push 3 knocking a character clear over a pit to land in a heap on the other side.

Some powers specifically have this effect, and it's probably not a good idea to extend it to others. Rely on how you imagine the power working in the world. If you see the blow lifting a creature off the ground, particularly if it leaves him or her prone at the end of the push, you can decide that the power throws the target over hindering terrain along the way.

## Precipitous Terrain

When you design an encounter area, don't put 1st-level characters in a fight at the edge of an 80-foot cliff. The 8d10 points of damage from falling off that cliff would be lethal even to the group's fighter.

The table below classifies the distances of falls according to their severity by character level. A painful fall does significant damage to characters of the indicated levels, but shouldn't kill a character who's not yet bloodied. A perilous fall might kill a bloodied character, and could leave even a character at full health bloodied. A deadly fall could kill a fragile character, will probably make a character bloodied, and threatens significant harm even to a character who has more hit points than any of his companions.

### FALL SEVERITY BY CHARACTER LEVEL

| Level | Painful | Perilous | Deadly |
|-------|---------|----------|--------|
| 1st–5th | 20 ft. | 30 ft. | 40 ft. |
| 6th–10th | 30 ft. | 50 ft. | 70 ft. |
| 11th–15th | 40 ft. | 70 ft. | 110 ft. |
| 16th–20th | 60 ft. | 90 ft. | 140 ft. |
| 21st–25th | 80 ft. | 110 ft. | 170 ft. |
| 26th–30th | 90 ft. | 130 ft. | 200 ft. |

# AQUATIC COMBAT

Fighting underwater is tricky business for land-dwelling adventurers and creatures. Water provides resistance against movement, swirling currents grab and drag a swimmer along, and tempestuous waters immobilize all but expert swimmers.

## AQUATIC COMBAT

When fighting underwater, the following modifiers apply:

- ✦ Creatures using powers that have the fire keyword take a -2 penalty to attack rolls.
- ✦ Characters using weapons from the spear and crossbow weapon groups take no penalties to attack rolls with those weapons while fighting underwater. Characters using any other weapon take a -2 penalty to attack rolls.
- ✦ Creatures move using their swim speed. A creature without a swim speed must use the Athletics skill to swim, as described in the *Player's Handbook*.
- ✦ **Aquatic:** Creatures native to watery environments have the aquatic ability. They gain a +2 bonus to attack rolls against opponents that do not have this ability. Aquatic monsters, such as sahuagin, are noted as such.

## UNDERWATER TERRAIN

The most important underwater terrain is the water itself–especially when the water is moving.

### UNDERWATER TERRAIN

- ✦ **Current:** A current drags creatures along its path. When you swim into a current, you move a distance and direction according to the current's strength and in the direction where it flows. This is a slide effect, with the distance and direction determined by the current. If you wish to fight against a current, you can spend squares of movement to reduce the distance the current slides you. You can reduce the distance partially, or decrease it down to zero, provided that you have enough movement to do so.

    If a current slides you into another square with a current, you ignore that square's current. This applies to all squares the current moves you into, including the destination.

    Current terrain on maps indicates the direction the current slides you and the distance in squares that the current moves you.

- ✦ **Other Terrain:** Difficult terrain, cover, and concealment all exist in watery realms. The ruins of a sunken ship provide cover, while dirt kicked up by powerful currents grants concealment. Choppy, storm-churned seas act as difficult terrain. Best of all, underwater battles allow for up-and-down movement. Creatures can attack the characters from all directions, not just along the ground.

## MOVEMENT IN THREE DIMENSIONS

Aquatic and aerial encounters force you to think in three dimensions. Any DM who has had a monster directly below a PC knows how annoying it is to stack several miniatures in one square.

Define an arbitrary elevation, preferably the one where most of the encounter takes place, as "ground" level. Creatures are all positioned above or below the action relative to that altitude.

Placing a small d6 or d4 next to a figure is a good way to measure its distance above or below this level. The number on the die shows how many squares the creature is above or below the baseline. Use dice of one color to mark creatures below the fight and another color for those above.

When a monster is directly above or below a PC, you can squeeze its miniature into the same place. Although crowded, placing the two miniatures in the same square still works well enough. If you are worried about figures being knocked over or accidentally pushed into the wrong square, pull the miniatures off the table and use smaller proxies, such as the dice that measure elevation, in their place.

Determining range against creatures above or below you is straightforward. Look at the distance between the two creatures as if they were at the same elevation, counting squares as normal. Then count the difference between their elevations. Use the higher of these two numbers.

Since D&D counts diagonal movement the same as movement across the edges of squares, this method works out well. If a creature is far away from another, you can trace a path that shifts upward via diagonals for free. The opposite is true for a creature that is almost directly above another: As you trace its range up to it, you can choose a path that shifts sideways diagonally and up.

# MOUNTED COMBAT

A valiant knight and his fearless warhorse charge a blue dragon. The dwarf cavalry of the Barrier Peaks takes to its hippogriffs to repel a flight of rampaging harpies. A drow scout patrol rides monstrous spiders across a cavern's ceiling, watching for surface dwellers foolish enough to blunder into its territory. From a mundane horse to a snarling wyvern, mounted D&D warriors have many options.

Mounts offer three basic advantages to riders. They are faster than most humanoids, they can offer movement modes such as flight and swimming, and the more ferocious of them combine their fighting abilities with their riders' attacks.

The mounted combat rules define the relationship between a rider and a mount. The rules combine the actions and options of the two creatures, as though mount and rider were a single creature.

## ENCOUNTERS WITH PC MOUNTS

These rules exist to let the PCs use mounts in the easiest, most balanced way. When you decide that the evil wizard rides a wyvern, you add the NPC and the monster to the encounter as normal and let them take their full actions separately. The evil wizard moves along with the wyvern, but both monsters get to attack. The encounter is balanced because you accounted for both of their XP values.

You can allow the PCs and the creatures they ride to get their own sets of actions, especially if a character rides a powerful, intelligent monster such as a dragon. However, at that point you have effectively added an additional member to the party. If you do this, add an additional XP value of monsters to the encounter equal to the mounts' XP value. When granting the PCs experience, subtract these "bonus" monsters from the XP total.

You should use this rule if the mount's level is at the party's level or higher, or if its level is no more than two below the characters' level. Lower-level mounts are too weak to have a big effect on the encounter. As usual, use your common sense. If a lower-level mount manages to prove a big help to the party, add extra creatures and hold back XP as above.

## MOUNTS

- **Size:** Your mount must be larger than you, and no smaller than Large size.
- **Adjacent:** You must be adjacent to a creature to mount it.
- **Willing:** You can use a creature as a mount only if it is willing.
- **Saddles:** The rules assume that you ride a creature with a saddle. If you lack a saddle, you take a –2 penalty to attack rolls, AC, and Reflex defense while mounted.

- **Mounted Combat:** Anyone can simply ride along with a beast of burden without using the Mounted Combat feat. The Mounted Combat feat allows you to make the most of a mount's abilities. When you have the Mounted Combat feat and you ride a creature, you gain access to any special mount abilities it confers to its rider. (Not every creature has these abilities.) While you are riding a creature with Mounted Combat, the creature can make any Athletics, Acrobatics, Endurance, or Stealth checks using your base skill check bonus rather than its own if yours is better.

### MOUNT AND RIDER

- **Space:** You and your mount occupy the mount's space. If it is ever important to determine the precise location within the mount's space that you occupy, you choose.
- **Targeting:** Targeted attacks can target you or your mount, as the attacker chooses. A close attack or an area attack affects both you and your mount if its area includes either of you.
- **Mount Benefits:** Many mounts offer special attacks or benefits they can use or grant to their riders. These abilities range from flat bonuses, such as an AC bonus to the rider, to special attacks that the mount can use. The *Monster Manual* details the benefits that many creatures grant if you meet a minimum level and have the Mounted Combat feat. If you don't meet a mount's prerequisites, you can ride it, but you don't gain the mount's special benefits.
- **Opportunity Attacks:** If your mount's movement provokes an opportunity attack, the attacker chooses to target either you or your mount. If you provoke an opportunity attack by making a ranged attack, the attacker must target you.
- **Forced Movement:** If an attack that forces movement targets you but not your mount, you can choose for your mount to also be affected, so that you and your mount continue to move together. If you don't want your mount to be affected, you can be pushed off your mount if the forced movement carries you out of the mount's space.

### MOUNTS IN COMBAT

- **Mounting and Dismounting:** Mounting or dismounting a creature is a standard action.
- **Initiative:** You and your mount both act on your initiative count. If you and your mount separate, you both continue acting on the same initiative count.
- **Actions:** On your turn, you and your mount combined can take a normal set of actions—a standard action, a move action, and a minor action. You divide these actions as you wish. Most commonly, your mount takes a move action to walk or fly, and

you take a standard action to attack. You and your mount also share a single immediate action. If you and your mount separate, you still share one set of actions on that turn.

- ✦ **Attacking Mounts:** Your mount can use a standard action to attack instead of you. If you don't have the Mounted Combat feat, your mount takes a -2 penalty to all its attack rolls.
- ✦ **Charge:** If you charge, you can move your mount's speed and either make a melee basic attack yourself or let your mount make a melee basic attack.
- ✦ **Squeezing:** If your mount squeezes, it and you both take the associated penalties.
- ✦ **Mounts in Enclosed Spaces**: Mounts native to outdoor areas don't like being cramped into tight dungeon rooms and corridors, and take a -2 penalty to attacks and defenses if forced into a confined space. Mounts native to subterranean regions (such as blade spiders and carrion crawlers) don't take this penalty, and the penalty doesn't apply in an underground area large enough to seem like it's outdoors (at least 50 feet in every direction).
- ✦ **Knocked Prone:** An attack that knocks your mount prone also forces you to dismount. You move into a space of your choice adjacent to the now-prone mount.

  If an attack knocks you prone, you immediately attempt a saving throw to avoid being dismounted. This saving throw works just like a normal saving throw, except you make it as soon as you are knocked prone, not at the end of your turn.

  *Lower than 10:* Failure. You are dismounted and fall prone in an open space of your choice adjacent to the mount.

  *10 or higher:* Success. You remain in the saddle and are not knocked prone.

## Mounts in the Game

Mounts are the most fun when used as part of wilderness adventures, mass battles, and other situations where the characters have open spaces to fight in and long distances to cover. In such situations, you can give the PCs' enemies mounts of their own.

Keep an eye out for traps, narrow corridors that require squeezing, and other effects that make mounts less than useful in dungeons. In addition, wild animals such as griffons typically dislike enclosed spaces. Apply a -2 penalty to such a creature's attacks and defenses if it is forced inside. Be sure to make such penalties clear to the players so that their characters can plan and react appropriately.

If you have any doubts about the effect that mounts have on the campaign, keep them on the sidelines or create story reasons to limit them. For example, the PCs might gain the use of a flight of griffons, but only when they undertake specific missions on the elf

king's behalf. Be forthright with the players. Let them know that they can have cool mounts within the limits you set before they get a chance to use them. Open communication and honesty are the best answers to any problems that arise in the game.

# Flying

The rules for fighting in the air stress abstraction and simplicity over simulation. In real life, a flying creature's ability to turn, the speed it must maintain to stay aloft, and other factors put a strict limit on flight. In D&D, flying creatures face far fewer limitations.

## The Fly Action

Unless otherwise noted below, a flying creature moves like a creature that walks on the ground. It can turn as often as it wants, move backward, and so on. Unless a special ability or a portion of the fly action says otherwise, it moves like it does for any other mode.

### FLY: MOVE ACTION

- ✦ **Movement:** Fly a number of squares up to your fly speed.
- ✦ **Moving Up and Down:** While flying, you can fly straight up, straight down, or diagonally up or down. There is no additional cost for moving up or down.
- ✦ **Remaining in the Air:** If you fail to fly at least 2 squares during your turn, whether due to not moving far enough or simply not using the fly action, you crash at the end of your turn.
- ✦ **Landing and Crashing:** If a creature flies to a surface it can hold onto or rest upon, it can land. A creature that accidentally flies into an object, such as an invisible wall, immediately crashes.
- ✦ **Double Fly:** If you fly twice in a row on the same turn, you can fly a total number of squares equal to double your speed. Normally, you cannot end a move in an ally's space. If you double fly, you can pass through an ally's space even if your first fly action would otherwise leave you in its space.
- ✦ **Provokes Opportunity Attacks:** If you leave a square that is adjacent to an enemy, that enemy can make an opportunity attack.
- ✦ **No Opportunity Attacks:** A flying creature cannot make opportunity attacks.
- ✦ **Knocked Prone:** A flying creature that is knocked prone crashes.

## Crashing

Flight is a fast form of movement that allows a traveler to avoid obstacles and swoop over enemies, but it comes with a major drawback. Tumbling from the sky and crashing to the earth is risk enough to keep many adventurers safe on the ground.

**Crashing:** Most of the time, a creature that falls from the air slams into the ground and takes falling damage as normal (see page 284 of the *Player's Handbook*). However, sometimes a creature is high enough in the air or is a skilled enough flier that it can avoid a crash landing.

✦ **Safe Distance:** A flying creature that crashes immediately drops a distance equal to its fly speed. If it reaches the ground, it lands safely.

✦ **Falling:** If the flier has not yet reached the ground, it crashes.

✦ **Crashes:** A creature that crashes falls all the way to the ground and takes falling damage.

**High-Altitude Crashes:** Some encounters take place high above the ground. You need only the following two rules if a flying creature crashes thousands of feet above the ground.

✦ **Extreme Altitudes:** It is possible that a creature far above the ground can spend more than a round falling to the ground. As a rule of thumb, a creature that crashes falls 100 squares after checking for its safe distance. If it is still in the air, it can attempt to stop its descent by flying again.

✦ **Halting a Descent:** Halting a descent is a special Athletics check made as a standard action. It is a DC 30 check, with a bonus to the check equal to the creature's fly speed. On a success, the creature pulls out of its fall and stops falling. It must still use a move action to fly.

## Special Flying Rules

Many flying creatures have additional abilities related to flight. Here are the common abilities that modify flight.

**Altitude Limit:** A monster that has an altitude limit can't fly more than the indicated number of squares off the ground. If it flies higher than this limit, it crashes at the end of its turn even if it drops back below the limit.

**Clumsy Flying:** A clumsy flier takes a –4 penalty to attack rolls and defenses while flying. These creatures are ill suited to fighting in the air.

**Clumsy Grounded:** A creature that is clumsy when grounded takes a –4 penalty to attack rolls and defenses when on the ground, not flying. Such creatures are at home while flying, and due to their anatomy or training fare poorly on the ground. For example, a bat is agile in the air but clumsy on the ground.

**Hover:** A monster that can hover can shift and make opportunity attacks while flying. It remains flying even if it does not move the minimum distance normally needed to remain aloft. It stays in the air even if it takes no move actions to fly.

**Overland Flight:** Overland flight applies to creatures that fly to move from place to place but remain on the ground to fight. A creature using overland flight loses its minor, immediate, and standard actions while it flies, and can use its move action only to fly. The number associated with overland flight is the number of squares the monster moves with a single move action. If it takes actions to do anything else, it crashes.

## Aerial Terrain

Difficult terrain for a flying creature includes flying debris, swirling air currents, and other factors that interfere with flight. Clouds provide concealment, while towers, floating castles, and other structures provide cover. In addition, use the rules for current under "Aquatic Combat" (see page 45) to model strong gusts of wind.

## Fight in the Skies

It's fun to knock someone from the skies, but it can be a real drag when fights take place far, far above the surface. The distance a creature falls when crashing is great enough that it likely must spend several rounds doing nothing but moving to return to the melee. You don't need to invent reasons why a combatant that crashes but manages to recover quickly returns to the fight. If anything, a monster that rises back to the melee just as the characters think they have won makes for a nasty surprise.

Keep in mind the possibility of a crash when building encounters in the air. Creatures that knock their foes prone are the biggest cause of crashes.

On the other hand, the threat of a crash adds a lot of tension to the game. Use it in moderation, or plan your adventures to account for splitting the party between characters who stay in the air and those who crash.

## Aerial Combat Complexities

When you are running a battle in the air, ground-based elements allow you to add in terrain and a lot more complexity than you might find in a clear sky. Grounded monsters using ranged weapons are the easiest element to add, while soaring rock spires, towers, and other tall terrain details give the characters and their enemies stuff to swoop around.

In an enclosed environment, such as an Underdark cavern or an enormous building, ledges can hang above the fliers, mounted on the chamber's roof or high on its walls. Add in these platforms to attack fliers from two directions or give walking creatures a chance to jump down upon fliers who draw too close. A readied action to jump on a passing flier makes for an interesting complication or a truly heroic action.

## Using a Reference Point

The dwarf crew of an airship works furiously to coax as much speed from its arcane engines as possible. Meanwhile, a flight of marauding gnolls on winged demons draws ever closer to the ship. The characters take to the upper deck, ready to repel the approaching boarders. During the battle, the ship continues to roar forward, the gnolls pushing their mounts to match the pace.

When running this sort of battle at your table, with the ship in the center of the activity, designate the ship as a reference point. On the ship's initiative count, it "moves" forward–but instead of moving the ship, reposition all the creatures flying around it. If the ship flies 10 squares to the east, you can reproduce this event by relocating all the gnolls and their mounts 10 squares to the west. The ship and the gnolls are in the same relative positions as if you had actually moved the ship, but by keeping the ship stationary, you avoid having to reposition the centerpiece of the battle grid.

# DISEASE

When creatures are exposed to a disease–from the bite of a disease-carrying monster, immersion in filthy swamp water, or infected food–they risk contracting the disease.

---

**DISEASE**

+ **Infection:** When you are exposed to a disease, you risk becoming infected. If you are infected, you suffer the initial effect of the disease and begin to move on the disease track.

---

*Monster Attacks:* Make a saving throw at the end of the encounter. If the saving throw fails, you are infected.

*Other Exposure:* For other kinds of exposure (environmental or food), the disease makes an attack roll. If the disease's attack hits, you are infected.

*Prolonged Exposure:* If a character spends a long time exposed to disease, the disease makes one attack roll per day of exposure.

+ **Disease Track:** Every disease has at least three states, arrayed on a a row of effects called the disease's track: cured (the target is no longer affected), the disease's initial effect, and the disease's final state.

*Initial Effect:* When you become infected, you suffer the disease's initial effect.

*Moving on the Disease Track:* As the disease progresses, you might get worse, moving on the track toward the final state, or you might improve until you are cured. Some effects continue until you are cured, persisting regardless of where you are on the disease's track, until you improve to the cured state. Other effects end when you move to a better or worse state on the track.

+ **Disease Progression:** Once you're infected, make an Endurance check after each extended rest to see if you improve, worsen, or maintain your current condition. A disease specifies two target Endurance DCs: a lower DC to maintain and a higher DC to improve.

## EXAMPLE DISEASES

| Blinding Sickness | Level 9 Disease |
|---|---|
| *Often spread in tainted water, blinding sickness leaves its victims sightless.* | **Attack:** +12 vs. Fortitude<br>**Endurance** improve DC 26, maintain DC 22, worsen DC 21 or lower |

| The target is cured. | ◀ | **Initial Effect** The target loses one healing surge that it cannot regain until cured. | ◀▶ | The target's vision is blurred. Creatures beyond 10 squares of it have concealment. | ▶ | **Final State** The target is blinded. |
|---|---|---|---|---|---|---|

| Mummy Rot | Level 11+ Disease |
|---|---|
| *This disease, delivered by the attack of a mummy, fills the lungs of its victims with dust, making it progressively harder for them to breathe* | **Attack:** See mummy lord and mummy champion templates, page 179.<br>**Endurance** improve DC 20 + one-half mummy's level, maintain DC 16 + one-half mummy's level, worsen DC 15 + one-half mummy's level or lower |

| The target is cured. | ◀ | **Initial Effect** The target regains only half the normal number of hit points from healing effects. | ◀▶ | The target regains only half the normal number of hit points from healing effects. In addition, it takes 10 necrotic damage, which cannot be healed until the target is cured of the disease. | ▶ | **Final State** The target dies. |
|---|---|---|---|---|---|---|

| Cackle Fever | Level 12 Disease |
|---|---|
| *The symptoms of cackle fever include high fever, disorientation, and frequent bouts of hideous laughter.* | **Attack:** +16 vs. Fortitude<br>**Endurance** improve DC 28, maintain DC 25, worsen DC 24 or lower |

| The target is cured. | ◀ | **Initial Effect** The target begins each day with no action points. Each time the target becomes bloodied, it laughs uncontrollably and is dazed (save ends). Both of these effects apply until the target is cured. | ◀▶ | The target cannot gain or use action points. | ▶ | **Final State** The target is catatonic and unable to take any actions. |
|---|---|---|---|---|---|---|

## Shakes

**Level 14 Disease**

This disease causes involuntary twitches and tremors that grow progressively worse.

**Attack:** +18 vs. Fortitude
**Endurance** improve DC 29, maintain DC 27, worsen DC 26 or lower

The target is cured. ◄ | **Initial Effect** The target's speed is reduced by 1 until cured. | ◄► The target is slowed. | ► **Final State** The target is immobilized.

## Mindfire

**Level 16 Disease**

In the initial stages, victims of mindfire complain of burning pain in the head. Later, they sink into stupor.

**Attack:** +18 vs. Will
**Endurance** improve DC 31, maintain DC 26, worsen DC 25 or lower

The target is cured. ◄ | **Initial Effect** The target gains vulnerable 10 psychic until cured. | ◄► Each time the target becomes bloodied, it becomes dazed and takes ongoing 10 psychic damage (save ends both). | ► **Final State** The target is dazed.

## Hellfever

**Level 21 Disease**

Those who suffer from hellfever complain of alternating sensations of searing fire and freezing cold.

**Attack:** +24 vs. Fortitude
**Endurance** improve DC 34, maintain DC 29, worsen DC 28 or lower

The target is cured. ◄ | The initial effect's penalty becomes -1. | ◄► **Initial Effect** The target takes a -2 penalty to attacks and checks until cured. | ◄► The target is weakened. | ► **Final State** The target is dazed.

## Slimy Doom

**Level 23 Disease**

Abyssal parasites devour the internal organs of the victims, turning them into quivering slime.

**Attack:** +26 vs. Fortitude
**Endurance** improve DC 33, maintain DC 30, worsen DC 29 or lower

The target is cured. ◄ | The target regains one of its lost healing surges. The target loses this healing surge again if its condition worsens. | ◄► **Initial Effect** The target loses two healing surges until cured. | ◄► Each time the target becomes bloodied, it gains ongoing 10 necrotic damage (save ends). If this damage reduces the target to 0 hit points, it turns into infectious slime from the inside out, dying horribly. | ► **Final State** At the moment of the failed Endurance check and each time the target takes damage, the character gains ongoing 30 necrotic damage (save ends). If this damage reduces the character to 0 hit points, it turns into infectious slime from the inside out, dying horribly.

*Maintain:* If the check result beats the lower DC but doesn't beat the higher one, your condition remains the same.

*Improve:* If the check result beats the higher DC, your condition improves–move one step to the left on the disease track.

*Worsen:* If the check result doesn't beat either DC, your condition worsens–move one step to the right on the disease track.

*Cure:* When you reach the left edge of the track, you are cured and stop making Endurance checks.

*Final State:* When you reach the right edge of the track, the final state of the disease takes effect. Once the disease is in its final state, you no longer make Endurance checks to improve. Often, the only way to recover from the final state is through the Cure Disease ritual.

✦ **Heal Skill:** An ally can use a Heal check in place of your Endurance check to help you recover from a disease, as described in the *Player's Handbook*.

# POISON

A scorpion's sting or serpent's fang is a painful attack, but the sting or bite becomes deadly with the addition of the creature's natural venom. Poison can be harvested from creatures or created through magical and alchemical mixtures. If poison is applied to a weapon, such weapon attacks become more deadly.

## POISON

✦ **Poison Vector:** Poison can be applied with a weapon, to a trap, to darts or needles, smeared in such a way as to seep in through the skin, or dispersed in a powder or gas so it's inhaled. Poison in food or drink takes effect when it's ingested unless otherwise noted. The poison attacks the victim when it makes contact through any of these means. Some poisons, as noted in their descriptions, can be administered only by specific means, such as in food or by a weapon that has been coated with the poison.

- ✦ **Poison Characteristics:** Poisons are consumable items (similar to magic items). They affect you with an attack power. Some poisons have aftereffects, which apply after you save against the initial attack.
- ✦ **Poisoned Weapon Attacks:** You must apply a poison to a weapon. The poison takes effect the next time the weapon hits and deals damage. The poison's effect is a secondary attack against the same target. If a poisoned weapon hits multiple targets, the poison attacks only the first target hit.

    *Apply a Poison:* Apply poison to a weapon. This is a standard action. Poison applied to a weapon loses its potency at the end of the encounter or after 5 minutes have passed.

## Stormclaw Scorpion Venom — Level 5 Poison

*This purple-black venom attacks the nerves.*

**Poison** 250 gp
**Attack:** +5 vs. Fortitude; ongoing 5 poison damage and immobilized (save ends both).
*Aftereffect:* The target is immobilized (save ends).

## Deathjump Spider Venom — Level 5 Poison

*Looking like nothing so much as black mud, this poison is a favorite weapon of lizardfolk darters.*

**Poison** 250 gp
**Attack:** +8 vs. Fortitude; ongoing 5 poison damage and slowed (save ends both).

## Carrion Crawler Brain Juice — Level 5 Poison

*This venom is a clear, green liquid with a vile odor.*

**Poison** 250 gp
**Attack:** +8 vs. Fortitude; ongoing 5 poison damage and slowed (save ends both).
*First Failed Save:* The target is immobilized instead of slowed (save ends).
*Second Failed Save:* The target is stunned instead of immobilized (save ends).

## Ground Thassil Root — Level 5 Poison

*This poison is a flavorless, blue powder.*

**Poison** 250 gp
**Attack:** +8 vs. Fortitude; slowed (save ends).
*First Failed Save:* The target is immobilized instead of slowed (save ends).
*Second Failed Save:* Target unconscious for 1d4 hours.
**Special:** Thassil root can be delivered only by way of food or drink. It makes its first attack 2d6 minutes after its victim consumes it. All saving throws against this poison are made with a -2 penalty.

## Dark Toxin — Level 10 Poison

*This poison, used by dark stalkers, looks like liquid shadow and smells like mushrooms.*

**Poison** 1,250 gp
**Attack:** +13 vs. Fortitude; ongoing 5 poison damage (save ends).

## Drow Poison — Level 10 Poison

*Distilled from demonic ichor in the temples of Lolth, this poison is the drow race's favorite means of acquiring new slaves.*

**Poison** 1,250 gp
**Attack:** +13 vs. Fortitude; the target takes a -2 penalty to attack rolls (save ends).
*First Failed Save:* The target is also weakened (save ends).
*Second Failed Save:* The target falls unconscious until the end of the encounter.

## Hellstinger Scorpion Venom — Level 15 Poison

*A vibrant blue color makes this pasty toxin look harmless.*

**Poison** 6,250 gp
**Attack:** +18 vs. Fortitude; ongoing 10 poison damage and weakened (save ends both).
*Aftereffect:* The target is weakened (save ends).

## Blood of Zehir — Level 15 Poison

*This deadly red venom is said to come from the veins of the serpent-god.*

**Poison** 6,250 gp
**Attack:** +18 vs. Fortitude; ongoing 10 poison damage and dazed (save ends both).

## Demonweb Terror Venom — Level 15 Poison

*This deadly poison, also called deathblade, is highly prized by assassins.*

**Poison** 6,250 gp
**Attack:** +18 vs. Fortitude; ongoing 10 poison damage, slowed, and -2 penalty to defenses (save ends all).

## Black Lotus — Level 15 Poison

*When prepared as a poison, black lotus is ground into a fine, black powder that causes terrifying hallucinations.*

**Poison** 6,250 gp
**Attack:** +20 vs. Fortitude; while bloodied, the target uses its standard action each round to make a basic attack against the nearest creature, whether enemy or ally (save ends). The effect applies again each time the target is bloodied until it completes an extended rest.
**Special:** The target takes a -5 penalty to Perception checks until it completes an extended rest. Black lotus can be delivered only by way of food or drink. It makes its first attack 1d6 rounds after its victim consumes it.

## Insanity Mist — Level 20 Poison

*This fine mist smells cloyingly sweet and attacks the mind.*

**Poison** 31,250 gp
**Attack:** +23 vs. Will; stunned (save ends).
*Aftereffect:* The target is dazed (save ends).
**Special:** This poison works only when it is inhaled in mist form.

## Pit Toxin — Level 25 Poison

*The fiery red venom from the fangs of a pit fiend sizzles when exposed to air.*

**Poison** 156,250 gp
**Attack:** +28 vs. Fortitude; ongoing 15 poison damage and weakened (save ends both).

# CHAPTER 4

# BUILDING ENCOUNTERS

THIS CHAPTER gives you the building blocks you need to build your own combat encounters. Noncombat encounters are discussed in Chapter 5.

Dynamic monster groups combined with interesting terrain and other features make for lively combat encounters.

This chapter includes the following sections.

✦ **Monster Roles:** Combat encounters involve groups of monsters occupying different roles. A varied group of monsters presents a more interesting and challenging encounter than a group of identical foes.

✦ **Encounter Components:** Here's the simple step-by-step process of how to build an encounter to challenge your players. Start with an experience point target, then choose monsters and other threats to create an exciting encounter.

✦ **Encounter Templates:** You can create a whole range of encounters to challenge your characters using five simple procedures.

✦ **Encounter Settings:** Where an encounter takes place is sometimes as important as the monsters in the encounter. This section discusses physical features and terrain of both the mundane and fantastic varieties.

WILLIAM O'CONNOR

The key to designing interesting and varied groups of monsters for an encounter lies in the monster roles: artillery, brute, controller, lurker, minion, skirmisher, and soldier. Each role has its own place in a typical encounter. The role of every monster is given in a monster entry at the top right of the creature's statistics block in the *Monster Manual*. Most combat encounters involve groups of monsters occupying different roles. A group of varied monsters makes for a more interesting and challenging encounter than a group of identical foes.

In the context of monster roles (here and elsewhere in the game rules), the terms "controller" and "leader" have meanings and applications that are different from the class roles of controller and leader, as described in Chapter 4 of the *Player's Handbook*.

## ARTILLERY

Artillery monsters excel at ranged combat. These creatures rain arrows, explosive fireballs, and similar attacks on the party from a distance. They're well protected against ranged attacks, but more vulnerable in melee. They often spread damage out over multiple characters in an area.

Use artillery monsters in an encounter to hang behind soldiers and brutes and rain damage down on the characters from protected positions. Because they're more fragile than average monsters, they count on being protected by a line of brutes or soldiers, or skirmishers that help them to draw off attacks.

## BRUTE

Brute monsters specialize in dealing damage in melee. Brutes have relatively low defenses but high hit points. They don't hit as often as other monsters, but they deal a lot of damage when they hit. They don't move around a lot, and they're often big.

### TIPS FROM THE PROS

Some encounters make it easy to single out targets for particularly deadly attacks. They have identifiable leaders or significant threats that make great targets for daily powers or concentrated damage from the party's strikers. Others consist of similar creatures, with no obvious leader. Include a mix of both kinds of encounters in your adventures. The two kinds of encounters appeal to different kinds of classes—strikers like clear-target encounters, while controllers love mobs—and encourage different tactics.

*—James Wyatt*

Use brutes in an encounter to threaten the party while shielding other monsters with their great size and imminent threat. Brutes are easy to run, so put multiple brutes of the same kind in an encounter to provide the baseline muscle for the monsters.

## CONTROLLER

Controller monsters manipulate their enemies or the battlefield to their advantage. They restrict enemy options or inflict lasting conditions, alter terrain or weather, or bend the minds of their adversaries.

Position controller monsters just behind a front line of melee-focused monsters, and use them to attack the PCs at short range with their control powers. Most controllers can stand their ground in melee, so they often wade right in beside the brutes and soldiers. Controller monsters can be complex to run in numbers, so limiting an encounter to one or two controllers of the same type is usually a good idea.

## LURKER

Lurker monsters have some ability that lets them avoid attacks, whether by striking from hiding or by turning into an invulnerable statue while regaining strength. They usually deliver one devastating attack every few rounds, while concentrating on defense in between.

Use lurkers as surprise additions to encounters with other monsters or as sneaky assassins that circle around the main action of a fight, darting in from time to time with a well-timed strike. Lurkers study the party while the player characters are busy handling brutes and soldiers, gauging the PCs' weaknesses.

## MINION

Sometimes you want monsters to come in droves and go down just as fast. A fight against thirty orcs is a grand cinematic battle. The players get to enjoy carving through the mob like a knife through butter, feeling confident and powerful. Unfortunately, the mechanics of standard monsters make that difficult. If you use a large number of monsters of a level similar to the PCs, you overwhelm them. If you use a large number of monsters of much lower level, you bore them with creatures that have little chance of hurting the PCs but take a lot of time to take down. On top of that, keeping track of the actions of so many monsters is a headache.

Minions are designed to serve as shock troops and cannon fodder for other monsters (standard, elite, or solo). Four minions are considered to be about the same as a standard monster of their level. Minions are designed to help fill out an encounter, but they go down quickly.

A minion is destroyed when it takes any amount of damage. Damage from an attack or from a source that doesn't require an attack roll (such as the paladin's *divine challenge* or the fighter's *cleave*) destroys a minion. If a minion is missed by an attack that normally deals damage on a miss, however, it takes no damage.

Use minions as melee combatants placed between the PCs and back-rank artillery or controller monsters.

## SKIRMISHER

Skirmisher monsters use mobility to threaten the player characters. Their combat statistics define the baseline for monsters, but their mobility is their defining feature.

Use skirmishers as the mobile strikers in an encounter, the creatures that move to attack vulnerable PCs from the sides and rear. They often have powers that let them dart in, attack, and retreat in one action. Skirmishers like to fight alongside soldiers and brutes because those monsters tend to stay in one place and draw a lot of the party's attention, giving the skirmishers room to maneuver around this front line.

## SOLDIER

Soldier monsters specialize in drawing the characters' attacks and defending other monsters. They have high defenses and average hit points. Their attacks are accurate, but they don't do exceptional damage. They tend not to move around, and they often have powers that hinder other creatures from moving around them.

Use soldiers in an encounter to keep the party in place, preventing its members from attacking the artillery or controller monsters behind the soldiers or chasing after the skirmishers. Soldiers often have abilities that allow them to work well together, so a group of identical soldiers works well in an encounter with other monsters.

## ELITE MONSTERS

Elite monsters are tougher than standard monsters and constitute more of a threat than standard monsters of their main role and level. An elite monster counts as two monsters of its level. Elite monsters are worth twice as many XP and are twice as dangerous. Elite monsters make great "mini-bosses," allowing you to add a tougher opponent to a mix of monsters without creating an entirely new monster. A group of ogres led by an elite ogre reduces the number of ogre figures on the table without diminishing the encounter's level.

## SOLO MONSTERS

Solo monsters are specifically designed to appear as single opponents against a group of PCs of the same level. They function, in effect, as a group of monsters. They have more hit points in order to absorb the damage output of multiple PCs, and they deal more damage in order to approximate the damage output of a group of monsters.

A solo monster is worth the same amount of XP as five monsters of its level. It provides the same level of challenge as five monsters.

A solo monster might have tendencies that flavor it toward the brute, soldier, skirmisher, lurker, artillery, or controller role. Each type of chromatic dragon, for example, leans toward a different role. Red dragons have soldier tendencies, while blue dragons behave much like artillery monsters. However, a solo monster can never completely take on a different role, because the roles are largely defined by how monsters interact with other monsters in an encounter. Every solo monster has to be able to stand and fight on its own.

## LEADER

"Leader" is not a stand-alone role. It is an additional quality or subrole of some brutes, soldiers, skirmishers, lurkers, artillery, and controllers.

Leaders are defined by their relationship to the monsters under their command. A leader monster, like a leader PC, grants bonuses and special abilities to its followers, improving their attacks or defenses, providing some healing, or enhancing their normal abilities. Aside from one special ability to enhance its allies, a leader functions as its primary role indicates.

Add a leader to an encounter with monsters that gain the greatest benefit from the leader's abilities. For example, a leader that gives a defense bonus to nearby creatures is a great leader for brutes, who have weak defenses otherwise.

Building an encounter is a matter of choosing threats appropriate to the characters and combining them in interesting and challenging ways. The threats at your disposal include all the monsters in the *Monster Manual*, monsters and nonplayer characters of your own design, traps and hazards, and skill challenge elements. Encounter-building is a mixture of art and science as you combine these threats together.

Just as individual threats have a level that measures their danger, an encounter as a whole has a level. Build an encounter by choosing a level for the encounter. The level you choose determines the total XP reward you're aiming for. You then select threats (monsters, traps, or NPCs) until you reach the target number, which is the minimum number of XP that an encounter of a given level can contain.

Think of it as spending XP against a budget. The encounter level gives you an XP budget, and you "buy" individual monsters, traps, or other threats to build the encounter until you've exhausted your budget.

## STEP-BY-STEP ENCOUNTERS

1. **Choose an encounter level.** Encounter level is relative to the number of characters in the party.

   An easy encounter is one or two levels lower than the party's level.

   A standard encounter is of the party's level, or one level higher.

   A hard encounter is two to four levels higher than the party's level.

2. **Determine your XP budget.** Multiply the number of characters in the party by the XP value of a monster of the encounter's level.

3. **Spend your XP budget.** You don't have to spend the exact amount. But if you go too high, the encounter level might increase, and if you don't spend the exact amount, you'll end up with a lower-level encounter.

## Considerations

✦ **Levels of Individual Threats:** Choose threats within two or three levels of the characters' level.

   Threats in an easy encounter can be as many as four levels below the party's level.

   Threats in a hard encounter can be as many as three to five levels above the party's level.

✦ **Mix Roles:** Use two or three brute or soldier monsters, then spice up the group with other roles and different kinds of threats.

# ENCOUNTER LEVEL

A standard encounter should challenge a typical group of characters but not overwhelm them. The characters should prevail if they haven't depleted their daily resources or had a streak of bad luck. An encounter that's the same level as the party, or one level higher, falls in this standard range of difficulty.

You can offer your players a greater challenge or an easier time by setting your encounter level two or

## EXPERIENCE POINT REWARDS

| Monster Level | Standard Monster | Minion | Elite | Solo |
|---|---|---|---|---|
| 1 | 100 | 25 | 200 | 500 |
| 2 | 125 | 31 | 250 | 625 |
| 3 | 150 | 38 | 300 | 750 |
| 4 | 175 | 44 | 350 | 875 |
| 5 | 200 | 50 | 400 | 1,000 |
| 6 | 250 | 63 | 500 | 1,250 |
| 7 | 300 | 75 | 600 | 1,500 |
| 8 | 350 | 88 | 700 | 1,750 |
| 9 | 400 | 100 | 800 | 2,000 |
| 10 | 500 | 125 | 1,000 | 2,500 |
| 11 | 600 | 150 | 1,200 | 3,000 |
| 12 | 700 | 175 | 1,400 | 3,500 |
| 13 | 800 | 200 | 1,600 | 4,000 |
| 14 | 1,000 | 250 | 2,000 | 5,000 |
| 15 | 1,200 | 300 | 2,400 | 6,000 |
| 16 | 1,400 | 350 | 2,800 | 7,000 |
| 17 | 1,600 | 400 | 3,200 | 8,000 |
| 18 | 2,000 | 500 | 4,000 | 10,000 |
| 19 | 2,400 | 600 | 4,800 | 12,000 |
| 20 | 2,800 | 700 | 5,600 | 14,000 |
| 21 | 3,200 | 800 | 6,400 | 16,000 |
| 22 | 4,150 | 1,038 | 8,300 | 20,750 |
| 23 | 5,100 | 1,275 | 10,200 | 25,500 |
| 24 | 6,050 | 1,513 | 12,100 | 30,250 |
| 25 | 7,000 | 1,750 | 14,000 | 35,000 |
| 26 | 9,000 | 2,250 | 18,000 | 45,000 |
| 27 | 11,000 | 2,750 | 22,000 | 55,000 |
| 28 | 13,000 | 3,250 | 26,000 | 65,000 |
| 29 | 15,000 | 3,750 | 30,000 | 75,000 |
| 30 | 19,000 | 4,750 | 38,000 | 95,000 |
| 31 | 23,000 | 5,750 | 46,000 | 115,000 |
| 32 | 27,000 | 6,750 | 54,000 | 135,000 |
| 33 | 31,000 | 7,750 | 62,000 | 155,000 |
| 34 | 39,000 | 9,750 | 78,000 | 195,000 |
| 35 | 47,000 | 11,750 | 94,000 | 235,000 |
| 36 | 55,000 | 13,750 | 110,000 | 275,000 |
| 37 | 63,000 | 15,750 | 126,000 | 315,000 |
| 38 | 79,000 | 19,750 | 158,000 | 395,000 |
| 39 | 95,000 | 23,750 | 190,000 | 475,000 |
| 40 | 111,000 | 27,750 | 222,000 | 555,000 |

three levels higher or one or two levels lower than the party's level. It's a good idea to vary the difficulty of your encounters over the course of an adventure, just as you vary other elements of encounters to keep things interesting (see "Encounter Mix," page 104).

Encounter level is relative to the number of characters in the party. The *Monster Manual* and published adventures show levels for encounters based on an assumed party size of five characters. However, notice that a 9th-level encounter for five characters (2,000 XP) is a 7th-level encounter for six characters or a 10th-level encounter for four.

# TARGET XP REWARD

To find your total XP budget, multiply the number of characters in the party by the XP value of a monster whose level is equal to the encounter level you chose.

**Target XP** = (XP value for a monster of the encounter's level) × (number of characters in the party)

The Target Encounter XP Totals table shows XP targets for parties of four, five, or six characters. For larger or smaller groups, find the XP value for a standard monster of the encounter's level on the Experience Rewards table and multiply it by the number of characters in the party.

# SPENDING YOUR XP BUDGET

The simplest way to spend your XP budget on an encounter is to use a number of monsters equal to the number of characters, with each monster's level equal to the encounter level. If you're building a 7th-level encounter for five characters, five 7th-level monsters fit the bill perfectly. A solo monster of that level is also an ideal encounter all by itself.

You don't have to hit your XP target exactly. If you don't, just keep an eye on the XP targets for encounters a level above or below the level you chose. If you set out to build a 10th-level encounter for five characters (target XP 2,500), but you spend only 2,200 XP, you've created a 9th-level encounter.

Once you've picked the monsters and traps you want to use in your encounter, make a note of the total XP reward for that encounter. Keep it for the end of the encounter when you award XP to the players.

**Level:** As you select individual threats to make up your encounter, keep the level of those threats in mind. Monsters or traps more than four levels below the party's level or seven levels above the party's level don't make good challenges. They're either too easy or too hard, even if the encounter's level seems right. When you want to use a single monster to challenge the PCs—or a large mob of monsters, for that matter— try using minions, elites, and solo monsters instead.

*Examples:* A 14th-level monster fits within the XP budget for a 5th-level encounter for five characters, but its attacks usually hit the PCs, while its defenses are out of their reach. Similarly, an encounter made up of fifty 1st-level monsters uses the XP budget for a 14th-level encounter for five characters, but the monsters don't provide any challenge to 14th-level characters.

**Roles:** An encounter with a group of monsters that all have the same role is less interesting than one with a mix of roles. On the other hand, a group of five monsters with five different roles is *too* interesting—or, more to the point, too complex. A good rule of thumb is to pick a brute or soldier monster and use two or three of them. Pick one or two monsters of other roles to round out the encounter.

Brutes and soldiers create the front line of the combat and give skirmishers, lurkers, artillery, and controllers the room they need to succeed. When you start making encounters, this general rule makes for interesting combats. You can still create a great deal of variety by slightly adjusting encounters to take advantage of the strengths of the latter four roles.

## TARGET ENCOUNTER XP TOTALS

| Encounter Level | Target Encounter XP | | |
|---|---|---|---|
| | 4 PCs | 5 PCs | 6 PCs |
| 1 | 400 | 500 | 600 |
| 2 | 500 | 625 | 750 |
| 3 | 600 | 750 | 900 |
| 4 | 700 | 875 | 1,050 |
| 5 | 800 | 1,000 | 1,200 |
| 6 | 1,000 | 1,250 | 1,500 |
| 7 | 1,200 | 1,500 | 1,800 |
| 8 | 1,400 | 1,750 | 2,100 |
| 9 | 1,600 | 2,000 | 2,400 |
| 10 | 2,000 | 2,500 | 3,000 |
| 11 | 2,400 | 3,000 | 3,600 |
| 12 | 2,800 | 3,500 | 4,200 |
| 13 | 3,200 | 4,000 | 4,800 |
| 14 | 4,000 | 5,000 | 6,000 |
| 15 | 4,800 | 6,000 | 7,200 |
| 16 | 5,600 | 7,000 | 8,400 |
| 17 | 6,400 | 8,000 | 9,600 |
| 18 | 8,000 | 10,000 | 12,000 |
| 19 | 9,600 | 12,000 | 14,400 |
| 20 | 11,200 | 14,000 | 16,800 |
| 21 | 12,800 | 16,000 | 19,200 |
| 22 | 16,600 | 20,750 | 24,900 |
| 23 | 20,400 | 25,500 | 30,600 |
| 24 | 24,200 | 30,250 | 36,300 |
| 25 | 28,000 | 35,000 | 42,000 |
| 26 | 36,000 | 45,000 | 54,000 |
| 27 | 44,000 | 55,000 | 66,000 |
| 28 | 52,000 | 65,000 | 78,000 |
| 29 | 60,000 | 75,000 | 90,000 |
| 30 | 76,000 | 95,000 | 114,000 |

Here are templates you can fill in with monsters of your own choosing that combine different roles and levels into dynamic encounters.

**Encounter Template Format:** In each of these templates, the letter $n$ represents the level of the encounter you want to build. The templates assume a party of five PCs. For such a group, the easy encounters are about level $n - 2$, the standard encounters are level $n$ or level $n + 1$, and the hard encounters are between level $n + 2$ and $n + 4$.

If you have three or four players, you can also use the easy encounters as standard encounters and the standard encounters as hard encounters. Likewise, if you have six or seven players, use the standard encounters as easy encounters and the hard encounters as standard ones.

The example encounters given in this section serve to illustrate the sorts of adversaries you can produce from the creatures in the *Monster Manual*.

## BATTLEFIELD CONTROL

One controller monster with several skirmishers of similar level can limit the movement of its enemies without hampering its allies. The controller's ability to hinder enemies heightens the skirmishers' movement advantage. Challenging terrain or hindering terrain (see page 61) in which the monsters can move more easily than the PCs can replace the controller.

| Easy: | Controller of level $n - 2$ |
| | 6 skirmishers of level $n - 4$ |
| Standard: | Controller of level $n + 1$ |
| | 6 skirmishers of level $n - 2$ |
| Hard: | Controller of level $n + 5$ |
| | 5 skirmishers of level $n + 1$ |

**Easy Example for 5th-level PCs:** 1 goblin hexer (level 3 controller) and 6 goblin warriors (level 1 skirmisher). Level 3 encounter, 750 XP.

**Standard Example for 5th-level PCs:** 1 harpy (level 6 controller) and 6 orc raiders (level 3 skirmisher). Level 5 encounter, 1,150 XP.

**Hard Example for 5th-level PCs:** 1 gibbering mouther (level 10 controller) and 5 gnoll claw fighters (level 6 skirmisher). Level 8 encounter, 1,750 XP.

## COMMANDER AND TROOPS

One commander monster in charge (a controller or soldier, but a lurker or skirmisher could also serve) leads a number of troops. The troops are usually melee focused (brutes and soldiers), but more challenging Commander and Troops encounters can feature some strategic artillery support.

| Easy: | Commander of level $n$ |
| | 4 troops of level $n - 3$ |
| Standard: | Commander of level $n + 3$ |
| | 5 troops of level $n - 2$ |
| Hard: | Commander of level $n + 6$ |
| | 3 troops of level $n + 1$ |
| | 2 artillery of level $n + 1$ |

**Easy Example for 8th-level PCs:** 1 troglodyte curse chanter (level 8 controller) and 4 rage drakes (level 5 brute). Level 5 encounter, 1,150 XP.

**Standard Example for 8th-level PCs:** 1 mezzodemon (level 11 soldier) and 5 evistro demons (level 6 brute). Level 8 encounter, 1,850 XP.

**Hard Example for 8th-level PCs:** 1 war troll (level 14 soldier), 3 trolls (level 9 brute), and 2 destrachans (level 9 artillery). Level 11 encounter, 3,000 XP.

## DRAGON'S DEN

Some monsters are so powerful that they pose a threat to a whole adventuring party just by themselves. Dragons, of course, are the most famous example, but other creatures such as beholders, purple worms, and hydras also fit the bill. Dragon's Den encounters pit the heroes against a single solo monster. Often the fight is in the monster's chosen den or lair, but sometimes it might be a chance encounter somewhere else—for example, when a hunting dragon spies the party traveling on a road far below and decides to drop in for a snack.

| Easy: | Solo monster of level $n - 2$ |
| Standard: | Solo monster of level $n$ or $n + 1$ |
| Hard: | Solo monster of level $n + 3$ |
| Hard: | Solo monster of level $n + 1$ |
| | Elite monster of level $n$ |

## DOUBLE LINE

A front line of brutes or soldiers protects a rear line of artillery or controller monsters. The front-line monsters keep their opponents from breaking through to attack the others behind them. The artillery and controllers in the back line use ranged attacks and try to avoid contact with the enemy.

You can modify the template by using a skirmisher or lurker to replace one of the rear-line foes. The front-line monsters protect the artillery or controller, while the lurker or skirmisher circles around behind the opponents or otherwise seeks advantageous positions.

| Easy: | 3 front line (brute/soldier) of level $n - 4$ |
| | 2 rear line (artillery/controller) of level $n - 2$ |
| Standard: | 3 front line (brute/soldier) of level $n$ |
| | 2 rear line (artillery/controller) of level $n$ |
| Standard: | 3 front line (brute/soldier) of level $n - 2$ |
| | 2 rear line (artillery/controller) of level $n + 3$ |

| Hard: | 3 front line (brute/soldier) of level $n + 2$ |
| | 1 controller of level $n + 4$ |
| | 1 artillery/lurker of level $n + 4$ |
| Hard: | 3 front line (brute/soldier) of level $n$ |
| | 2 artillery of level $n + 1$ |
| | 1 controller of level $n + 2$ |
| | 1 lurker of level $n + 2$ |

**Easy Example for 12th-level PCs:** 3 snaketongue warriors (level 8 soldier) and 2 venom-eye basilisks (level 10 artillery). Level 9 encounter, 2,050 XP.

**Standard Example for 12th-level PCs:** 3 blade spiders (level 10 brute) and 2 drow priestesses (level 15 controller). Level 12 encounter, 3,900 XP.

**Hard Example for 12th-level PCs:** 3 kuo-toa harpooners (level 14 soldier), 1 kuo-toa whip (level 16 controller), and 1 bodak skulk (level 16 lurker). Level 14 encounter, 5,800 XP.

# WOLF PACK

Some creatures hunt in packs of their own kind. These creatures are often skirmishers, and they sometimes adopt special tactics meant to distract opponents and make best use of combat advantage. One or more members of the pack act as soldiers, forming a front line; the others remain mobile, flanking opponents and ducking out of harm's way when possible. When the front line gets worn down, those creatures revert to their skirmisher role as fresh ones take their place.

| Easy: | 7 skirmishers of level $n - 4$ |
| Standard: | 7 skirmishers of level $n - 2$ |
| Standard: | 5 skirmishers of level $n$ |
| Hard: | 3 skirmishers of level $n + 7$ |
| Hard: | 4 skirmishers of level $n + 5$ |
| Hard: | 6 skirmishers of level $n + 2$ |

**Easy Example for 15th-level PCs:** 7 grimlock ambushers (level 11 skirmisher). Level 13 encounter, 4,200 XP.

**Standard Example for 15th-level PCs:** 5 angels of battle (level 15 skirmisher). Level 15 encounter, 6,000 XP.

**Hard Example for 15th-level PCs:** 4 black slaads (level 20 skirmisher). Level 18 encounter, 11,200 XP.

# SIMPLE SUBSTITUTIONS

You can create endless variations from these encounter templates without making the encounters any more complicated.

Elite, minion, and solo monsters are designed to be interesting challenges for PCs of their level, but they're tougher or weaker than one standard monster of the same level. For that reason, they don't count as individual monsters when you use them to build an encounter. Elite monsters count as two standard monsters and solo monsters count as five. It takes four minions to fill the place of one standard monster.

## SIMPLE ENCOUNTER SUBSTITUTIONS
✦ **Minion Monsters:** Replace one standard monster with several minion monsters of the same level.
✦ **Elite Monsters:** Replace two standard monsters with one elite monster of the same level.
✦ **Solo Monster:** Replace five standard monsters with one solo monster of the same level.
✦ **Traps and Hazards:** Replace one standard monster with a trap or hazard of the same level.

**Minion Monsters:** To incorporate minions into an encounter, replace one standard monster with four minions of the same level. A Commander and Troops encounter takes on a different feel when you replace standard brutes or soldiers with several times their number of minions—a vampire lord surrounded by his brood of vampire spawn, for example, or a war devil with a regiment of legion devils.

**Elite Monsters:** To incorporate an elite monster into an encounter, replace two standard monsters with an elite monster of the same role and level. You can also replace a single monster with an elite monster of the same role and level and increase the encounter's level by one.

You could modify the Commander and Troops template to use an elite monster as the commander. You then increase the encounter level—or you can remove one or two troops to keep the encounter level about the same. An elite commander can reduce the number of minion troops you use to fill out the encounter.

A Wolf Pack made up of elites can be smaller and more manageable. A group of three bulettes (9th-level elite skirmishers) is a bit easier to manage than a pack of six displacer beasts (9th-level skirmishers), but it's the same encounter level. You'll have fewer monsters to keep track of, and a little more room for them to maneuver on the battle grid.

**Solo Monsters:** A solo monster is usually an encounter all by itself, but you can also use solo monsters as part of larger groups. Any encounter template that includes at least five standard monsters of the same level can feature a solo monster instead of those standard monsters, though the solo monster might change the feel of the encounter significantly. A standard Commander and Troops encounter could include a commander of level $n + 3$ and a solo monster of level $n - 2$, leaving open the question of who's really in command.

If you have a party that's larger or smaller than five characters, it works reasonably well to increase a solo monster's level by one for each additional character above five, or decrease it by one for each character below five. So, use a 10th-level solo monster for a group of six 9th-level characters, or an 11th-level solo monster for a group of seven.

**Traps and Hazards:** A well-placed trap or hazard can contribute just as much to an encounter as a monster, but the encounter feels quite different. Replace a monster with a trap or hazard of the same level.

An encounter that occurs in a small, bare dungeon room is hard to make memorable, no matter what the monsters in it are doing. To maximize the fun for everyone around the table, follow these guidelines when crafting the chambers, caverns, or battlefields for your encounters.

## INTERESTING AREAS

Your first consideration in crafting interesting encounter spaces is the size and shape of the room or encounter area and the placement of the monsters and players characters.

**Room to Move:** Make sure everyone has enough room to move around. For most encounters, the minimum is an area roughly 8 to 10 squares on a side (which happens to be the size of the largest D&D Dungeon Tiles). For an important encounter, consider a space as large as 16 or 20 squares on a side (two of those 8-square-by-10-square dungeon tiles). A poster-size map like those included in DUNGEONS & DRAGONS Miniatures starter sets and in D&D adventures covers an area roughly 20 by 30 squares and makes a great area for a climactic battle. Folded in half (at about 15 by 20 squares), it also works well for other important fights.

**Bigger Creatures Need More Space:** Large and Huge creatures need more space. An encounter that includes Large monsters needs at least 16 squares by 10 squares. With Huge monsters, the encounter area should be at least 20 squares by 20 squares (or about three large D&D Dungeon Tiles). Gargantuan monsters work best on poster maps.

**Avoid Symmetry:** Symmetry is boring. Fighting in one square or rectangular room after another is dull and doesn't allow for much tactical variety. Let rooms branch out into corridors, alcoves, and antechambers, and find ways to draw some of the fighting into these areas. Also, build rooms using all three dimensions. Large platforms and raised areas, depressions and pits, along with galleries and overlooks, are interesting and can produce fun tactical situations.

**Fantasy It Up:** Your goal is not to create a realistic area for your encounter. Sprinkle fantastic features liberally throughout your encounters, and every once in a while put in fantastic features of cinematic scope. A room where the PCs have to jump between floating platforms as they fight a wing of gargoyles, or avoid gouts of magma while fighting for their lives against a red dragon—those are encounter areas that take on a life of their own. They reinforce in everyone's mind that D&D is a fantasy game.

**Encounter Distance:** For outdoor encounters, start the characters 10 squares away from the monsters. If terrain or visibility suggests a short-range encounter

(dense forest or thick fog, for example), use 5 squares instead. In wide-open areas, such as rolling hills or farmland, use 20 squares. In open terrain, characters might see monsters at even greater distances, which gives them a chance to try to avoid an encounter entirely (especially if the monsters don't see them).

Don't start an outdoor encounter with either the characters or the monsters at the edge of the map. Leave room for everyone to move around, which for some characters often means getting away to a safer distance from the monsters.

## TERRAIN FEATURES

It's easy to overlook the effects of terrain when building adventures and encounters. After all, the party's enemies are the monsters, not the dungeon stairs, the low rock wall, or the crumbled statues in the dungeon room. Yet, terrain provides the context for an encounter. A mob of goblin archers is easy to defeat when only empty terrain lies between it and the party. Take the same goblins, put them on the opposite side of a wide chasm, and the characters face a much tougher challenge.

### TYPES OF TERRAIN FEATURES

+ **Difficult Terrain:** It costs 1 extra square of movement to enter a square of difficult terrain.
+ **Blocking Terrain:** Blocking terrain prevents movement, blocks line of sight and line of effect, and provides cover.
+ **Challenging Terrain:** Challenging terrain requires a skill check or ability check to successfully cross it.
+ **Hindering Terrain:** Hindering terrain prevents movement or damages creatures that enter it.
+ **Obscured Terrain:** Obscured terrain provides concealment and blocks line of sight if a target is far enough away from you. However, it has no effect on movement.
+ **Cover Terrain:** Cover terrain provides cover (see page 43), making ranged attacks more difficult.

## DIFFICULT TERRAIN

Difficult terrain slows down characters without blocking line of sight. In encounter design, difficult terrain is a useful tool to make a path less appealing without removing it as an option. It gives you some of the benefits of walls and other terrain that blocks movement without the drawback of constricting the party's options. It costs 1 extra square of movement to enter a square of difficult terrain.

Too much difficult terrain proves frustrating, since shifting and attacking becomes impossible. Use difficult terrain in small quantities. The ideal patch of difficult terrain is just big enough to force the characters to spend an extra round moving down a particular path or taking a position in an encounter area.

Avoid using much, if any, difficult terrain in areas where you expect the PCs and monsters to fight in melee. Difficult terrain prevents shifting, which can turn a melee into a static slugfest. That might make for an occasional change of pace, but it makes the game boring if it happens too often.

**Examples:** Rubble, uneven ground, shallow water, fallen trees, a steep slope.

## Blocking Terrain

Blocking terrain prevents movement and blocks line of sight. The characters might be able to use the Athletics skill to climb over such obstacles, but otherwise this type of terrain prevents movement.

Blocking terrain channels the encounter's flow and cuts down on the range at which the PCs can attack the monsters (and vice versa). Using blocking terrain, you can present two or three distinct paths in an encounter area and different challenges down each one. For example, the characters come under attack when they enter an intersection. Orc warriors charge down two corridors, while an orc shaman casts spells from a third. If the PCs charge the shaman, they risk attack from two sides. If they fall back, they can meet the warriors along one front, but the shaman is safely away from the melee.

Don't use too much blocking terrain. Fights in endless narrow corridors are boring. While the fighter beats on the monster, the rest of the party must rely on ranged attacks.

**Examples:** Walls, doors, impassable rubble.

## Challenging Terrain

Challenging terrain requires a skill check or ability check to cross. Fail the check, and something bad happens to you. Challenging terrain makes skills more important. It adds an active element of risk to the game.

Athletics checks and Acrobatics checks are often required for challenging terrain. Moving across slick ice requires Acrobatics. Slogging through deep mud requires Athletics. Running over a thin beam requires Acrobatics. Use the Skill Check Difficulty Class table below to select a relevant DC for the party's level.

A successful check allows a character to move at his speed across the terrain. Some challenging terrain is also difficult terrain.

The type of terrain determines what happens when characters fail their checks. Climbing characters might fall. Characters wading through mud must pay 1 extra square of movement to enter the square. Characters moving across ice fall prone in the first square of ice they enter.

Too much challenging terrain wears down the party or slows the action if the characters have a few unlucky skill checks. If the terrain has a high DC or if the characters are cautious, they can treat it as hindering terrain (see below) instead.

**Examples:** Ice, deep water, deep mud, thin beam across a chasm.

### SKILL CHECK DIFFICULTY CLASS

| Party Level | Easy | Moderate | Hard |
|---|---|---|---|
| 1st–3rd | 15 | 20 | 25 |
| 4th–6th | 18 | 22 | 26 |
| 7th–9th | 20 | 24 | 28 |
| 10th–12th | 22 | 26 | 30 |
| 13th–15th | 23 | 27 | 31 |
| 16th–18th | 25 | 29 | 33 |
| 19th–21st | 27 | 31 | 35 |
| 22nd–24th | 28 | 32 | 36 |
| 25th–27th | 29 | 33 | 37 |
| 28th–30th | 30 | 34 | 38 |

## Hindering Terrain

Hindering terrain prevents movement (or severely punishes it) or damages creatures that enter it, but allows line of sight.

Hindering terrain can be interesting because it encourages ranged attacks. You can shoot an arrow over hindering terrain, while it is impossible or risky to run through it to attack in melee.

Too much hindering terrain makes melee characters and monsters worthless. It is best used to protect a monster or two, or as a favorable defensive position that the PCs can exploit.

**Examples:** Pits, deep water, lava, fire.

## Obscured Terrain

Obscured terrain provides concealment and blocks line of sight if a target is far enough away from you. However, it has no effect on movement.

The following rules expand on the material found in Chapter 9 of the *Player's Handbook*.

### OBSCURED TERRAIN

✦ **Lightly Obscured:** Squares of dim light, fog, smoke, heavy snow, or rain are lightly obscured.

*Concealment:* A creature has total concealment against you if 5 or more lightly obscured squares stand between you and it (including the nearest square of the creature's space). Closer creatures have concealment, but not total concealment.

*Vision:* You can see through lightly obscured squares, but you take a –5 penalty to Perception checks to see or spot things.

✦ **Heavily Obscured:** Squares of heavy fog or heavy smoke are heavily obscured.

Obscured terrain lends a sense of mystery to an encounter. The characters can't see what lurks ahead, but their enemies have open space they can move through to attack. It restricts ranged attacks similar to blocking terrain does, but it allows more movement. Encounters are a little more tense and unpredictable.

Obscured terrain becomes a problem when it shuts down the fight. The characters likely stick close together, and if the monsters can ignore the concealing terrain due to some magical effect, the fight might be unfair rather than tense.

**Examples:** Fog, mist, zones of magical darkness.

## Cover Terrain

Cover terrain provides cover, making ranged attacks more difficult. See "Cover" in Chapter 3 on page 43.

Cover terrain forces ranged attackers to move if they want to shoot around it. It also helps creatures avoid ranged attacks.

Too much cover makes the encounter too difficult for ranged attackers.

**Examples:** Low walls, piles of rubble.

# Terrain and Roles

Monster roles provide the best pointer for how to use terrain. Each role has different preferences for the terrain it thrives in. When you build an encounter, think about the monsters you want to use and how terrain can help them.

**The Natural Method:** It makes logical sense that creatures seek out favorable terrain. If you create an area map first, think about how your villain would exploit the terrain by intelligently deploying his followers. Even wild animals are clever enough to utilize terrain. For example, a lion hides in wait by a spring. The spring draws thirsty prey, and it blocks many routes of escape.

**The Staged Method:** If you build encounters purely with an eye toward the game experience, start by picking out monsters, and create terrain to maximize their advantages.

## Artillery

These monsters thrive on wide, open spaces and difficult terrain. An open space allows them to rain attacks on the party at a distance, while difficult terrain forces melee characters to waste precious time moving to engage the artillery. Any terrain that blocks movement or slows it down without affecting line of sight is an artillery monster's best friend. Artillery also likes having some cover nearby where it can gain some protection from the party's ranged attacks.

## Brutes and Soldiers

Brutes and soldiers both like to get into melee while avoiding the party's ranged attacks. They favor twisty, dense terrain that has enough room for melee, but makes it difficult for ranged attackers to get in shots from a distance. Brutes and soldiers also like choke points that make it difficult for rogues and other strikers to get behind them.

## Controllers

Controllers like the same sort of terrain as brutes and soldiers, but with one key difference: A controller likes slightly larger spaces where its allies can take advantage of its attacks. If an area is too narrow, a controller and his soldier buddies can't both attack the party. Controllers like wide spaces, but not necessarily long ones. Long spaces allow ranged attackers to pick off the controllers and their allies at a distance. Wide ones allow the monsters to all attack at once while keeping the action at relatively close range.

## Lurkers

Lurkers love obscured terrain and areas thick with blocking terrain. They usually need cover to hide from the PCs or to escape out of the party's reach. However, lurkers also like wide corridors and areas that give them lots of approaches to the characters. A lurker wants to slip past the party's defender, making narrow passages and easily controlled chokepoints bad for such a monster.

## Skirmishers

Skirmishers are a little like lurkers in that they want open spaces to attack the party from multiple directions. On the other hand, if the terrain is too open, skirmishers can't easily evade the party's attacks. The ideal skirmisher terrain is a mix of blocking or obscured terrain and open terrain, such as a series of linked dungeon rooms. A skirmisher can attack in one room, then slip around the corner to a nearby room to prepare its next strike.

# Building an Encounter Script

Terrain and monsters never combine in a vacuum. The characters' abilities and tactics, the encounter's purpose in the overall adventure, and the goal of the encounter all play a role in determining the right terrain for an encounter. An encounter script in your mind, a simple walk-through of the encounter, is a great tool for figuring out how to add and use terrain.

Building an encounter script is a simple process. Start with the basics of the encounter area. You might have the monsters picked out or the area mapped, depending on how you have designed the area. With either of those factors in mind, walk through the likely outcome of the encounter.

Suppose that the main villain in your adventure is a wizard and his four ogre bodyguards. Looking over the wizard's spells, you see that he has lots of area of effect attacks. The four ogre bodyguards are brutes.

Assume that the party fights these monsters in a huge, featureless room. It might help to break out a grid and miniatures, so you can better visualize what happens.

The characters who excel in melee run forward to attack, while the ogres move to intercept them. The ranged characters hang back and try to take out the wizard. Meanwhile, the wizard uses his area attacks.

Run the fight in your head, looking at it from the characters' and the monsters' points of view. Consider likely tactics and goals the PCs have, and then do the same for the monsters. What kinds of actions can you expect both sides to take? How does each side respond to the other? Answer these questions with an eye toward making things easier for the monsters and harder for the PCs. A few points become clear:

✦ The wizard has trouble using area attacks against PCs who are in melee with the ogres. He can blast the PCs, but he might also catch his minions in the attack.

✦ The ogres need enough room to crowd around the party, but if the room is too spacious, the PCs can run around the ogres and attack the wizard.

✦ The wizard needs cover for protection against ranged attacks, or the ogres need some way to threaten such PCs.

Run down your list of concerns, and think of how you can use terrain to respond to each of them. Here are some potential complications you can add:

✦ The ogres need to spread out, so be sure to add lots of open space for them to maneuver.

✦ Alternatively, you could give them a path that lets them maneuver around the party. For instance, the passage leading into the encounter area loops around to the east and west. The ogres wait where the two entrances meet, and two of them rush down whichever passage the PCs don't use.

✦ In contrast, the wizard wants only a narrow path to her position. Hindering terrain, such as a short bridge over a pit, restricts access to the wizard. Best of all, one of the ogres can take up position here and force the PCs to fight through it. One spot of hindering terrain should be enough.

4

ANNE STOKES

Creating a script is an iterative process. Keep walking through the scenario, thinking of how the PCs and monsters might act in response to the terrain that solves the problems you foresee, until you have just the right balance of challenge and complication. In the example above, walk through the encounter again, injecting the terrain elements mentioned above. Does the encounter feel fun? What other elements do you want to add?

# GETTING TERRAIN MIX RIGHT

Dressing up an encounter with terrain is an art, not a science. Only during and after an encounter, when you can see if it worked the way you wanted, can you judge if your decisions were good ones. Experience is your best guide. Keep the following points in mind to try to use terrain well.

**1. Terrain has a purpose.** Some terrain is just supposed to look cool. Some terrain serves to slow down the party. Look at each section of the encounter area and make sure it fulfills some purpose.

**2. Terrain encourages choices.** Do the PCs fight the goblins coming down the corridor, or do they focus on the bugbear torturer? If every fight has the PCs on one side of the room and the monsters on the other, things get boring fast. Build areas where the PCs and monsters can take a lot of different paths to attack each other.

**3. Terrain encourages movement.** A crumbling wall provides cover against a beholder's attacks. An ogre runs to close a portcullis, trapping the PCs in the dungeon unless they can intercept it. Terrain should give characters and monsters a reason to move toward it or away from it. An easily defended position, such as a narrow doorway, is a magnet for the PCs if they are outnumbered. On the other hand, if the PCs outnumber the monsters, they want to push the fight to an open space. If both sides are standing around trading blows round after round, your terrain isn't doing its job.

**4. Terrain makes fights more interesting.** After an encounter, the players should remember the terrain as well as the monsters that occupied it. Part of this memorability comes from the terrain's tactical aspects, but your description also plays a big role. Search for reasons to add memorable terrain to the battlefield. Using generic rubble as terrain is useful, but you can add to the experience by describing the rubble in a temple to Torog as heaps of ancient, broken skulls. That terrain has the same mechanical effect as ordinary rubble but injects an element of creepiness into the atmosphere.

# SAMPLE MUNDANE TERRAIN

Difficult terrain might take the form of a steep staircase in a dungeon or shifting sands on a stormy beach. This section offers help in applying the basic terrain categories to the features that characters commonly find in their adventures.

**Terrain and Skill Checks or Ability Checks:** When terrain requires a skill check or ability check, use the Difficulty Class by Level table (page 42) to set a DC that's appropriate to the characters' level. Some of the examples below show DCs for breaking down doors or opening locks, and also show the level at which a character should be able to break down the door with a Strength check of moderate difficulty. Thus, that level is a good rule of thumb for dungeon design. Don't put an iron door in a dungeon designed for 10th-level characters unless you intend it to be difficult for them to break through.

## DUNGEON DRESSING

Dungeon dressing is a category of mundane terrain that covers everything you expect to find in a dungeon.

**Walls:** Most dungeon walls are masonry or carved out of solid rock. Characters can use Athletics checks to climb a wall and break right through a wall with an incredible Strength check.

### DCS TO CLIMB OR BREAK THROUGH WALLS

| Wall | Climb DC | Break DC |
|------|----------|----------|
| Masonry wall (1 ft. thick) | 20 | 35 |
| Hewn stone wall (3 ft. thick) | 20 | 43 |
| Natural stone wall (3 ft. thick) | 10 | 43 |
| Wooden wall (6 in. thick) | 30 | 26 |

**Doors:** Opening a door takes a minor action, or a standard action if the door is stuck and requires a Strength check. A door might be locked, or it could have a window in it that provides superior cover to anyone firing through it.

### DCS TO BREAK DOWN DOORS

| Strength Check to | DC | Level |
|-------------------|----|----|
| Break down wooden door | 16 | 3 |
| Break down barred door | 20 | 9 |
| Break down stone or iron door | 25 | 18 |
| Break down adamantine door | 29 | 29 |
| Break through force portal | 38 | — |

Characters can open locked doors by using Thievery to pick the lock instead of breaking down the door. This is a standard action as part of a skill challenge. See "Open Lock" on page 189 of the *Player's Handbook*.

**Portcullises:** A portcullis is a metal gate that swings shut or drops down from the ceiling. It provides cover, and a Strength check allows a character to lift it or pull it open.

## DCS TO OPEN PORTCULLISES

| Strength Check to | DC | Level |
| --- | --- | --- |
| Force open wooden portcullis | 23 | 15 |
| Force open iron portcullis | 28 | 26 |
| Force open adamantine portcullis | 33 | 30+ |

**Secret Doors and Trapdoors:** In the confines of a dungeon, some doors are disguised as part of the wall, floor, or ceiling. A successful hard difficulty Perception check allows a PC to spot an average version of one of these portals. They make great ambush points for monsters or hiding places for treasure.

**Small Statues and Pillars:** These terrain features are difficult terrain that provides cover. You can move through their spaces because they are small enough to squeeze past.

**Big Statues and Pillars:** These are blocking terrain. As a rule of thumb, a big statue or pillar completely fills one or more squares.

**Tapestries and Curtains:** It costs 1 square of movement to move through a tapestry or curtain hung to partition a room or hallway. Tapestries and curtains block line of sight.

**Stairs:** Stairs are difficult terrain, unless the steps are sufficiently broad or the slope of their ascent is gentle.

**Pools:** Shallow pools, those waist-deep or less to a character, are difficult terrain. Characters must use Athletics checks to swim through deeper pools.

**Ladders:** Characters can climb ladders without making Athletics checks. A PC moves at one-half speed when going up or down a ladder.

**Ledges and Platforms:** Low ledges or platforms (below waist-high) are difficult terrain. Higher ones require Athletics checks to jump or climb onto.

## DAMAGING OBJECTS

Like characters, objects have hit points and defense scores (except for Will defense; see Object Immunities and Vulnerabilities, below).

An object's AC, Fortitude, and Reflex defense depend entirely on its size. (As you can tell from the following table, it's pretty easy to hit an object; so easy, in fact, that many DMs just skip the attack roll unless the situation is particularly dramatic.)

An object's hit point total generally depends on two factors: its size and its material. As a rule, larger or thicker objects have more hit points than smaller or thinner ones. Objects made of stone or metal have more hit points than those made of wood or glass.

Exceptions to this general rule abound. An object that's big but full of delicate moving parts might have fewer hit points than a smaller, more solid object, because it doesn't take as much damage to render that object functionally useless.

To determine an object's hit points, first find its size on the Object Properties table below. Then apply any appropriate multipliers based on its material or composition. If more than one multiplier is appropriate, it doesn't matter what order you apply them in. A Large iron clockwork contraption, for instance, should have around 60 hit points (40 for Large, × 3 for iron, × 0.5 for intricate construction).

An object reduced to 0 hit points is destroyed or otherwise rendered useless. At your judgment, the object might even still be more or less whole, but its functionality is ruined—a door knocked from its hinges or a clockwork mechanism broken internally, for example.

### OBJECT PROPERTIES

| Object Size | AC/ Reflex | Fortitude | Base HP | Example |
| --- | --- | --- | --- | --- |
| Tiny | 10 | 5 | 5 | Bottle, book |
| Small | 8 | 8 | 10 | Treasure chest, manacles |
| Medium | 5 | 10 | 20 | Door, statue |
| Large | 4 | 12 | 40 | Wagon, vault door |
| Huge | 3 | 15 | 100 | Big statue |
| Gargantuan | 2 | 20 | 200 | Even bigger statue |

| Material or Composition | Hit Point Multiplier |
| --- | --- |
| Very fragile | × 0.25 |
| Fragile/intricate | × 0.5 |
| Reinforced | × 1.5 |
| Paper or cloth | × 0.1 |
| Glass or ice | × 0.25 |
| Leather or hide | × 0.5 |
| Wood | None |
| Stone | × 2 |
| Iron or steel | × 3 |
| Adamantine | × 5 |

## IMPROVISED TERRAIN EFFECTS

The D&D game would become a bloated mess if we tried to cover every possible obstacle or terrain. If you want to use something not covered in this chapter, refer to the examples here as a guideline. Don't be afraid to make something up based on a logical interpretation of what you think should happen.

**Find a Match:** Look at the sample terrain, find the closest match, and use those rules.

**Charge Extra Movement:** If a feature is difficult to move into or through, increase the squares of movement needed to cross it by 1, 2, or 3.

**Skill and Ability Checks:** Is there a chance that a character could try to enter a space and fail? If so, ask for an appropriate check. Athletics is good for obstacles that can be overcome by leaping or climbing, while Acrobatics fits those that demand finesse and agility. Use the Difficulty Class by Level table (page 42) to aid you.

## Object Immunities and Vulnerabilities

Usually, it doesn't matter what kind of attack you make against an object: Damage is damage. However, there are a few exceptions.

All objects are immune to poison damage, psychic damage, and necrotic damage.

Objects don't have a Will defense and are immune to attacks that target Will defense.

Some unusual materials might be particularly resistant to some or all kinds of damage. In addition, you might rule that some kinds of damage are particularly effective against certain objects and grant the object vulnerability to that damage type. For example, a gauzy curtain or a pile of dry papers might have vulnerability 5 to fire because any spark is likely to destroy it.

# Outdoor Terrain

From a dense forest to a scorched desert, the characters face a wide variety of outdoor terrain.

**Trees:** Trees are difficult terrain that provides cover. Big trees are blocking terrain.

**Undergrowth:** Low, thick trees, small plants, and other undergrowth are difficult terrain.

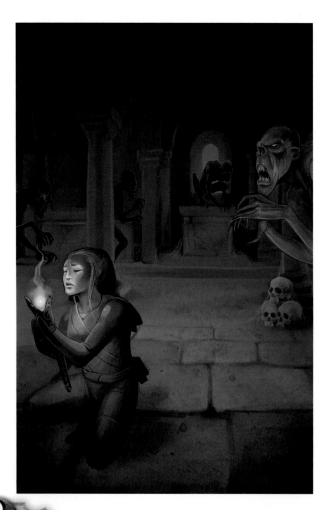

**Foliage, Leaves, and Vines:** Screening foliage, leaves, and vines are all concealing terrain if the plant material hangs down low enough or projects outward enough to block sight. Such plant matter might also be difficult terrain if the branches are thick or difficult to move through.

**Sand and Dirt:** Soft, shifting sand or dirt is difficult terrain. Hard-packed sand and dirt is normal terrain.

**Hills:** A slope is difficult terrain, though shallow or gentle slopes are normal terrain.

**Ice:** Slick ice patches are difficult terrain. You might also require an Acrobatics check for a character to avoid falling. See the relevant DCs under "Balance" in the Acrobatics skill in the *Player's Handbook* (page 180).

**Swamp:** Swamp is a combination of shallow pools and mud. It is difficult terrain.

## Constructed Terrain

Fortifications are built to repel attacks, giving you a lot of interesting terrain options.

**Streets:** The best maintained streets are normal terrain, but potholes and poor maintenance in the rough parts of town can make them difficult terrain.

**Windows:** Windows provide line of sight and grant cover. Opening a window is a minor action, and moving through one large enough for a creature to fit itself through costs 1 extra square of movement.

**Arrow Slits:** Arrow slits are small holes designed to provide archers with maximum protection while they fire. An arrow slit grants a ranged attacker superior cover while granting him or her a clear view of the battlefield. The firer determines the target's cover from the square just outside the slit.

**Murder Holes:** Murder holes use the same rules as arrow slits, except that they are placed in the ceilings of chambers to allow archers above to rain fire on attackers below.

**Catwalks:** Narrow catwalks are difficult terrain. You might also require an Acrobatics check to avoid falling. See the relevant DCs under "Balance" in the Acrobatics skill in the *Player's Handbook* (page 180).

**Furniture:** It costs 1 extra square of movement to move on top of a table or chair, but no extra movement to move off. A character can also crawl beneath a table, gaining cover against standing foes.

## Light Sources

Many dungeons and caverns are illuminated to some degree, since only a few monsters are truly at home in pitch blackness. The Example Light Sources table lists light sources, both mundane and magical. (It expands on the table in the *Player's Handbook*, page 262.) The table describes the radius (in squares) of the light, the brightness, and the duration of the light effect. You can alter these numbers as you see fit in the context of a specific terrain you make.

The last entries on the table show the light emitted by fire creatures–fire elementals, hell hounds, or immoliths, for example. Only creatures made of fire (which includes most creatures that have the fire keyword) shed this much light.

### EXAMPLE LIGHT SOURCES

| Source | Radius | Brightness | Duration |
|---|---|---|---|
| Candle | 2 | dim | 1 hour |
| Torch in wall sconce | 5 | bright | 1 hour |
| Lantern | 10 | bright | 8 hours/pint |
| Campfire | 10 | bright | 8 hours |
| Sunrod | 20 | bright | 4 hours |
| Phosphorescent fungi | 10 | dim | ongoing |
| Sacrificial brazier | 10 | bright | 8 hours |
| Fireplace/oven | 5 | bright | 8 hours/load of fuel |
| Forge | 2 | bright | 8 hours/load of fuel |
| Magma | 40 | bright | ongoing |
| Tiny fire creature | 2 | bright | ongoing |
| Small fire creature | 5 | bright | ongoing |
| Medium fire creature | 10 | bright | ongoing |
| Large fire creature | 20 | bright | ongoing |
| Huge or Gargantuan fire creature | 40 | bright | ongoing |

# VISION AND SPECIAL SENSES

Many creatures see in the dark much better than humans do. Some creatures even see in complete lightlessness. Other creatures get along in the dark by using other senses–uncanny hearing, sensitivity to vibrations and air movement, or an acute sense of smell.

**Normal Vision:** Creatures that have normal vision see normally in areas of bright light. Areas of dim light are lightly obscured. Areas of darkness are totally obscured.

**Low-Light Vision:** Creatures that have low-light vision see normally in areas of bright and dim light. Areas of darkness are totally obscured.

**Darkvision:** Darkvision lets creatures see normally regardless of light.

**Blindsight** and **Tremorsense:** Creatures that have blindsight or tremorsense ignore obscured squares or invisibility within range. They can see creatures in range regardless of these conditions. Beyond that range, they rely on vision (unless they're blind).

# SAMPLE FANTASTIC TERRAIN

The D&D world is rife with magic, and this power spawns wondrous terrain. Massive spiderwebs choke ancient passages. Elemental energy surges through a cavern, granting strength to fire-based spells.

**Tier and Skill Checks and Ability Checks:** Throughout these examples, the term "per tier" is used to show how an effect should scale. Multiply the per tier value by one for heroic tier, two for paragon, and three for epic. If a terrain feature grants a +1 bonus to attack rolls per tier, the bonus is +1 at heroic tier, +2 at paragon tier, and +3 at epic tier.

Terrain scales in order to keep it relevant as PCs and monsters gain higher attack bonuses and hit points. It is an element of game balance and a reflection of the greater magical power present in paragon or epic locations.

## BLOOD ROCK

The site of ceremonial sacrifices, a great slaughter, or some other calamity, the spirit of death hovers over blood rock. A creature standing in a square of blood rock can score a critical hit on a natural die roll of 19 or 20.

## CAVE SLIME

This thin, blue slime is harmless but extremely slick. A creature that enters a square filled with cave slime must succeed at an Acrobatics check or fall prone. Use the Difficulty Class by Level table (page 42) to set a DC that's appropriate to the character's level.

## CHOKE FROST

Choke frost is found in the deepest caves of the distant north or in the lairs of creatures of elemental ice. This light, white mist congeals into thick ice as creatures or other sources of heat move through it. Each time a creature enters a square of choke frost, it takes a –1 penalty to speed. As a move action, a creature can negate this penalty. Creatures that have the cold keyword are immune to this effect.

## CLOUDSPORE

These strange, Underdark mushrooms are normal terrain, but as soon as a creature enters a square of these mushrooms, the mushrooms create a thick cloud of spores. The square provides concealment (see page 281 of the *Player's Handbook*) for 5 minutes. Once a square has discharged a cloud, it cannot do so again for 24 hours.

## EMBER MOSS

This strange Underdark moss is a useful ingredient in creating everburning torches and sunrods. It is highly flammable and burns bright. A character in a square with ember moss takes an extra 5 damage from all fire attacks and takes a -4 penalty to saving throws to end ongoing fire damage.

## FONT OF POWER

Due to planar energy, the presence of a powerful artifact, or some other factor, this terrain boosts certain kinds of attacks. Pick one power keyword, such as fire, charm, or arcane. Attacks that have that keyword gain a +5 bonus per tier to damage.

## GRAB GRASS

This thick, tough grass grows in deep forests of the Feywild or in areas where the Feywild's magic filters into the material world. A creature that falls prone in a square of grab grass must make a Strength check to stand up. Use the Difficulty Class by Level table (page 42) to set a DC appropriate to the character's level.

## GRASPING SLIME

This black, viscous goo feeds on Underdark insects and vermin by trapping them in place and slowly digesting them. It poses no threat to larger creatures, but its clinging substance can cause a creature to become stuck. Grasping slime is difficult terrain. Use the Difficulty Class by Level table (page 42) to set an Athletics DC appropriate to the character's level to pass through the slime. On a failed check, the creature enters the slime, but its move ends immediately.

## ILLUSIONS

Illusions can mimic any terrain. Creatures that realize that an object is an illusion ignore its effects, while those that do not realize the truth behind the illusion react to it as appropriate. Use characters' passive Insight checks to determine if they notice something "not right," but don't allow them to make active checks without good reason. Once a character has reason to be suspicious, he can make an Insight check as a minor action to attempt to disbelieve an illusion. Use the Difficulty Class by Level table (page 42) to set a DC appropriate to the character's level and the relative difficulty you wish to assign to disbelieving the illusion.

Illusions don't do any actual damage, and interacting with them might reveal their true nature. For example, a character who walks into an illusory pit doesn't fall to the ground. At that point, the character realizes the pit is fake.

## ILLUSORY WALL

An illusory wall blocks line of sight. Creatures can walk through it without penalty, though obviously creatures that believe the illusion aren't likely to try doing so. Some illusory walls are similar to one-way mirrors in that they are transparent from one side (allowing a viewer to see creatures on the other side) while from the other side they appear to be normal walls (blocking line of sight, and looking like normal wall terrain).

## LOADSTONE

This strange rock dramatically increases the weight of all objects. It is difficult terrain, and ranged attacks that trace line of sight through it take a -2 penalty to attack rolls.

## MIRROR CRYSTAL

Mirror crystal causes strange twists and turns in space. A creature standing on mirror crystal can look down and see all the other mirror crystal spaces within 20 squares. Creatures can make ranged attacks through mirror crystal, targeting any creature on or adjacent to another square of mirror crystal. The range to a creature attacked through mirror crystal is 1 square.

## PILLAR OF LIFE

This tall stone pillar is infused with life energy. Any creature that begins its turn adjacent to it regains 5 hit points per tier.

## SACRED CIRCLE

A sacred circle is dedicated to a specific deity and infused with divine energy. A creature that shares that deity's alignment gains a +2 bonus to attack rolls while standing in the circle. A sacred circle typically fills an area 3 squares by 3 squares.

## SLIDES

A slide is coated with a slick substance and designed to send characters tumbling, offering quick transport at a price. A slide is difficult terrain. A character who enters a slide square must make an Acrobatics check. Use the Difficulty Class by Level table (page 42) to set an Acrobatics DC appropriate to the character's level. A creature that fails immediately moves to the end of the slide, falls prone, and ends its move.

## SPIDERWEBS

The webs of giant spiders are difficult terrain. A character who enters a spiderweb must make an Athletics check or Acrobatics check or become immobilized. Trapped creatures can use the escape action to free themselves from the web. Use the Difficulty Class by Level table (page 42) to set an appropriate DC for the characters' levels. Spiderwebs also provide concealment.

## TELEPORTERS

Teleporters are magical gates that whisk characters from one spot to another. A creature that enters a teleporter's space immediately moves to the teleporter's destination square. The square can be another teleporter to allow for two-way travel. In that case, the creature automatically moves adjacent to the destination teleporter.

## WHIRLWIND

Whirlwinds form in areas infused with elemental energy (often in water or air). A whirlwind's current pulls creatures along its path. This is a slide effect. A creature that enters a whirlwind moves a distance and direction determined by the strength of the whirlwind. An affected creature can fight against the wind by spending squares of movement to reduce the distance the wind slides it. Only one whirlwind square can affect a creature at a time. If the wind slides the creature through or into another whirlwind square, that square has no effect. A whirlwind can also move creatures upward. A creature that ends its turn outside of a whirlwind square and aloft falls to the ground (if it is not flying–see "Flying," page 47).

# Noncombat Encounters

No D&D game consists of endless combat. You need other challenges to spice up and add variety to adventures. Sometimes these challenges are combined with combat encounters, making for really interesting and strategic situations. Other times, an encounter completely revolves around character skills and social interactions. This chapter is your guide to running and creating encounters that feature skill challenges, puzzles, traps, and hazards.

This chapter includes the following sections.

✦ **Skill Challenges:** When characters make skill checks in response to a series of changing conditions, with success or failure being uncertain, they're in a skill challenge. Scouring the jungle for a hidden temple or persuading the duke to send aid to defend the pass might both be skill challenge encounters, relying heavily on very different skills. Learn to run skill challenges, creating your own according to the guidelines presented here, and see how to combine skill challenges with combat encounters to create truly memorable situations.

✦ **Puzzles:** Some D&D adventures feature puzzles. Some DMs believe puzzles should test the characters, and see puzzles as a form of skill challenge. Others see puzzles as a challenge for the players, and welcome the variety and hands-on nature of puzzles that they can solve personally or as a group. Use puzzles as either sort of challenge in your game.

✦ **Traps and Hazards:** Traps and hazards are inanimate threats to life, limb, mind, or spirit. They fill roles similar to monsters in encounters or stand as encounters on their own. Learn how to use traps and hazards, and select from numerous examples to use or modify for your adventures.

An audience with the duke, a mysterious set of sigils in a hidden chamber, finding your way through the Forest of Neverlight—all of these present challenges that test both the characters and the people who play them. The difference between a combat challenge and a skill challenge isn't the presence or absence of physical risk, nor the presence or absence of attack rolls and damage rolls and power use. The difference is in how the encounter treats PC actions.

Skill challenges can account for all the action in a particular encounter, or they can be used as part of a combat encounter to add variety and a sense of urgency to the proceedings.

## The Basics

To deal with a skill challenge, the player characters make skill checks to accumulate a number of successful skill uses before they rack up too many failures and end the encounter.

**Example:** The PCs seek a temple in dense jungle. Achieving six successes means they find their way. Accruing three failures before achieving the successes, however, indicates that they get themselves hopelessly lost in the wilderness.

## Designing Skill Challenges

More so than perhaps any other kind of encounter, a skill challenge is defined by its context in an adventure. Adventurers can fight a group of five foulspawn in just about any 8th- to 10th-level adventure, but a skill challenge that requires the PCs to unmask the doppelganger in the baron's court is directly related to the particular adventure and campaign it's set in.

Follow these steps to design skill challenges for your adventures.

### Step 1: Goal and Context

What's the goal of the challenge? Where does the challenge take place? Who is involved in this challenge? Is it a stand-alone skill challenge or a skill challenge as part of a combat encounter?

Define the goal of the challenge and what obstacles the characters face to accomplish that goal. The goal has everything to do with the overall story of the adventure. Success at the challenge should be important to the adventure, but not essential. You don't want a series of bad skill checks to bring the adventure to a grinding halt. At worst, failure at the challenge should send the characters on a long detour, thereby creating a new and interesting part of the adventure.

Give as much attention to the setting of the skill challenge as you do to the setting of the rest of the adventure. You might not need a detailed map full of interesting terrain for a skill challenge, but an interesting setting helps set the tone for the encounter.

If the challenge involves any kind of interaction with nonplayer characters or monsters, detail those characters as well. In a complex social encounter, have a clear picture of the motivations, goals, and interests of the NPCs involved so you can tie them to character skill checks.

A skill challenge can serve as an encounter in and of itself, or it can be combined with monsters as part of a combat encounter.

### Step 2: Level and Complexity

What level is the challenge? What is the challenge's complexity?

Choose a grade of complexity, from 1 to 5 (1 being simple, 5 being complex).

**SKILL CHALLENGE COMPLEXITY**

| Complexity | Successes | Failures |
|---|---|---|
| 1 | 4 | 2 |
| 2 | 6 | 3 |
| 3 | 8 | 4 |
| 4 | 10 | 5 |
| 5 | 12 | 6 |

Level and complexity determine how hard the challenge is for your characters to overcome. The skill challenge's level determines the DC of the skill checks involved, while the grade of complexity determines how many successes the characters need to overcome the challenge, and how many failures end the challenge. The more complex a challenge, the more skill checks are required, and the greater number of successes needed to overcome it.

Set the complexity based on how significant you want the challenge to be. If you expect it to carry the same weight as a combat encounter, a complexity of 5 makes sense. A challenge of that complexity takes somewhere between 12 and 18 total checks to complete, and the characters should earn as much

---

### IS THIS A CHALLENGE?

It's not a skill challenge every time you call for a skill check. When an obstacle takes only one roll to resolve, it's not a challenge. One Diplomacy check to haggle with the merchant, one Athletics check to climb out of the pit trap, one Religion check to figure out whose sacred tome contains the parable—none of these constitutes a skill challenge.

experience for succeeding as they would for a combat encounter of the same level (it's the same as taking on five monsters of the challenge's level). For quicker, less significant challenges, or for challenges that work as part of a combat encounter, set the complexity lower. (Figure that each complexity is the equivalent of that number of monsters of the challenge's level.)

Set a level for the challenge and DCs for the checks involved. As a starting point, set the level of the challenge to the level of the party, and use moderate DCs for the skill checks (see the Difficulty Class and Damage by Level table on page 42).

If you use easy DCs, reduce the level of the challenge by one. If you use hard DCs, increase the level of the challenge by two. You can also adjust the level of the challenge by reducing the number of failures needed to end the challenge. Cut the number of failures needed in half, and increase the level of the challenge by two. (You can also mix DCs in the same challenge, as described on page 74.)

**Example:** A complexity 3 challenge using hard DCs and cutting the number of failures needed in half increases this skill challenge's level by four.

## STEP 3: SKILLS

What skills naturally contribute to the solution of the challenge? How do characters use these skills in the challenge?

Certain skills lead to the natural solutions to the problem the challenge presents. These should serve as the primary skills in the challenge. Give some thought to which skills you select here, keeping in mind the goal of involving all the players in the action. You know what skills your player characters are good at, so make sure to include some chances for every character to shine. In general, it's a good idea to include a mix of interaction skills (Bluff, Diplomacy), knowledge-based skills (Arcana, Nature), and physical skills (Athletics, Acrobatics) in the challenge, either as primary or as secondary skills. These general sorts of skills play to the strengths of most characters.

Start with a list of the challenge's primary skills, then give some thought to what a character might do when using that skill. You don't need to make an

exhaustive list, but try to define categories of actions the characters might take. Sometimes characters might decide to do exactly what you anticipate, but often you need to take what a player wants to do and find the closest match to the actions you've outlined.

When a player's turn comes up in a skill challenge, let that player's character use any skill the player wants. As long as the player or you can come up with a way to let this secondary skill play a part in the challenge, go for it. If a player wants to use a skill you didn't identify as a primary skill in the challenge, however, then the DC for using that secondary skill is hard. The use of the skill might win the day in unexpected ways, but the risk is greater as well. In addition, a secondary skill can never be used by a single character more than once in a challenge.

Always keep in mind that players can and will come up with ways to use skills you do not expect. Stay on your toes, and let whatever improvised skill uses they come up with guide the rewards and penalties you apply afterward. Remember that not everything has to be directly tied to the challenge. Tangential or unrelated benefits, such as making unexpected allies from among the duke's court or finding a small, forgotten treasure, can also be fun.

### ADDING A SKILL CHALLENGE TO A COMBAT ENCOUNTER

You can also add a skill challenge to a combat encounter, using it as you would a monster to determine the correct challenge level. For example, combine three standard 7th-level monsters with a 7th-level trap with a complexity of 2 and you have a 7th-level combat encounter. While some of the party deals with the monsters, the rest try to overcome the trap with skill checks before the walls crash together and kill everyone in the chamber.

EVA WIDERMANN

## STEP 4: OTHER CONDITIONS

What other conditions might apply to the challenge?

Do the ogre mercenaries demand payment every 10 minutes they allow you to talk to them? Or is there an energy-draining field in the Labyrinth of Shadows that applies increasing penalties over the length of the characters' intrusion? These other conditions can impose a sense of urgency on a skill challenge or comprise part of the penalty for failing at the challenge.

If you put a monetary cost on the challenge (as in the example of the ogre mercenaries), try to make up that cost in treasure if the characters succeed at the challenge. If they fail, the cost is part of the penalty they pay.

It's also a good idea to think about other options the characters might exercise and how these might influence the course of the challenge. Characters might have access to utility powers or rituals that can help them. These might allow special uses of skills, perhaps with a bonus. Rituals in particular might grant an automatic success or remove failures from the running total.

## STEP 5: CONSEQUENCES

What happens if the characters successfully complete the challenge? What happens if they fail?

When the skill challenge ends, reward the characters for their success (with challenge-specific rewards, as well as experience points) or assess penalties for their failure.

A skill challenge's complexity, combined with its level, defines its value in experience points. A skill challenge is worth the same XP as a number of monsters of its level equal to its complexity. Thus, a 7th-level challenge with a complexity of 1 is worth 300 XP (the same as one 7th-level monster), while a 7th-level challenge with a complexity of 5 is worth 1,500 XP—the same as a 7th-level combat encounter.

You can also decide to allocate some of the adventure's treasure to the challenge.

Beyond those fundamental rewards, the characters' success should have a significant impact on the story of the adventure. Additional rewards might include information, clues, and favors, as well as simply moving the adventure forward.

If the characters fail the challenge, the story still has to move forward, but in a different direction and possibly by a longer, more dangerous route. You can think of it like a room in a dungeon. If the characters can't defeat the dragon in that room, they don't get the experience for killing it or the treasure it guards, and they can't go through the door on the opposite side of the room. They might still be able to get to the chamber behind the door, but by taking a different and more arduous path. In the same way, failure in a skill challenge should send the characters down a different route in the adventure, but not derail them entirely.

In addition, failing a skill challenge might make some future encounters more difficult. The angry baron might throw more obstacles in the characters' path or, alerted to their plans, increase his defenses.

## RUNNING A SKILL CHALLENGE

Begin by describing the situation and defining the challenge. Running the challenge itself is not all that different from running a combat encounter (see Chapter 3). You describe the environment, listen to the players' responses, let them make their skill checks, and narrate the results. The skill challenge description outlines the skills that are useful for the challenge and the results of using them.

Roll initiative to establish an order of play for the skill challenge. If the skill challenge is part of a combat encounter, work the challenge into the order just as you do the monsters.

In a skill challenge encounter, every player character must make skill checks to contribute to the success or failure of the encounter. Characters must make a check on their turn using one of the identified primary skills (usually with a moderate DC) or they must use a different skill, if they can come up with a way to use it to contribute to the challenge (with a hard DC). A secondary skill can be used only once by a single character in any given skill challenge. They can also decide, if appropriate, to cooperate with another character (see "Group Skill Checks," below).

Sometimes, a player tells you, "I want to make a Diplomacy check to convince the duke that helping us is in his best interest." That's great—the player has told you what she's doing and what skill she's using to do it. Other times, a player will say, "I want to make a Diplomacy check." In such a case, prompt the player to give more information about how the character is using that skill. Sometimes, characters do the opposite: "I want to scare the duke into helping us." It's up to you, then, to decide which skill the character is using and call for the appropriate check.

You can also make use of the "DM's best friend" rule to reward particularly creative uses of skills (or penalize the opposite) by giving a character a +2 bonus or –2 penalty to the check. Then, depending on the

### OPPOSED CHECKS

For speed and simplicity, skill challenges use only flat DCs to oppose the PCs' skill checks. Opposing them with skill check results builds too much randomness into the system.

If you want to include opponents' checks in your skill challenges, use their passive checks (10 + base skill check bonus). Insight and Perception are the skills most often used in this way.

success or failure of the check, describe the consequences, and go on to the next action.

## GROUP SKILL CHECKS

Sometimes a skill challenge calls for a group skill check. When the party is climbing a cliff, everyone needs to roll an Athletics check to climb. In this case, allow one character to be the lead climber. This character makes the actual check to gain a success or failure. The others make checks to help the lead character, in effect aiding that character, but their checks provide neither a success nor a failure toward resolving the challenge. Each ally that gets a result of 10 or higher provides a +2 bonus to the lead character's check (to a maximum bonus of +8).

## INFORMING THE PLAYERS

In a combat encounter, the players already know a great deal about how to overcome the challenge. They know that the monsters possess defenses and hit points, and that everyone acts in initiative order. Furthermore, they know exactly what happens when their own attacks hit—and after a few rounds, they have a good sense of the likelihood of their attacks hitting.

But a skill challenge is a different story. When the PCs are delving through the Underdark in search of the ruined dwarven fortress of Gozar-Duun, they don't necessarily know how the game adjudicates that search. They don't know what earns successes, to put it in game terms, until you tell them.

You can't start a skill challenge until the PCs know their role in it, and that means giving them a couple of skills to start with. It might be as simple as saying, "You'll use Athletics checks to scale the cliffs, but be aware that a failed check might dislodge some rocks on those climbing below you." If the PCs are trying to sneak into the wizard's college, tell the players, "Your magical disguises, the Bluff skill, and knowledge of the academic aspects of magic—Arcana, in other words—will be key in this challenge."

## INTERRUPTING A SKILL CHALLENGE

Most of the time, skill challenges are completed in relatively short order. For skill challenges on a long time scale, however, break the action as necessary. Just keep track of successes and failures. For example, a skill challenge could be set up that calls for checks once per hour, once per day, or once per week or longer. Sometimes success or failure in the encounters between checks can earn one or more successes and failures in the larger skill challenge. When assassins strike in the middle of a negotiation, for example, fighting them off might impress the duke and earn a success or two that counts toward completing the skill challenge.

## MULTIPLE SKILLS ENGAGE MULTIPLE PLAYERS

Engage multiple PCs by making a spread of skills relevant. It makes some sense for one character trained in Diplomacy to do all the talking, but it's no more fun than one character doing all the fighting. Instead, multiple skills are relevant in every skill challenge, just as a wizard and a rogue are both important in combat. In a skill challenge, every character has something to do, so no player is bored. Whether it's the use of a primary or secondary skill, or whether a character is cooperating to help another character make a check, every character participates in a skill challenge.

As always, give the players the information they need to make smart choices. Make it clear what skills are useful in a challenge. The players don't have to know every skill that can earn them successes at the start, but they must know some. And make sure to tell them when a check result provides a success or a failure—if the players don't know if they're doing well or not, they don't know how to proceed. You can't engage players if they don't know how to interact with the challenge.

## REWARD CLEVER IDEAS

Thinking players are engaged players. In skill challenges, players will come up with uses for skills that you didn't expect to play a role. Try not to say no. Instead, let them make a roll using the skill but at a hard DC, or make the skill good for only one success. This encourages players to think about the challenge in more depth and engages more players by making more skills useful.

However, it's particularly important to make sure these checks are grounded in actions that make sense in the adventure and the situation. If a player asks, "Can I use Diplomacy?" you should ask what exactly the character might be doing to help the party survive in the uninhabited sandy wastes by using that skill. Don't say no too often, but don't say yes if it doesn't make sense in the context of the challenge.

**Example:** The cleric wants to know if his Religion skill can give him some idea where the cultists would build their temple. If he beats a hard DC, he's sure that the cultists would build their temple near a river. The fighter wants to climb a tree with Athletics to get a good vantage point on the surrounding forest, thinking that gaps in the trees might indicate the presence of a river. That's an easy DC check. Once these characters use the skills in that way, though, they can't use them again—Religion and Athletics, in this case, are good for only one success in this particular challenge.

## Skill Checks

Skill challenges require the players to make rolls at specific times. Call for these checks according to the pace of the narrative and the nature of the challenge. This might be each round on their turns, during each short or extended rest, or some other time frame as determined by the challenge in question.

Skill checks usually count as successes or failures for the challenge, but sometimes a specific use of a certain skill in a challenge just provides a minor benefit or penalty.

**Examples:** When forging a trail through the jungle, every character has to make an Endurance check after each extended rest to stay healthy. Characters who fail lose one healing surge until the challenge ends, but the party doesn't accrue any failures for these checks.

In the middle of tense negotiations with the duke, the castellan might interrupt to challenge the PCs on a point of etiquette. Success on a Diplomacy check doesn't count as a success toward the challenge total, but it could provide a bonus to the next check in interacting with the duke, or win a small favor from the castellan.

## Encounters Have Consequences

Skill challenges have consequences, positive and negative, just as combat encounters do. When the characters overcome a skill challenge, they earn the same rewards as when they slay monsters in combat—experience and perhaps treasure. The consequences of total defeat are often obvious: no XP and no treasure.

Success or failure in a skill challenge also influences the course of the adventure—the characters locate the temple and begin infiltrating it, or they get lost and must seek help. In either case, however, the adventure continues. With success, this is no problem, but don't fall into the trap of making progress dependent on success in a skill challenge. Failure introduces complications rather than ending the adventure. If the characters get lost in the jungle, that leads to further challenges, not the end of the adventure.

---

### WHY HEALING SURGES?

Sometimes the penalty for failing a skill check is the cost of a healing surge. That can mean that a grueling trek across hostile terrain is sapping the characters' overall vitality, in which case the healing surges don't return until the group gets back to a more hospitable environment. Other times, the cost of a healing surge is just a shorthand method for taking damage. A character injures himself, but he's not in combat, so he can spend a healing surge to restore the lost hit points. If the encounter shifts quickly into combat with no time for a short rest in between, you can give out actual hit point damage instead.

---

# Sample Skill Challenges

Use the following skill challenge templates as the basis for skill challenges you design for your adventures. The level and complexity values are suggestions only; adjust as necessary to meet the needs of your adventure.

## The Negotiation

*The duke sits at the head of his banquet table. Gesturing with a wine glass, he bids you to sit. "I'm told you have news from the borderlands."*

This skill challenge covers attempts to gain a favor or assistance from a local leader or other authority figure. The challenge might take only as long as a normal conversation, or it could stretch on for days as the characters perform tasks to earn the NPC's favor.

**Setup:** For the NPC to provide assistance, the PCs need to convince him or her of their trustworthiness and that their cause helps the NPC in some way.

**Level:** Equal to the level of the party.

**Complexity:** 3 (requires 8 successes before 4 failures).

**Primary Skills:** Bluff, Diplomacy, Insight.

*Bluff (moderate DCs):* You try to encourage the NPC to aid your quest using false pretenses. Characters can cooperate to aid a lead character using this skill.

*Diplomacy (moderate DCs):* You entreat the NPC for aid in your quest. First success with this skill opens up the use of the History skill (the NPC mentions an event from the past that has significance to him).

*Insight (moderate DCs):* You empathize with the NPC and use that knowledge to encourage assistance. First success with this skill reveals that any use of the Intimidate skill earns a failure.

*History (easy DC):* You make an insightful remark about the significant event from the NPC's past. This is available only after one character has gained a success using the Diplomacy skill, and it can be used only once in this way during the challenge.

*Intimidate:* The NPC refuses to be intimidated by the PCs. Each use of this skill earns a failure.

**Success:** The NPC agrees to provide reasonable assistance to the characters. This could include treasure.

**Failure:** The characters are forced to act without the NPC's assistance. They encounter more trouble, which may be sent by the NPC out of anger or antagonism.

### Example in Play

*The initiative order for this skill challenge is as follows:* Jarret (20), Kathra (17), Elias (12), Baredd (8), and Uldar (3). The Duke (played by the DM) doesn't make skill checks, but does respond appropriately to each character's check in a round.

## Round 1

**Jarret:** I'm going to try to handle this with diplomacy. My good Duke, if you grant our petition for aid, it will not only help us complete our quest, but it will also secure your duchy from the ravages of the goblin horde for a season or more. Surely you can see the sense of that. (*Makes a Diplomacy skill check and gets a success.*)

**Duke:** Hmm, well said. I do remember the Battle of Cantle Hill. Nasty business. (*The DM informs the players that the History skill can now be used to aid in this challenge.*)

**Kathra:** I'm trained in History! I make a History check to see what I know about that battle. (*Makes a History check and gets a success.*)

**DM:** You know that the Duke fought in the Battle of Cantle Hill before he rose to his current station. It was a terrible battle between the people of the duchy and a horde of goblins from the nearby mountains. The duchy barely won the day, thanks in large part to the actions of the Duke.

**Kathra:** Well, then I tell the Duke that I remember the tale of that battle well, and how he bravely fought off the goblins to save the duchy. Help us today, and such a battle won't have to be repeated!

**Duke:** I'm listening. Continue. (*The DM says that Kathra's response is worth a +2 bonus to Elias's check.*)

**Elias:** I get a +2 bonus? Great! I'm going to use it to help our cause with a well-placed bluff. Duke, I know for a fact that the goblin leader is raising an army even as we speak. If we don't enter the mountain and disrupt that army, the goblins will overrun the duchy before the next moon rises! (*Makes a Bluff check with a +2 bonus and gets a success.*)

**Duke:** An army? I won't sit by and let history repeat itself. Still, you are asking for a lot. . . .

**Baredd:** Enough of this talking! It's time for action! I try to intimidate the Duke into helping us. Look, Duke, the goblins are the least of your worries. Agree to our demands, or we might have to take what we want. (*Makes an Intimidate check, unaware that such an action is an automatic failure.*)

**Duke:** How dare you! I will not be threatened by the likes of you!

**Uldar:** Okay, calm down, everyone. We're all friends here. I empathize with your desire to protect your people, Duke, and I assure you that we want to accomplish the same thing. But to do that, we really need your assistance. (*Makes an Insight check and gets a success.*)

**Duke:** Yes, well, I do not respond well to threats and intimidation. (*The DM explains as an aside that such attempts always gain a failure.*) Still, as long as we understand each other, let's continue.

*At the end of the round, the PCs have achieved 4 successes and 1 failure. The skill challenge continues.*

## The Dead Witness

*Bones creak as the corpse shudders and inhales. In a breathy whisper, it asks, "Who disturbs my eternal slumber and risks my wrath? Leave me be or suffer the consequences."*

After invoking the Speak with Dead ritual, the characters must convince a reluctant corpse to give up its knowledge. It refuses to be compelled by the power of the ritual—at least not without a little persuasion. This takes the form of a conversation that typically lasts 10 minutes or so. If the PCs are successful, the corpse answers the questions placed before it as usual, even going so far as to answer an extra question. If the PCs fail in this challenge, the corpse remains silent and its anger lingers to make the next encounter with undead more challenging than it would have otherwise have been.

With appropriate changes, you could also use this challenge for other rituals used to gain knowledge or information.

**Setup:** To learn what the corpse knows, the PCs must give it a reason to help.

**Level:** Equal to the level of the party.

**Complexity:** 2 (requires 6 successes before 3 failures).

**Primary Skills:** Bluff, Diplomacy, History, Insight.

*Bluff (moderate DCs):* You falsely suggest that you share a connection with the corpse, whether it be family, religion, purpose, or the like. If the corpse catches the PC in a lie (the check fails), you can allow it to tell a lie as one of its answers.

*Diplomacy (moderate DCs):* You explain why you need the information, truthfully detailing the needs of your quest.

*History (moderate DCs):* You bring up events that relate to the corpse's past life, or you disclose what happened after its death to make it feel more at ease talking to you.

*Insight (moderate DCs):* You try to connect with the corpse on an emotional level to make it more open to answering your questions. First success with this skill opens up the use of the Religion skill (the corpse mentions that it never received last rites before it died).

*Religion (easy DC):* You perform the death rites appropriate to the corpse's faith. This is available only after one character has gained a success using the Insight skill, and it can be used only once in this way during the challenge.

**Success:** The corpse answers one additional question (in addition to the number of questions provided by the ritual) before time runs out.

**Failure:** The corpse answers no questions. Further, the ill will generated by the reluctant corpse makes the next encounter the PCs have with undead monsters more difficult (increase the level of the monsters by one or two).

## Urban Chase

*Merchants scream and shoppers yell as your quarry shoves her way through the market. You're not exactly sure what's at stake yet, but you know you have to move faster than she is and catch up to her before she gets away.*

The PCs are hot on the heels of the only woman who can tell them what they need to know. Or the PCs try to escape as their enemies chase after them. A typical chase plays out in rounds, but it could take from minutes to hours in the game world.

**Setup:** To catch up with or to escape from the NPCs, you have to navigate the cityscape faster and smarter than your opponent.

**Level:** Equal to the level of the party.

**Complexity:** 5 (requires 12 successes before 6 failures).

**Primary Skills:** Acrobatics, Athletics, Perception, Streetwise.

*Acrobatics (moderate DCs):* You dodge past an obstacle, vault over a crowd, or cross a narrow passage to close or lengthen the distance between you and your opponent. A failed check indicates that you take a spill and lose one healing surge, in addition to counting as a failure for the challenge.

*Athletics (moderate DCs):* You run fast, scale a wall, leap a fence, or swim across a canal to gain an advantage in the chase. A failed check indicates that you get banged up and lose one healing surge, in addition to counting as a failure for the challenge.

*Perception (easy DCs):* You spot a shortcut, notice a hiding space, or otherwise aid your cause. Using this skill doesn't count as a success or failure for the challenge, but instead provides a +2 bonus or a –2 penalty to the next character's skill check.

*Streetwise (hard DCs):* You know enough about the layout of urban settlements to use the environment to your best advantage during a chase.

**Success:** If the PCs are chasing a quarry, they catch up to their quarry (who might be carrying a monetary reward); this could lead directly to a combat encounter. If the PCs are being chased, they evade pursuit or lead their pursuers into an ambush (which leads directly to a combat encounter).

**Failure:** The PCs lose sight of their quarry and have to work harder to find her later. She might take refuge in a den of thieves before they catch her, forcing them to deal with cutthroats or a crime boss to get back on the track of the adventure. If the PCs were being chased, their pursuers catch up with them, and a combat encounter starts immediately.

# The Interrogation

*The orc captive snarls at you, hatred gleaming in his eyes.*

In this skill challenge, the PCs try to extract information from a prisoner. An interrogation can take minutes or hours, sometimes even days.

**Setup:** To convince an NPC to give you the information you want, you need to strike a deal or break the NPC's will to resist your persistent questions.

**Level:** Equal to the level of the party.

**Complexity:** 1 (requires 4 successes before 2 failures).

**Primary Skills:** Bluff, Diplomacy, Intimidate.

*Bluff (moderate DCs):* You try to trick the NPC into revealing a vital piece of information. A failure closes off this approach and increases the DCs of other checks to hard for the duration of the challenge.

*Diplomacy (moderate DCs):* You try to reason with or bargain with the NPC, offering something in good faith for the information you require. At the end of the challenge, if three or more successes came from this approach, you must do everything in your power to hold up your end of the bargain.

*Intimidate (moderate DCs):* You threaten the NPC. A failure closes off this approach and increases the DCs of other checks to hard for the duration of the challenge.

**Success:** The PCs learn valuable information from the NPC, and he might agree to spy for them or otherwise give more information in the future.

**Failure:** The NPC refuses to give any useful information, or gives information that is incorrect or dangerously inaccurate. The PCs might walk into an ambush, or give the wrong code phrase, or otherwise run into trouble due to the false information they received.

# Lost in the Wilderness

*After running for two hours, you are finally able to lose the pursuing orcs. Unfortunately, you now have no idea where you are.*

The PCs try to survive long enough to find their way out of an unfamiliar wilderness. Checks in this challenge might occur once per hour or once per day of travel through the strange region.

**Setup:** You must use your knowledge of the wilderness to survive long enough to find your way back to a familiar area or to a settlement of some sort.

**Level:** Equal to the level of the party.

**Complexity:** 2 (requires 6 successes before 3 failures).

**Primary Skills:** Endurance, Nature, Perception.

*Endurance (moderate DCs):* At least two characters in the party must make Endurance checks each turn to resist the debilitating effects of wandering in the wilderness and dealing with exposure to the elements. A failed check indicates that all members of the party lose one healing surge, in addition to counting as a failure for the challenge.

*Nature (moderate DCs):* At least one character in the party must make a Nature check each turn to help the group find its way through the wilderness, avoid natural hazards, and forage sufficient food and water for the period in question. A failed check indicates that all members of the party lose one healing surge, in addition to counting as a failure for the challenge. If the party is traveling through the Underdark, replace Nature checks with Dungeoneering checks.

*Perception (easy DCs):* You notice something that helps you better survive the trek. Using this skill doesn't count as a success or failure for the challenge, but instead provides a +2 bonus or –2 penalty to the next character's Endurance or Nature check.

**Success:** The PCs emerge from the wilderness near a friendly settlement, onto a familiar road, or are otherwise back on track and out of imminent danger.

**Failure:** The PCs stumble into a monster's lair. This leads to a combat encounter at their level + 2. After dealing with the monster lair, they must complete another "Lost in the Wilderness" skill challenge to find their way back to familiar environments or otherwise get back on track for the adventure.

## DISCOVERING SECRET LORE

*Your knowledge has failed you. Time to research the answer to the mystery before you.*

In this skill challenge, PCs try to learn more about a clue they've discovered during their adventures. It involves research in local libraries and attempts to gather information from sages and other scholars. The challenge might take a matter of minutes, hours, or even days for particularly complex or obscure clues.

**Setup:** To find the information they need, the PCs must search libraries and consult with loremasters.

**Level:** Equal to the level of the party.

**Complexity:** 3 (requires 8 successes before 4 failures).

**Primary Skills:** Arcana, Diplomacy, Religion.

*Arcana (moderate DCs):* You visit libraries and sift through vast stacks of lore in search of a useful clue. Success brings the research one step closer to fruition. Failure indicates that this particular line of research ran into a dead end.

*Diplomacy (moderate DCs):* You visit a sage or scholar, hoping to curry favor and learn a useful bit of information that will bring you one step closer to discovering the secret lore. This approach requires a character to spend gold pieces equal to the level of the challenge × 100. You pay the cost, whether the check results in a success or a failure. A success provides a +2 bonus to the next Arcana check or Religion check, as well as counting as a success for completing the challenge. A failure likewise provides a -2 penalty, as well as counting toward the completion of the challenge.

*Religion (moderate DCs):* You delve into religious lore or seek omens and the counsel of priests to further your research. Success brings the research one step closer to fruition. Failure indicates that this particular line of research ran into a dead end.

**Success:** The PCs solve the riddle or otherwise gain the information they need.

**Failure:** The PCs uncover flawed or incomplete information. As they proceed forward, they operate at a disadvantage. Perhaps they find the wrong answer to a riddle, causing a trap to detonate or cutting off the aid they could have gotten from a magic item or ritual. Or they might translate the lore incorrectly, leading to all kinds of mistakes and misadventures as they otherwise work to complete their quest.

## COMBAT ENCOUNTER

*As the monsters attack, you notice that the chamber is also filling with a deadly green gas.*

This is an example of a combat encounter that includes a skill challenge. While some of the PCs deal with the attacking monsters, others work to disable or destroy the trap before it can overcome the adventurers. Skill uses in combat are usually standard actions, as described in the *Player's Handbook*.

**Setup:** To successfully complete this encounter, the PCs must defeat the monsters and overcome the challenge of the trap.

**Level:** Equal to the level of the party.

**Complexity:** 2 (requires 6 successes before 3 failures). Includes three monsters of the same level as the party.

**Primary Skills:** Arcana, Endurance, Perception, Thievery.

*Arcana (hard DCs):* You call upon your knowledge of magical effects to study the trap and determine some method to help defeat it.

*Endurance (moderate DCs):* Every character in the party must make an Endurance check each turn as a free action to resist the debilitating effects of the trap. Using this skill doesn't count as a success or failure for the challenge, but a success provides a +2 bonus to the character's defenses for the next attack the trap makes, and a failed check indicates that the character takes a -2 penalty for the next attack the trap makes.

*Perception (easy DCs):* You try to notice something to help overcome the trap. Using this skill doesn't count as a success or failure for the challenge, but instead provides a +2 bonus or -2 penalty to the next character's Thievery check.

*Thievery (moderate DCs):* (A character must first make a successful Perception check to find the mechanism to disable the trap.) You work to disable the trap.

**Success:** If a PC gains 6 successes before attaining 3 failures, he or she disables the trap. It no longer damages the party.

**Failure:** If a PC attains 3 failures before gaining 6 successes, the trap completes its cycle. This could mean that it explodes and does considerably more damage, or that it reaches its fully functional state and becomes more deadly (increasing its attack bonus and damage) for the rest of the encounter.

# PUZZLES

Puzzles in a D&D game present a unique form of challenge, one that tests the capabilities of the players at the table instead of their characters. Combat is a tactical challenge for the players, and many traps and skill challenges present puzzlelike elements, but they also involve plenty of die rolling to represent the characters' abilities. A puzzle, generally speaking, does not.

Furthermore, puzzles present a challenge to players that's usually independent of their experience with the game. Experienced players have an edge in combat or skill challenges because of their familiarity with the rules and situations of the game. Unless a puzzle relies on game knowledge, it's just as accessible to someone who has never played D&D before as it is to the hardened veteran. That makes a puzzle a great challenge to throw in front of a group that includes both experienced and new players—as long as you know that the new players have some interest in and facility with puzzles. It gives the new players a chance to join in the game on an equal footing.

The basic nature of puzzles—that they rely on player ability—is the reason that some people love puzzles in the game and some people dislike them. Players who enjoy puzzles and are reasonably good at solving them generally like running into them in the course of an adventure. Players who don't like puzzles, or who balk at the idea that a 25th-level wizard with a 26 Intelligence can't solve a simple number square, find puzzles an intrusion into the game. Looking at the motivations of your players (see Chapter 1), you'll find that puzzles engage some explorers and many thinkers, and they can grab a surprising number of watchers, but instigators, power gamers, and slayers quickly get impatient with them. If your group consists mostly of the latter types of players, it's best to steer away from puzzles.

As with all types of challenges, don't overuse puzzles. A dungeon that is nothing but one puzzle after another can be fun for a little while, but before long the players will start wondering whether they're playing D&D or just working through a book of puzzles. Watch your players for signs of boredom or frustration, and head them off with hints or even a combat encounter sprung on the characters to interrupt their work on the puzzle.

## Is a Puzzle an Encounter?

Although this discussion of puzzles appears in a chapter about noncombat encounters, a puzzle isn't always an encounter. An encounter, by definition, involves a meaningful risk of failure. It's possible for a puzzle to fit that definition, particularly if it's paired with a trap or if it involves an encounter with a monster such as a sphinx. Other puzzles, though, aren't encounters. They might be obstacles in the characters' path, but ones they can find other ways around. As a rule of thumb, you can treat a puzzle as an encounter if there's a definite time limit to solving it, particularly if there's physical or other serious risk to failing to solve the puzzle in that time. Otherwise, it's not an encounter.

## Using Puzzles

A puzzle can be an intriguing way to start an adventure: The earl is kidnapped, and a cryptogram is found in his bedchamber. A cryptic prophecy leads the characters to seek—or prevent—its fulfillment. A map makes no sense until the characters read it in a mirror, and then it leads them to the dungeon. A sphinx has taken up residence in a mountain pass and won't let anyone through unless they can answer a riddle—and so far, no one has.

More commonly, puzzles can serve exactly the same role as other obstacles and challenges in the game, including monsters, hazards, and physical barriers—they stand between the characters and their goal, forcing the characters to solve them or find a way around them. The treasure chest won't open until the characters place the colored stones in the correct spaces on the grid, following a simple rule: Each row, each column, and each subsection of the grid must contain exactly one of each color of stone. The door to the ancient shrine can be opened only by saying nine prayers to the god the shrine was dedicated to, whose name is concealed in a puzzle. The minotaurs have trapped their captives in the heart of a sprawling labyrinth.

Some puzzles conceal a message that's important for the characters to learn, anything from "The baron is a mind flayer" to "The third door holds no trap." Word puzzles work well for concealed messages, particularly cryptograms, word searches (the leftover letters spell the message), and quotation puzzles.

Other puzzles are a matter of the players figuring something out in the context of the adventure. Given a limited set of facts about the three sons of Emperor Darvan the Mad and the three crypts beneath the ruined imperial palace, the characters need to determine which son is buried in the Crypt of the Disgraced—a complex logic puzzle.

---

### THE "GET A CLUE" CHECK

One way to appease the frustrated player who thinks his high-Intelligence character should be able to solve puzzles he can't is to allow the player to roll Intelligence checks or various skill checks to help solve the puzzle. With a successful check (use the Difficulty Class and Damage by Level table, page 42, leaning toward the hard DCs), give the player a hint—a small part of the puzzle, one right move, or a clue toward a new way of thinking about the puzzle.

# TYPES OF PUZZLES

**Riddles** are a form of puzzle with an illustrious history going back to the Greek legends of the sphinx, not to mention *The Hobbit*. That classic form of the "What am I?" riddle basically consists of a series of clues couched in intentionally obscure language. Solving such a riddle is a matter of understanding the less obvious meaning of the riddle's words. For example:

> *In daytime I lie pooled about,*
> *At night I cloak like mist.*
> *I creep inside shut boxes and*
> *Inside your tightened fist.*
> *You see me best when you can't see,*
> *For I do not exist.*

Apparent paradoxes, plays on words, and metaphor conceal the riddle's answer: darkness.

**Cryptograms** are written word puzzles in which the letters are replaced with other letters or symbols. An easy cryptogram uses a pattern of substitution, such as using the next letter of the alphabet (use B for A, C for B, and so on). Harder ones use no pattern, matching letters more or less at random. Instead of letters, you can use runes or other symbols to spell out a message.

**Word searches** are grids of letters that conceal words written horizontally, vertically, or diagonally across the grid, forward or backward. You can give the players a list of words to find, or use tightly themed words (the names of gemstones, for example) and force the players to find all the words themselves. Word searches can conceal a message either by reading the letters left behind when all the words have been found, or by arranging the words themselves into sentences.

**Quotation puzzles** are perfect for concealing messages. In a quotation box, a message is laid out in a grid, then the letters in each column are arranged in alphabetical order instead of their natural order. The players have to rearrange the letters to spell out the message. An acrostic is similar, but the letters of the message are scrambled and divided up among different words. Players decipher clues to identify the words, then match the letters of those words to letters in the message using a numbered key. Many newspapers run acrostic puzzles on a regular basis.

**Crossword puzzles** include crisscross puzzles, where the goal is to fit all the words from a list into a provided grid of crossing lines, and fully crossed puzzles like you find in most newspapers. A crisscross can hide a message spelled out by shaded squares in the grid, while a fully crossed puzzle is better as an obstacle the characters must solve to get past.

Another common newspaper puzzle is easy to adapt as an obstacle puzzle: a **number grid**. In place of numbers, you can use any set of distinct symbols, colored gems, coins, or other items. Given a few numbers or symbols already placed, the object is straightforward: fill in the grid so that each number or symbol occurs exactly once in each row, once in each column, and once in each subsection of the grid. (A typical number grid is 9 × 9, with nine 3 × 3 subsections.)

In a **logic puzzle**, the players figure out an answer by using clues to winnow all the possibilities down to a single answer. For example:

> *Emperor Darvan the Mad had three sons. The oldest, Fieran, was killed by his brother's hand. Madrash knew no fury. Delvan was the youngest.*
> *The three sons wielded three legendary swords, which were buried with them. Fury's Heart was never touched by a righteous hand. Night's Embrace was untainted by royal blood. Death's Chill slew the orc chieftain Ghash Aruk.*
> *Having learned that much, the adventurers now stand in the antechamber before the crypts of the three brothers and read the inscriptions on their doors. The Crypt of the Disgraced holds the son who murdered his brother. The Crypt of the Innocent holds the blameless son who died of old age. The Crypt of the Righteous, undimmed by night, holds the paladin son.*
> *The characters need to determine which son and which sword lie in the Crypt of the Disgraced.*

A careful reading of the clues and application of logic reveal that the Crypt of the Disgraced holds Delvan, who used Fury's Heart to murder his brother.

**Mazes** are classic puzzles often associated with minotaurs (thanks to Greek legend), but you should use them with caution in a dungeon adventure. Exploration that consists purely of a description of turns and dead ends is not exactly riveting, and usually involves only the DM and the player who is trying to make a map. Used with caution—and spiced with traps and monsters—a maze can be an effective puzzle. Typically, dungeon builders design mazes to keep someone from leaving (as Daedalus did to imprison the original minotaur), to keep something safe from intruders, or as a trap, to prevent those who wander in from ever getting out. (As a trap, a maze works best if a wall or rubble falls behind the characters when they enter, preventing them from simply retracing their steps.)

# DESIGNING PUZZLES

Unless you have a particular fondness or facility for creating puzzles, the best way to design puzzles for your D&D game is to steal shamelessly. You can find shelves full of puzzle books and magazines in any bookstore, and the Internet has an abundant supply. Sometimes you can use puzzles exactly as you find them, but other times a puzzle works best if you tweak and customize it to the game's setting and the context of the adventure.

## RIDDLES

A lot of published riddles are very culture-specific or aimed at young children, or else so well known that they don't offer your players any challenge. However, it's not too hard to change the details of a riddle and give it a new face that makes it harder to figure it out. For example, consider the classic riddle of the sphinx: "What goes on four legs in the morning, two legs in the afternoon, and three legs in the evening?"

That riddle is well known enough that you probably can't use it in an adventure as it is. But if you change its fundamental metaphor (the time of day) and couch the idea of going about on varying numbers of legs in a new metaphor, you can disguise the riddle:

> In spring four pillars hold me up,
> a shining dome above the earth.
> In summer two pillars support me,
> a doorway into mystery.
> In autumn three pillars stand beneath me,
> a temple of the Bright City.
> In winter my pillars are crumbled to dust,
> a ruin of ancient glory.

The answer to the riddle is the same—a person, who crawls on hands and knees as an infant, walks on two legs in the prime of life, and uses a cane for support in old age. Using the seasons instead of the time of day as a metaphor for the stages of life is a simple change, and it adds a natural fourth couplet to further disguise the riddle. Instead of the fairly literal mention of legs in the original riddle, we switch to the metaphor of pillars and add different metaphors for the person in each stage of life.

When you're making a riddle of your own, synonyms and metaphors are your friends. Start with an idea of the riddle's answer, which ideally is a clue to the plot of your adventure. Then brainstorm a list of the qualities that thing possesses. Once you have that list, you can couch each quality in metaphorical or intentionally obscure language, and you have a basic riddle.

## CRYPTOGRAMS

Cryptograms are the easiest puzzles to create. You can make a simple one by choosing a pattern, such as replacing each letter with another one some number of letters later in the alphabet (wrapping around to the beginning when you reach Z, of course). Or just make yourself a key, taking care not to use the same letter twice (unless you want a fiendishly difficult puzzle). If you find published cryptograms that use symbols you like, you can adopt those symbols for your own puzzle. Once you have your key, run the letters of your message through it and give the result to your players.

## WORD SEARCHES AND CROSSWORDS

You might have a hard time finding word searches that are at all relevant to the world that D&D characters know, but word searches are also pretty easy to construct. Start with a blank grid (such as a piece of graph paper), then make a list of words that share some common theme. One approach is to use the words of the message you want the players to piece together. Or you might use the names of gemstones, aberrant monsters, or rulers from the ancient dynasties of Bael Turath for a really difficult challenge (difficult because unfamiliar words are harder to spot than familiar ones). Then place those words into the grid in every direction (don't forget backward, including diagonals). Start with the longest words, and work down to the shortest. If you want the players to piece together a message from the letters that aren't used to make words, make sure you leave room for those letters. Once you have all your words placed, fill in the empty squares, either with the letters of your hidden message or with random letters.

Making a crossword puzzle is a very similar task. In both kinds of puzzles you're arranging words from a list in intersecting patterns.

## QUOTATION PUZZLES

A quotation box is easy to design. First, write out the short message you want to deliver, then count the number of letters in the message. (A message longer than 120 letters gets pretty unwieldy.) Don't count spaces or punctuation, but do include hyphens and apostrophes. Divide the number of letters by 3 for an easy puzzle, 6 for a really hard puzzle, or some number in between.

Then take a piece of graph paper and count out squares across equal to your new number, rounding up. Count squares down equal to the number you used to divide the total. Then write out the message, putting

---

### PUZZLES AND PROPS

When you include a puzzle in an adventure, it's a great opportunity to use a prop (see page 25). Even if the prop is nothing more than a riddle written out on paper, it gives the players something to hold, to look at, and to pass around the table as they try to solve it. Sometimes you can use actual puzzles as props—puzzle boxes, tangrams, and other manipulative puzzles are a good place to start. You can buy a blank jigsaw puzzle and draw a map or write a riddle on it before taking it apart—and scattering the pieces in different parts of a dungeon (or even different dungeons!). Stores that sell books and educational games for children typically have a good selection of puzzle toys that can be reasonably challenging for adults.

one letter in each square and drawing lines between squares at the ends of words. When you reach the end of a line, continue in the leftmost square of the next line. When you're done, if you have any blank squares at the end, fill them in with black squares.

Below your message, write down the letters in each column, rearranging them into alphabetical order. Those are the letters you'll then copy onto a new piece of paper for the players to solve.

An acrostic is harder to create, but if you understand how to solve them it's a fairly obvious process. The real challenge is in finding clued words that use all of the letters in the original message, without using any letters twice or leaving any out.

## Number Grids

There's no reason to create your own number grid when there's an abundance of puzzles you can steal. The puzzle will feel more esoteric to your players if you replace the numbers with symbols, colored gemstones in a grid carved into stone doors, or letters that spell out a nine-letter word. (Remember that your nine-letter word can't use the same letter twice!) As with a cryptogram, make yourself a key—you might replace every occurrence of the number 1 with a C, for example. If your puzzle spells out a word in one row or column, you might want to give the players a clue to the word to help them solve the puzzle.

## Logic Puzzles

Logic puzzles are also pretty easy to steal and adapt. If you come across a puzzle in which you need to correctly match each of three children with the color of his shirt and his favorite fruit, you can translate each child into one of Emperor Darvan's three sons, each color into one of the three legendary swords, and each fruit into a crypt. The trick is in translating the clues.

Fundamentally, each clue in a logic puzzle amounts to a fact such as, "Object A isn't connected to object 2," whether A is a crypt or a fruit and 2 is a sword or a color. Sometimes a puzzle uses a positive assertion instead ("Object A is connected to object 2"), but that makes the puzzle simpler. If you boil the clues from your example puzzle down into that form, it gets easier to translate them.

The real fun of a logic puzzle is presenting it in your adventure. Unlike a puzzle you find in a magazine, the clues don't have to be presented neatly arranged in one place—the entire adventure can consist of assembling clues that are scattered through ancient libraries and crumbling ruins. You can also use a logic puzzle as the structure of a mystery adventure, as the characters piece together clues that ultimately reveal a killer, a motive, and a an accomplice.

# Puzzle as Skill Challenge

*The voice flowed out of the statue, a cold, distant sound. "What are the four virtues of Keblor Kest? Answer now, before time runs out!"*

You can also set up a puzzle as a skill challenge. In this example, the PCs make appropriate skill checks to simulate their characters solving the clues of the puzzle. If they achieve the listed number of successes before failures, they solve the puzzle and earn the reward. If they achieve the listed number of failures first, however, they fail to solve the puzzle and must suffer the consequences.

**Setup:** To open the door to the secret chamber, the PCs must solve the riddle of the statue. After each success, the voice says, "Good, you remember Keblor's greatness." After each failure, the voice says, "You know nothing of Keblor's greatness and time is running out!"

**Level:** Equal to the level of the party.

**Complexity:** 1 (requires 4 successes before 2 failures).

**Primary Skills:** Arcana, History, Insight, Religion.

*Arcana (moderate DCs):* You call upon your knowledge of magical lore to remember one of the four virtues.

*History (hard DCs):* You call upon your knowledge of history to remember some forgotten bit of information pertaining to the four virtues of Keblor Kest.

*Insight (moderate DCs):* You try to discern something to help support the rest of your party. Using this skill doesn't count as a success or failure for the challenge, but instead provides a +2 bonus or -2 penalty to the next character's Arcana, History, or Religion skill check.

*Religion (easy DCs):* As a religious figure of some renown, this skill provides the best route to solving the puzzle of the statue. You call upon your knowledge of religious lore to remember one of the four virtues.

**Success:** If the PCs gain 4 successes before attaining 2 failures, the party solves the riddle, and the statue slides open to reveal the entrance to the secret chamber.

**Failure:** If the PCs attain 2 failures before gaining 4 successes, the party fails to solve the riddle before time runs out. The statue animates and attacks the party. Start a combat encounter.

# TRAPS AND HAZARDS

One wrong step in an ancient tomb triggers a series of scything blades that cleave through armor and bone. The seemingly innocuous vines that hang over a cave entrance grasp and choke at anyone foolish enough to push through them. A narrow stone bridge leads over a pit filled with hissing, sputtering acid. In the D&D game, monsters are only one of many challenges that adventurers face.

If it can hurt the party, but it isn't a monster, it's either a trap or a hazard.

## TRAP OR HAZARD?

What's the difference between a trap and a hazard? Traps are constructed with the intent to damage, harry, or impede intruders. Hazards are natural or supernatural in origin, but typically lack the malicious intent of a trap. Though both feature similar risks, a pit covered with a goblin-constructed false floor is a trap, while a deep chasm between two sections of a troglodyte cave constitutes a hazard.

Traps tend to be hidden, and their danger is apparent only when they are discovered with keen senses or a misplaced step. The danger of a hazard is usually out in the open, and its challenge determined by the senses (sometimes far too late) or deduced by those knowledgeable of the hazard's environs.

The common link between traps and hazards revolves around peril—both to adventurers and monsters. Because of this similarity, traps and hazards feature similar rules, conventions, and presentations.

## PERCEIVING TRAPS AND HAZARDS

When the party is within line of sight of a trap, compare each character's passive Perception check with the DCs of the traps in the room. A PC whose passive Perception is equal to or higher than the DCs notices the trap or the relevant aspect of the trap. Other skills might also play a role in allowing PCs to notice traps or identify hazards, such as Dungeoneering and Nature.

Of course, PCs can always try an active Perception check as a minor action to find any traps they missed with their passive check. PCs most often decide to roll an active Perception check when some aspect of the trap becomes apparent.

## TRIGGERING TRAPS AND HAZARDS

Traps and hazards act without a hint of intelligence, so their behavior is predictable, even if it's sometimes random. A trap is constructed to go off when certain conditions are met—from a character stepping on a pressure-sensitive flagstone in the floor to intruders entering the evil temple without wearing the symbol of the deity it's dedicated to. When triggered, traps and hazards either attack or activate and roll initiative, acting every round in initiative order.

## ATTACKS AND EFFECTS

A trap's attack is limited only by the imagination of its creator. A blade cuts across the corridor, making melee attacks. Flames shoot out in close blasts. Rubble drops from the ceiling in an area burst. Arrows shoot out from the wall, making ranged attacks. Trap attacks use the same rules as creature attacks, but a trap's ranged attacks and area attacks do not provoke opportunity attacks.

## COUNTERING TRAPS AND HAZARDS

While the best way to counter a trap or hazard is to avoid it, sometimes that's not possible. That leaves characters with three approaches to countering the obstacle: break it, disable it, or outsmart it.

Destroying a trap or hazard with a weapon or attacks is often difficult, if not impossible—arrow traps are typically protected by walls or shielding, magic traps have a habit of blowing up when attacked, and very few attacks can counter that huge boulder rumbling down the corridor. But attacking and destroying a trap may be the best way to defeat it in a pinch.

Most traps can be disabled or delayed with the Thievery skill. Sometimes other skills and abilities can supplement the Thievery check. When a character delays a trap, the trap stops functioning for a period of time (until the end of the character's next turn, with a 50% chance each round that it reactivates after that). Disabling a trap takes the trap out of commission until someone makes the effort to repair or reset it. While it's delayed or disabled, the trap effectively isn't there.

You can outsmart a trap or hazard. Figuring out a trap's location and avoiding the pressure plates is a sure way of doing this, but more subtle and interesting methods sometimes apply. Many traps have interesting countermeasures other than destroying, delaying, or disabling them that make it possible for a variety of characters to foil or even defeat them.

## PLACING TRAPS AND HAZARDS

Traps and hazards fit into an encounter much like an additional monster. Every trap or hazard has a level (and an appropriate XP value for that level), so you can figure it in as part of an encounter that includes monsters to determine the appropriate reward for defeating it. For example, an encounter for five 10th-level PCs might include four 10th-level monsters and one 10th-level trap. Defeating the trap, just like defeating the monster, earns the party 500 XP.

# Trap and Hazard Roles

Although traps and hazards can take the place of a monster in your encounter design, they aren't monsters. They attack differently, their effects can debilitate, and they can be difficult to spot at first. What traps and hazards usually don't do is choose from a variety of attacks, move into advantageous position, or even choose their target. And they typically don't take actions that aren't strictly defined by their construction or nature. That is the fundamental difference between a trap or hazard and a monster.

Because of these differences, traps and hazards have their own roles that loosely correspond to monster roles. Like monster roles, they give you an idea of how a trap or hazard is supposed to fit into an encounter, how it tends to act, and how it might interact with the monsters and terrain in the encounter. There are four trap roles: blaster, lurker, obstacle, and warder.

## Blaster

If a trap or hazard creates damaging areas of effect or attacks multiple targets from a distance in a regular and programmed way, it's a blaster. Traps that propel missile weapons, create exploding blasts each round, or hurl magical effects from a spell turret all represent blaster traps.

Blaster traps often serve a role similar to that of artillery monsters, but can also work as a buffer for monsters of other roles. Since many traps are harder to damage than monsters, blaster traps are a first or second line of defense that artillery or controller monsters hide behind.

## Lurker

Lurker traps attack and then disappear or dissipate, making them harder to attack or counter. A pendulum trap that strikes only to retract back into the wall each round, and strange motes of energy from the Shadowfell that attack the life force of those nearby before flickering out of existence for a few moments, are examples of lurker traps.

Lurker traps fulfill the same role as lurker monsters. They attack and move away, and can be hard to counter without organized effort on the part of the characters.

## Obstacle

As the name implies, an obstacle trap or hazard impedes movement, and it might stun or daze creatures to further slow them down. Obstacles are barriers and perils that characters can get past, but they have to spend some effort or take some damage, or both, to do so. Electrified squares on a floor that demand puzzle-solving to get around, magical glyphs that require Arcana to decipher and avoid, or falling portcullises that channel movement through a maze of corridors are a few examples of interesting obstacle traps.

Obstacles complement brutes and skirmishers. Carefully placed obstacles offer the brute an amount of battlefield control and allow the skirmisher's expanded movement options to shine. These perils can be extremely powerful when used in concert with soldiers and controllers, since their very presence can bolster the battlefield control that marks those two roles.

## Warder

A warder trap or hazard functions as an alarm, alerting nearby guards or monsters while also doing damage to the characters who triggered it. A warder attacks to begin the encounter, dealing its damage or other effect and raising its alarm. Thereafter, some warders continue to attack and sound the alarm, while others do their thing initially and then become inactive.

A warder can complement a variety of monster roles, but typically works best with groups of soldiers, controllers, and lurkers. It gives these monsters time to prepare an organized defense against intruders who have already been weakened by the trap.

## Elite and Solo Traps

Much like monsters, traps can also be designated as elite or solo threats. It's relatively easy to convert any trap or hazard to an elite version with quick adjustments to its DCs and attacks. Many of the traps and hazards presented in this section include ways that you can upgrade them to elite as part of their presentations.

---

## Winging It

There is always more than one way to approach a trap or hazard. Even the best designed traps feature potential design holes that a player might exploit to counter a trap. Sometimes the best or the most fun ideas for countering a trap or hazard come as a flash of inspiration during play.

Remember the first rule of improvisation: Try not to say no. When a player suggests a plausible countermeasure for a trap, even if that possibility isn't included in the trap's presentation, figure out the best way to resolve that using the rules: a skill check or ability check against an appropriate DC, an attack, or the use of a power. You can always use the DCs that are included in the trap's description as example DCs for using other skills and abilities.

In short, always find ways to reward quick thinking and fun when it comes to traps and hazards. Outsmarting traps, hazards, and villains (and even the DM) is fun for players, and first and foremost, your game should be fun.

---

On the other hand, solo traps and hazards are rare and complex things that usually occur only as a skill challenge.

# USING TRAPS AND HAZARDS

More so than monsters, traps and hazards take finesse to run and place in an adventure. Some traps and hazards behave just like monsters in an encounter, attacking on their turn in the initiative order. Others attack once, usually when the characters blunder into them. Some even behave as skill challenges, requiring multiple successes to defeat before something dramatic occurs.

## SAMPLE TRAPS AND HAZARDS

| False-Floor Pit | Level 1 Warder |
|---|---|
| Trap | XP 100 |

*A covered pit is hidden near the center of the room. Timber covered with flagstones is rigged to fall when a creature walks on it, dropping the creature into a 10-foot-deep pit.*

**Trap:** A 2-by-2 section of the floor hides a 10-foot-deep pit.

**Perception**
✦ DC 20: The character notices the false stonework.

**Trigger**
The trap attacks when a creature enters one of the trap's four squares.

**Attack**
**Immediate Reaction     Melee**
**Target:** The creature that triggered the trap.
**Attack:** +4 vs. Reflex
**Hit:** Target falls into pit, takes 1d10 damage, and falls prone.
**Miss:** Target returns to the last square it occupied and its move action ends immediately.
**Effect:** The false floor opens and the pit is no longer hidden.

**Countermeasures**
✦ An adjacent character can trigger the trap with a DC 10 Thievery check (standard action). The floor falls into the pit.
✦ An adjacent character can disable the trap with a DC 25 Thievery check (standard action). The floor becomes safe.
✦ A character who makes an Athletics check (DC 11, or DC 21 without a running start) can jump over the pit.
✦ A character can climb out with a DC 15 Athletics check.

**Upgrade to Elite (200 XP)**
Increase the Perception and Thievery DCs by 2. The pit is 20 feet deep and filled with poisoned spikes. A character who falls into the pit takes 3d10 damage + ongoing 5 poison damage (save ends).

| Rockslide | Level 1 Lurker |
|---|---|
| Hazard | XP 100 |

*Rocks fall from above.*

**Hazard:** Rocks tumble down to a target square and make a burst 3 attack.

**Perception**
Characters can't use Perception to detect this hazard.

**Additional Skills:** Nature or Dungeoneering
A DC 20 Nature or Dungeoneering check notices a rock formation is unstable.

**Initiative** +3

**Trigger**

The trigger for a rockslide can be random, caused by the actions of others, or timed. When triggered, the rockslide rolls initiative. Between the trigger and the rockslide's attack, characters in the area know that a rockslide is beginning and the area it will affect.

**Attack**
**Standard Reaction     Close burst 3**
**Targets:** Creatures in burst
**Attack:** +4 vs. Reflex
**Hit:** 2d6 + 2 damage
**Miss:** Half damage
**Sustain Standard:** The rockslide continues for 1d4 rounds. The burst area is difficult terrain during and after the rockslide.

**Countermeasures**
✦ A character in the area can take advantage of natural openings in the slide to avoid damage by making a DC 25 Nature or Dungeoneering check. With a successful check, a character takes half damage (no damage if it misses).

| Spear Gauntlet | Level 2 Obstacle |
|---|---|
| Trap | XP 125 |

*Hidden spears thrust upward from the floor in response to pressure. The individual trigger plates and spear-thrusting devices are connected to a key-operated control panel on the wall nearby.*

**Trap:** Five squares in the room contain hidden spears that thrust up to attack when triggered.

**Perception**
✦ DC 20: The character notices the trigger plates.
✦ DC 25: The character notices the hidden control panel.

**Trigger**
The trap, five squares placed randomly in the room, attacks when a creature enters one of the trigger squares or starts its turn on a trigger square. When the trap is triggered, all five spears thrust up at the same time, attacking anyone standing on a trigger square.

**Attack**
**Opportunity Action     Melee**
**Target:** All creatures on trigger squares when the trap activates.
**Attack:** +7 vs. AC
**Hit:** 1d8 + 3 damage

**Countermeasures**
✦ A character who makes a successful Athletics check (DC 6 or DC 11 without a running start) can jump over a single pressure plate square.
✦ An adjacent character can disable a trigger plate with a DC 25 Thievery check.
✦ A creature adjacent to the control panel can disable the entire trap with a DC 20 Thievery check.
✦ A DC 20 Dungeoneering check grants the party a +2 bonus to Thievery checks to delay or disable the trap.
✦ A character can ready an action to attack the spears (AC 13, other defenses 10; hp 10). When the spears in one square are destroyed, that trigger plate becomes useless.
✦ A character can attack a trigger plate or the control panel (AC 12, other defenses 10; hp 30; resist 5 all). Destroying a trigger plate renders it useless, and destroying the control panel disables the entire trap.

**Upgrade to Elite (250 XP)**
Increase the number of trapped squares to 10 and increase the DCs for Perception and Thievery checks by 2.

## Magic Crossbow Turret
**Trap**

**Level 3 Blaster**
**XP 150**

*A pair of armored crossbow turrets drops down from the ceiling on the far edge of the room, peppering creatures with quarrels.*

**Trap:** Two crossbows attack each round on their initiative after they are triggered.

**Perception**

✦ DC 20: The character notices the trigger plates.
✦ DC 25: The character notices the location of the hidden turret emplacements.
✦ DC 25: The character notices the location of the hidden control panel.

**Initiative** +3

**Trigger**

The trap activates and rolls initiative when a character enters one of the four trigger squares in the room.

**Attack**

**Standard Action**      **Ranged** 10

**Targets:** Each crossbow attacks one intruder. It magically distinguishes intruders from natives of the dungeon.

**Attack:** +8 vs. AC

**Hit:** 2d8 + 3 damage

**Countermeasures**

✦ A character who makes a successful Athletics check (DC 6 or DC 11 without a running start) can jump over a single trigger plate square.
✦ An adjacent character can disable a trigger plate with a DC 25 Thievery check.
✦ Attacking a trigger plate (AC 12, other defenses 10) only triggers the trap.
✦ A character can attack a turret (AC 16, other defenses 13; hp 38). Destroying a turret stops its attacks.
✦ A character can engage in a skill challenge to deactivate the control panel. DC 20 Thievery. Complexity 2 (6 successes before 3 failures). Success disables the trap. Failure causes the control panel to explode (close blast 3, 2d6 + 3 damage to all creatures in blast) and the trap remains active.

**Upgrade to Elite (300 XP)**

Increase the Perception and Thievery DCs by 2. Increase the number of turrets to four.

## Doomspore
**Hazard**

**Level 3 Obstacle**
**XP 350**

*Usually found in large, natural caverns, or in areas tainted by the Shadowfell, these patches of large, toadstool-shaped fungus can grow to be about 3 feet tall. When disturbed, a doomspore unleashes a cloud of deadly spores.*

**Hazard:** A doomspore fills a square (the square is difficult terrain). When triggered, it releases a cloud of spores.

**Perception**

No check is necessary to notice the fungus.

**Additional Skill:** Dungeoneering

✦ DC 20: The character identifies the fungus as doomspore.

**Trigger**

When a creature enters a square of doomspore, or kicks or pokes at it from an adjacent square, or attacks it in any way, the fungus releases a cloud of spores. A bloodied character in the initial burst or that begins its turn in a doomspore cloud is attacked by the poison.

**Attack**

**Standard Action**      **Close** burst 1

**Target:** Bloodied creature in burst

**Attack:** +6 vs. Fortitude

**Hit:** 1d10 poison damage and ongoing 5 poison damage (save ends).

**Effect:** The cloud provides concealment for creatures inside it. The cloud persists until the end of the encounter or for 5 minutes. Once a patch of doomspore creates a cloud, it can't create another one for 24 hours.

**Countermeasures**

✦ A character can move into a square of doomspore without triggering the cloud by making a DC 25 Dungeoneering check. The character's move must end in the doomspore's square.

**Upgrade to Elite (700 XP)**

✦ Increase the Dungeoneering DCs by 2.
✦ Increase the damage to 3d10 poison damage and ongoing 5 poison damage (save ends).

## Pendulum Scythes
**Trap**

**Level 4 Lurker**
**XP 175**

*Scything blades sweep across the room in a seemingly random pattern, cutting swaths at 5-foot intervals.*

**Trap:** Each row of squares in the chamber features a scything blade. On its turn, a blade sweeps through one row of squares at random, attacking all creatures in the row.

**Perception**

✦ DC 17: The character notices thin, shallow cuts running across the dungeon floor at 5-foot intervals.
✦ DC 22: The character notices thin slots across the ceiling of the room, corresponding with the cuts across the floor. A character who makes a DC 15 Dungeoneering check recognizes these as signs of a scything blades trap.
✦ DC 22: The character spots the pressure plates at the room's entrance.
✦ DC 27: The character notices the hidden control panel if it is within line of sight.

**Initiative** +6

**Trigger**

The trap rolls initiative when a creature enters one of the six squares of pressure plates at the room's entrance. As a standard action, a creature can trigger the trap using the control panel at the far end of the room, if it has the key.

**Attack**

**Standard Action**      **Melee**

**Targets:** All creatures in a row of squares. Roll randomly each round to determine the row the trap attacks.

**Attack:** +9 vs. AC

**Hit:** 2d8 + 4 damage and secondary attack
    **Secondary Attack:** +7 vs. Fortitude
    **Hit:** Push 1 (in the direction of the blade's movement), knock target prone, and ongoing 5 damage (save ends).

**Countermeasure**

✦ A character who makes a DC 22 Dungeoneering check as a minor action can determine the row of squares the trap will attack on its next turn.
✦ A character can ready an action to attack a pendulum blade (AC 15, other defenses 12; hp 48). Destroying a blade renders that row of squares safe from attack.
✦ A character can engage in a skill challenge to deactivate the control panel. DC 22 Thievery. Complexity 1 (4 successes before 2 failures). Success disables the trap. Failure causes 1d4 + 1 blades to attack each round.

**Upgrade to Elite (350 XP)**

Two blades attack each round on separate initiative counts. The characters' enemies know the logic of the blades' attacks and avoid the rows the blades attack.

## Whirling Blades
**Trap**

Level 5 Obstacle
XP 200

*Blades rise out of hidden compartments and spin wildly across the chamber.*

**Trap:** A whirling blades contraption emerges and spins like a top, moving its speed in a random direction and attacking each round.

**Perception**

✦ DC 22: The character notices trigger plates around the chamber.

✦ DC 27: The character notices the hidden control panel.

**Initiative** +7      **Speed** 4

**Trigger**

When a character moves into a trigger square, the whirling blades contraption emerges and attacks.

**Attack**

**Standard Action**      **Close** burst 1

**Targets:** All creatures in burst

**Attack:** +10 vs. AC

**Hit:** 3d8+3 damage

**Countermeasures**

✦ A character can engage in a skill challenge to deactivate the control panel. DC 22 Thievery. Complexity 2 (6 successes before 3 failures). Success disables the trap. Failure causes the whirling blades to act twice in the round (roll a second initiative for the trap).

✦ A character can attack the whirling blades contraption (AC 16, other defenses 13; hp 55; resist 5 all) or the control panel (AC 14, other defenses 11; hp 35; resist 5 all). Destroying either disables the entire trap.

## Treacherous Ice Sheet
**Hazard**

Level 5 Obstacle
XP 200

*A slick sheet of ice creates a hazardous obstacle.*

**Hazard:** This sheet of ice fills 10 contiguous squares, turning them into difficult terrain.

**Perception**

No check is necessary to notice the ice.

**Additional Skill:** Nature

✦ DC 22: The character identifies the squares of treacherous ice.

**Trigger**

The ice attacks when a creature enters or begins its turn in a square of treacherous ice. It also attacks when a creature stands up from prone in a square of treacherous ice.

**Attack**

**Opportunity Action**      **Melee**

**Target:** Creature on the ice

**Attack:** +8 vs. Reflex

**Hit:** 1d6+2 damage and fall prone. If the creature is already prone, no damage but its turn ends immediately.

**Countermeasures**

✦ With a DC 27 Acrobatic check and a move action, a character can move into a square of treacherous ice without risk of falling. If the check fails or the character move more than 1 square, the ice attacks.

**Upgrade to Elite (400XP)**

✦ Increase the Nature checks and the attack modifiers by 2.

✦ Increase the size of the sheet to 20 squares.

## Poisoned Dart Wall
**Trap**

Level 6 Blaster
XP 250

*Darts fire from the wall, filling the chamber with danger.*

**Trap:** Each round on its initiative, the trap fires a barrage of poison darts that randomly attack 2d4 targets in range.

**Perception**

✦ DC 22: The character notices the small holes in the walls.

✦ DC 27: The character notices the tripwire trigger.

**Initiative** +7

**Trigger**

When a character moves across the tripwire at the entrance of the chamber, the trap rolls initiative.

**Attack**

**Standard Action**      **Ranged** 20

**Targets:** 2d4 targets in range

**Attack:** +11 vs. AC

**Hit:** 1d8+2 damage and ongoing 5 poison damage (save ends).

**Countermeasures**

✦ An adjacent character can disable the tripwire with a DC 30 Thievery check.

✦ A character who moves no more than 1 square on a turn gains a +5 bonus to AC against the dart attacks.

**Upgrade to Elite (500 XP)**

✦ Increase the DCs for Perception and Thievery checks by 2.

✦ The trap fires 4d4 darts that deal 1d8+2 damage and ongoing 10 poison damage (save ends).

## Glyph of Warding
**Trap**

**Level 7 Warder**
**XP 300**

*A hidden glyph around the door suddenly glows and explodes as you try to open it.*

**Trap:** A magical glyph wards a portal, ready to explode with arcane fury when the trap is triggered.

### Perception
✦ DC 28: The character notices the glyph.

**Additional Skill:** Arcana

✦ DC 24: The character spots the glyph and provides a +2 bonus to Thievery checks made to disable it.

### Trigger
When a creature tries to open the guarded portal or pass through it, the glyph explodes.

### Attack
**Immediate Reaction**    **Close** burst 3

**Targets:** All creatures in burst

**Attack:** +10 vs. Reflex

**Hit:** The glyph is designed with one of the following effects:
✦ 4d6+4 fire damage and ongoing 5 fire damage (save ends)
✦ 4d6+4 cold damage and immobilize (save ends)
✦ 4d6+4 thunder damage and dazed (save ends)
✦ 4d6+4 lightning damage and dazed (save ends)
✦ 4d6+4 acid damage and ongoing 5 acid damage (save ends)
✦ 4d6+4 necrotic damage and -2 attack penalty (save ends)
✦ 4d6+4 radiant damage and blinded (save ends)

### Countermeasure
✦ An adjacent character can disable the glyph with a DC 28 Thievery check.

### Upgrade to Elite (600 XP)
✦ Increase the DCs of Perception, Thievery, and Arcana checks by 4.
✦ Add to the glyph's attack:
*Aftereffect:* 4d6+4 damage of the same type as the glyph's original damage.

## Daggerthorn Briar
**Hazard**

**Level 7 Obstacle**
**XP 300**

*Found in deep woods and in the Feywild, daggerthorn briar is a bloodthirsty plant that some hard-hearted nobles use to guard the grounds of their villas.*

**Hazard:** A single briar patch of daggerthorn fills 10 contiguous squares, turning them into difficult terrain.

### Perception
No check is necessary to notice the briars.

**Additional Skill:** Nature

✦ DC 24: The character identifies the patch as daggerthorn briar.

### Trigger
The briars attack when a creature enters or begins its turn in or adjacent to a square of daggerthorn briar.

### Attack
**Opportunity Action**    **Melee**

**Target:** Creature in or adjacent to briar

**Attack:** +12 vs. AC

**Hit:** 2d10 + 5 damage and immobilized until escape. The attack deals 3d10 + 5 damage if the target is bloodied.

### Countermeasures
✦ Immobilized characters can use the Acrobatics or Athletics (DC 20) to free themselves.
✦ A character can attack a square of daggerthorn briar (AC 18, other defenses 15; hp 70; vulnerable 10 fire). Once a square is destroyed, it cannot attack and is no longer difficult terrain.

### Upgrade to Elite (600 XP)
✦ Increase Nature DCs and attack rolls by 2.
✦ Increase size to 15 squares.
✦ Elite daggerthorn is not vulnerable to fire.

## Flame Jet
**Trap**

**Level 8 Blaster**
**XP 350**

*Two hidden nozzles let loose a blast of flame.*

**Trap:** When the trap is triggered, two hidden nozzles in the walls attack each round on their initiative.

### Perception
✦ DC 24: The character notices the nozzles.
✦ DC 28: The character notices the control panel on the far side of the room.

**Initiative** +5

### Trigger
When a character enters the blast area of one of the flame jets, it makes its first attack as an immediate reaction. It then rolls initiative, attacking each round.

### Attack
**Immediate Reaction or Standard Action**    **Close** blast 3

**Targets:** All creatures in blast

**Attack:** +11 vs. Reflex

**Hit:** 3d8+4 fire damage and ongoing 5 fire damage (save ends).

**Miss:** Half damage, no ongoing damage.

### Countermeasures
✦ An adjacent character can disable one flame jet with a DC 24 Thievery check.
✦ A character can engage in a skill challenge to deactivate the control panel. DC 28 Thievery. Complexity 1 (4 successes before 2 failures). Success disables the trap. Failure causes the control panel to explode (close blast 3, 3d8 + 4 damage to all creatures in blast) and the trap remains active.

### Upgrade to Elite (700 XP)
✦ Increase the Perception and Thievery checks by 2.
✦ Increase the number of nozzles to 6, or to 3 with a larger area of close blast 5.

## Caustic Geyser
Hazard

Level 9 Blaster
XP 400

*A geyser of acidic liquid explodes from the ground.*

**Hazard:** The geyser becomes active when triggered. Thereafter, it attacks every round on its initiative.

### Perception
✦ DC 28: The character detects the geyser before moving within 6 squares of it.

**Additional Skill:** Nature or Dungeoneering
✦ DC 24: The character recognizes the danger of the geyser before moving within 6 squares of it.

**Initiative** +3

### Trigger
The geyser rolls initiative when one or more characters move within 6 squares of it.

### Attack
**Standard Action**     **Close** burst 3
**Targets:** Creatures in burst
**Attack:** +12 vs. Reflex
**Hit:** 3d8+4 acid damage and followup.
   *Followup:* +10 vs. Fortitude.
     **Hit:** Ongoing 5 acid damage and blinded (save ends).
**Miss:** Half damage.

### Countermeasure
✦ A character in the burst can minimize the damage of the geyser with a DC 28 Acrobatics check made as an immediate interrupt before the geyser's attack. With a successful check, the character takes half damage if the geyser hits and no damage if it misses.

## Electrified Floor
Trap

Level 10 Obstacle
XP 500

*A stretch of hallway contains glowing blue floor tiles. When the wrong tile is stepped upon, an electrifying shock is triggered.*

**Trap:** This trap consists of 10 randomly positioned squares that contain electrified tiles. When the trap is triggered, it attacks.

### Perception
✦ DC 26: The character can discern if any adjacent squares contain electrified tiles.

**Additional Skill:** Arcana
✦ DC 22: The character's knowledge provides a +2 bonus to Thievery checks to disable a tile.

### Trigger
When a creature enters or begins its turn in an electrified square, the trap attacks that creature.

### Attack
**Opportunity Action**     **Melee** 1
**Target:** Creature in a trapped square
**Attack:** +13 vs. Fortitude
**Hit:** 2d10 + 6 lightning damage. On a critical hit, the target is stunned (save ends).
**Miss:** Half damage.

### Countermeasures
✦ A character who makes a successful Athletics check (DC 6 or DC 11 without a running start) can jump over a single trapped square.
✦ An adjacent character can disable a tile with a DC 26 Thievery check.

### Upgrade to Elite (1,000 XP)
✦ Increase the DCs for Perception and Thievery checks by 2.
✦ The trap's attacks deal 3d10 + 6 lightning damage and target is stunned (save ends).

## Spectral Tendrils
Trap

Level 13 Obstacle
XP 800

*Ghostly tendrils whip from the ground to lash at you.*

**Trap:** This trap consists of a continuous field of 10 squares. When a creature steps into the area of this attack, spectral tendrils lash out and attack the creature.

### Perception
✦ DC 27: The character notices something strange about the area ahead, as though a ghostly mist hangs just above the ground.

**Additional Skill:** Arcana
✦ DC 23: The character recognizes some terrain feature, usually a fresco or other art, that serves as the trap's focus.
✦ DC 31: The character's knowledge provides a +2 bonus to Thievery checks to disable the trap.

### Trigger
When a creature enters or begins its turn in a trapped square, the trap attacks.

### Attack
**Opportunity Action**     **Melee**
**Target:** Creature in trapped square
**Attack:** +18 vs. AC
**Hit:** 2d10 + 6 necrotic damage and dazed until the end of the target's next turn.
   *Aftereffect:* Dazed until the end of the target's next turn.

### Countermeasures
✦ A character who makes a DC 27 Acrobatics check can move through a trigger square without provoking the attack. The squares count as difficult terrain.
✦ An adjacent character can disable a trigger plate with a DC 31 Thievery check.

## Cave-In
Hazard

Level 13 Lurker
XP 800

*A disruption of some sort sets off a chain reaction that doesn't end until all the room is covered in rubble.*

**Hazard:** When triggered, rocks and debris fall from above to fill the area with attacks. It attacks a different part of the area each turn, on its initiative.

### Perception
✦ DC 31: The character sees that the ceiling appears unstable.

**Additional Skill:** Dungeoneering
✦ DC 26: Same as for Perception, above.

**Initiative** +6

### Trigger
The trigger for a cave-in can be random, caused by the actions of others, or timed. When triggered, the cave-in rolls initiative. Between the trigger and the cave-in's attack, characters in the area know that a cave-in is beginning. On its turn, the cave-in attacks a random square within the encounter area.

### Attack
**Standard Action**     **Close** burst 1
**Targets:** All creatures in burst
**Attack:** +16 vs. Reflex
**Hit:** 2d12 + 8 damage
**Miss:** Half damage.
**Effect:** The burst area becomes difficult terrain.
**Sustain Standard:** The cave-in attacks each round, targeting a different square.

### Countermeasure
✦ A character who makes a DC 31 Dungeoneering check as a minor action can determine the square the trap will attack on its next turn.

## Altar of Zealotry
**Trap**

Level 15 Lurker
XP 1,200

*The altar ahead appears twisted and evil, and it radiates a disturbing feeling of maliciousness and dread.*

**Trap:** Taking the form of a large altar devoted to a dread god, this shrine attempts to dominate those who approach it. The trigger area is the entire shrine. It draws its energy from living creatures not devoted to its deity, and functions only as long as such creatures are within the shrine.

**Perception**

No check is required to see the altar.

**Additional Skill:** Religion

✦ DC 27: The character recognizes the nature of the altar.

**Initiative** +6

**Trigger**

When characters enter the area, the trap activates and rolls initiative. The trap continues its attacks until no living unbelievers remain in the area.

**Attack**

**Standard Action**          **Ranged** sight

**Target:** A random creature not wearing the holy symbol of the deity it is dedicated to

**Attack:** +19 vs. Will

**Hit:** Target is dominated (save ends).

*Aftereffect:* Target is dazed (save ends).

**Countermeasure**

✦ A character can attack the altar (AC 26, other defenses 24; hp 125; resist 10 all). Destroying the altar disables the trap.

**Upgrade to Elite (2,400 XP)**

✦ The altar can attack twice each round.

## Field of Everflame
**Hazard**

Level 18 Blaster
XP 2,000

*As you move forward, the shimmering haze of heat around you erupts into a field of blazing fire.*

**Hazard:** When a gate or portal to a fiery region of the Elemental Chaos remains open for several centuries, a small area around it can become imbued with the magic of everflame. While the place appears normal to all but the most knowledgeable observer, it's a place dangerous to creatures not accustomed to the flaming heart of the Elemental Chaos. A field of everflame is usually 20 contiguous squares.

**Perception**

✦ DC 33: The faintest shimmer in the air marks the area as a hazard of some sort.

**Additional Skill:** Arcana

✦ DC 29: The character recognizes the area as a field of everflame.

**Trigger**

When a living creature enters or begins its turn within the area, the hazard is triggered and attacks, bursting into visible flame around the creature. (The rest of the area remains difficult to see.)

**Attack**

**Opportunity Action**          **Melee**

**Target:** Living creature within the field

**Attack:** +21 vs. Fortitude

**Hit:** 2d10 + 5 fire damage and ongoing 10 fire (save ends).

**Miss:** Half damage.

**Upgrade to Elite (4,000 XP)**

✦ Increase the attack bonus by 2.

✦ The field is so powerful that it ignores fire resistance.

## Kinetic Wave
**Trap**

Level 19 Blaster
XP 2,400

*The object ahead suddenly glows with power, and a wave of kinetic energy rushes forth, smashing into you like an ocean wave.*

**Trap:** When a creature steps within 5 squares of a particular object, often an altar, portal, or other obvious item of power, the object starts to exude kinetic energy that pushes living creatures away.

**Perception**

Characters can't use Perception to detect this trap.

**Additional Skill:** Arcana

✦ DC 31: The character recognizes the object as the focus of a kinetic trap.

**Initiative** +8

**Trigger**

When a creature comes within 5 squares of the focus object, the trap activates and rolls initiative.

**Attack**

**Standard Action**          **Close** burst 5

**Target:** All creatures in burst

**Attack:** +22 vs. Reflex

**Hit:** 3d12 + 5 damage and push 3 squares and knock prone.

**Countermeasures**

✦ An adjacent character can disable the trap with a DC 31 Thievery check.

✦ A character can attack the focus object (AC 30, other defenses 27; hp 69). Destroying the focus disables the trap.

## Entropic Collapse
**Hazard**

Level 23 Warder
XP 5,100

*The chamber swirls with dust, as though no one has disturbed the place in a long, long time.*

**Hazard:** When a creature casts a spell or carries a magic item into an ancient, dusty room, it triggers a temporary unweaving of the strands of time. Although reality reasserts itself a few moments later, the damage to the psyches of those who have glimpsed beyond time takes longer to heal. The dust typically covers 10 contiguous squares in a room.

**Perception**

✦ DC 36: The character notices that the swirling dust appears to glow with a faint luminescence.

**Additional Skill:** Arcana

✦ DC 32: The character notices and identifies the telltale dust glow that often presages entropic collapses.

**Trigger**

When a character carrying a magic item enters a square that contains the dust, or when a character in a square that contains the dust casts a spell, the hazard attacks.

**Attack**

**Opportunity Action**          **Close** burst 5

**Targets:** All creatures in burst

**Attack:** +29 vs. Will

**Hit:** 5d6 + 8 psychic damage and dazed (save ends).

**Miss:** Half damage and dazed (save ends).

**Special:** Immortals, animates, and undead are immune to the effects of an entropic collapse.

## Symbol of Suffering — Level 24 Warder
**Trap** — XP 6,050

*A glowing symbol wards the area ahead.*

**Trap:** Anyone familiar with magic recognizes the symbol as a powerful ward against approach. But its exact nature isn't known until a creature steps close enough to comprehend it. Once triggered, the symbol inflicts excruciating pain.

### Perception
✦ DC 28: The character notices the glowing symbol.
**Additional Skill:** Religion
✦ DC 32: The character recognizes the nature of the symbol.

### Trigger
When a creature approaches within 5 squares of the symbol, the trap attacks. Once a creature has entered the area, it can remain in the area without suffering further attacks. The trap attacks again when another creature enters the area, or if a creature leaves and reenters the area.

### Attack
**Opportunity Action     Close** burst 5
**Attack:** +27 vs. Will
**Hit:** 3d6 + 9 psychic damage and slowed until the beginning of the target's next turn.
*Aftereffect:* Ongoing 15 psychic damage and immobilized (save ends both).

### Countermeasure
✦ An adjacent character can disable the trap with a DC 36 Thievery check or a DC 32 Arcana check.

## Soul Gem — Level 26 Solo Blaster
**Trap** — XP 45,000

*A strange, many-faceted gem in the center of the chamber suddenly emits blasts of blinding light.*

**Trap:** This fist-sized cut crystal is often embedded in a statue or placed on a pedestal in the center of a room. When a creature steps within 5 squares of the soul gem, it starts emitting blasts of radiant power from its many facets.

### Perception
✦ DC 29: The character spots the strange gem.
**Additional Skill:** Arcana
✦ DC 33: The character recognizes the soul gem.
**Initiative** +8

### Trigger
When a creature moves within 5 squares of the soul gem, it rolls initiative and attacks.

### Attack
**Standard Action     Close** blast 5
**Target:** All creatures in blast
**Attack:** +29 vs. Fortitude
**Hit:** 4d10 + 5 radiant damage and ongoing 5 radiant damage and stunned (save ends).
*Aftereffect of stun:* Dazed (save ends).
**Special:** Each round, roll 1d8 to determine the direction of the blast. The blast is centered on one square of the gem's space, starting with the north square and moving clockwise around the gem's space.

### Countermeasures
✦ A character can engage in a skill challenge to detach the soul gem from its socket and thereby disable it. DC 37 Thievery. Complexity 1 (4 successes before 2 failures). Success detaches the gem and disables the trap. Failure causes the gem to explode (close burst 8, 4d10 + 5 radiant damage and stunned (save ends) to all creatures in burst).
✦ A character can attack the gem (AC 33, other defenses 29; hp 100; resist 15 all). When reduced to 0 hit points, the gem explodes in a close burst 8, as above. Destroying the gem disables the trap.

## Sphere of Annihilation — Level 29 Lurker
**Hazard** — XP 15,000

*A strange sphere of impenetrable blackness hovers before you.*

**Hazard:** A sphere of pure blackness fills one square or, alternatively, is set into the wall of one square. It doesn't provide cover or block movement.

### Perception
No check is required to see the sphere.
**Additional Skill:** Arcana
✦ DC 34: The character recognizes the sphere's nature.

### Trigger
When a creature enters the sphere's square or the sphere enters a creature's square, the sphere attacks.
**Special:** A character holding a special talisman attuned to the sphere's can control it. With a move action and a DC 25 Arcana check, he can move the sphere up to 6 squares. The sphere hovers in the air. A special ritual is required to create and attune the talisman, which is a level 29 magic item.

### Attack
**Opportunity Action     Melee** 0
**Target:** One creature
**Attack:** +32 vs. Fortitude
**Hit:** 6d6 + 10 damage and ongoing 15 damage (save ends). A creature reduced to 0 hit points by the sphere's damage is destroyed, reduced to a pile of fine gray dust.

### Countermeasure
✦ Destroying or disenchanting the talisman is the only way to destroy the sphere. The talisman has AC 38, other defenses 35, hp 200; resist 15 all.

# CHAPTER 6

# ADVENTURES

**THIS CHAPTER** teaches you how to build and modify adventures. An adventure is just a series of encounters. How and why these encounters fit together–from the simplest to the most complex–is the framework for any adventure.

An adventure revolves around a particular expedition, mission, or series of tasks in which the PCs are the heroes. Think of it as a distinct story in which all the elements are tied together. An adventure might stem from a previous one and lead to yet another, but a single adventure also stands on its own.

Several sessions might be required for your group to complete an adventure, or it might be over in one session. If you're using a published adventure, the adventure is probably going to take you many sessions to complete. An adventure from *D&D Insider's* DUNGEON *Magazine* might take as long, or you might be able to finish it in one night of play.

This chapter includes the following sections.

✦ **Published Adventures:** Running a purchased adventure is straightforward. Look here for tips on modifying the adventure to suit your world, your players, and your overall vision for the campaign.

✦ **Fixing Problems:** Whether you're using a published adventure or one you wrote yourself, problems come up. Here is advice on how to address some common ones.

✦ **Building an Adventure:** When you're building your own adventures, think about the beginning, the middle, and the ending of the adventure, and try to make sure they all feel satisfying and fit together.

✦ **Quests:** Quests are the hooks that lead characters into dangerous adventure.

✦ **Encounter Mix:** A good adventure presents a variety of challenges.

✦ **Adventure Setting:** Flesh out your setting's personality, from broad concept to small details, mapping, outdoor settings, and event-based adventures that don't rely on maps.

✦ **Cast of Characters:** Monsters and nonplayer characters bring an adventure to life.

Published adventures are readily available on *D&D Insider*, in Wizards of the Coast products such as campaign guides, and as stand-alone products. If your campaign is episodic in nature (a series of adventures that are only loosely connected), you can easily run your whole campaign using published adventures. That's a great solution if you don't have a lot of time for preparation. Even if your campaign is more story-driven, you can make good use of published adventures with a little bit of preparation.

## Hook Them In

The first thing to consider is how to stitch the published adventure into your campaign. In order for it to feel like a seamless part of your campaign's story, you need to weave threads out from it in both directions: backward into the previous adventures and forward into the following ones.

### Plan Forward

As you're planning your game sessions, always be thinking about the adventure you're going to run next. Look for ways to plant story hooks that lead characters from their current adventure to the next one. Two or three sessions before you're going to start the next adventure, look through it and find an NPC, location, or plot point that you can work into the current adventure.

### Use Adventure Hooks

Most published adventures provide adventure hooks designed to draw characters into the plot of the adventure. Look for ways to incorporate those hooks into your current adventure, rather than abruptly throwing them in front of the players at the start of the next one. Plot is a strong linking tool, and the more you can weave an adventure hook into the course of another adventure, the better. For example, one of the adventure hooks for *The Keep on the Shadowfell* has the characters learn of a ruined fortress that might contain treasures from a fallen empire. You could just tell the characters at the start of the adventure that they've learned of this place, but the adventure starts to feel like part of your campaign if they find a history of this ruined fortress while on another adventure.

### Tie in NPCs and Groups

A nonplayer character or group can be another strong connection between adventures. If a helpful merchant gives the characters useful information in one adventure, the PCs are more likely to listen to him when he comes asking for help in the next one. Try to give recurring characters distinctive features or mannerisms, so the players remember them from one adventure to the next.

Look for ways to connect characters in different adventures to each other. If one adventure involves a cultist of Zehir and another one pits the PCs against the cult of Asmodeus, change one or the other (or both!) so these two cults are devoted to the same deity. If the next adventure you want to run pits the characters against a hidden cult of Bane, alter a character or a group of bandits in the current adventure so they're Bane worshipers (carrying his symbol in their gear).

### Plant Location Hooks or Maps

Locations are also good linking tools, from the classic treasure map depicting the site of the next adventure to nervous locals talking about the haunted tower in the mountains while the characters are exploring the ruins in the forest. Consider planting a partial map from your next adventure somewhere in the current adventure—on the body of the main villain is a particularly strong choice.

## Simple Fixes

Even if you don't have time to weave threads between adventures, you can use a few simple techniques to put a unique stamp on a published adventure to make it fit better in your campaign.

### Change Names

If your campaign is based in Golden Huzuz, the City of Delights, ruled by the Grand Caliph Khalil al-Assad, it might be a little jarring for the PCs to travel to the nearby village of Brindinford and speak to Baron Euphemes. Fortunately, names are easy to change. Brindinford becomes Halwa, the baron turns into Amir Ghalid al-Fahad, and the architectural details of the city change to match the rest of your campaign. You're ready to go!

### Alter the Setting

It rarely snows anywhere within a thousand miles of Golden Huzuz, but you just found an adventure involving a trek across a frozen tundra to an ancient, monumental ruin. You might be tempted to pass over that adventure as useless to your campaign, but an adventure's setting is easy to alter.

Altering a setting can be as simple as scanning the descriptive text for details of the setting and changing those details to match what you have in mind. Rather than frigid wind blowing sharp ice crystals through the air, describe gusts of arid wind driving stinging sand into the characters' faces.

## Adjust Monsters

If you've changed an adventure's setting, you might feel like you need to change some monsters as well. Maybe a white dragon feels out of place in the desert outside Golden Huzuz (although its presence could add a strange mystery to the adventure, which you could follow up on in a later one). A quick glance at the *Monster Manual*'s list of monsters organized by level makes these changes easy. If the adult white dragon is out of place, maybe an oni night haunter combined with some ogre savages fits better with what you have in mind.

## Scale Levels

What do you do if the adventure you want to run is written for a group of a different level from your player's characters? First, bear in mind that an encounter two or three levels above the PCs isn't a killer encounter. It might be more challenging, but it shouldn't wipe them out. Likewise, an encounter two or three levels below them can still provide an appropriate challenge.

If you still want to adjust the levels of encounters in a published adventure, you can do it three ways: change the numbers of monsters in the encounters, change the monsters' levels, or change the monsters entirely.

Chapter 4 tells you how to adjust the level of an encounter by adding or removing monsters. You can easily increase or decrease an encounter's level by up to three or four. For example, if you want to use a published 10th-level encounter against a 14th-level party, you're looking to add 2,500 XP. (See the Experience Rewards table and the Target Encounter XP Totals table on pages 56 and 57.) You could double the monsters in the encounter, or just throw a 15th-level elite monster into the encounter. Taking two 14th-level monsters out of a 14th-level encounter makes it a fine encounter for 10th-level characters.

Chapter 10 provides some ways to adjust the levels of monsters or turn normal monsters into elite or solo monsters. Adjusting a monster's level by two to four is as simple as adjusting its attacks and defenses by 1 or 2 points. Turning a single monster in an encounter into an elite monster raises the encounter level by one, and turning one monster into a solo monster raises the level by four.

Finally, you can use the *Monster Manual*'s list of monsters by level to swap out monsters for similar monsters of a different level. Many monsters have versions or variations at a range of levels, so you can replace a 7th-level carrion crawler with a 17th-level enormous carrion crawler, or vice versa. (But watch out for the sizes of encounter areas.)

## Bring Them Out

Transitioning characters out of a published adventure, whether you're bringing them back into the main storyline of your campaign with an adventure you've written yourself or moving them on to the next published adventure you want to run, is just another way of looking at the issue of bringing characters into the adventure in the first place.

### Weave in More Threads

Use the same techniques described in "Hook Them In" to plant seeds for the next adventure you want to run into the published adventure. If you have established villains in your own campaign, insert one of those villains (or a member of a villainous organization) into the closing encounters of the published adventure (or throughout the course of the adventure) to remind the players of the larger story that encompasses the current adventure.

### Twist the Ending

Another interesting technique is a jarring exit, in which the players suddenly learn that the adventure they've just completed was a diversion from the main story of the campaign. Perhaps it was just an interesting side trek, or perhaps the villains intentionally misled them in order to get them out of the way for a time: "You return triumphantly from your latest adventure, only to find that while you were away in the western hinterlands, the Knights of Zehir deposed the baron and took control of Starhold Keep!"

Don't overuse this technique, though. Players who feel as though they're constantly being duped and dragged down the wrong path quickly grow frustrated.

### Use Unresolved Questions

If you haven't designed your own adventures before, a great way to start is by looking at the situation at the end of a published adventure. The adventure might pose unresolved questions for the characters, villains might have escaped, or the characters might have left sections of the dungeon unexplored. Your players will thank you for an opportunity to tie up those loose ends instead of hurtling on into an unrelated adventure. The rest of this chapter provides plenty of advice about how to create adventures, and if you use a published adventure as a starting point, you are off to a great start.

Published adventures, for better or worse, can't account for every character action. Occasionally, the characters decide to go exactly the wrong way, pursuing a path not covered in the adventure at all. They discover a shortcut that the adventure designer didn't anticipate and skip right to the climactic battle of the adventure. They traipse through encounter after encounter without breaking a sweat or unleashing any daily powers.

What do you do?

You can ask your players to show mercy and do what the adventure expects them to do. Understanding players will agree, but it leaves a sour taste in their mouth. Instead, remember the first rule of improvising: Say yes, and go from there. (See page 28 for more advice about improvising.)

## WANDERING OFF COURSE

You can often steer wandering characters back to the main plot line of the adventure, but be careful not to be too heavy-handed about it. Entice them back to where you want them to be, don't pick them up and drop them there. Don't bore them back to the adventure, either. Making the characters wander through the wilderness for weeks on end without a single encounter communicates your displeasure clearly, but it's a painful way of steering the characters.

**Use Extra Encounters:** Use extra encounters you prepared ahead of time to fill in the gaps in the adventure, and make sure those encounters are just as fun and pulse-pounding as the rest of the encounters in the adventure. Then plant hooks in those encounters to lead the players back to prepared material.

**Generate Random Encounters:** If you don't have prepared encounters, make something up. Chapter 10 provides ways to generate random dungeons and random encounters. At worst, you need a way to fill a few encounters from these improvisational tools until the end of the session. You can spend your preparation time before the next session figuring out how to get the adventure back on track.

**Let It Go and Move On:** Sometimes the adventure you're running isn't worth steering the characters back to. The characters might have strayed off course on purpose because they found the adventure unsatisfying. Don't keep leading the players back to an adventure that has failed to capture their interest unless you're sure you can resurrect their interest in the next encounter. If the characters wander away from an adventure, it might be time to bring out the next adventure.

## SKIPPING TO THE END

Sometimes adventure designers fail to account for the capabilities of high-level characters or the resourcefulness of clever players, and the players find a way to skip over most of the adventure and get right to the climactic fight. Again, it's better to say yes and go from there, rather than coming up with an arbitrary reason why their plan doesn't work. Let the players feel clever, and reward their ingenuity.

**Promote a Lesser Villain:** Just because the climactic battle is over, the adventure need not end. If the PCs defeat the scheming villain early on, one of his lieutenants or subordinates—a character the players left alive in their rush to the end of the adventure—might step up and continue the master's plans, and the adventure can continue on very much as written.

**Introduce More Plot Twists:** Another way characters might skip to the end of an adventure is by jumping to a conclusion that the adventure assumes they won't reach until they've accumulated a lot more information. Perhaps they immediately guess or figure out that the baron is a rakshasa in disguise, or deduce that the murdered noblewoman isn't dead, but faked her own death for some reason. The fact that the characters intuited the plot isn't necessarily an indication of bad adventure design. Giving the players too much information is better than giving them too little and leaving them searching for the fun (see below). You can keep things moving by introducing plot twists. For instance, the baron is a rakshasa, but he's working against the real villain of the adventure.

**Move On, and Scavenge for Future Improvisation:** Once again, if the players skip a whole lot of adventure, it might be that trying to salvage the adventure is more trouble than it's worth. It doesn't have to be a total waste, though. You can scavenge encounters and locations from it for your next adventure.

### A CAKEWALK

Whether your characters are higher in level than the adventure intended, or better equipped, or just more inventive and tactically savvy, sometimes they overcome the encounters you throw at them without ever feeling seriously challenged. Fortunately, solving that problem is easy.

You can adjust encounter levels upward using the three techniques described in the previous pages: add monsters, increase monster levels, or substitute monsters. You can also alter terrain to give the monsters a home field advantage and challenge the players' tactical mastery. Watch what your players do and use the same tactics against them.

These changes are easy enough to make during your preparation time, but you can also make them on the fly if you need to. Extra monsters can arrive as reinforcements. A dramatic event (such as an earthquake) can alter the battlefield and give the players a little more to worry about at the same time. The monsters are more threatening when the PCs also have to avoid collapsing ceilings and yawning chasms. A monster or villain might suddenly manifest a new ability when it becomes bloodied. It could even suddenly transform into an elite, a solo monster, or an entirely different monster. The world of the D&D game is a fantastic place, so as long as the events you describe seem like they fit in the world, you can get away with a lot of adjustment as you go.

## SEARCHING FOR THE FUN

Sometimes characters wander about, growing increasingly frustrated with you and the adventure, not because they've strayed off the intended course, but because they missed some important bit of information the adventure assumes they'll come across. Don't make the players search for the fun in the adventure. The fun should be within easy reach, even if the answers to the mysteries they face aren't.

Here's another case where encounters you've prepared in advance can save the day. When things start grinding to a halt, a bad guy kicks in the door, a thrilling combat encounter ensues, and the characters conveniently find the information from the bad guy or what he was carrying to kick-start the plot of the adventure. You don't have to use a combat encounter, but don't hesitate to spring some kind of unexpected occurrence on the characters.

These added encounters can also introduce interesting new twists to a plot. If the characters get lost while trying to solve a mystery, perhaps a stranger invites them to his house and gives them the clue they're looking for. Why? What's the stranger's interest in all this? He could be an indifferent observer, or he could have some stake in the outcome of their investigation. Perhaps he wants a favor from the PCs in exchange for his help (and negotiates for that favor in a tension-filled skill challenge). Perhaps he's looking for some other information he hopes they'll drop in the course of their conversation with him. Perhaps unraveling the mystery eventually leads the characters to a confrontation with a hated rival of this stranger. The possibilities are limitless, and a little creative improvisation can create lots of room for exciting plot twists and wrinkles in your campaign.

When you build an adventure, you're building a frame to hang encounters on. Building that structure is a process of answering some simple questions.

You don't have to answer these questions in any particular order. You might start from a quest: One of your players wants a specific magic sword, so the adventure gives her a place to find that sword. A cool villain or monster might be the springboard for a setting or series of events. An interesting setting idea might call for particular inhabitants and plot. The climax might suggest a story leading up to it.

### COMPONENTS OF AN ADVENTURE

**Structure**
+ How does the adventure start and end?
+ What happens in between?

**Quests**
+ What is the situation?
+ What led up to this situation?
+ Does solving the situation require going somewhere?
+ Does solving the situation require responding to events?
+ Why do the PCs care?
+ What are the PCs' goals?

**Setting**
+ Where is the situation taking place?
+ What is this setting's original purpose?
+ What is the setting used for now?
+ What kind of terrain and locations can you find there?
+ What's interesting and dangerous there besides monsters?
+ How do you build an event-based adventure?

**Cast**
+ Who and what inhabits the setting?
+ Does the adventure have a villain?
+ Who else cares about the situation?
+ Which characters are helpful, neutral, or hostile?

## THINGS TO BEAR IN MIND

When you design an adventure, remember the motives that bring your players to the table. Doing so is a sure way to help everyone have more fun. See Chapter 1 for more on player motives.

Consider your adventure's place in the campaign. If the adventure centers on a wondrous location, it gives players a sense of a world that has a reality beyond their characters. An adventure that engages the PCs because it involves them on a personal level gives a sense that the characters have a place in the world. Both senses are valuable to your game. See Chapter 8 for more on campaigns.

## ADVENTURE STRUCTURE

All good adventures have a clear structure. Like a novel or a story, an adventure has a clear beginning, middle, and ending.

## BEGINNING

An adventure's beginning is a proposal of a problem, sometimes suggesting the adventure's end. An adventure can begin with a roleplaying encounter in which the PCs find out what they must do and why. It can start with a surprise attack on the road, or the heroes stumbling upon something they were not meant to see. Whatever form it takes, the players should be hooked into the adventure by the time the beginning is over.

Reach out and grab the players with the adventure's beginning. If the adventure starts with someone asking the PCs to do something for them, you are inviting them to say no. Players never say no to rolling initiative. Starting with action is a solid lead-in that clearly shows adventure is afoot.

### GOOD BEGINNINGS . . .
+ Show the players that adventure is afoot.
+ Make the players want to be involved, rarely forcing them.
+ Are exciting but short—one game session.

## MIDDLE

The middle of an adventure is where most of the action occurs. An adventure's middle might reveal new quests or change the goal altogether as the PCs make discoveries. Whatever the case, a good middle requires the PCs to make important choices and gives the sense that the adventure is building toward an end.

### GOOD MIDDLES . . .
+ Include a variety of challenges and clear choices.
+ Build excitement, but give some time for reflection.
+ Draw the players and the PCs in and onward.

## ENDING

The ending of an adventure speaks to the proposal of the beginning and the substance of the middle in a satisfying way. An ending is often a confrontation with a major villain, but it can also be a tense negotiation, a narrow escape, or the acquisition of a prize. Endings needn't be triumphant for the PCs, but they should make sense in the larger context of the whole adventure.

### GOOD ENDINGS . . .
+ Tie together the beginning and middle.
+ Fit with character actions and choices.
+ Allow the players and PCs to clearly see success or failure.
+ Might provide new beginnings.

## GOOD STRUCTURE

Good structure makes use of the tenets of good beginnings, middles, and ends.

**Hooks:** From the beginning, players should want their characters to be involved in the challenge the adventure proposes. The "hook" used to pull the characters into the adventure must be compelling or personal, or both, to the players and their characters. Here is where knowing your players and their characters' goals pays off (see "Player Motivations" on page 8, "Party Background" on page 10, "Campaign Details" on page 11, and "Using Character Backgrounds" on page 11). Use that knowledge to make compelling hooks.

**Choices:** Player and character choices must matter in a good adventure. Not only must they matter, but also in at least a few cases, those choices must be important to an adventure's end. Your communication skills and information flow become especially important here (see Chapter 2: Running the Game). You must give the players enough information, even in simple situations, for them to make meaningful decisions.

**Challenges:** A good adventure provides varied challenges that test the PCs and stimulate the players. Create different encounters to emphasize attack, defense, skill use, problem-solving, investigation, and roleplaying. Make sure the encounters invite the player behavior you want by drawing out and rewarding that behavior. Know the characters' capabilities so you can build encounters that test those resources. Chapter 4 gives more advice for building good encounters.

**Excitement:** The tension should build in a good adventure. Event-based adventures are easy to fashion in this way, but setting-based adventures can have building tension too. See "Adventure Setting" (page 106).

**Climax:** Even the simplest adventures should have dramatically decisive moment when crucial knowledge or decisive action pays off, or the villain gets what's coming to him. A sprawling dungeon complex or a long event-based adventure might have several such instances, with a big payoff at the ultimate end.

A tough fight doesn't by itself constitute a climactic encounter. The last encounter should be the most fantastic and epic in the adventure. Don't give the players an exciting encounter on a bridge with swinging blades and goblin archers mounted on worgs, and then let them kill the goblin king alone in a bare cave.

**Meaningful Victory:** Whatever the goal of the adventure, the characters' success should be meaningful. Players should care about what happens if they fail.

## POOR STRUCTURE

Watch out for some common pitfalls that can wreck your adventure structure and leave your players dissatisfied or even angry.

**Bottlenecking:** Don't let the characters' ability to move forward in or complete the adventure hinge on a single action, such as finding the secret door to the villain's lair. If the characters don't find the door, the adventure comes to a grinding halt. Make sure that the characters can move ahead with the adventure in at least two different ways. Instead of punishing characters with a bottleneck if they fail to find the right clues, reward them with an extra edge if they do find those clues.

**Railroading:** If a series of events occurs no matter what the characters do, the players end up feeling helpless and frustrated. Their actions don't matter, and they have no meaningful choices. A dungeon that has only a single sequence of rooms and no branches is another example of railroading. If your adventure relies on certain events, provide multiple ways those events can occur, or be prepared for clever players to prevent one or more of those events. Players should always feel as though they're in control of their characters, the choices they make matter, and that what they do has some effect on the end of the adventure and on the game world.

**Cluelessness:** On the flip side, don't give the players so many options that they can't make any meaningful decisions. Even though that open-ended situation is far from railroading, too many options is still frustrating to the players. Give hints, nudge them however you like, but try to keep the action, the story, and the pace of the game going.

**Sidelining:** The player characters should always be the central heroes in the adventure. If NPCs can do everything the characters can, why are the characters even on the adventure? Along similar lines, don't bring in a powerful character as a deus ex machina to save the characters from disaster. The characters should take the consequences and reap the rewards of their actions.

**Squelching:** D&D characters are powerful, and as their powers grow, it is harder to build encounters to challenge them. Know what the characters are capable of, and then design to reward the clever use of those powers. Don't resort to weird effects that shut down the characters' capabilities.

**Anticlimax:** An unsatisfying end to an adventure can be a real disappointment to the players. Make sure to end the adventure with a bang and a big payoff.

Quests are the fundamental story framework of an adventure—the reason the characters want to participate in it. They're the reason an adventure exists, and they indicate what the characters need to do to solve the situation the adventure presents.

The simplest adventures revolve around a single quest, usually one that gives everyone in the party a motivation to pursue it. More complex adventures involve multiple quests, including quests related to individual characters' goals or quests that conflict with each other, presenting characters with interesting choices about which goals to pursue.

### BASIC QUEST SEEDS

**Adversaries**
+ Capture
+ Compete with to accomplish another task
+ Defeat
+ Discover hidden
+ Drive away
+ Escape from
+ Hide from
+ Infiltrate
+ Thwart activities or plans

**Allies, Extras, and Patrons**
+ Escort to a location
+ Establish a relationship with
+ Help perform a specific task
+ Hide or protect from attack, kidnapping, or other harm
+ Rescue from existing danger
+ Settle a debt

**Events**
+ Deal with the aftermath
+ Flee or hide from ongoing weird or harmful
+ Mistaken identity
+ Prevent or stop weird or harmful
+ Transported to a strange place
+ Win a contest, race, or war

**Items or Information**
+ Deliver to a place or person
+ Destroy, perhaps by a particular method
+ Hide
+ Retrieve for an ally or patron
+ Recover for personal use

**Locations**
+ Escape from
+ Explore
+ Protect from attack or damage
+ Seal off
+ Secure for another use
+ Survive in

## USING BASIC QUEST SEEDS

When you're devising a simple adventure, one to three basic seeds are enough to get you started. A classic dungeon adventure uses three: The characters set out to explore a dangerous place, defeat the monsters inside, and take the treasure they find. One simple quest can be enough, such as a quest to slay a dragon.

You can combine any number of basic seeds to create a more multifaceted adventure. The more seeds you throw in the mix, the more intricate your adventure will be. You might add timing elements to one or more of the seeds to create more depth in your adventure.

Once you have your seed or seeds, you can start getting specific. Go back and answer the questions in "Components of an Adventure" on page 100, keeping your quest seeds in mind. Again, you don't need to follow any particular order. You might come up with a set of monsters you want to use first, you might invent a cool place or item, or you might choose a seed or three. You can then use Chapter 4 and the "Adventure Setting" section of this chapter to help flesh out your adventure.

## MAJOR QUESTS

Major quests define the fundamental reasons that characters are involved. They are the central goals of an adventure. A single major quest is enough to define an adventure, but a complex adventure might involve a number of different quests. A major quest should be important to every member of the party, and completing it should define success in the adventure. Achieving a major quest usually means either that the adventure is over, or that the characters have successfully completed a major chapter in the unfolding plot.

Don't be shy about letting the players know what their quests are. Give the players an obvious goal, possibly a known villain to go after, and a clear course to get to their destination. That avoids searching for the fun—aimless wandering, arguing about trivial choices, and staring across the table because the players don't know what to do next. You can fiddle with using another secret villain or other less obvious courses, but one obvious path for adventure that is not wrong or fake should exist. You can count on the unpredictability of player actions to keep things interesting even in the simplest of adventure plots.

Thinking in terms of quests helps focus the adventure solidly where it belongs: on the player characters. An adventure isn't something that can unfold without their involvement. A plot or an event can unfold without the characters' involvement, but not an adventure. An adventure begins when the characters get involved, when they have a reason to participate and a goal to accomplish. Quests give them that.

# Minor Quests

Minor quests are the subplots of an adventure, complications or wrinkles in the overall story. The characters might complete them along the way toward finishing a major quest, or they might tie up the loose ends of minor quests after they've finished the major quest.

Often, minor quests matter primarily to a particular character or perhaps a subset of the party. Such quests might be related to a character's background, a player goal, or the ongoing events in the campaign relevant to one or more characters. These quests still matter to the party overall. This game is a cooperative game, and everyone shares the rewards for completing a quest. Just make sure that the whole group has fun completing minor quests tied to a single character.

Sometimes minor quests come up as sidelines to the main plot of the adventure. For example, say the characters learn in town that a prisoner has escaped from the local jail. That has nothing to do with the main quest. It pales in importance next to the hobgoblin raids that have been plundering caravans and seizing people for slaves. However, when the characters find and free some of the hobgoblins' slaves, the escaped prisoner is among them. Do they make sure he gets back to the jail? Do they accept his promise to go straight—and his offer of a treasure map—and let him go free? Do they believe his protestations of innocence and try to help him find the real criminal? Any of these goals can launch a side quest, but clearly the characters can't pursue all of them. This situation gives them the opportunity to roleplay and make interesting choices, adding richness and depth to the game.

# Designing Quests

Design quests so that they have a clear start, a clear goal, and clear consequences. Any quest should provide a ready answer for when the players ask, "What should we do now?"

## Level

Give the quest a level based on how difficult it is to accomplish. A good rule of thumb is to set the quest at the level you expect the characters to be when they complete it. For example, if completing a quest requires overcoming several encounters well above the party's level, the average level of those encounters is a fine level for the quest.

## Start

A quest's start is where the characters begin the quest if they choose to accept it. It might be a person who assigns the quest. It might be an observation they make that leads them to adopt a quest of their choosing. It's a point of reference that the players can refer to and that the characters might be able to return to.

## Goal

The goal of a quest is what the characters have to accomplish to succeed on the quest. Goals should be as clear as you can make them. Goals can change as the characters uncover information, but such changes should also be clear.

## Outcome

The reward for success and the cost of failure should be or become clear to the players and their characters. Like goals, outcomes can change over the course of an adventure as the PCs expose the truth.

## No Redundant Quests

Don't reward the characters twice for the same actions. Quests should focus on the story reasons for adventuring, not on the underlying basic actions of the game—killing monsters and acquiring treasure. "Defeat ten encounters of your level" isn't a quest. It's a recipe for advancing a level. Completing it is its own reward. "Make Harrows Pass safe for travelers" is a quest, even if the easiest way to accomplish it happens to be defeating ten encounters of the characters' level. This quest is a story-based goal, and one that has at least the possibility of solution by other means.

## Conflicting Quests

You can present quests that conflict with each other, or with the characters' alignments or goals. The players have the freedom to make choices about which quests to accept, and these can be great opportunities for roleplaying and character development.

## Player-Designed Quests

You should allow and even encourage players to come up with their own quests that are tied to their individual goals or specific circumstances in the adventure. Evaluate the proposed quest and assign it a level. Remember to say yes as often as possible!

---

### QUEST CARDS

You can give the players index cards to help them keep track of their quests. Each card should include the quest level, the start of the quest, the goal, and the possible outcomes the characters are aware of. This helps remind the players what they're trying to do, which can be important when a quest spans several gaming sessions. Quest cards can also help players keep their objectives in mind when they reach a decision point in an adventure.

Leave space on the cards for players to make notes about the quest, including changes to the quest's goals or possible outcomes.

When you're building an adventure, try to vary the encounters you include, including combat and non-combat challenges, easy and difficult encounters, a variety of settings and monsters, and situations that appeal to your players' different personalities and motivations. This variation creates an exciting rhythm. Adventures that lack this sort of variety can become a tiresome grind.

## COMPLEXITY

Encounters can be complex in several different ways. An encounter with five different kinds of monsters is complex for the players and for you, so mix those up with wolf pack encounters (a group made up of a single kind of monster; see page 59 in Chapter 4) as well as more straightforward encounter types.

Some encounters are complex in their relationship to the plot, such as a tangled interaction in which the characters have to unravel each adversary's motivations and hidden agendas, or even a combat encounter that raises new questions about what's going on in the adventure. Make sure to mix those up with encounters in which it's completely clear what's going on.

Rooms with lots of interesting terrain, cover, and room features make for great combat encounters, but you should keep some variation in that level of complexity. You don't have to resort to a straight-up, face-to-face melee in a tiny room, but some encounters can be less tactically interesting than others.

## DIFFICULTY

If every encounter gives the players a perfectly balanced challenge, the game can get stale. Once in a while, characters need an encounter that doesn't significantly tax their resources, or an encounter that makes them seriously scared for their characters' survival—or even makes them flee.

The majority of the encounters in an adventure should be moderate difficulty—challenging but not overwhelming, falling right about the party's level or one higher. Monsters in a standard encounter might range from three levels below the characters to about four levels above them. These encounters should make up the bulk of your adventure.

Easy encounters are two to three levels below the party, and might include monsters as many as four levels lower than the party. These encounters let the characters feel powerful. If you build an encounter using monsters that were a serious threat to the characters six or seven levels ago, you'll remind them of how much they've grown in power and capabilities since the last time they fought those monsters. You

might include an easy encounter about once per character level—don't overdo it.

Hard encounters are two to three levels above the party, and can include monsters that are five to seven levels above the characters. These encounters really test the characters' resources, and might force them to take an extended rest at the end. They also bring a greater feeling of accomplishment, though, so make sure to include about one such encounter per character level. However, be careful of using high-level soldiers and brutes in these encounters. Soldier monsters get really hard to hit when they're five levels above the party, and brutes can do too much damage at that level.

Monsters that are more than eight levels higher than the characters can pretty easily kill a character, and in a group they have a chance of taking out the whole party. Use such overpowering encounters with great care. Players should enter the encounter with a clear sense of the danger they're facing, and have at least one good option for escaping with their lives, whether that's headlong flight or clever negotiation.

On average, it takes a character eight to ten encounters to gain a level, with the possible addition of a major quest. For a group of nine encounters, here's how they might be broken down.

### ENCOUNTER DIFFICULTY

| Level of Encounter | Number of Encounters |
|---|---|
| Level − 1 | 1 encounter |
| Level + 0 | 3 encounters, 1 major quest |
| Level + 1 | 3 encounters |
| Level + 3 | 1 encounter |

## FANTASY

The D&D game is all about fantasy, so don't feel restricted by realism when coming up with weird and interesting adventure elements. Allow movies, video games, and other media to inspire you. Imagine cool encounter situations and locales, and then include them in your adventure.

That does not mean that every encounter has to be incredibly fantastic. Some monsters provide all the fantasy an encounter needs. Fighting a dragon is such a staple of the fantasy genre that you can't forget you're playing a fantasy game in the middle of that battle. On the other hand, encounters with humanoid monsters such as orcs and bugbears can start to feel mundane, and those encounters can use a fantasy injection. A floating cloud castle or similar fantastic location, an add-on monster such as a rage drake or a wyvern, or a strange magical effect such as shifting shadow tendrils that provide concealment—these elements remind the players that their characters live in a fantastic world that doesn't obey the natural laws of the real world.

## MONSTERS

In addition to using different monster groups to vary the complexity of your encounters, try to vary the kinds of monsters the characters face in ways that are more basic as well. Don't fill a dungeon with nothing but humanoid monsters, at the risk of losing the sense of fantasy and wonder. Make sure to include minions and solo monsters from time to time, so not every fight pits five PCs against five monsters. Use different encounter templates, and vary the composition of those groups as well, using controllers and soldiers for some encounters, artillery and brutes for others.

You can also create variation within the same kinds of monsters, which is particularly useful when the story of the adventure seems to demand a lot of battles with the same kinds of monster. When the characters strike into the hobgoblin stronghold, use the different hobgoblins presented in the *Monster Manual* (as well as goblins and bugbears), make sure to include plenty of nonhumanoid guard monsters, and then use the templates in Chapter 10 to create new hobgoblin variations. The hobgoblin leader might be a vampire or a mummy, or just a 10th-level fighter built as an NPC. Or he could be a solo monster, a whirlwind of flashing blades and killer moves. Or he could be some kind of aberrant monstrosity dredged from your worst nightmares and created using the guidelines in Chapter 10. The players will remember that encounter for years.

## NPCs

Memorable nonplayer characters are best built on stereotype. The subtle nuances of an NPC's personality are lost on the players. Just don't rely on the same stereotype for every NPC you make. Not every villain has to be a cackling megalomaniac, not every ally is honest and forthright, and not every bartender is loud and boisterous. Variety in NPCs is the spice of your adventures and lends depth to your campaign.

## PLAYER MOTIVATIONS

Make sure to include a variety of encounters designed to appeal to the different motivations of your players. See Chapter 1 for more about these motivations, but remember these encounter elements for different types of players.

**Actor:** Interaction encounters are the actor's natural habitat. Plenty of decision points give the actor a chance to consider what his character would do and act out the deliberation and debate.

**Explorer:** The explorer loves cool settings and fantastic environments. Make sure a sense of new wonders over the next hill or down the next dungeon staircase abounds.

**Instigator:** Traps give the instigator a chance to make things happen, though deadly traps can bring the wrath of the other players down on the instigator's head. Interaction encounters with lively NPCs, especially if you're ready for those encounters to turn into combat, give the instigator plenty to work with.

**Power Gamer:** Combat encounters give the power gamer a place to shine. Cool rewards, including quest rewards, keep this player happy.

**Slayer:** Use more combat encounters. The slayer enjoys a variety of complexity in combat encounters and can get bored during other encounters.

**Storyteller:** This player thrives on encounters that advance the story of the adventure and the campaign and gladly pursues quests that tie into her background and specific goals.

**Thinker:** Puzzle encounters, difficult decisions, and tactically interesting combats give the thinker plenty to work with.

**Watcher:** You never know when or if a watcher will latch onto an element that catches his interest, so give him variety. Varied encounters give him opportunities to get more involved without forcing it on him.

## TRAPS AND HAZARDS

Not every combat encounter consists only of monsters and terrain. Include traps as part of monster mixes as well as traps that stand alone as encounters in their own right. Other hazards add spice to encounters as well. Don't overlook these components of encounter design, but don't overuse them, either. Monsters are the staple of D&D encounters for a good reason. They're exciting, tactically challenging, and visually interesting.

## FUN

Fun is one element you shouldn't vary. Every encounter in an adventure should be fun. As much as possible, fast-forward through the parts of an adventure that aren't fun. An encounter with two guards at the city gate isn't fun. Tell the players they get through the gate without much trouble and move on to the fun. Niggling details of food supplies and encumbrance usually aren't fun, so don't sweat them, and let the players get to the adventure and on to the fun. Long treks through endless corridors in the ancient dwarven stronghold beneath the mountains aren't fun. Move the PCs quickly from encounter to encounter, and on to the fun!

The Vault of the Drow, the Tomb of Horrors, the Forge of Fury, and the Keep on the Shadowfell—all those names describe two things: adventures published over the last 30 years of D&D history, and the settings in which those adventures take place. One element that all the best adventures share is a compelling and evocative setting. When you're building an adventure, think about what makes an awe-inspiring and memorable setting.

One good way to think about setting is to work backward: imagine a great climactic battle against the ultimate villain of the adventure. You don't need to have any idea who that villain is just yet, but thinking about the setting might give you ideas. Of course, if you have a villain in mind, that might inspire setting ideas as well. If you want your players fighting a red dragon in that last encounter, something volcanic or otherwise fiery is a good starting point. Alternatively, if some fantastic terrain inspires you, run with that. Perhaps you want to set that great climactic battle in an enormous Underdark cavern where two mighty armies of drow clashed centuries ago, staining the rock with their accursed blood. From that starting point, you could build an expansive Underdark adventure that eventually leads the characters into that cavern and its blood rock.

## TYPES OF SETTINGS

Adventure settings in the D&D world tend to fall into four categories. The first consideration in thinking about a setting is what type of setting you want: an underground "dungeon," a wilderness environment, a city or other settlement, or a fantastic different world (or plane of existence).

### UNDERGROUND

Many D&D adventures revolve around a dungeon setting. That's why the game is called DUNGEONS & DRAGONS. The word "dungeon" might conjure images of dry, bare stone corridors with manacles on the walls, but dungeons in the D&D game also include great halls built into the walls of a volcanic crater, natural caverns extending for miles beneath the surface of the earth, and ruined castles that provide gateways to other planes.

Underground settings are such a staple of D&D adventures because dungeon environments are cleanly defined, separated from the outside world and set apart as a special, magical environment. More important, dungeons physically embody good adventure design: they offer choices (branching passages and doorways) but not too many choices. They're limited environments that clearly define the options

available. The rooms and corridors constrain the characters' movement, but the characters can explore them in any order they choose, so they have a feeling of control and meaningful choices.

Many dungeons are ancient ruins, long abandoned by their original creators and now inhabited only by monsters looking for underground lairs or humanoids setting up temporary camps. Some undying remnants of the original inhabitants might also linger in the ruins—undead, constructs, or immortal guardians set in place to keep watch over treasures or other important locations. The dungeon's rooms might contain hints of their previous purpose—rotting remnants of furnishings piled together into kruthik nests, or faded tapestries hanging behind a crumbling throne. Rumors of ancient treasures or artifacts, historical information, or magical locations might lure adventurers into these ruins.

Other dungeons are currently occupied, presenting a very different sort of environment for the characters to explore. Whether they originally created the dungeon or not, intelligent creatures now inhabit it, calling its chambers and passages home. It might be a fortress, a temple, an active mine, a prison, or a headquarters. The inhabitants organize guards to defend it, and they respond intelligently to the characters' attacks, especially if the characters withdraw and return later. Characters might fight or sneak their way into an occupied dungeon to discover the secrets of an underground cult, stop the orcs from pillaging nearby towns, or prevent a mad necromancer from animating undead legions to conquer the barony. Or they might seek to reclaim the ancient dwarven fortress from the goblins that have taken it over, making it safe for habitation once again.

Sometimes dungeons are built to hold something—whether a mighty artifact or the body of a revered ruler—and keep it safe. A dungeon might also serve as a prison for a powerful demon or primordial that couldn't be destroyed at the time. These dungeons are usually sealed, often trap-laden, and sometimes inhabited only by monsters that can survive the passage of ages—undead, constructs, immortal guardians, devils, or angels.

Some dungeons aren't built at all. They're sprawling networks of natural caverns stretching deep below the earth. Taken as a whole, this expanse of naturally occurring dungeon is called the Underdark. It is an almost lightless region of subterranean wilderness. Within those caverns, adventurers might find cities of the drow, ruins of long-forgotten dwarf strongholds, or the hidden tomb of a mind flayer lich. Many kinds of monsters call the Underdark home, making it among the most dangerous areas of the world.

Finally, many dungeons combine two or more of these elements. For example, imagine that the dwarves of an ancient civilization built a sprawling subterranean complex where they thrived in splendor for many years. Then they dug too deep. Their tunnels opened into the natural caverns of the Underdark. Some horrible evil emerged from the lightless depths and destroyed the dwarven civilization. Centuries later, most of the original complex lies in ruins. Here and there among its sprawling passages, though, ragged bands of degenerate dwarves, enclaves of scheming drow, and a tribe of savage orcs have made their homes, and they live in a perpetual state of war against each other. Somewhere in the ruins is the tomb of the last dwarf queen, said to hold the mighty *Axe of the Dwarvish Lords*. Lastly, the ruins still connect to the Underdark. All four dungeon types come together in this single dungeon.

## WILDERNESS

Not every adventure has to take place in a dungeon. A trek across the wilderness to the heart of the Blackmire or the Desert of Desolation could be an exciting adventure in itself.

When designing a wilderness adventure, it helps to think of the great outdoors as a big dungeon. The characters should have a destination in mind, so that helps make the route they will take predictable. Roads, paths, and terrain features can channel the PCs along predefined paths, rather than allowing them to wander freely around a vast and open map. The PCs still have plenty of choices—from simple choices such as whether to walk along the bottom or the top of a gorge, to larger choices such as whether to skirt the edge of the swamp or cut through the middle, taking days off the journey but exposing the characters to greater danger.

In cases where the terrain doesn't channel the characters to specific locations, think about the adventure in more of an event-based structure, with encounters connected by a flowchart of events and choices rather than defined by geographical location. See "Event-Based Adventures" on page 115 for more ideas.

Most wilderness areas should seem familiar but have fantastic elements. The creatures flitting among the branches of the Wyrmclaw Forest might be tiny dragonets rather than birds. They're not any more dangerous than birds (until the characters encounter a needlefang drake swarm), but they add a fantastic and flavorful element to the wilderness environment. Once in a while, though, break up the familiar wilderness with truly wondrous locations: trees that hover above the ground and send roots snaking through the air, auroras of many-colored light dancing in the depths of a lake, coldfire flames cascading across the surface of a glacier, or a swamp filled with pools of acid.

## CIVILIZED

From the smallest village to the largest metropolis, urban environments offer limitless opportunities for adventure. Humanoids make the most cunning and devious foes, and NPCs found within the boundaries of the adventurers' hometown are often the most memorable villains.

Urban settings need not be mundane—not any more than wilderness or dungeon areas. Wealthy citizens might ride hippogriffs between the towers of the upper-class families. A mysterious local wizard might live in a tower floating above the city. The storm sewers might crawl with wererats or hide a secret enclave of aboleths. The baron might be a rakshasa or a doppelganger. Magic and danger don't always come from normal humanoid threats.

Adventures based in settled areas don't usually focus on exploring a location and killing its inhabitants. However, cities can hold mini-dungeons (such as the aboleths' sewers or the floating tower of the rakshasas) that combine elements of underground and urban settings. City adventures also work well as event-based adventures in which the setting is a backdrop for the unfolding drama.

## PLANAR

The world is not the only dangerous place full of dungeons. The Shadowfell and the Feywild hold countless opportunities for even low-level adventurers to seek treasure and glory, and the Elemental Chaos and the dominions of the Astral Sea are proving grounds for the most powerful characters. These different worlds offer the most magical, fantastic settings for D&D adventures. The Elemental Chaos is full of mountains floating through the air, stone slabs drifting on rivers of liquid fire, and clouds of pure lightning. The dominions of the gods in the Astral Sea are as different as the deities themselves, from Zehir's Endless Night to Pelor's shining palace at the pinnacle of Celestia.

Planar adventures sometimes resemble wilderness adventures with more fantastic terrain. However, such adventures have plenty of opportunities for dungeon exploration—the fey Labyrinth of Eldren Faere or the Endless Crypts of Morth Dire in the Shadowfell—and even urban encounters in the City of Brass or the Bright City.

# SETTING PERSONALITY

A great way to think about the setting for your adventure is to imagine its personality. A dungeon built as a hobgoblin stronghold has a very different flavor from an ancient temple-city inhabited by yuan-ti, and both are different from a place where the alien energy of the Far Realm has warped and twisted all life into aberrant forms. A setting's personality lends its flavor to the adventure as a whole.

Deciding on a setting's overall personality helps you create all the little details that make it come to life. That said, here and there you can throw in elements that don't fit the overall theme. While fighting their way through the hobgoblin stronghold, if the characters find a secret door leading to an ancient shrine to Bahamut built by the dungeon's original creators, they get a sense of a bigger world beyond their adventures, a taste of history, and a larger view of the dungeon's place in the world.

## CREATOR AND INHABITANTS

A setting's creator and current inhabitants can have a profound impact on the personality of that setting. A forest haunted by ettercaps and spiders is a very different place from one where the Feywild draws near the world and the fey lead their hounds on monthly wild hunts. An ancient dwarven stronghold takes on a different flavor when a minotaur cult moves into its ruins.

When large creatures create dungeons or cities, they build things to scale. A fortress crafted by titans can be hard for humans to negotiate, even if only goblins and dark creepers inhabit it now. On the flip side, adventurers (except halflings) find a kobold warren to be close quarters. The difference between grand battles in the stately halls of the titan ruins and running skirmishes in the cramped tunnels of the kobolds leads to a marked difference in the personality of those two settings.

Some other fundamental elements of a setting's structure can be shaped by the nature of its creator. A lost temple of the yuan-ti, choked by overgrown jungle plants, might use ramps instead of stairs. A place carved by beholders would use empty shafts to connect different levels. Flying creatures in general approach the construction and use of their lairs very differently from land-bound creatures, potentially creating challenging dungeons for adventurers to explore.

A setting's environment might also be closely related to who built it or lives in it. A fortress built into the side of an active volcano might have been built by fire giants or be inhabited by salamanders. A towering palace of ice in the frigid northern wastes could be the work of ice archons, or it might be a temple to the Raven Queen. These are cases in which distinguishing between the setting's original creator and its current inhabitants can be very interesting. Perhaps dwarves built the volcano fortress, but they were wiped out when the volcano erupted a hundred years ago. Now the volcano is home to salamanders. Or its current inhabitants could be relatively normal creatures that rely on magic rituals to keep them protected from the volcano's heat and ongoing activity.

Cultural details, at both a large scale and a small one, bring a setting's personality to life in your players' minds. Great bearded faces carved on the doors of a dwarven stronghold (perhaps defaced by the orcs who live there now), spiderweb decorations in a citadel of the drow, grisly battle trophies impaled on spears around a gnoll camp, and a statue of Pelor in the ruined temple are all details that tell the PCs something about who built the setting or who currently inhabits it. Cultural details such as these can also tie different settings together, perhaps suggesting an interesting storyline. Imagine that in three different dungeons, all the gold coins the characters find were minted by the ancient tiefling empire of Bael Turath. Does this cultural detail hint at some historical element linking these three dungeons?

A more dramatic sort of cultural detail has to do with the types of rooms or buildings you might find in the setting. A drow stronghold might have pens for slaves, a number of torture chambers, and elaborate temples to Lolth. A kobold warren or dragonborn ruin might have egg incubation chambers. An expansive complex with a dusty library and museum has a different feel from one full of armories, barracks, and prisons.

## HISTORY

Many of the elements just discussed speak to the setting's history. The race or culture that originally created a dungeon gives it a great deal of its personality, and the history of the site between its creation and the present is no less significant.

The D&D world has a glorious history of expansive empires and prosperity. In the present day, the empires of the past lie in ruin, replaced by petty baronies and vast expanses of lawless wilderness. This world has endless opportunities for adventure: ancient ruins to explore, lost treasures to be recovered, savage hordes to drive away from settled lands, and terrible monsters haunting the dark places of the world. The exact history of your own campaign world, of course, is yours to design if you so choose, but these basic assumptions make for a world of opportunity from the adventurer's point of view.

Does this dungeon hold the last ancient monster of its kind, a powerful being that fiercely defends its last stronghold? Were its long-dead rulers the last known possessors of the Regalia of the Seven Kingdoms? Was it built as a prison for a primordial or demon prince whose influence still lingers in the place? Do the residents of the city in the remote jungle not know that the empire of Nerath has fallen? These are all ways you can tie the history of a setting into adventures you place there, shaping its flavor and feel.

A word of warning: Let background be background. Unless the background is essential to your adventure, don't spend a lot of time detailing the history of a dungeon in exhaustive detail. Use history to spice up the setting and provide the interesting details that help bring it to life in the players' minds, then move on to focus on the adventure.

## ENVIRONMENT

Sometimes a setting's surroundings give it all the personality it needs. A ruined castle in the Shadowfell, a monastery drifting through the Elemental Chaos, or the classic dungeon built into an active volcano are all settings that have a distinct personality regardless of their history or inhabitants. You might find inspiration in the jungle-choked ruins of Angkor Wat or decide to create a coral labyrinth in a tropical sea. The environment in these cases is the primary element of the setting's personality, which you can then enhance by choosing the right inhabitants and creating an appropriate history.

## ATMOSPHERE

A subtle but important way to communicate your setting's personality to the players is through the background sensory details you use in your descriptions—the ambience the characters experience in the place. Remember to consider all five senses, as well as harder-to-define gut feelings and emotional responses characters might have to the setting. As the characters enter a natural cavern complex, they might see a dim blue glow radiating from the walls, hear the distant dripping of water, smell the slightly acrid scent of wet earth, and feel the cool air even as the weight of the earth and stone above them seems to press down on their spirits. When they creep down the stairs of an ancient crypt, describe the dust-covered cobwebs, skittering beetles, dry air, and perhaps the haunting sense of a presence deep within the tomb that watches their every move, anticipating their arrival.

You don't need to pile atmospheric details into your very first description of an adventure setting. Make a note of the ambience of the place, perhaps listing a variety of details that might appear to every sense, and break them out to add some flair to your narratives as the adventure progresses.

ROB ALEXANDER

# Setting Details

You can design the details of settings in your adventures in three ways: the natural method, the staged method, and the best method. The strengths of the first two methods fuse to create the best method while countering their weaknesses.

## The Natural Method

With this method, you picture a location in your mind and draw it out on your map. If the goblins live in a ruined castle, you take care to design a castle first, add in crumbled walls and ruined areas to reflect its age, and then determine how the goblins live in the place. Logic, story, and realism guide your design. The areas you map have a history, they were built for a purpose, and those two factors guide your design.

The natural method is the best method because it creates realistic, believable environments that reflect the story and your campaign world.

The natural method is the worst method because it can cause you to worry too much about realism, especially realism that is lost on the players. Taken too far, worrying about "real" encounter areas can force you to build boring ones. Remember, you are the creator and final arbiter of the game, not a rule, someone else's sense of realism, or any other outside factor.

## The Staged Method

This method embraces the encounter area as a setting for a game. It sets aside worries about realism or a sense that a location existed as something other than the place for a fight. With the staged method, you treat encounter areas as stages for the action, just like a director or novelist. The only thing that matters is how much excitement and fun the encounter yields.

The staged method is the best way to go because it promotes action, adventure, and excitement. It forces you to design toward a clear goal of making things fun.

The staged method is the worst approach because it places artifice above everything. Like a paper-thin façade, it works as long as no one pushes against it. If the players stop to think about the area, or if you try to make sense of it in terms of story and narrative, it falls flat.

## The Best Method

The aptly named best method is a fusion of the natural and staged approaches. Build encounter areas within the context of the campaign's story and history, but keep an eye out for creating fun, interesting encounters. In truth, the two methods are completely compatible, particularly when you add monsters to the mix.

For instance, a ruined castle might have an entrance gate with battlements above it. The goblin lord of the place assigns archers to watch the gate from this position. When the PCs attack, the archers rain arrows down upon them while the characters must rush through the gate and up the crumbling stairs to reach the goblins.

A dungeon filled with puzzles and weird monsters was built that way because Emperor Darvan the Mad constructed it to defend his most valuable treasures. The alleyways around the syndicate's headquarters are rife with traps and ambush points because the Lord of Shadows is always ready for an attack by his rivals. Encounter areas never spring from a vacuum. They are built, designed, or chosen by monsters and intelligent creatures for a reason.

Even wholly natural terrain lends itself to this approach. While the characters travel along the road, bandits attack when they reach an area of rough ground that offers plenty of cover for the bandit archers. A bulette hunts in a box canyon, trapping animals in a dead end.

## Dungeon Rooms

The rooms in a dungeon setting show what the place was built for, and they show how the inhabitants live their lives. When you add rooms to a site, consider the story they tell about the place and its dwellers. Rooms, as well as the arrangement of them, should make sense within the context of their intended purpose and current use. Don't forget that fantastic elements can be a part of the scene—illusions instead of art, or unusual passages and rooms for creatures that have a distinctly nonhuman body or mindset.

**DUNGEON ROOM POSSIBILITIES**

| | |
|---|---|
| Arena | Nursery |
| Armory | Observatory |
| Audience chamber | Prison |
| Burial site | Quarters |
| Communication center | Storeroom |
| Cookery | Temple |
| Dumping grounds | Training area |
| Guard post | Transportation |
| Library | Water supply |
| Museum | Workshop |

## Terrain Features

In natural settings, whether outdoors or underground, large-scale terrain features tend to define the environment. In outdoor environments, look for fantasy art or even real-world photography that depicts dramatic natural settings. A forest does not need to be just a battle grid dotted with trees and undergrowth when even a casual Internet search can bring up dozens of beautiful pictures of dramatic forest landscapes. Not only do your players have a more vivid scene to imagine, but an encounter can also become a lot more interesting when it takes place on a forested hill with a stream tumbling down its rocky side.

## OUTDOOR TERRAIN POSSIBILITIES

| | | |
|---|---|---|
| Basin | Esker | Mesa |
| Bluff | Fissure | Mound |
| Canyon | Glacier | Oasis |
| Chasm | Gorge | Overlook |
| Cliff | Grove | Plateau |
| Crater | Hill | Ravine |
| Crevice | Island | Sinkhole |
| Delta | Lake | Stream |
| Dune | Meadow | Wetland |

## UNDERGROUND TERRAIN POSSIBILITIES

| | |
|---|---|
| Column | Pool |
| Flowstone | Stalactite |
| Gypsum flower | Stalagmite |

## CITY BUILDINGS

Even in a fantastic city, a lot of buildings are mundane places—the ropemakers, tanneries, and provisioners' shops that support the day-to-day life of the city's people. Those don't usually make great adventure sites, though. Use them for color as characters move through the city. The types of businesses found in a city can say a lot about the city's personality. (Does the city have a slave auction yard or abundant hostels where the poor can find food and shelter? Does it host three temples to Bahamut, or a great fortress-temple to Bane?)

Look to more exotic and interesting sites for the important scenes in an urban adventure. Sites that can take a role as part of an encounter are always a good choice—a mill with wheels and gears turning a giant millstone is terrain that smart players (or monsters) can use to their advantage. Moving parts, built-in hazards, and verticality—the risk of falling with a wrong step—make city sites more interesting than a stereotypical tavern brawl.

### INTERESTING CITY SITES

| |
|---|
| Battlements |
| Bridges, balconies, and rooftops |
| Forge (smithy or smelting furnace) |
| Mill (windmill, water wheel) |
| Monument (pyramid or ziggurat) |
| Rooftops |
| Ruins from an ancient, larger city on the same site |
| Temple (with magical traps and hazards) |
| Tower (bell tower, clock tower, watch tower) |
| Waterways (storm sewers, aqueducts, canals) |

### FANTASTIC FLAVOR

| |
|---|
| Defensive walls of magical fire or thorns |
| Floating buildings—towers, palaces, or whole neighborhoods |
| Hippogriff stables or behemoths as beasts of burden |
| Magical lamps or an artificial sun |
| Monstrous or magical sentinels (treants or golems) |
| Planar connections (shadow district or fey garden) |

## UPSCALE TRADES AND SERVICES (EXAMPLES)

| | | |
|---|---|---|
| Alchemist | Cartographer | Ritual caster |
| Assassin | Goldsmith | Sage |
| Bank | Jeweler | Scribe |
| Bookseller | Moneychanger | Spice merchant |

## AVERAGE TRADES AND SERVICES (EXAMPLES)

| | | |
|---|---|---|
| Armorer | Butcher | Painter |
| Auctioneer | Cartwright | Provisioner |
| Baker | Mason | Stable |
| Blacksmith | Messenger | Tavern |

## POOR TRADES AND SERVICES (EXAMPLES)

| | | |
|---|---|---|
| Almshouse | Fishmonger | Pawn shop |
| Basketweaver | Fuller | Tanner |
| Brickmaker | Gambling hall | Warehouse |
| Burglar | Miller | |

# FURNISHINGS AND FEATURES

Spice up dungeon or city rooms with furnishings or other minor features whose primary purpose is flavor. Any detail you add to a room not only brings the setting to more vivid life in your players' minds, it can also spur unusual and creative ideas in encounters, such as tipping over a brazier of burning coals or pulling a tapestry down over opponents. (Refer to "Actions the Rules Don't Cover" in Chapter 3 on page 42 when these situations come up.) Some of these features might count as difficult terrain or grant cover (see "Encounter Settings" on page 60 in Chapter 4).

### SAMPLE FURNISHINGS AND FEATURES

| | | |
|---|---|---|
| Alcove | Altar | Arrow slit |
| Balcony | Barrel | Bed |
| Bench | Bookcase | Brazier |
| Cage | Caldron | Carpet |
| Chair | Chandelier | Chasm |
| Chest | Collapsed wall | Crate |
| Curtain | Dome | Evil symbol |
| Fallen stones | Fire pit | Forge |
| Fountain | Gong | Hole |
| Idol | Ladder | Loose masonry |
| Manacles | Mirror | Mosaic |
| Murder hole | Oven | Painting |
| Pedestal | Peephole | Pillar |
| Platform | Pool | Portcullis |
| Ramp | Relief | Sconce |
| Screen | Shaft | Shelf |
| Shrine | Statue | Stool |
| Stuffed beast | Sunken area | Table |
| Tapestry | Torture device | Throne |
| Trash | Tub | Wall basin |
| Weapon rack | Well | Workbench |

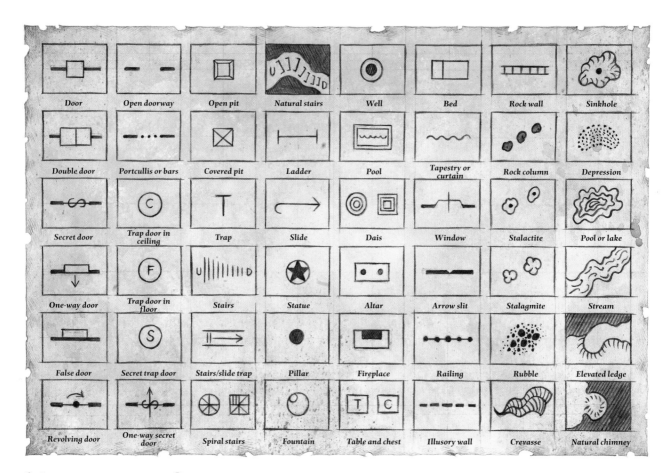

| | | | | | | | |
|---|---|---|---|---|---|---|---|
| Door | Open doorway | Open pit | Natural stairs | Well | Bed | Rock wall | Sinkhole |
| Double door | Portcullis or bars | Covered pit | Ladder | Pool | Tapestry or curtain | Rock column | Depression |
| Secret door | Trap door in ceiling | Trap | Slide | Dais | Window | Stalactite | Pool or lake |
| One-way door | Trap door in floor | Stairs | Statue | Altar | Arrow slit | Stalagmite | Stream |
| False door | Secret trap door | Stairs/slide trap | Pillar | Fireplace | Railing | Rubble | Elevated ledge |
| Revolving door | One-way secret door | Spiral stairs | Fountain | Table and chest | Illusory wall | Crevasse | Natural chimney |

# MAPPING THE SITE

Once you've come up with a concept for your adventure's setting, you probably need a map. An adventure map can take many forms—from an exquisitely detailed dungeon map that shows every feature in every 5-foot square to a sketchy outline of how one encounter might lead to one or two or three others, depending on the route the characters choose. Whatever your map looks like, it serves the fundamental purpose of mapping out your adventure, not just its setting. The map is a visual representation of how all the encounters that make up the adventure fit together. The map is also like a flowchart, in which each decision point (a branch in a corridor, a room with multiple exits) leads along a different course to new decision points. By looking at your map, you can tell where the characters' decisions lead them. If they leave the room by the north door, you look at your map and see that it leads them into the great hall, lined with pillars, where the fire giant king holds court. If they leave by the secret door to the southeast, you look at the map and follow the secret tunnel as it winds to the hidden vaults below the great hall.

Chapter 11 includes a short adventure with a dungeon map you can use as example and inspiration for your own maps. Each encounter also includes a map of the encounter area in greater detail. Although in the case of that adventure, the encounter areas are all close to each other in a relatively limited space, that doesn't have to be true. Your adventure map could be circled numbers representing encounter areas with lines between them, and each line possibly representing hours or even days of travel. Your adventure might have decision points along those lines that aren't encounter areas: "After about two hours, you reach a point where the passage splits. The left branch starts with a short flight of stairs and seems to lead gently upward beyond them, while the right branch slopes sharply downward. Which way do you go?" It is fine if your map glosses over long stretches of travel to keep the adventure moving.

Sometimes an encounter map is literally a flowchart, when the setting is less important than the plot, and encounters are more like events. Decision points on such a map aren't literal rooms with multiple exits, but they work just the same way: If the characters convince the baron to send soldiers to the pass, they lead a squad to the pass the next day, and their next encounter is with a group of hobgoblins in the pass. If they fail to convince the baron, their next encounter is a team of assassins sent by the vizier that attacks them that night.

## DRAWING THE MAP

When you're setting out to draw a dungeon map, start with a blank sheet of graph paper. With one square on the graph paper representing 5 feet of distance, you can easily translate the encounter areas on your map to the battle grid when combat breaks out.

Your map should include all the important features of a room, although flavor details can rest in descriptive text or notes rather than appearing on the map. Consider all the elements that apply from the following list.

### MAP ELEMENTS
✦ Boundaries and walls
✦ Doors and passages
✦ Furnishings
✦ Hazards
✦ Numbers or letters for key locations
✦ Obstacles
✦ Secret areas
✦ Terrain
✦ Territory for factions
✦ Traps

Unless cartography is fun for you, don't worry about the drawing quality in your mapping. Your map is a tool to help you keep track of the adventure and convey the setting to the players. It just needs to be clear and easy for you to use. Make notes on it that will help you describe the area and run the encounters.

**Map Symbols:** You can use symbols to indicate map features. The map symbol illustration here shows one way to depict common features of adventure settings, but use whatever symbols work best for you.

## ADVENTURE MAP AND BATTLE GRID

When you map encounter areas, keep in mind that you're going to have to transfer your map to the battle grid when the characters enter the area. Don't make areas that are too big to fit on your table (or your gridded surface). If you use *D&D Dungeon Tiles* for your battle grid, consider building each area with the tiles first, then transferring it to the map. That way, you are sure you can build the location again when the encounter starts.

### DRAWING DIAGONAL WALLS

Here's a tip for drawing diagonal walls on the battle grid: Don't draw the walls through the corners of squares. Instead, start at the middle of a square's edge and go through the middle of the adjacent square's edge. This way, where creatures can stand is always clear: A square with a corner cut off is a legal square, but a creature can't occupy a space that's just the corner of a square.

## THE MAP KEY

The key for your map is the substance of your adventure. For each room on the adventure map, your key describes what's in the room—its physical features, as well as the encounter that waits there. The key turns a room sketched on graph paper with the numeral 1 in the middle of it into an encounter on the battle grid designed to entertain and intrigue your players.

### ELEMENTS OF A KEY/ENCOUNTER DESCRIPTION
✦ Room description
✦ Monsters
✦ Traps
✦ Hazards
✦ Monster tactics
✦ Encounter XP value
✦ Treasure, if any
✦ Rules for terrain and features in the room

The encounter areas presented in Chapter 11 are reasonably well detailed, but you don't necessarily need the same level of detail in your own adventures. Particularly if you don't have a lot of time to prepare, it can be enough to jot quick notes about each encounter. Even so, try to include at least enough detail to spur you to give an expanded description when you're running the encounter. Here's an example of the sort of quick notes you might make for a room:

### ROOM 1–FOULSPAWN GUARDS (2,100 XP)
Smell like rotting flesh mixed with chemical odor. Strange shadows—don't seem to follow light, things moving?
  2 foulspawn berserkers
  1 foulspawn seer
  2 foulspawn manglers
Berserkers attack when the characters enter the room. Next round, seer enters on balcony (10 ft. up) and manglers sneak in through side doors (Stealth +12).
**Treasure:** Seer wears an *amulet of protection* +2 (+2 defenses).

Whatever format works best for your reference during the game is the format you should use. Some DMs like having a page neatly organized for each encounter, while others use index cards. Still others write the contents of each room directly on the map and don't bother with a key at all, trusting their ability to improvise any further details. Your own preference is what matters, along with the preparation time you have available.

# Outdoor Settings

A dungeon makes a great adventure setting because it offers choices without presenting too many options. The characters can turn right or left, and that choice can make a significant difference in the adventure, but they can't go in a completely different direction than you planned for. Because the players' options are limited, planning for all possibilities is easy. Just determine what's in every dungeon room, and you've covered all your bases.

By contrast, an outdoor setting seems to present limitless options. The players can move in any direction they want to over the trackless desert, and you might think you'd have to detail every square mile of the desert in order to be prepared for every possibility. Either that, or you design an encounter in an oasis, the characters miss the oasis because they wandered off course, and the result is a boring adventure with uninterrupted slogging across bare rock and dry sand.

The solution is to think of an outdoor setting very much like you think about a dungeon. First, most terrain—even trackless desert—does present some clear pathways. The reason that roads seldom run straight is that they follow the contours of the land, finding the most level or otherwise easiest pathways across uneven ground. Valleys and ridges channel travel in a certain direction. Mountain ranges present a forbidding barrier except for natural or constructed passes. Even an apparently trackless desert has easier routes and harder ones—regions of wind-blasted rock that are easier to walk on than shifting sand.

Second, you don't have to be precise about where you place encounters on your outdoor maps. A part of your brain might cling to the realism of saying, "But the oasis is right there," but the oasis is not there. The oasis isn't real. It exists precisely where you need it to exist, which is in the path of the player characters as they make their way across the desert. It might be 80 miles into their journey, or however far they travel in three days.

You might want to draw a sketch of an outdoor map for an adventure. However, keep it on the free-form side. Just as you do in a dungeon, think about decision points and encounter areas and how to connect them, rather than focusing on the exact terrain between. A decision point might be a fork in the road, or the choice to ford a river, continue down its closer bank, or build a raft and paddle downstream. The ford might lead to one encounter, while either walking or rowing downstream might lead to another. The adventure continues, no matter which route the characters choose.

Thinking about outdoor adventures in this way presents some risk of overpreparing. If the characters' goal is to get from one place to another, and the adventure is the encounters they have along the way, they're significantly more likely to miss encounters you have planned than they are in a dungeon where they're inclined to explore every room. You can approach this problem in two ways: You can grin and bear it, taking care not to put too much effort into each encounter and knowing that the characters will skip over some of them. Or, you can throw every encounter in the characters' way, regardless of the choices they make.

That might seem like railroading, but it's not—at least, not any moreso than a normal dungeon is. As long as the players feel as though they're making meaningful choices along the way, the end result can be that they go through the same encounters they would have if they would have made completely different choices. Their choices should influence the *order* in which the encounters occur, just as they do in a dungeon. For example, opponents from one encounter might flee and appear again as reinforcements in a later encounter.

Another way to think about outdoor travel is as an extended skill challenge. The "Lost in the Wilderness" skill challenge example in Chapter 5 (page 79) shows how to make a journey through the wilds into an important part of an adventure. You can interrupt the skill challenge with combat encounters at several points along the way—the higher the complexity of the challenge, the longer it will take to complete, and thus the more often it is liable to be interrupted. Using the skill challenge system in this way makes the players feel as though the episode of outdoor travel is full of meaningful choices and a chance for their characters' skills to matter in the game.

## Varying Adventure Settings

Present a variety of settings within both a single adventure and over the course of several adventures. It's almost a cliché of the game, but one outdoor encounter on the way to the dungeon—or an outdoor encounter that leads the characters to the dungeon—can be an exciting way to lay the foundation of an adventure, cluing the players in to the nature of the threat they face.

A mix of dungeon, outdoor, urban, and even planar adventuring also keeps a campaign interesting. You might even structure your campaign so that characters routinely travel the world, with one adventure in steamy tropical rainforest and the next set in the frozen tundra.

# EVENT-BASED ADVENTURES

If a good outdoor adventure map is a sort of abstraction of a dungeon map, then the "map" for a purely event-based adventure is even more so. But the idea of a dungeon map as flowchart is a great metaphor for how to structure an adventure around events and decisions instead of around physical space.

An event-based adventure focuses on the things the characters do rather than the places they go. Each decision—as well as the outcome of each encounter—leads to direct consequences. Typically, event-based adventures rely heavily on skill challenges, particularly those that involve interactions with nonplayer characters. They might involve solving a mystery (which you might also think of as a logic puzzle), plunging into a tangled web of diplomacy and intrigue, or tracking down a hidden cult operating in the bell tower of the abandoned temple. An event-based encounter is a great way to involve the actors, storytellers, and thinkers in your group, but you can keep slayers happy with frequent combat encounters thrown into the mix.

The setting of an event-based adventure is often a city (though it can be anything). An event-based structure works well for urban adventures because you don't have to map every building in the city. What's important is whom the characters interact with. However, you can also use this structure for outdoor or dungeon encounters, particularly in cases where the opponents are organized and intelligent, rather than dumb brutes who lurk in their dungeon lairs until characters come along to fight. Consider an ancient ruin now inhabited by three different factions: yuan-ti in one quarter, minotaurs in another, and drow in the cellars, sewers, and caverns below. Such an adventure has an element of exploration, but more interesting is how the characters might play the three factions against each other, making the events of the adventure far more important than the setting—particularly since the inhabitants of the ruin move around regularly, rather than appearing in fixed encounter locations.

Certain points on the event flowchart for your adventure might be sites—small dungeons or just city building. At those points, you set the flowchart "adventure map" aside and turn to a smaller map, let the characters explore that site and complete the encounters there, then return to the flowchart, following one branch or another depending on the outcome of those encounters. These mini-dungeons are a good way to vary the pace and feel of the adventure and so to appeal to different player motivations.

Similarly, have encounter areas mapped for the combat encounters you do plan for an event-based adventure. Assassins might attack the characters anywhere in the city, when the time is right, but if you have a few interesting encounter maps available to choose from (a marketplace, a tavern, a warren of back alleys) you can pick the right one for the event when it occurs.

Even more than in most adventures, the overall structure of an event-based adventure is essential. You want events to hook the characters in immediately, build excitement slowly, and reach a climactic moment, a crucial encounter. That crucial encounter might be an all-out fight against the mind flayer impersonating the baron or a final showdown with the castellan to determine the duke's final decision, but it should be the most exciting and tension-filled encounter in the whole adventure. Pay close attention to the advice about good and bad structure (see page 101). It's easy to bottleneck or railroad the players in an event-based adventure.

Another useful tool for organizing an event-based adventure is with a timeline. Certain events might occur at specific times in the adventure regardless of the characters' actions (a solar eclipse, a new nonplayer character arriving on the scene, a festival day, or some other event beyond the player characters' control), or events on the timeline could trigger unless the characters manage to prevent them. A timeline is a great way to make sure an event-based adventure stays on track by adding new elements to the mix at regular intervals. It can also put time pressure on the characters to accomplish their goals before certain inevitable events occur. If the villains are scheming to assassinate the earl during the festival, the characters have a limited time to unravel the plot and stop it.

Finally, have a few more-or-less random combat encounters prepared to kick-start the action if things start to bog down. Rather than drop a clue in the characters' lap, have someone kick down their door and start a fight, dropping the clue in the process. That way, the players feel like they earned the clue, and the encounter also gets their adrenaline flowing and ratchets up the excitement a notch.

6

An adventure's cast–the monsters and nonplayer characters involved–brings it to life. Cast members are tools that facilitate the game. Many cast members are monsters or NPCs for the PCs to face and defeat. They require little work aside from placing them in encounters and a little attention to behavior that makes them interesting to roleplay. Others are extras directly involved with the PCs–employers and other support characters who require at least a little detail for roleplaying purposes. Still others are unique villains or monsters that require statistics and roleplaying details you create.

Every cast member has a purpose, a reason for appearing in the adventure. The most fundamental purposes are straightforward: Is the character an ally or patron to the characters, their enemy, or an extra with a walk-on role? When you populate your adventure, you can give some of the cast notable purposes. However, such purposes are relevant only if they'll matter to the PCs. Don't bother with such details if no way exists for the PCs to interact with them.

Sometimes a cast member can serve multiple purposes, and the purposes of some cast members can change as a reaction to the characters' actions or events in the world. An ally or patron could become an enemy, or fade into the background and become a mere extra. Enemies can reconcile and even become allies.

## ALLIES AS EXTRA CHARACTERS

Sometimes you want an ally or patron nonplayer character to accompany the player characters on part or all of an adventure. You might do it for story reasons, or just because you like having a character of your own to play when the player characters leave the comforts of civilization. An ally can be a way to introduce clues to the characters, or might be along just so she can betray the characters (and turn into an enemy) at the worst possible moment.

When a nonplayer character participates in an encounter, that character earns an equal share of experience points. You should build encounters to challenge the party that includes the ally. Allies are within their rights to demand a share of treasure earned as well, though in that case you should add treasure to the adventure to account for the ally.

Resist the temptation to use allied nonplayer characters as a way to railroad the players, and don't ever let an ally become the focus of an adventure. Keep the spotlight firmly on the player characters where it belongs.

## ALLIES

An ally is a cast member that helps the PCs in some way, large or small. Allies come in all sorts, from the sagacious peasant who knows and can relate all the local legends, to the guard captain who fights alongside the characters as they hold off the hobgoblin invaders. Allies don't need to give their help for free, but they often do.

Allies can serve a number of roles in an adventure. An ally might be an explorer who shares her maps with the characters or guides them through the wilderness. Or he might be the priest the characters turn to when they need a Raise Dead ritual performed. A deity might even assign an angel of protection to ward a character on a particularly dangerous and important adventure. If you plan a twist in your game, an ally might have darker qualities that make the character later become an enemy.

An ally needs only as much detail as its role in the game requires. A sage who exists only to provide an important clue doesn't need any more detail than a quirk of appearance or mannerism to help you play her at the table. But the explorer-guide who accompanies the characters on part of their adventure needs full combat statistics in addition to those small details.

## PATRONS

A patron employs the characters, providing help or rewards as well as hooks to adventure. Most of the time, a patron has a vested interest in the characters' success and doesn't need to be persuaded to help. However, circumstances or hidden schemes might make a patron cagey or even treacherous. A patron might cease to care about the characters after they complete a particular task. Let these circumstances guide the detail you give a patron. A name and a few choice interactions are all you need for a patron who serves as an adventure hook, but you might need further facets for a recurring patron–or one who might become an ally or enemy. At the least, give some thought to why the patron wants what he does and why he hires the characters to pursue his goals instead of doing it himself.

## ENEMIES

Enemies oppose or hinder the characters. Simple monsters are enemies, as are dastardly villains you make up. Most enemies need combat statistics more than roleplaying details, although an enemy in a skill challenge might need more extensive personality notes and motivations. Enemies who play a significant role in an adventure–the villains featured in climactic encounters, as well as recurring villains who vex the characters in adventure after adventure—should always be more than their combat statistics. They don't need extensive personal histories that explain why they became so evil, but tales of their past evils can be a good way to build player anticipation for that climactic battle. A memorable personality, preferably something that becomes apparent before the final battle, also brings a villain to life. Mocking verses, in flowery language, scrawled in blood beside each victim speak volumes about the villain the characters seek.

Also consider the motivations of an important enemy. Is he an evil cultist who offers sacrifices to Orcus in a cellar shrine? A scheming mastermind who plans to take over the barony? A mercenary criminal who does anything if the price is right? A crazed lunatic who delights in torture with no real purpose? Villains with different motivations can give very different flavor to the adventures they appear in.

## Extras

Extras are characters and creatures that exist to make the world seem more real. In a movie, they're the people in the background that the main characters rarely interact with. The duke's servants, townsfolk who witness (and scatter away from) a street brawl, and tavernkeepers are extras. In a D&D game, you might keep basic and short notes on extras you think might become part of a brief encounter. Many DMs make up extras on the spot when the PCs go somewhere unexpected. Often you need to know only what kinds of extras to expect in an area of your adventure or settlement.

## Bringing the Cast to Life

One way to ease the job of roleplaying a wide variety of characters is to give each one a distinctive trait—something the heroes remember that character by. If the tavern keeper on duty during the day is hard of hearing and the one on duty at night speaks loudly (and tactlessly), the players have an easier time remembering which is which. Traits that have an easy, obvious effect on how you play that character are best. It's one thing to tell the players that a criminal contact has bad breath, but it's quite another to play him so that he ends every sentence with a noticeable exhalation of breath toward the characters. If your voice and acting talents are up to the challenge, creating distinctive voices for important characters is a great way to make sure they stick in the players' minds, and different facial expressions can create a vivid picture of different characters.

Another important thing to remember as you bring this enormous supporting cast to life is to be consistent. Creating a distinct daytime and nighttime tavernkeeper is great. Randomly using one of two different personalities whenever the heroes visit a tavern is just random. When you invent a new character's personality, make a note of it, so you can refer back to it when the heroes return to the same place later.

One of the great things about establishing consistency like this is that it can be very effective when you break it. If characters visit their favorite tavern at noon and find the night keeper on duty, they wonder why, which can be a wonderfully subtle way to draw the heroes into an adventure.

## Variant Behavior

Surprise your players occasionally by making familiar creatures act in unusual or bizarre ways for their kind. The variant behavior should be explainable if the PCs can discover the cause. Perhaps the setting changes those who stay within it too long. Maybe the presence or influence of one or more creatures has swayed others to behave in an unusual way.

Variant behavior can go in many directions. An evil creature might instead behave in a more benevolent fashion, or it could be limited in some way that prevents or suppresses its natural tendencies. Innocent creatures might be forced to fight for the bad guys, causing the PCs a moral quandary. Weak creatures might have stronger yet subservient allies.

CHAPTER 7

# REWARDS

EXPERIENCE POINTS, treasure, action points, and intangible rewards keep characters moving on from encounter to encounter, level to level, and adventure to adventure. Small rewards come frequently, while large rewards provide a big boost once in a while. Both are important.

Without frequent small rewards, players begin to feel like their efforts aren't paying off. They're doing a lot of work with nothing to show for it. Without occasional large rewards, encounters feel like pushing a button to get a morsel of food—a repetitive grind with no meaningful variation.

Characters gain experience points (XP) for every encounter they complete. They gain action points when they reach milestones, generally after every two encounters. They gain treasure as they complete encounters—not after every encounter, but sporadically over the course of an adventure. They gain a level after completing eight to ten encounters (including quests).

Gaining a level (see page 27 of the *Player's Handbook*) is the most significant reward the game has to offer, but even that reward has its own tidal rhythm. Characters gain new attack powers at odd-numbered levels, and they gain new feats, ability score increases, and global adjustments to all their attacks and defenses at even-numbered levels. Both are exciting, but they feel different.

This chapter includes the following sections.

✦ **Experience Points:** Every monster slain, skill challenge, puzzle solved, and trap disabled is worth an XP reward. As characters gain XP, they move toward new levels.

✦ **Quests:** Completing quests brings rewards just like completing encounters.

✦ **Action Points:** Action points encourage characters to take on more encounters before stopping to take an extended rest.

✦ **Treasure:** Whether it's coins, gems, art objects, or magic items, treasure is the reward characters can put to use right away.

HOWARD LYON

Experience points (XP) are the fundamental reward of the game, just as encounters are the building blocks of adventures and campaigns. Every encounter comes with an experience reward to match its difficulty.

## XP REWARDS

The Experience Point Rewards table provides XP values for monsters of every level. Use the "Standard Monster" column for NPCs, traps, and noncombat encounters (skill challenges and puzzles).

**EXPERIENCE POINT REWARDS**

| Monster Level | Standard Monster | Minion | Elite | Solo |
|---|---|---|---|---|
| 1 | 100 | 25 | 200 | 500 |
| 2 | 125 | 31 | 250 | 625 |
| 3 | 150 | 38 | 300 | 750 |
| 4 | 175 | 44 | 350 | 875 |
| 5 | 200 | 50 | 400 | 1,000 |
| 6 | 250 | 63 | 500 | 1,250 |
| 7 | 300 | 75 | 600 | 1,500 |
| 8 | 350 | 88 | 700 | 1,750 |
| 9 | 400 | 100 | 800 | 2,000 |
| 10 | 500 | 125 | 1,000 | 2,500 |
| 11 | 600 | 150 | 1,200 | 3,000 |
| 12 | 700 | 175 | 1,400 | 3,500 |
| 13 | 800 | 200 | 1,600 | 4,000 |
| 14 | 1,000 | 250 | 2,000 | 5,000 |
| 15 | 1,200 | 300 | 2,400 | 6,000 |
| 16 | 1,400 | 350 | 2,800 | 7,000 |
| 17 | 1,600 | 400 | 3,200 | 8,000 |
| 18 | 2,000 | 500 | 4,000 | 10,000 |
| 19 | 2,400 | 600 | 4,800 | 12,000 |
| 20 | 2,800 | 700 | 5,600 | 14,000 |
| 21 | 3,200 | 800 | 6,400 | 16,000 |
| 22 | 4,150 | 1,038 | 8,300 | 20,750 |
| 23 | 5,100 | 1,275 | 10,200 | 25,500 |
| 24 | 6,050 | 1,513 | 12,100 | 30,250 |
| 25 | 7,000 | 1,750 | 14,000 | 35,000 |
| 26 | 9,000 | 2,250 | 18,000 | 45,000 |
| 27 | 11,000 | 2,750 | 22,000 | 55,000 |
| 28 | 13,000 | 3,250 | 26,000 | 65,000 |
| 29 | 15,000 | 3,750 | 30,000 | 75,000 |
| 30 | 19,000 | 4,750 | 38,000 | 95,000 |
| 31 | 23,000 | 5,750 | 46,000 | 115,000 |
| 32 | 27,000 | 6,750 | 54,000 | 135,000 |
| 33 | 31,000 | 7,750 | 62,000 | 155,000 |
| 34 | 39,000 | 9,750 | 78,000 | 195,000 |
| 35 | 47,000 | 11,750 | 94,000 | 235,000 |
| 36 | 55,000 | 13,750 | 110,000 | 275,000 |
| 37 | 63,000 | 15,750 | 126,000 | 315,000 |
| 38 | 79,000 | 19,750 | 158,000 | 395,000 |
| 39 | 95,000 | 23,750 | 190,000 | 475,000 |
| 40 | 111,000 | 27,750 | 222,000 | 555,000 |

## EARNING XP

Characters earn XP for every encounter they overcome. The XP reward for completing an encounter is the sum of the XP values for each monster, NPC, trap, or hazard that makes up the encounter. You noted or assigned this number when you built the encounter, to judge its difficulty against your players. (Published adventures note the XP value of each encounter they contain.) Divide the XP total for the encounter by the number of players present to help overcome it, and that's how many XP each character gets.

**Overcoming an Encounter:** What counts as overcoming an encounter? Killing, routing, or capturing the opponents in a combat encounter certainly counts. Meeting the success conditions of a skill challenge is overcoming it. Remember that an encounter, by definition, has a risk of failure. If that risk isn't present, it's not an encounter, and the characters don't earn XP. If the characters accidentally trigger a trap as they make their way down a hallway, they don't get XP because it wasn't an encounter. If the trap constitutes an encounter or is part of an encounter, though, they do earn XP if they manage to disarm or destroy it.

Say the characters avoid a hydra to get into the treasure vault it guards. Do they get XP for overcoming the challenge of the hydra? No. If the treasure was the object of a quest, they get the reward for completing the quest (see Quest Rewards on page 122), which should include XP as well as treasure. But because they didn't have an encounter with the hydra, they didn't overcome the challenge. (If they sneak past, trick, or defeat the hydra in an encounter, they do earn XP.)

**XP for Combat Encounters:** The *Monster Manual* indicates the XP reward each monster is worth. That number comes from the Experience Rewards table on this page, and it depends on the monster's level. A minion is worth one-quarter of the XP of a standard monster of its level. An elite monster is worth twice as much XP, and a solo monster is worth five times as much XP.

If you apply a template to a monster (see page 175), you turn it into an elite or solo monster (see "Creating New Solos," page 185) and therefore adjust its XP value. Likewise, if you alter a monster's level, its XP value changes.

A nonplayer character counts as a monster of his or her level for calculating XP. Traps and hazards that serve as combat complications also have levels. If the characters overcome a combat encounter where a trap or hazard presented a threat during the encounter, give them XP for the trap or hazard even if they didn't disable or neutralize it. They overcame the challenge it presented most directly, which was its danger during the combat.

**XP for Noncombat Encounters:** Noncombat encounters that carry risk also carry reward. A skill challenge has a level and a difficulty that combine to determine the XP your characters earn for successfully completing the challenge. A skill challenge counts as a number of monsters of its level equal to its complexity—so a 7th-level challenge with a complexity of 3 counts as three 7th-level monsters, or 900 XP.

If a puzzle constitutes an encounter (see "Is a Puzzle an Encounter?" on page 81), treat it as a monster. If the puzzle is the entire encounter, treat it as a solo monster. If it's part of an encounter that also includes traps or monsters, count it as one or two monsters, depending on how hard it is and how important it is for the characters to solve it.

## VARYING THE RATE OF ADVANCEMENT

The experience point numbers in the game are built so that characters complete eight to ten encounters for every level they gain. In practice, that's six to eight encounters, one major quest, and one minor quest per character in the party.

If you were to start a campaign with 1st-level characters on January 1st, play faithfully for four or five hours every week, and manage to finish four encounters every session, your characters would enter the paragon tier during or after your session on June 24th, reach epic levels in December, and hit 30th level the next summer. Most campaigns don't move at this pace, however; you'll probably find that the natural rhythms of your campaign produce a slower rate of advancement that's easier to sustain.

If you double the XP rewards you give out, your characters will gain a level at least every other session, and hit 30th level in thirty-five sessions, or about eight months. That can be great for a campaign that runs during the school year (allowing some time for holiday breaks).

If you want to limit your campaign to a single tier (ten levels), you could cut the XP rewards in half and stretch that campaign out to nearly a year. Characters gain levels a little less often than once a month.

## SIMPLER EXPERIENCE POINTS

If you want to, you can treat experience points the same way you handle action points (see "Awarding Action Points" on page 123): Tell the players that they gain a level after they complete eight to ten encounters. Don't count really easy encounters, count really hard encounters as two, and don't worry about precise XP totals. As with action points, harder and easier encounters balance each other out over the course of that level.

## EXPERIENCE AT THE TABLE

Awarding experience points is a simple process, but it can raise a few sticky issues at the table. It's worth setting a few table rules for how you give out those rewards.

## XP PER ENCOUNTER

Some DMs prefer to give XP after every encounter. That way, they don't have to keep track of a running XP total for the session. The players are the only ones who have to worry about how many XP they've earned. Others prefer to award XP when the characters stop for an extended rest or at the end of a gaming session. It's purely a matter of personal preference, but be mindful of the pace of the session. Don't stop to give out XP if it's going to bring the game to a halt at a tense moment.

## LEVELING UP

Some DMs let characters gain the benefits of a new level as soon as they have the required XP to reach that level, while others prefer to wait until the characters take an extended rest or even until the end of a session before letting characters level up. That decision is entirely up to you. If your players are particularly slow about advancing their characters and are taking a long time to pore over the options available to them, it might be best to wait until the end of a session. If leveling up would completely shatter the pace of the session, put it off until they take an extended rest at least.

## ABSENT PLAYERS

One issue that's going to come up is how to handle experience for characters who weren't present for a session. As with other table rules, decide on a policy and stick to it, although it's all right to make an exception for the player who misses a lot of sessions for a good reason.

The game works better in a lot of ways if you just assume that the characters all gain experience and advance levels at the same rate, even if their players miss a session. You don't have to worry about players lagging behind the others, and players who miss a session don't feel like they're less effective. D&D is a cooperative game, and it's more fun when all the players are on a level playing field, able to make equal contributions to the group's success. All the players can share in the excitement of gaining a level at the same time. And it makes tracking XP much easier. In fact, a group could decide to delegate the job of tracking XP to a single player, who could announce when the characters go up a level.

The alternative, of course, is to give XP only to the characters who are present and who participate in each encounter. If a character is dead while the rest of the party faces an encounter, that character doesn't get XP for the encounter. If a player misses a session, that character doesn't get XP for the whole session. The result is that players who never miss a session get ahead of those who miss the occasional game, and eventually they wind up a level or more ahead. There's nothing wrong with that.

## QUEST REWARDS

When the characters finish a major quest that they've been pursuing for several sessions, divide the XP reward among all the characters who participated in the quest, even those who aren't present in the particular session when the PCs complete it. That's only fair—a major quest is like an encounter that stretches over multiple game sessions, and everyone who participates deserves to share in the reward.

## EXTENDED ABSENCES

Even if you don't give characters XP for sessions they missed, consider making an exception for a player who has to step out of the game for a long period because of a significant life event. When a player misses two

months of gaming because of work or school or family, it's pretty punishing to return to the game three levels behind the other characters. Discuss the situation with the other players, but strongly consider advancing the character to the same level as the rest of the group or maybe a level behind.

## CATCHING UP

If letting absent characters keep pace with the rest of the group is too hard to swallow but you don't want characters lagging behind, you can let them catch up a little more slowly. When a player misses a session, let the character lag behind for the next session, but award the character the XP he missed at the end of the session. Therefore, all the characters present have the same XP total at the end every session.

If a player misses multiple sessions in a row, you might require that player to attend the same number of sessions he missed before awarding the missed XP. Ultimately, it depends on how much bookkeeping you're willing to do in order to let the character catch up at the rate you want.

# QUESTS

Completing quests earns rewards for the PCs. These rewards primarily take the form of treasure (both money and items) and experience points, but quests can also have less concrete rewards. Perhaps someone owes them a favor, they've earned the respect of an organization that might give them future quests, or they've established a contact who can provide them with important information or access.

Fundamentally, a minor quest is worth the same as one monster of the quest's level, in terms of both XP and treasure rewards. A major quest is worth a whole encounter of its level. As with other rewards, all the PCs share in the rewards for quests, even if the quest was meant for an individual member of the group.

Completing a major quest is equivalent to completing an encounter, so it really feels like a significant accomplishment. The XP reward varies based on the number of characters in the group, just as the XP value for an encounter does. When a group of characters completes a 10th-level major quest, each individual in the group gets 500 XP, regardless of how many characters are in the group.

Completing a minor quest is equivalent to defeating a single monster, and that XP reward is divided among all the characters in the group. Since minor quests are more likely to be individual quests, the number of characters in the group helps determine how many minor quests the characters complete. When a group of four adventurers completes a 9th-level minor quest, each character gets 100 XP. When they complete four minor quests, they earn 400 XP.

**QUEST XP REWARDS**

| PC Level | Major Quest Reward | | | Minor Quest Reward |
|---|---|---|---|---|
| | 4 PCs | 5 PCs | 6 PCs | |
| 1st | 400 | 500 | 600 | 100 |
| 2nd | 500 | 625 | 750 | 125 |
| 3rd | 600 | 750 | 900 | 150 |
| 4th | 700 | 875 | 1,050 | 175 |
| 5th | 800 | 1,000 | 1,200 | 200 |
| 6th | 1,000 | 1,250 | 1,500 | 250 |
| 7th | 1,200 | 1,500 | 1,800 | 300 |
| 8th | 1,400 | 1,750 | 2,100 | 350 |
| 9th | 1,600 | 2,000 | 2,400 | 400 |
| 10th | 2,000 | 2,500 | 3,000 | 500 |
| 11th | 2,400 | 3,000 | 3,600 | 600 |
| 12th | 2,800 | 3,500 | 4,200 | 700 |
| 13th | 3,200 | 4,000 | 4,800 | 800 |
| 14th | 4,000 | 5,000 | 6,000 | 1,000 |
| 15th | 4,800 | 6,000 | 7,200 | 1,200 |
| 16th | 5,600 | 7,000 | 8,400 | 1,400 |
| 17th | 6,400 | 8,000 | 9,600 | 1,600 |
| 18th | 8,000 | 10,000 | 12,000 | 2,000 |
| 19th | 9,600 | 12,000 | 14,400 | 2,400 |
| 20th | 11,200 | 14,000 | 16,800 | 2,800 |
| 21st | 12,800 | 16,000 | 19,200 | 3,200 |
| 22nd | 16,600 | 20,750 | 24,900 | 4,150 |
| 23rd | 20,400 | 25,500 | 30,600 | 5,100 |
| 24th | 24,200 | 30,250 | 36,300 | 6,050 |
| 25th | 28,000 | 35,000 | 42,000 | 7,000 |
| 26th | 36,000 | 45,000 | 54,000 | 9,000 |
| 27th | 44,000 | 55,000 | 66,000 | 11,000 |
| 28th | 52,000 | 65,000 | 78,000 | 13,000 |
| 29th | 60,000 | 75,000 | 90,000 | 15,000 |
| 30th | 76,000 | 95,000 | 114,000 | 19,000 |

Even though the XP reward for a major quest is the same as the reward for an encounter, don't count a quest as an encounter for the purposes of earning action points. Characters need to complete two actual encounters to gain an action point.

If you want to, you can attach a treasure reward to a quest as well as XP. Treat a quest just like an encounter for purposes of treasure. You can assign one or more treasure parcels (see page 126) to its completion, or you can put all the treasure in the dungeon. Sometimes the person who gave the PCs a quest gives them a payment for completing it. Sometimes the characters collect a bounty on the head of a dangerous criminal or receive a goodwill offering collected by the families and friends of the prisoners they rescued and escorted back to safety.

# MILESTONES

If the characters complete multiple encounters without resting, they reach milestones. "Reaching a milestone" means completing two encounters without taking an extended rest. For every two encounters the characters complete between extended rests, they reach a milestone.

## AWARDING ACTION POINTS

When characters reach milestones, they get action points. Action points help balance the depletion of character resources (expended daily powers and healing surges) by providing a new resource that can help characters adventure longer before taking an extended rest.

Characters have 1 action point when they complete an extended rest. When they reach a milestone, they gain another action point. They gain additional action points after every milestone. When they take an extended rest, they lose any unspent action points and start the next day with 1 action point again.

## VARYING ACTION POINT REWARDS

You're well within your rights to tell the players that an encounter doesn't count toward a milestone. An encounter that's two or more levels lower than the characters is really easy, and it shouldn't contribute toward a milestone.

Likewise, if the characters overcome an encounter that's really hard, you can count it as two encounters, so they reach a milestone right away. An encounter that's four or more levels higher than the characters should count as two encounters.

If you vary encounter difficulty within a more normal range—one level below to two or three levels above the characters' level—just count each encounter as one. The harder encounters balance out the easier ones.

EVA WIDERMANN

Treasure rewards come in two basic flavors: magic items and monetary treasure. Magic items include all the magic weapons, armor, gear, and wondrous items detailed in the *Player's Handbook* and other sources. Monetary treasure includes coins (silver, gold, and platinum), precious gems, and valuable objects of art. Over the course of an adventure, characters acquire treasure of all kinds.

## Monetary Treasure

Monetary treasure doesn't have a level, but it has a similar economy. Gold coins are the standard coins of treasure hoards from 1st level through the paragon tier. At the lowest levels, characters might find silver coins as well, but that mundane coinage disappears from dungeon treasures after about 5th level.

In the mid-paragon tier, platinum coins start appearing in treasures. One platinum piece (pp) is worth 100 gp and weighs the same as 1 gold piece, so it's a much easier way to transport the quantities of wealth that high-level characters possess. By the time characters reach epic level, they rarely see gold any more. Platinum is the new standard.

In the mid-epic tier, a new currency comes into play: astral diamonds. These precious gems are used as currency in the Elemental Chaos and in any divine dominions that have commercial economies. One astral diamond (ad) is worth 100 pp or 10,000 gp, and 10 ad weigh as much as one gold or platinum coin—so 500 ad weigh one pound. Astral diamonds never completely replace platinum, but they're a useful measure of wealth in the high epic tier. Astral diamonds are most commonly found in strings of five or ten, linked together in settings of mithral or silver.

## Gems

Precious gems are as good as currency. Characters can cash them out at full value or use them to purchase expensive items. Gemstones come in four common values: 100 gp, 500 gp, 1,000 gp, and 5,000 gp. The most common examples of each value are shown on the lists below. (Numerous kinds of gems exist.) Astral diamonds are technically gemstones worth 10,000 gp apiece, but they are more often used as currency in their own right.

### GEMSTONES

**100 gp Gems:** amber, amethyst, garnet, moonstone, jade, pearl, peridot, turquoise
**500 gp Gems:** alexandrite, aquamarine, black pearl, topaz
**1,000 gp Gems:** emerald, fire opal, sapphire
**5,000 gp Gems:** diamond, jacinth, ruby

Gems appear in treasures beginning at 1st level. In the paragon tier, 100 gp gems are rare. Gems worth 500 gp start appearing in 5th-level treasures and fade out in the paragon tier. Gems worth 1,000 gp appear from the middle of the heroic tier to the high end of the paragon tier. The most precious gems occur only in paragon and epic treasures.

## Art Objects

Art objects include idols of solid gold, necklaces dripping with gems, old paintings of ancient monarchs, bejeweled golden chalices, and more. Art objects found as treasure are at least reasonably portable, as opposed to enormous statues (even if they are made of solid platinum) or tapestries woven with gold thread.

In the heroic tier, characters commonly find art objects worth 250 gp or 1,500 gp. At paragon levels, items worth 2,500 gp or 7,500 gp appear. At high paragon and epic levels, items worth 15,000 gp and 50,000 gp appear in treasures as well. Examples of each category of item appear on the lists below.

### ART OBJECTS

**250 gp Art Objects:** gold ring with 100 gp gem, bone or ivory statuette, gold bracelet, silver necklace, bronze crown, silver-plated sword, silk robe
**1,500 gp Art Objects:** gold ring with 1,000 gp gem, gold or silver statuette, gold bracelet with 500 gp gems, gold necklace with 100 gp gems, silver tiara or crown with 100 gp gems, ivory comb with 500 gp gems, cloth of gold vestments
**2,500 gp Art Objects:** gold or platinum ring with 1,000 gp gems, gold or silver statuette with 500 gp gems, gold necklace with 500 gp gems, gold crown with 500 gp gems, gold chalice with 100 gp gems, ceremonial gold breastplate
**7,500 gp Art Objects:** platinum ring with 5,000 gp gem, gold statuette with 1,000 gp gems, mithral necklace with 1,000 gp gems, adamantine crown with 1,000 gp gems, adamantine box containing elemental flame, black tunic woven of pure shadow
**15,000 gp Art Objects:** mithral ring with an astral diamond, gold statuette with 5,000 gp gems, gold necklace with 5,000 gp gems, mithral tiara with 5,000 gp gems, cup of celestial gold that glows with a soft inner light, silvery cloak of astral thread, enormous emerald or sapphire

---

### ASTRAL DIAMONDS

Astral diamonds are clear, faceted crystals that glow with a faint silvery light. Some legitimate operations mine astral diamonds in the divine dominions that float through the Astral Sea, particularly in Mount Celestia and the hinterlands of the Bright City. Secret mines also exist in other dominions. Abandoned dominions are poor sources for astral diamonds, but characters venturing to those desolate landscapes might find both operating mines and abandoned ones that are dangerous epic dungeons.

**50,000 gp Art Objects:** bracelet formed of cold elemental lightning, gown woven of elemental water, brass ring with bound elemental fire, celestial gold statuette with astral diamonds, royal attire of astral thread with 5,000 gp gems, enormous diamond or ruby

Many of the most precious art objects include material from the Elemental Chaos or the Astral Sea and its dominions. None have any magical effect, however, and even elemental fire is stripped of its heat in the crafting process so it can't do any damage (to its wearer or an enemy).

# Magic Items

All the magic items in the *Player's Handbook* have a level. When characters risk life and limb in adventures, they find magic items of higher level than their own level. Players enjoy finding powerful items, and they have a strong incentive to use those items rather than sell or disenchant them for a fraction of their value. When they use their own resources to acquire magic items, they buy or create items of their own level or lower. These items are useful and can be important, but they don't have the wonder and excitement of the items players find on their adventures—and that's intentional.

# Awarding Treasure

While experience points are fundamentally an encounter-based (or quest) reward, treasure is a larger-scale reward doled out over the course of an adventure. You plan treasure in terms of the eight to ten encounters it takes characters to advance from one level to the next.

During the course of gaining that level, expect a group of five characters to acquire four magic items ranging in level from one to four levels above the party level. In addition, they should find gold and other monetary treasure equal to the market price of two magic items of their level. So a 6th-level party would find four magic items, one each of levels 7 through 10, and gold worth two 6th-level items, or 3,600 gp.

At the start of an adventure, look at the adventure in chunks of eight to ten encounters. (Include major quest rewards as if they were encounters, and if the party completes five minor quests, include those five rewards as a single encounter as well.) For each of those chunks, look at the treasure parcels on the following pages. Find the level of the characters as they work through those encounters, and note the parcels of treasure you will give out over the course of the encounters.

If your group has more than five characters, add a parcel for each additional character, as shown below. If you have fewer than five characters, remove parcels accordingly.

## CHARACTER GROUP SIZE AND TREASURE PARCELS

**8 Characters:** Add three parcels: a magic item of Level + 3, a magic item of Level + 2, and a magic item of Level + 1.

**7 Characters:** Add two parcels: a magic item of Level + 2 and a magic item of Level + 1.

**6 Characters:** Add one parcel: a magic item of Level + 2.

**5 Characters:** Use the parcels as given.

**4 Characters:** Remove parcel 3 (a magic item of Level + 2).

**3 Characters:** Remove parcel 2 (a magic item of Level + 3) and parcel 4 (a magic item of Level + 1).

**2 Characters:** Remove parcel 1 (a magic item of Level + 4), parcel 2 (a magic item of Level + 3), and parcel 4 (a magic item of Level + 1).

**1 Character:** Remove parcel 1 (a magic item of Level + 4), parcel 2 (a magic item of Level + 3), parcel 4 (a magic item of Level + 1), and parcel 5.

If you want to, you can give the characters one parcel of treasure after each encounter they complete (including one for a major quest reward, if appropriate). It's more interesting, however, to combine some parcels into larger hoards and leave some encounters with no treasure at all. Sometimes it's a good idea to include treasures with no associated encounter, such as a hidden cache of gold or stashed item that the characters can find with careful searching after they've overcome a few encounters. In any event, when you give out one parcel of treasure, cross it off your list.

The trickiest part of awarding treasure is determining what magic items to give out. Tailor these items to your party of characters. Remember that these are supposed to be items that excite the characters, items they want to use rather than sell or disenchant. If none of the characters in your 6th-level party uses a longbow, don't put a 10th-level longbow in your dungeon as treasure.

A great way to make sure you give players magic items they'll be excited about is to ask them for wish lists. At the start of each level, have each player write down a list of three to five items that they are intrigued by that are no more than four levels above their own level. You can choose treasure from those lists (making sure to place an item from a different character's list each time), crossing the items off as the characters find them. If characters don't find things on their lists, they can purchase or enchant them when they reach sufficient level.

Each set of ten treasure parcels includes one less magic item than there are characters in the party. That's not meant to be unfair, just to make sure that characters gain magic items at a manageable rate. Make sure that over the course of several levels of adventuring, you award items evenly to all the characters, so that over the course of, say, five levels, every character has acquired four useful and exciting items. The monetary rewards included in the treasure parcels should also allow characters to buy or enchant items of their level or lower.

# Treasure Parcels

The lists in the following pages show treasure parcels for each character level from 1st to 30th.

**Mix:** The first four parcels at each level are individual magic items, and the rest are monetary treasure parcels. Each monetary treasure parcel is expressed in three different ways—various amounts of coinage, gems, and art objects, and sometimes potions or elixirs.

**Combining Parcels:** Remember that you can combine parcels to make some larger treasures. Try to find a balance between the excitement of finding a large treasure hoard and the regular reward of finding several smaller treasures. As a quick rule of thumb, over the course of eight to ten encounters, use one treasure hoard of three parcels, two treasures of two parcels each, and three treasures with a single parcel. That leaves two to four encounters with no treasure reward.

**Potions:** Keep an eye on how many potions you give the characters. Don't give out more than about three to five potions over the course of a level. The potions in these lists include only those that are in the *Player's Handbook*—potions of healing, vitality, recovery, and *life*. If you want to include potions from other sources, insert them into parcels using their market price as part of a monetary treasure parcel's value.

## Heroic Tier Treasure Parcels

### Party Level 1 — Total Monetary Treasure: 720 gp

1. Magic item, level 5
2. Magic item, level 4
3. Magic item, level 3
4. Magic item, level 2
5. 200 gp, or two 100 gp gems, or two *potions of healing* + 100 gp
6. 180 gp, or one 100 gp gem + 80 gp, or one *potion of healing* + 130 gp
7. 120 gp, or one 100 gp gem + 20 gp, or one *potion of healing* + 70 gp
8. 120 gp, or 100 gp + 200 sp, or one 100 gp gem + 200 sp
9. 60 gp, or one *potion of healing* + 10 gp, or 50 gp + 100 sp
10. 40 gp, or 400 sp, or 30 gp + 100 sp

### Party Level 2 — Total Monetary Treasure: 1,040 gp

1. Magic item, level 6
2. Magic item, level 5
3. Magic item, level 4
4. Magic item, level 3
5. 290 gp, or two 100 gp gems + 90 gp, or two *potions of healing* + 190 gp
6. 260 gp, or one 250 gp art object + 10 gp, or two *potions of healing* + one 100 gp gem + 60 gp
7. 170 gp, or one 100 gp gem + 70 gp, or one 100 gp gem + one *potion of healing* + 20 gp
8. 170 gp, or 150 gp + 200 sp, or one 100 gp gem + 70 gp
9. 90 gp, or one *potion of healing* + 40 gp, or 60 gp + 300 sp
10. 60 gp, or 30 gp + 300 sp, or one *potion of healing* + 10 gp

### Party Level 3 — Total Monetary Treasure: 1,355 gp

1. Magic item, level 7
2. Magic item, level 6
3. Magic item, level 5
4. Magic item, level 4
5. 380 gp, or one 250 gp art object + 130 gp, or two *potions of healing* + two 100 gp gems + 80 gp
6. 340 gp, or three 100 gp gems + 40 gp, or one *potion of healing* + one 250 gp art object + 40 gp
7. 225 gp, or two 100 gp gems + 25 gp, or one 100 gp gem + one *potion of healing* + 75 gp
8. 225 gp, or two 100 gp gems + 250 sp, or 180 gp + 450 sp
9. 110 gp, or one *potion of healing* + 60 gp, or 80 gp + 300 sp
10. 75 gp, or 50 gp + 250 sp, or one *potion of healing* + 25 gp

### Party Level 4 — Total Monetary Treasure: 1,680 gp

1. Magic item, level 8
2. Magic item, level 7
3. Magic item, level 6
4. Magic item, level 5
5. 470 gp, or one 250 gp art object + two *potions of healing* + 120 gp, or four 100 gp gems + 70 gp
6. 420 gp, or one 250 gp art object + 170 gp, or three 100 gp gems + one *potion of healing* + 70 gp
7. 280 gp, or two 100 gp gems + 80 gp, or one 100 gp gem + two *potions of healing* + 80 gp
8. 280 gp, or one 250 gp art object + 30 gp, or 250 gp + 300 sp
9. 140 gp, or one 100 gp gem + 40 gp, or one *potion of healing* + 90 gp
10. 90 gp, or 50 gp + 400 sp, or one *potion of healing* + 40 gp

### Party Level 5 — Total Monetary Treasure: 2,000 gp

1. Magic item, level 9
2. Magic item, level 8
3. Magic item, level 7
4. Magic item, level 6
5. 550 gp, or two 250 gp art objects + 50 gp, or one 500 gp gem + 50 gp
6. 500 gp, or one 250 gp art object + 250 gp, or five 100 gp gems
7. 340 gp, or three 100 gp gems + 40 gp, or one 250 gp art object + one *potion of healing* + 40 gp
8. 340 gp, or one 250 gp art object + 90 gp, or 300 gp + 400 sp
9. 160 gp, or one 100 gp gem + 60 gp, or one *potion of healing* + 110 gp
10. 110 gp, or one 100 gp gem + 10 gp, or one *potion of healing* + 60 gp

### Party Level 6 — Total Monetary Treasure: 3,600 gp

1. Magic item, level 10
2. Magic item, level 9
3. Magic item, level 8
4. Magic item, level 7
5. 1,000 gp, or one 500 gp gem + one 250 gp art object + 250 gp, or two 250 gp art objects + 500 gp
6. 900 gp, or one 500 gp gem + 400 gp, or one 250 gp art object + 650 gp
7. 600 gp, or four 100 gp gems + 200 gp, or one 250 gp art object + two *potions of healing* + 250 gp
8. 600 gp, or two 250 gp art objects + 100 gp, or two 100 gp gems + 400 gp
9. 300 gp, or one 250 gp art object + 50 gp, or one *potion of healing* + two 100 gp gems + 50 gp
10. 200 gp, or two 100 gp gems, or two *potions of healing* + 100 gp

## Party Level 7 — Total Monetary Treasure: 5,200 gp

1 Magic item, level 11
2 Magic item, level 10
3 Magic item, level 9
4 Magic item, level 8
5 1,500 gp, or two 500 gp gems + 500 gp, or one 1,000 gp gem + 500 gp
6 1,300 gp, or one 500 gp gem + 800 gp, or five 250 gp art objects + one *potion of healing*
7 850 gp, or three 250 gp art objects + two *potions of healing*, or six 100 gp gems + 250 gp
8 850 gp, or two 250 gp art objects + 350 gp, or four 100 gp gems + 450 gp
9 400 gp, or one 250 gp art object + 150 gp, or three *potions of healing* + 250 gp
10 300 gp, or one 250 gp art object + 50 gp, or three 100 gp gems

## Party Level 8 — Total Monetary Treasure: 6,800 gp

1 Magic item, level 12
2 Magic item, level 11
3 Magic item, level 10
4 Magic item, level 9
5 1,900 gp, or one 1,000 gp gem + 900 gp, or one 1,500 gp art object + 400 gp
6 1,700 gp, or one 1,500 gp art object + 200 gp, or three 500 gp gems + 200 gp
7 1,100 gp, or two 500 gp gems + 100 gp, or one 1,000 gp gem + 100 gp
8 1,100 gp, or two 250 gp art objects + 600 gp, or eleven 100 gp gems
9 600 gp, or one 500 gp gem + 100 gp, or two 250 gp art objects + one 100 gp gem
10 400 gp, or one 250 gp art object + 150 gp, or four 100 gp gems

## Party Level 9 — Total Monetary Treasure: 8,400 gp

1 Magic item, level 13
2 Magic item, level 12
3 Magic item, level 11
4 Magic item, level 10
5 2,400 gp, or two 1,000 gp gems + 400 gp, or one 1,500 gp art object + 900 gp
6 2,100 gp, or four 500 gp gems + 100 gp, or one 1,500 gp art object + 600 gp
7 1,400 gp, or one 1,000 gp gem + 400 gp, or four 250 gp art objects + 400 gp
8 1,400 gp, or two 500 gp gems + 400 gp, or three 250 gp art objects + 650 gp
9 700 gp, or seven 100 gp gems, or five *potions of healing* + 450 gp
10 400 gp, or four 100 gp gems, or one 250 gp art object + 150 gp

## Party Level 10 — Total Monetary Treasure: 10,000 gp

1 Magic item, level 14
2 Magic item, level 13
3 Magic item, level 12
4 Magic item, level 11
5 2,800 gp, or one 2,500 gp art object + 300 gp, or two 1,000 gp gems + 800 gp
6 2,500 gp, or one 1,500 gp art object + one 1,000 gp gem, or two 1,000 gp gems + one 500 gp gem
7 1,700 gp, or one 1,000 gp gem + 700 gp, or one 1,500 gp art object + 200 gp
8 1,700 gp, or one 1,500 gp art object + two 100 gp gems, or six 250 gp art objects + 200 gp
9 800 gp, or three 250 gp art objects + 50 gp, or eight 100 gp gems
10 500 gp, or two 250 gp art objects, or one 500 gp gem

# PARAGON TIER TREASURE PARCELS

## Party Level 11 — Total Monetary Treasure: 18,000 gp

1 Magic item, level 15
2 Magic item, level 14
3 Magic item, level 13
4 Magic item, level 12
5 5,000 gp, or two 2,500 gp art objects, or one 5,000 gp gem
6 4,000 gp, or four 1,000 gp gems, or two 1,500 gp art objects + one 1,000 gp gem
7 3,000 gp, or two 1,500 gp art objects, or three 1,000 gp gems
8 3,000 gp, or one 2,500 gp art object + 500 gp, or one *potion of vitality* + two 1,000 gp gems
9 2,000 gp, or two 1,000 gp gems, or one 1,500 gp art object + 500 gp
10 1,000 gp, or two 500 gp gems, or one *potion of vitality*

## Party Level 12 — Total Monetary Treasure: 26,000 gp

1 Magic item, level 16
2 Magic item, level 15
3 Magic item, level 14
4 Magic item, level 13
5 7,200 gp, or one 5,000 gp gem + two 1,000 gp gems + 200 gp, or seven 1,000 gp gems + 200 gp
6 7,000 gp, or seven 1,000 gp gems, or two 2,500 gp art objects + 2,000 gp
7 4,400 gp, or two 1,500 gp art objects + 1,400 gp, or four 1,000 gp gems + 400 gp
8 4,400 gp, or one 2,500 gp art object + one 1,500 gp art object + 400 gp, or one *potion of vitality* + three 1,000 gp gems + 400 gp
9 2,000 gp, or two 1,000 gp gems, or one 1,500 gp art object + 500 gp
10 1,000 gp, or one 1,000 gp gem, or one *potion of vitality*

## Party Level 13 — Total Monetary Treasure: 34,000 gp

1 Magic item, level 17
2 Magic item, level 16
3 Magic item, level 15
4 Magic item, level 14
5 9,500 gp, or one 7,500 gp art object + 2,000 gp, or three 2,500 gp art objects + two *potions of vitality*
6 8,500 gp, or three 2,500 gp art objects + 1,000 gp, or eight 1,000 gp gems + one 500 gp gem
7 5,700 gp, or two 2,500 gp art objects + 700 gp, or one 5,000 gp gem + 700 gp
8 5,700 gp, or three 1,500 gp art objects + 1,200 gp, or five 1,000 gp gems + one 500 gp gem + 200 gp
9 2,800 gp, or one 2,500 gp art object + 300 gp, or two *potions of vitality* + 800 gp
10 1,800 gp, or one 1,000 gp gem + 800 gp, or one 1,500 gp art object + 300 gp

## Party Level 14 — Total Monetary Treasure: 42,000 gp

1 Magic item, level 18
2 Magic item, level 17
3 Magic item, level 16
4 Magic item, level 15
5 12,000 gp, or 120 pp, or four 2,500 gp art objects + 2,000 gp
6 10,000 gp, or two 5,000 gp gems, or one 7,500 gp art object + one 2,500 gp art object
7 7,000 gp, or one 5,000 gp gem + two 1,000 gp gems, or four 1,500 gp art objects + 1,000 gp
8 7,000 gp, or one 5,000 gp gem + two *potions of vitality*, or seven 1,000 gp gems
9 4,000 gp, or one 2,500 gp art object + one 1,500 gp art object, or two 1,500 gp art objects + 1,000 gp
10 2,000 gp, or two 1,000 gp gems, or one 1,000 gp gem + one *potion of vitality*

## Party Level 15 — Total Monetary Treasure: 50,000 gp

1. Magic item, level 19
2. Magic item, level 18
3. Magic item, level 17
4. Magic item, level 16
5. 14,000 gp, or 140 pp, or one 7,500 gp art object + one 5,000 gp gem + one 1,500 gp art object
6. 12,000 gp, or 120 pp, or one 7,500 gp art object + 4,500 gp
7. 8,500 gp, or one 7,500 gp art object + 1,000 gp, or one 7,500 gp art object + one 1,000 gp gem
8. 8,500 gp, or one 5,000 gp gem + one 2,500 gp art object + 1,000 gp, or eight 1,000 gp gems + 500 gp
9. 5,000 gp, or one 5,000 gp gem, or one 2,500 gp art object + one 1,500 gp art object + one *potion of vitality*
10. 2,000 gp, or two *potions of vitality*, or two 1,000 gp gems

## Party Level 16 — Total Monetary Treasure: 90,000 gp

1. Magic item, level 20
2. Magic item, level 19
3. Magic item, level 18
4. Magic item, level 17
5. 25,000 gp, or 250 pp, or five 5,000 gp gems
6. 22,000 gp, or 220 pp, or two 7,500 gp art objects + one 5,000 gp gem + 2,000 gp
7. 15,000 gp, or two 7,500 gp art objects, or three 5,000 gp gems
8. 15,000 gp, or one 7,500 gp art object + one 5,000 gp gem + two *potions of vitality* + 500 gp, or four 2,500 gp art objects + one 5,000 gp gem
9. 8,000 gp, or one 5,000 gp gem + one 2,500 gp art object + 500 gp, or one 7,500 gp art object + 500 gp
10. 5,000 gp, or one 5,000 gp gem, or two 1,500 gp art objects + two *potions of vitality*

## Party Level 17 — Total Monetary Treasure: 130,000 gp

1. Magic item, level 21
2. Magic item, level 20
3. Magic item, level 19
4. Magic item, level 18
5. 36,000 gp, or 360 pp, or two 15,000 gp art objects + one 5,000 gp gem + one *potion of vitality*
6. 33,000 gp, or 330 pp, or four 7,500 gp art objects + three 1,000 gp gems
7. 22,000 gp, or 220 pp, or four 5,000 gp gems + two 1,000 gp gems
8. 22,000 gp, or two 7,500 gp art objects + one 5,000 gp gem + 2,000 gp, or four 5,000 gp gems + two *potions of vitality*
9. 11,000 gp, or two 5,000 gp gems + 1,000 gp, or one 7,500 gp art object + two *potions of vitality* + 1,500 gp
10. 6,000 gp, or one 5,000 gp gem + 1,000 gp, or four 1,500 gp art objects

## Party Level 18 — Total Monetary Treasure: 170,000 gp

1. Magic item, level 22
2. Magic item, level 21
3. Magic item, level 20
4. Magic item, level 19
5. 48,000 gp, or 480 pp, or three 15,000 gp art objects + one 2,500 gp art object + 500 gp
6. 42,000 gp, or 420 pp, or two 15,000 gp art objects + two 5,000 gp gems + 2,000 gp
7. 29,000 gp, or 290 pp, or three 7,500 gp art objects + one 5,000 gp gem + one 1,500 gp art object
8. 29,000 gp, or five 5,000 gp gems + 4,000 gp, or one 15,000 gp art object+ one 7,500 gp art object + three *potions of vitality* + 3,500 gp
9. 15,000 gp, or three 5,000 gp gems, or two 7,500 gp art objects
10. 7,000 gp, or one 5,000 gp gem + two *potions of vitality*, or seven 1,000 gp gems

## Party Level 19 — Total Monetary Treasure: 210,000 gp

1. Magic item, level 23
2. Magic item, level 22
3. Magic item, level 21
4. Magic item, level 20
5. 60,000 gp, or 600 pp, or four 15,000 gp art objects
6. 52,000 gp, or 520 pp, or three 15,000 gp art objects + seven 1,000 gp gems
7. 35,000 gp, or 350 pp, or seven 5,000 gp gems
8. 35,000 gp, or four 7,500 gp art objects + one 5,000 gp gem, or two 15,000 gp art objects + three 1,000 gp gems + two *potions of vitality*
9. 18,000 gp, or one 15,000 gp art object + three *potions of vitality*, or three 5,000 gp gems + three 1,000 gp gems
10. 10,000 gp, or two 5,000 gp gems, or one 7,500 gp art object + one 2,500 gp art object

## Party Level 20 — Total Monetary Treasure: 250,000 gp

1. Magic item, level 24
2. Magic item, level 23
3. Magic item, level 22
4. Magic item, level 21
5. 70,000 gp, or 700 pp, or 600 pp + two 5,000 gp gems
6. 61,000 gp, or 610 pp, or four 15,000 gp art objects + 1,000 gp
7. 42,000 gp, or 420 pp, or two 15,000 gp art objects + two 5,000 gp gems + 2,000 gp
8. 42,000 gp, or 400 pp + two *potions of vitality*, or eight 5,000 gp gems + two 1,000 gp gems
9. 21,000 gp, or 210 pp, or four 5,000 gp gems + one *potion of vitality*
10. 14,000 gp, or twp 5,000 gp gems + one 2,500 gp art object + 1,500 gp, or one 7,500 gp art object + one 5,000 gp gem + one *potion of vitality* + 500 gp

# Epic Tier Treasure Parcels

## Party Level 21 — Total Monetary Treasure: 4,500 pp

1. Magic item, level 25
2. Magic item, level 24
3. Magic item, level 23
4. Magic item, level 22
5. 1,250 pp, or two *potions of recovery* + one 50,000 gp art object + five 5,000 gp gems, or two 50,000 gp art objects + five 5,000 gp gems
6. 1,120 pp, or 1,000 pp + two 5,000 gp gems + two *potions of vitality*, or one 50,000 gp art object + four 15,000 gp art objects + 2,000 gp
7. 750 pp, or five 15,000 gp art objects, or 700 pp + one 5,000 gp gem
8. 750 pp, or 600 pp + three 5,000 gp gems, or 500 pp + one *potion of recovery*
9. 380 pp, or two 15,000 gp art objects + one 5,000 gp gem + three *potions of vitality*, or five 7,500 gp art objects + 500 gp
10. 250 pp, or five 5,000 gp gems, or three 7,500 gp art objects + 2,500 gp

## Party Level 22 — Total Monetary Treasure: 6,500 pp

1. Magic item, level 26
2. Magic item, level 25
3. Magic item, level 24
4. Magic item, level 23
5. 1,800 pp, or 1,500 pp + six 5,000 gp gems, or three 50,000 gp art objects + two 15,000 gp art objects
6. 1,600 pp, or 1,000 pp + four 15,000 gp art objects, or three 50,000 gp art objects + two 5,000 gp gems
7. 1,100 pp, or 600 pp + two *potions of recovery*, or two 50,000 gp art objects + two 5,000 gp gems
8. 1,100 pp, or 500 pp + four 15,000 gp art objects, or 600 pp + ten 5,000 gp gems
9. 550 pp, or one *potion of recovery*+ six 5,000 gp gems, or seven 7,500 gp art objects + 25 pp
10. 350 pp, or two 15,000 gp art objects + one 5,000 gp gem, or seven 5,000 gp gems

## Party Level 23    Total Monetary Treasure: 8,500 pp

1. Magic item, level 27
2. Magic item, level 26
3. Magic item, level 25
4. Magic item, level 24
5. 2,400 pp, or 2,000 pp + two 15,000 gp art objects + two 5,000 gp gems, or four 50,000 gp art objects + two 15,000 gp art objects + two 5,000 gp gems
6. 2,100 pp, or 1,600 pp + one 50,000 gp art object, or two *potions of recovery* + four 15,000 gp art objects
7. 1,400 pp, or 1,000 pp + one *potion of recovery* + one 15,000 gp art object, or two 50,000 gp art objects + two 15,000 gp art objects + two 5,000 gp gems
8. 1,400 pp, or 450 pp + one 50,000 gp art object + three 15,000 gp art objects, or one *potion of recovery*+ two 50,000 gp art objects + three 5,000 gp gems
9. 700 pp, or four 15,000 gp art objects + two 5,000 gp gems, or two *potions of recovery* + four 5,000 gp gems
10. 500 pp, or one *potion of recovery* + five 5,000 gp gems, or one 50,000 gp art object

## Party Level 24    Total Monetary Treasure: 10,500 pp

1. Magic item, level 28
2. Magic item, level 27
3. Magic item, level 26
4. Magic item, level 25
5. 3,000 pp, or one *potion of life* + 20 ad, or six 50,000 gp art objects
6. 2,500 pp, or 20 ad + one *potion of recovery* + five 5,000 gp gems, or 1,000 pp + three 50,000 gp art objects
7. 1,750 pp, or 1,000 pp + one *potion of recovery* + one 50,000 gp art object, or 15 ad + five 5,000 gp gems
8. 1,750 pp, or 1,500 pp + one 15,000 gp art object + two 5,000 gp gems, or 1,500 pp + one *potion of recovery*
9. 900 pp, or six 15,000 gp art objects, or one 50,000 gp art object + 400 pp
10. 600 pp, or two 15,000 gp art objects + one *potion of recovery* + 5,000 gp, or 300 pp + six 5,000 gp gems

## Party Level 25    Total Monetary Treasure: 12,500 pp

1. Magic item, level 29
2. Magic item, level 28
3. Magic item, level 27
4. Magic item, level 26
5. 3,500 pp, or 20 ad + one *potion of life* + one 50,000 gp art object, or 30 ad + two *potions of recovery*
6. 3,200 pp, or 20 ad + two *potions of recovery* + one 50,000 gp art object + 200 pp, or 30 ad + four 5,000 gp gems
7. 2,000 pp, or 20 ad, or 10 ad + four 15,000 gp art objects + eight 5,000 gp gems
8. 2,000 pp, or 1,000 pp + two 50,000 gp art objects, or four 50,000 gp art objects
9. 1,000 pp, or one *potion of life*, or twenty 5,000 gp gems
10. 800 pp, or five 15,000 gp art objects + one 5,000 gp gem, or one 50,000 gp art object + six 5,000 gp gems

## Party Level 26    Total Monetary Treasure: 22,500 pp

1. Magic item, level 30
2. Magic item, level 29
3. Magic item, level 28
4. Magic item, level 27
5. 6,250 pp, or 50 ad + 750 pp + one 50,000 gp art object, or twelve 50,000 gp art objects + one *potion of recovery*
6. 5,600 pp, or 40 ad + one *potion of life* + two *potions of recovery* + two 5,000 gp gems, or 50 ad + one 50,000 gp art object + 1,000 pp
7. 3,750 pp, or 20 ad + three *potions of recovery* + two 50,000 gp art objects, or 30 ad + one 50,000 gp art object + five 5,000 gp gems
8. 3,750 pp, or 20 ad + 1,750 pp, or one *potion of life* + 2,750 pp
9. 1,900 pp, or three 50,000 gp art objects + 400 pp, or 15 ad + 400 pp
10. 1,250 pp, or 10 ad + one *potion of recovery*, or one 50,000 gp art object + five 15,000 gp art objects

## Party Level 27    Total Monetary Treasure: 32,500 pp

1. Magic item, level 30
2. Magic item, level 30
3. Magic item, level 29
4. Magic item, level 28
5. 9,000 pp, or 90 ad, or 50 ad + one *potion of life* + six 50,000 gp art objects
6. 8,000 pp, or 80 ad, or 75 ad + two *potions of recovery*
7. 5,500 pp, or 55 ad, or 50 ad + 500 pp
8. 5,500 pp, or one *potion of life* + thirty 15,000 gp art objects, or 50 ad + three 15,000 gp art objects + 500 pp
9. 2,800 pp, or 25 ad + 300 pp, or 25 ad + one *potion of recovery* + one 5,000 gp gem
10. 1,700 pp, or 15 ad + 200 pp, or 10 ad + four 15,000 gp art objects + two 5,000 gp gems

## Party Level 28    Total Monetary Treasure: 42,500 pp

1. Magic item, level 30
2. Magic item, level 30
3. Magic item, level 30
4. Magic item, level 29
5. 12,000 pp, or 120 ad, or 60 ad + two *potions of life* + eight 50,000 gp art objects
6. 10,000 pp, or 100 ad, or 50 ad + five 50,000 gp art objects + 2,500 pp
7. 7,200 pp, or 70 ad + 200 pp, or 35 ad + six 50,000 gp art objects + 700 pp
8. 7,200 pp, or 50 ad + four 50,000 gp art objects + 200 pp, or 60 ad + one *potion of life* + 200 pp
9. 3,600 pp, or 35 ad + 100 pp, or six 50,000 gp art objects + two *potions of recovery* + 100 pp
10. 2,500 pp, or 25 ad, or five 50,000 gp art objects

## Party Level 29    Total Monetary Treasure: 52,500 pp

1. Magic item, level 30
2. Magic item, level 30
3. Magic item, level 30
4. Magic item, level 30
5. 15,000 pp, or 150 ad, or 100 ad + one *potion of life* + six 50,000 gp art objects
6. 13,000 pp, or 130 ad, or 100 ad + 3,000 pp
7. 8,750 pp, or 85 ad + 250 pp. or 40 ad + two *potions of life* + three *potions of recovery* + four 50,000 gp art objects
8. 8,750 pp, or 55 ad + two *potions of life* + 1,250 pp, or 60 ad + two *potions of life* + 750 pp
9. 4,500 pp, or 45 ad, or 30 ad + two 50,000 gp art objects + two *potions of recovery*
10. 2,500 pp, or 25 ad, or 15 ad + 1,000 pp

## Party Level 30    Total Monetary Treasure: 62,500 pp

1. Two magic items, level 30
2. Magic item, level 30
3. Magic item, level 30
4. Magic item, level 30
5. 17,500 pp, or 175 ad, or three *potions of life* + ten 50,000 gp art objects + 95 ad
6. 15,000 pp, or 150 ad, or 80 ad + two *potions of life* + ten 50,000 gp art objects
7. 10,000 pp, or 100 ad, or 50 ad + four *potions of recovery* + six 50,000 gp art objects + 1,000 pp
8. 10,000 pp, or 80 ad + 2,000 pp, or 25 ad + ten 50,000 gp art objects + 2,500 pp
9. 6,000 pp, or 60 ad, or 25 ad + five 50,000 gp art objects + 1,000 pp
10. 4,000 pp, or 40 ad, or two *potions of life* + four 50,000 gp art objects

# CHAPTER 8

# CAMPAIGNS

JUST AS a D&D adventure is a series of encounters strung together into an overarching story, a campaign is a larger story that ties those adventures together. When you're ready to construct your own campaign, let this chapter be your guide.

At its most fundamental level, a campaign is the story of the characters in your game. You don't have to give a lot more thought to it than that: It's fine to run adventures in an episodic format, with the characters as the only common element. But you can also weave themes through those adventures to build a greater saga of those characters' achievements in the world.

Planning an entire campaign seems a daunting task, but don't worry—you don't have to plot out every detail right from the start. You can start off with the basics, running a few adventures (whether published or those you design yourself), and later think about larger plotlines you want to explore. You're free to add as much or as little detail as you wish.

This chapter includes the following sections.

✦ **Published Campaigns:** An overview of how published campaigns can give your campaign a solid start and lots of fuel for adventures to come.

✦ **Campaign Theme:** Ideas for creating a campaign from adventures with a common link.

✦ **Super Adventures:** How to build a campaign consisting of just one long adventure.

✦ **Campaign Story.** Advice on developing the campaign, looking toward its conclusion, and planning how the characters will get there.

✦ **Beginning a Campaign.** How to get started—keep it small at first.

✦ **Running a Campaign.** Tying adventures together in a way that makes sense.

✦ **Ending a Campaign.** How to bring the story to its natural conclusion, in a fun and satisfying way.

You don't have to create an entire campaign from nothing. A published campaign makes starting and running a game as easy as possible.

Chapter 11 of this book presents a brief example of a published campaign. It includes a starting area, a short adventure, and plot hooks and story ideas for further development. You can continue from that starting point, using other published adventures (for example, *Keep on the Shadowfell*, *Thunderspire Labyrinth*, and *Pyramid of Shadows*) or designing stories of your own.

A complete campaign setting, such as the FORGOTTEN REALMS setting, goes quite a bit farther than this introduction. A published campaign isn't quite like a published adventure. You can run an adventure right away, with only a minimum of preparation, or customize it to fit your play group. Although you can start a published campaign as soon as you crack open the book, you'll get more out of using the tools and ideas it contains as inspiration for crafting your own adventures in that setting.

The *FORGOTTEN REALMS Campaign Guide* provides a starting area–the town of Loudwater–complete with interesting characters and encounters, but that's just a taste of what awaits. That town lies in the Gray Vale, just one region in a richly detailed fantasy world. The FORGOTTEN REALMS setting is full of mysterious ruins, evil plots, and deadly threats. You can build your own adventures from those details, use published ones set in that world, or draw on years of FORGOTTEN REALMS novels for inspiration. The *Campaign Guide* will help you weave those ideas together with story threads to bring the campaign setting to life. Your players can even make characters custom-fitted for the world, using the rules in the *FORGOTTEN REALMS Player's Guide*. Everything you need to keep a campaign going for years is readily available in these resources.

## CHARACTER ORIGIN AND BACKGROUND

The *Player's Guide* for a published campaign gives your players rules and background information to make characters who feel as though they belong in the setting. Your job is to find common threads to tie those characters together at the start of the campaign. In a FORGOTTEN REALMS campaign, for example, one player might bring a heroic scion native to the Gray Vale, reared on tales of her parents' and grandparents' adventures. Another might play a horse barbarian from Narfell, traveling the world in search of a way to free his homeland from the icy grip of winter. A

third character could be an escaped slave from Thay, haunted by years of servitude in that land of evil magic.

With just these simple backgrounds, your players have already given you a lot to work with. Start by learning more about Thay and Narfell in the *Campaign Guide* and think about what led those characters to the Gray Vale or why they met. You can also let your players take on that responsibility: They can play characters of any background, but they have to give a good reason for them to be in the starting area. (This tactic is also an incentive for players to learn more about the world.) Perhaps the escaped slave has heard whispered tales of the heroic scion's grandparents, who won renown fighting against the Red Wizards of Thay a hundred years ago, and has come seeking them. The slave might have run into the horse nomad during their travels, regaling him with tales of those legendary figures and inspiring him to seek them out as well. How will the two react when they find out that the great heroes' only surviving heir is no more accomplished an adventurer than they? Your campaign is off to an interesting start.

## THE CAMPAIGN START

A setting's *Campaign Guide* provides introductory material to familiarize yourself and your players with the setting. You can get going right away in the starting location, and the book supplies a few short adventures as well as pointers to further story ideas. While you're playing through these, look for hints, plots, and other hooks that grab the attention of you or your players. You can develop your campaign by following those ideas to interesting parts of the world.

On the flip side, you might first read through the *Campaign Guide* to find a story element that captures your imagination, then plant the seeds of that story in the very first adventure. To grow the campaign, work in some connection to the larger world–ties between the adventure's main antagonist and a larger villainous organization, or foreshadowing of some greater threat to come. Now you're ready for the next steps.

## NEXT STEPS

By the time you get close to wrapping up the introductory adventures of your campaign, you should have some idea of what to do next. Maybe you'd like to run another published adventure, or you feel ready to strike out on your own. Either way, you'll need to come up with a theme.

A campaign's theme has a clear direction and gives the players a sense of purpose. (There's more about campaign themes in the next section.) It might be an exciting villain whom you want to expand on, an organization that sponsors adventurers, or a world-shaking threat that grows more urgent as the campaign progresses. Your theme can carry your campaign all the way to epic levels, or be a short-term issue that evolves or disappears as time goes by. It might fit in neatly with elements at the start of the campaign or be completely unrelated—it's all right to shift gears, introducing new themes and plots after the players have gotten their feet wet.

A *Campaign Guide* is a treasury of good ideas, bundled with the tools you need to adapt them to your game. Use the guidelines in Chapter 6 to help you customize published adventures for the setting and choose the ones that work best with your campaign. Say you're running a FORGOTTEN REALMS campaign that revolves around the shades of Netheril. You can easily relate the plot of a published adventure to the far-reaching ambitions of the shades, regardless of geographic setting. You might make its key villain into a shade, then create other adventures featuring that organization more prominently. Ultimately, the characters might dare the floating cities of Netheril itself.

## MAKING IT YOURS

Even though you're using a published setting, always remember: It's still *your campaign*. You should never limit your creativity to what the book says—any book. A *Campaign Guide* is a source of ideas and a toolbox. You don't have to use that material exactly as it stands. You can and should change things you don't like, incorporate elements you like from other campaigns or adventures, and put your own distinctive stamp on the world.

Altering a published campaign to suit your tastes can be tricky if the setting is familiar to one or more of your players. It's a good idea to establish at the outset that not everything in the book is necessarily true in *your* version of the world. Otherwise, the game can get bogged down by arguments about the details, such as whether the adherents of this or that deity would do the things your adventure calls for them to do. It's your game, and the players should understand that its events make sense in your vision for the setting.

In short, use a *Campaign Guide* as it's intended—a springboard for creativity—and let your imagination run free. It doesn't matter whether you're putting your own personal stamp on a published campaign or making up your own and incorporating elements you like from a published setting. The campaign is just as much yours either way.

## LOOTING FREELY

Even if you want to create your own campaign, you don't have to do all the work yourself. A lot of really creative fantasy is already out there, and you can pick and choose from that rich body of material to make your game more colorful and exciting.

Perhaps you have an idea for a campaign with a strong elemental theme, ultimately pitting the characters against one or more primordials. Your world might incorporate the elemental-touched genasi race from the FORGOTTEN REALMS *Player's Guide,* but can also borrow heavily from other sources. The *Avatar: The Last Airbender* animated television show is full of wonderful imagery and ideas to suit an elemental plotline. The AL-QADIM campaign setting for the D&D game, published in the 1990s, drew on the legends of the Arabian Nights and featured efreets and elementals. What and how much you borrow doesn't matter. The final product is uniquely yours, and your players will marvel at its detail.

Just as the personality of a setting shapes the adventures that take place there, the theme of a campaign gives a distinctive flavor to its stories. A freewheeling series of adventures, in which the characters travel from one dungeon to another with little or no connection, feels very different from a years-long struggle against cultists of Orcus that culminates in a final showdown with the Demon Lord of the Undead himself.

This section gives overviews of some typical campaign themes, as well as different ways of handling them.

## EVOLVING THEMES

You don't have to stick with a single theme from the start of your campaign through thirty levels of play. The characters grow and change over the course of a campaign; so should your world. You can wrap up one storyline after a few levels and start a new one, or introduce multiple themes at various levels and weave them subtly together.

Breaks between tiers are natural points for concluding one theme and bringing in another. For example, the characters might spend their first twenty levels fighting the temples of evil gods, then discover the even greater threat of a primordial uprising. At epic levels, they have to join forces with the gods—including the evil ones who were their former enemies—to defeat the primordials.

## DUNGEON OF THE WEEK

This sort of campaign resembles an episodic television show. Each week, the main characters move from one distinct setting to another (a planet, a haunted house, an era of history, and so on). They solve that episode's problems, then go on their way to deal with the next. Once they're done, things return to pretty much the way they were at the start.

A "Dungeon of the Week" is the simplest kind of campaign to run, since it requires little effort beyond finding or creating adventures. Each story has its own main villain, unconnected to the antagonists of any other. The D&D world is dark and full of threats, and they don't need anything else in common.

## ON A MISSION

Only slightly more involved than an unconnected series of adventures, this campaign theme quickly links the characters' exploits with an overarching goal. It's easy to overlay a mission or similar story on otherwise independent sessions. The simplest is one of exploration: The characters set out to map the region, the continent, or the whole world, encountering threats along the way. Perhaps they seek the ancient capital of a fallen empire, or are trying to find their way back to the home they left to fight in a recent war.

Religion is a ready-made source of missions. For example, the characters could be pilgrims to some holy site, or members of a sacred order dedicated to defending the last bastions of civilization in an ever-darkening world. In more militant orders, they might be holy warriors dedicated to stamping out a particular kind of threat, such as aberrant creatures or demonic cultists. Whatever the story, it implies a stronger connection between adventures.

## ULTIMATE VILLAIN

Episodic adventures against a certain kind of opponent, such as in the "holy warrior" mission above, lead naturally to a campaign focused on a single villain who's ultimately behind everything. The characters might begin their careers fighting goblins and kobolds, only to discover that those monsters are the servants of foulspawn. Their continuing adventures lead them into the horrors of the Far Realm's influence, with battles against aboleths and illithids, climaxing in an epic struggle against a mind flayer mastermind and its swordwing minions. That aberrant mastermind need not have been directly involved in the characters' first adventures, but the existence of even the lowly foulspawn can be traced to its activities.

You can build a villain-focused campaign from the top down or from the bottom up. In the first method, you first choose an epic villain for the campaign's climactic battle (Orcus, for example), and then plan adventures toward that conclusion from the start of the campaign. In the case of Orcus, these encounters build on themes of cultists, demons, and undead. In the second method, you build encounters around low-level monsters that appeal to you (such as the foulspawn) and then create adventures involving similar or related monsters at higher levels.

## RECURRING VILLAINS AND SECRET WEAKNESSES

Players can become deeply invested in a campaign whose main villain keeps coming back to vex their characters. One way to ensure that the final battle with their nemesis really is climactic is to give the villain a secret weakness. In order to ultimately destroy their archenemy, the characters need to discover this weakness and then exploit it. Then that last battle will be more than just a race to see who runs out of hit points first.

For example, every lich has a phylactery, a magical receptacle for its soul that it keeps well hidden. The characters face the lich in combat and defeat it, believing they have ended its threat, only to find later that has returned to continue its evil schemes. Now they must discover the location of the phylactery, win their way past its magical and monstrous guardians, and ultimately fight the lich again, with the phylactery hanging in the balance. Destroying the item might itself become a quest in which time is of the essence—the characters might have to perform a particular ritual, or locate the forge of the phylactery's creation to melt it down. Such a theme can carry a campaign well into the paragon tier.

Epic-level characters might have to confront and overcome a creature of enormous power, such as the tarrasque, a demon lord, a deity, or a primordial. Such beings can be defeated only with special rituals or particular items. For example, the party must quest for and assemble the scattered pieces of the *Rod of Seven Parts* to have a hope of destroying the primordial called the Queen of Chaos. Even relatively ordinary foes can return again and again, protected by some means that the characters must discover and eliminate. A vile caliph performs a ritual to remove his still-beating heart and hides it in a chest at the center of a desert sandstorm. A wicked baron is cursed to rise

from the dead until the onyx shard that holds a splinter of his soul is found and destroyed.

Naturally, when the characters start pursuing the means to kill a powerful villain, their enemy is sure to get wind of their efforts sooner or later—and try to put a stop to it. The villain will be prepared when they arrive for the ultimate confrontation or, more likely, will send out agents or otherwise try to prevent them from completing their task. The villainous response to the party's actions can produce a wealth of adventures in itself.

## WORLD-SHAKING EVENTS

A campaign featuring a major villain often revolves around a diabolical plan that will result in significant changes to the world—presumably for the worse—which the characters must stop. In other campaigns, the world faces a crisis without a villain's involvement, and the characters have to prevent or at least minimize the impact of such an event.

Campaigns of this nature have a deadline that looms over the course of dozens of adventures. The dreaded event will take place at a certain time unless the characters succeed. Perhaps the Elemental Chaos is eating away at the stable fabric of creation, drawing the world toward ultimate entropy; the characters must collect scattered shards of divine energy to shore up the pillars of creation. Or a primordial entombed at the center of the earth is extending tendrils of reality-warping energy toward the surface, forming dungeons that spew forth hideous monstrosities. The characters must clear the dungeons and cut off their connection to the primordial before they engulf what shattered remnants of civilization remain. The threat to your world might be mundane in nature, but no less devastating—in the last days of a great empire's decline, orc hordes menace the frontiers while decadence and corruption undermine the empire's foundation.

## UNFOLDING PROPHECY

This type of campaign puts an interesting spin on world-shaking events, casting them as the unfolding fulfillment of an ancient prophecy. A villain might be helping to bring about the foretold doom, furthering his own plans, or try to keep the prophecy from coming true (for example, killing the child who is destined to destroy the villain).

The beauty of a well-crafted prophecy is its ambiguity. Classical myth is full of examples of tragic misinterpretation or ultimate vindication of what has been foretold. Since it's always open to a variety of interpretations, many different ways can exist to fulfill the prophecy. The villain might try to bring it about in one way, while the characters struggle to find a solution that betters the world instead of plunging it into ruin.

# Divine Strife

The ongoing struggle between good and evil is the basis for many tales, myths, and campaigns. In a conflict between two gods, or between groups of deities with different alignments, taking sides becomes a matter of cosmic importance.

In a campaign built around divine strife, the characters aren't just fighting evil creatures—they're servants of good deities warring with the agents of evil ones. They might be champions of a single god, such as Bahamut, dedicated to overthrowing the temples of Bane. In such a storyline, the enemies of their adventures are connected to the opposing deity: priests of Bane, hobgoblin warlords devoted to that lord of conquest, and angelic servitors of the god himself. Bane might be planning to seize power from Bahamut, or to conquer the Celestial Mountain where Bahamut, Moradin, and Kord reside. Or Bahamut might instigate the struggle, bent on exterminating an ancient enemy.

# Primordial Threat

Even more fundamental to the world than conflicts among deities is the gods' ancient war with the primordials, embodiments of chaos and elemental power. From the earliest times, gods and primordials fought over ownership of the cosmos, and the gods emerged victorious. The surviving primordials could yet arise as a threat to the whole of creation, seeking to return it to the Elemental Chaos of its birth.

In the early stages of such a campaign, the characters might battle a goblin cult of a minor fire spirit, then discover that it is just one manifestation of a worldwide madness. More cults dedicated to destructive elemental forces are springing up everywhere, channeling power to the entombed primordials in preparation for their escape. Ultimately, the epic-level characters might have to fight alongside the gods themselves to oppose these mighty foes.

# Fantasy Subgenres

Dungeons & Dragons is a fantasy game, but that broad category has room for a lot of variety. Many different subgenres of fantasy exist in both fiction and film. Do you want a horrific campaign inspired by the works of H.P. Lovecraft or Clark Ashton Smith? Or a world of muscled barbarians and nimble thieves, along the lines of the classic swords-and-sorcery books by Robert E. Howard and Fritz Leiber? The D&D game can handle either of these models, and many others.

## Horror

Vampires brood on the battlements of their accursed castles. Necromancers toil in dark dungeons to create colossi of undead flesh. Devils corrupt the innocent, and werewolves prowl the night. All these elements evoke horrific aspects of the fantasy genre.

If you want to put a horror spin on your campaign, you have plenty of material to work with. The *Monster Manual* is full of creatures that perfectly suit a storyline of supernatural horror. The most important element of such a campaign, though, isn't covered by the rules. You must create an atmosphere of building dread, through careful pacing and evocative description. Your players contribute too—they have to be willing to be scared. Whether you want to run a full-fledged horror campaign or a single creepy adventure, you should discuss your plans with the players ahead of time to make sure they're on board. Horror can be intense and personal, and not everyone is comfortable with such a game.

## Intrigue

The corrupt vizier schemes with the baron's oldest daughter to assassinate the baron. A hobgoblin army sends doppelganger spies to infiltrate the city before the invasion. At the embassy ball, the spy in the royal court makes contact with his employer.

Political intrigue, espionage, sabotage, and similar cloak-and-dagger activities can make for an exciting D&D campaign. In this kind of game, the characters might care more about skill training and making contacts than about attack powers and magic weapons. Roleplaying and interaction-focused skill challenges take on greater importance than combat encounters, and the party might go for several sessions without seeing a monster.

Again, make sure your players know ahead of time that this is the kind of campaign you want to run. Otherwise, a player might make a character such as a dwarf paladin focused on defense, only to find he is out of place among the half-elf diplomats and tiefling spies.

## Mystery

Who stole three legendary magic swords and hid them away in a remote dungeon, leaving a cryptic clue to their location? Who placed the duke into a magical slumber, and what can be done to awaken him? Who murdered the guildmaster, and how did the killer get into the guild's locked vault?

A mystery-themed campaign puts the characters in the role of investigators, perhaps traveling from town to town to crack tough cases the local authorities can't handle. Such a campaign emphasizes puzzles and problem-solving in addition to combat prowess.

A larger mystery might even set the stage for the whole campaign. Why did someone kill the characters' mentor, setting them on the path of adventure? Who really controls the Cult of the Red Hand? In this case, the characters might uncover clues to the greater mystery only once in a while; individual adventures might be at best tangentially related to that theme. A diet of nothing but puzzles can become frustrating, so be sure to mix up the kinds of encounters you present.

## SWASHBUCKLING

Rapier-wielding sailors fight off boarding sahuagin. Ghouls lurk in derelict ships, waiting to devour treasure hunters. Dashing rogues and charming paladins weave their way through palace intrigues and leap from balconies onto waiting horses below.

You can have grand fun modeling your campaign on the swashbuckling adventures of pirates and musketeers. The characters typically spend more time in cities, royal courts, and seafaring vessels than in dungeon delves, making interaction skills important (though not to the extent of a pure intrigue campaign). Nevertheless, the heroes might end up in classic dungeon situations, such as searching storm sewers beneath the palace to find the evil duke's hidden chambers.

A swashbuckling theme is slightly anachronistic for the medieval setting of the D&D game, so you might want to make some cosmetic changes—particularly where heavy armor is concerned. Rapiers and acrobatic combat moves don't go well with heavy, clanking metal. The paladin who normally wears a suit of plate mail might instead sport a relatively light breastplate. In this case, you might need to adjust the armor bonus to match that of plate in a standard campaign.

## SWORDS AND SORCERY

A grim, hulking fighter disembowels the high priest of the serpent god on his own altar. A laughing rogue spends ill-gotten gains on cheap wine in filthy taverns. Hardy adventurers venture into the unexplored jungle in search of the fabled City of Golden Masks.

A swords-and-sorcery campaign is old-school D&D, a tradition that goes right back to the roots of the game. Here you'll find a dark, gritty world of evil sorcerers and decadent cities, where the protagonists are more motivated by greed and self-interest than by altruistic virtue. Martial characters tend to be far more common than arcane or divine ones. In such a pulp fantasy setting, those who wield magic often symbolize the decadence and corruption of civilization.

## WAR

A hobgoblin army marches toward the city, leading behemoths and giants to batter down its walls and ramparts. Dragons wheel above a barbarian horde, scattering enemies as the raging warriors cut a swath through field and forest. Fire archons muster at an efreet's command, poised to assault an Astral fortress.

Warfare in a fantasy world is rife with opportunities for adventure. A war campaign isn't generally concerned with the specifics of troop movements, but instead focuses on the heroes whose actions turn the tide of battle. They might be sent on specific missions: capture a magical standard that empowers undead armies, gather reinforcements to break a siege, or cut through the enemy's flank to reach a demonic commander. In other situations, the party might support the larger army, by holding a strategic location until reinforcements arrive, killing enemy scouts before they can report, or cutting off supply lines. Information gathering and diplomatic missions might supplement the more combat-oriented adventures.

## WUXIA

When their mentor disappears mysteriously, his young students must hunt down the oni that's terrorizing the village. Accomplished heroes, masters of their respective martial arts, return home to free their village from a evil hobgoblin warlord. The rakshasa master of a nearby monastery is performing rituals to raise troubled ghosts from their rest.

Chinese martial-arts movies (or Japanese anime) form a distinct fantasy tradition. A campaign that draws on these elements can still feel very much like D&D. Players can define the appearance of their characters and gear however they choose, and powers might need cosmetic changes to flavor so that they better reflect such a setting. For example, when the characters use powers that teleport them or shift them several squares, they actually make high-flying acrobatic leaps. Climb checks don't involve careful searching for holds but let characters bounce up walls or from tree to tree. Warriors stun their opponents by striking pressure points. Such flavorful descriptions of powers don't change the nuts and bolts of the rules but make all the difference in the feel of a campaign.

# VARIATIONS ON A THEME

It's a good idea to mix things up once in a while, so that your players can enjoy a variety of adventures. Even if you're running a tightly themed campaign, you can stray now and then. If your campaign involves lots of intrigue, mystery, and roleplaying, your players might enjoy the occasional dungeon crawl—in the end, it might turn out to be related to a larger plot in the campaign. If most of your adventures are dungeon expeditions, shift gears with a good urban mystery (whose solution leads the party into a kind of dungeon crawl in an abandoned building or tower). If you run horror adventures week after week, try throwing in a villain who turns out to be quite ordinary, perhaps even silly. Comic relief is a great variation on almost any D&D campaign, though players usually provide it themselves!

Make sure you provide a variety of opponents as well. Even if your campaign is all about invading hobgoblins, your players will get tired of fighting an endless series of them, week after week. Hobgoblins are accomplished beast trainers, so mix in pets and war animals to vary your encounters. Even better, take a break once in a while from the hobgoblin armies and introduce a new threat. Perhaps gnolls from the nearby hills take advantage of the chaos of war to raid the characters' supply lines, providing a chance to fight a very different flavor of humanoid opponent.

A super adventure is a type of short campaign—really one long adventure—that focuses on a single, limited setting. The characters' exploration of this one site might form part of a larger campaign, or be itself the entire campaign. A super adventure combines the best features of a short campaign and a narrow theme. You don't need to tie adventures together or link different villains to a single grand plot. The climactic battle at the end is a tidy way to end a campaign—before you begin your next one!

Super adventures share a number of traits:

✦ They are limited to a single setting.

✦ They often allow for free-form, nonlinear exploration.

✦ They might involve different quests and multiple expeditions.

✦ They encourage character specialization.

Each of these attributes is discussed in more detail below.

## SINGLE SETTING

The setting for a super adventure has to be both large and compelling, providing enough material for characters to explore over several months of play. You might create a massive dungeon with many floors, each more dangerous than the last, or design a secluded wilderness site with small dungeons scattered throughout.

The adventure site could be a vast network of Underdark passages, leading the party ever deeper into the earth.

A super adventure demands the most compelling setting you can imagine, with a striking personality and lots of potential for interesting locations. Classic published super adventures have been set in the fabled ruins of Greyhawk; Castle Ravenloft with its mysterious lands; the Forbidden City, nestled in a crater choked with jungle overgrowth; and the Vault of the Drow, hidden deep underground. You might create a new classic of your own: the Blackmire, a miasma of madness and disease surrounding a slumbering primordial; or the haunted forest of Grimmendeep, which has swallowed many ancient castles in its tangled briars.

Designing a super adventure is easier if you divide the larger setting into smaller units. That way, you and your players can better keep track of where they are and what they're doing. A dungeon is a convenient and traditional design for separating encounter areas. Its multiple floors have limited connections, whether stairs or shafts, and each can have its own distinct personality. A vast locale such as Grimmendeep can also contain multiple smaller areas with a variety of flavors, though they're all overlaid by the larger site's personality (in this case, the choking roots and vines of the haunted forest).

## BIRTH OF THE SUPER ADVENTURE

It's my contention that the first super adventure was a slim, 28-page module called *Dwellers of the Forbidden City*, published by TSR, Inc., in 1981. "Proto-super adventure" might be a more accurate term. It was really just a setting that was ripe for exploration, combined with a single quest that barely scratched the surface of its possibilities.

The adventure as published called for the characters to track down goods recently stolen from merchant caravans. To do that, they had to find the Forbidden City, and a way into it, and track down a wizard who had made his home among the ruins. A straightforward quest—but what made it exceptional was the number of possible ways to accomplish that single goal. This adventure pioneered the idea of nonlinear exploration. No dungeon corridors channeled the characters' movements. There were at least four ways to get down into the crater where the Forbidden City lay, each one detailed as a mini-site within the larger setting. The characters could choose their approach and go whatever way they wanted to in the ruined city.

Within the city itself were three factions of monsters. The yuan-ti made their first appearance in this adventure, and they were accompanied by froglike bullywugs and humanoids of highly questionable heritage called mongrelmen. Long-armed, arboreal humanoids called tasloi rode giant wasps through the jungle trees. Fighting the bullywugs or the tasloi didn't bring the characters any closer to finding the lost caravan goods, but there they were anyway.

An all-too-brief section at the end of the adventure took a tentative next step, suggesting other quests that might bring the characters into the Forbidden City. With more detail, more fleshed-out quests, and another hundred pages or so, *Dwellers of the Forbidden City* would have been a spectacular super adventure—four years before the landmark release of *The Temple of Elemental Evil*, which more properly deserves that description.

—*James Wyatt*

# Nonlinear Exploration

You can design your super adventure's setting to let the characters choose which areas to explore and in what order, depending on the quests laid before them. This method requires more preparation time but rewards you and the players with a more interesting experience. The characters might decide to clear the drow out of the Phantom Tower before they deal with the raiders in the ruins of Dorbren Keep, for example. Those two locations are relatively small and self-contained, rather than full-fledged adventures, so you can have both ready for whatever the players decide to do.

Each adventure area should contain eight to ten encounters, so the characters will probably advance a level when they complete its challenges. But when adventurers can travel to any area in any order, building appropriate encounters can be tricky. Fortunately, adjusting encounter difficulty is fairly simple. To account for characters who have advanced a few levels, you can boost the monsters' levels to match, using the guidelines in Chapter 10, or add monsters to make the encounter more challenging.

When characters leave a part of your adventure setting and venture back later, it should change in response to their actions. This kind of detail helps the setting seem more real and alive to the players. Monsters the party has killed should (usually) stay dead—the site shouldn't just reset to the state it was in the first time around. But the second delve might well present new threats to the characters. Intelligent survivors of the characters' first intrusion into their domain react appropriately, bolstering their defenses or evacuating the area. New creatures might appear in areas left vacant, such as predators drawn to shelter and prey opportunities. A living setting provides repeat play value and continues to hold the players' interest.

A free-form environment such as this feels very natural—the opposite of railroading. The players' decisions seem to really make a difference to the course of the adventure. A possible problem is that the party might end up wandering around with no real idea of what to do. You can keep them from having to search for the fun by making liberal use of quests.

# Multiple Quests

A good way to start your super adventure, just as with any other adventure, is with a quest or two that draws the characters in. As the adventure unfolds, give them more quests that encourage them to move around the area. They might find clues in one area that send them to a different one. Quests might lead the party into a dungeon, back out again, and in again with a new purpose.

With a number of quests at hand, characters can look at all their options and choose one. A given quest might seem the obvious first thing to do, or it could simply be more interesting. It's better to offer too many quests than too few, but don't go too far in either direction. They can be major or minor, aimed at the whole group or tailored to individuals (whether known to the whole group or secret). At the outset, you might design individual quests based on each character's background and motivations. As the super adventure progresses, players might even suggest their own.

# Character Specialization

A super adventure usually has a narrow focus, such as a certain kind of environment or foe. Such a theme gives players the opportunity to choose specialized options for their characters that they might otherwise avoid. In a super adventure, the players know their characters will be fighting undead—or dragons or demons or gnolls, depending on the setting—for the duration of their careers.

Published super adventures often include material specifically designed to allow this kind of specialization. When you design your own super adventures, consider creating or borrowing elements that let characters focus on what they are called to do: specialized feats, powers, paragon paths, magic weapons and armor, and the like. Remember also that characters can retrain as they advance, changing specialized skills as needed to face new challenges.

The theme you choose for your campaign shapes the story it will tell. When you start a campaign, you should have some idea of its end and how the characters will get there. Fundamentally, the story is what the characters do over the course of the campaign.

Keep that point in mind—the story is theirs, not yours, and not that of any nonplayer character in your world. The players' job is to tell that story, develop their characters, and help chart the course of events through the choices they make. When you're writing a novel, you have control over the protagonists, but when you're creating a D&D campaign, they have free will and are apt to do unexpected things.

That said, you can do a lot to shape the campaign story. You provide the context—the setting, the background, and the quests that hook the characters. You determine how the world responds to their actions. You set the stage on which their story unfolds with the adventures you design. For that reason, all the advice in Chapter 6 about creating adventures applies to campaign design as well. Offer strong hooks and meaningful choices. Present varied and exciting challenges. If the characters go in drastically unexpected directions, try to coax them back to the story you want your game to tell without railroading them. Build the campaign to a climax that's even bigger than the smaller peaks of each adventure, and let the players feel as though their ultimate victory really makes a difference in the world.

When you're thinking about the story of your campaign as a whole, ask yourself these three questions.

✦ How does my campaign's theme shape its story?
✦ What significant events took place before the start of the campaign?
✦ What's going to happen in the campaign?

## THEME AND STORY

A campaign theme should suggest the outline of a story, or at least give some idea about how things are likely to end up. Here's advice on how to build a story using the themes discussed earlier in this chapter.

### DUNGEON OF THE WEEK

A highly episodic campaign doesn't need to have an overall story, but it could. As the characters explore, they might begin to uncover common elements that link the disparate dungeons together, ultimately leading to the "Mother of All Dungeons," figuratively or even literally speaking. You can also gradually nudge this sort of campaign toward any other theme, giving your campaign a new direction and ultimately an exciting conclusion.

### ON A MISSION

In this kind of campaign, the characters' purpose drives the story. How do they achieve their goal? That question is easier to answer for some missions than for others. If the characters are trying to explore a continent, their story might not end until they fill in every bit of coastline, riverbank, and mountain range on the map. But if they're on a holy quest to stamp out evil, imagining a satisfactory conclusion is a little harder. In such a case, consider evolving the theme somewhat over the course of the campaign. For example, the characters might uncover corruption within their own church, and their goal shifts to rooting it out—ultimately confronting whoever is behind the evil within.

### ULTIMATE VILLAIN

This campaign revolves around the characters' efforts to foil the villain's plot. Thus, this plot shapes the story of the campaign. Typically the ultimate villain exploits the plans of less powerful bad guys to further his or her ends. Think about those lesser antagonists along the way to the final conflict, and how their actions contribute to this greater goal. Do they know they're helping the mastermind, or are they oblivious to this larger purpose? The answers direct the progress of the story, leading to a climactic confrontation.

### WORLD-SHAKING EVENTS

When the foundations of the world tremble, the characters need some way to make a difference. How do these great events play out, and how do the characters influence them? Will they in fact avert the destruction or transformation of the world, and if so, how? It might be that they can't prevent the calamity, but their actions can determine what follows in its wake. Perhaps they can't stop the empire's fall, but they might drive the orc barbarians back from the frontiers, then destroy the decadent emperor and establish a republic—or a stronger empire with themselves as rulers.

### UNFOLDING PROPHECY

The prophecy itself is the story in this kind of campaign. You can imagine each "verse" of the prophecy as a series of forking paths: How one is fulfilled causes the following ones to unfold in different ways, with multiple interpretations all down the line. In the end, does the prophecy come to pass, or do the characters prevent whatever cataclysmic events it seemed to foretell? Perhaps they must venture to the Bright City and persuade Ioun herself to alter the prophecy. If they can't, they might have to battle their way to the loom where the strands of fate are woven into the tapestry of history, there to cut the thread.

## DIVINE STRIFE

This campaign theme suggests an escalating conflict against increasingly powerful servants of the characters' divine enemy. Ultimately, the party could face an evil god directly or play a pivotal role in a battle between gods. However you plan it, such a scenario needs to emphasize the characters' importance—watching helplessly on the sidelines while two gods duke it out isn't a fun or satisfying conclusion to a campaign. Perhaps Bane has imprisoned Bahamut, and the only way the characters can defeat him is to join together into a single, mighty avatar of Bahamut that combines their own abilities with an infusion of divine power. Some evil gods (such as Tiamat, Torog, and Zehir) are within the reach of 30th-level characters, who can win a final, epic struggle by themselves.

## PRIMORDIAL THREAT

When the gods fought the primordials at the beginning of the world, they became the first adventurers, working in parties of four or five to challenge individual enemies. In a campaign revolving around a primordial resurgence, the characters might fight alongside their divine allies. Or they could follow in the gods' footsteps, defeating a primordial as the pinnacle of their careers—and earning a well-deserved place among the gods as their final reward.

# EVOLVING THEMES

If you're thinking about evolving campaign themes, you're already considering the overall story. What events bring this change about? Are they the actions of the characters, or do they result from external influence? Characters on a mission of discovery might unearth a world-shaking threat at some point in their explorations and alter their focus to deal with it. A party embroiled in a conflict between two gods might become aware of a growing danger from a primordial. At that point, the characters have to persuade the divine enemies to set aside their differences long enough to overcome the greater threat. (But will one deity use the climactic battle with the primordial to attack the other when his back is turned?)

# WHAT HAS COME BEFORE

You should put some thought into the events that have brought your world to the point where the campaign begins. Don't overdo it, though. You need only as much history as necessary to set the stage for the story you have in mind.

The material in the D&D core rulebooks makes a few basic assumptions about the game world. Mighty empires rose and fell in the distant past: the dragonborn realm of Arkhosia, Bael Turath of the tieflings, and the eladrin Realm of the Twin Queens. Most recently, the human empire of Nerath covered much of the known world, uniting the civilized races into one great nation—but it, too, has fallen. If any empires remain, they are distant and foreign. The world as the characters know it is a dangerous place where civilized areas are small, flickering lights amid a greater darkness.

This historical sketch provides a background against which the D&D game makes sense. Why is the world full of dungeons, where characters fight monsters and find treasure? Because ancient fallen empires leave behind both ruins and precious artifacts. The encroaching darkness is full of creatures that make their lairs in those ruins and hoard those treasures. Why do dwarves, tieflings, eladrin, and humans cooperate in adventuring parties? Because the human empire brought the different races together in its towns and cities, and they still live beside one another in most remaining communities. As well, the threats of the darkness are driving people from their ancestral holdings—for example, burning forests scatter the elves, who seek refuge in human towns.

None of these principles are set in stone. You might adopt them wholly, tweak some of them to suit your campaign, or discard them completely in favor of a history of your own. They make a good starting point, though, for creating your own story. If you alter this assumed history, make sure you can explain the underlying assumptions of your campaign.

# THE CAMPAIGN OUTLINE

Once you have some idea of how your campaign theme will shape the story and have developed a historical backdrop, you can sketch out its major events. Such an outline must be in broad strokes, since the characters' actions have to make a difference, and their choices be meaningful. This sketch is likely to change significantly as your campaign progresses and new details are filled in. If nothing else, though, you'll at least have an idea of the campaign's climax and how the characters can get there. When they stray from your outline—and they will—you'll have some sense of what adventures to create to get them back on course.

One way to think about this outline is to divide it into adventuring tiers: heroic, paragon, and epic. You can use the *Monster Manual* to find out the kinds of threats the characters might face at each tier. Since characters need eight to ten encounters to gain a level, a tier consists of roughly a hundred encounters, or ten fairly short adventures. There are plenty of drow in the paragon tier, for example—perhaps at those levels the characters will be traveling through the Underdark realms. You can use that idea as a springboard for designing adventures to fit your broad story outline from 11th to 20th level.

The start of a campaign is a lot like the start of an adventure: You want to get quickly to the action, show the players that adventure awaits, and grab them right away. Give the players enough information to make them want to come back week after week to see how the story plays out.

## START SMALL

You've spent some time thinking about the big picture of your campaign's theme and story. Now it's time to start building adventures and fleshing out the details. Start small. Don't be intimidated by the size of the setting—focus on what's close at hand. You don't need to draw a map of the world right away, because the characters only know about the town where they start the game, and perhaps the nearby dungeon. You might have ideas about how this town's barony is at war with a nearby duchy, or some distant forest is crawling with yuan-ti, and you should make a note of those things. But right now, the local area is enough to get the game off the ground.

Above all, make sure you provide a common starting location for the characters—a place where they have met and decided to put their lives in each other's hands. This starting point might be the village where they grew up or a city that has attracted them from all over. Perhaps it's the dungeons of the evil baron's castle, where they are locked up for various reasons, throwing them into the midst of the adventure.

Whatever you choose, give that starting place only as much detail as it needs. You don't need to identify every building in a village or label every street in a large city. If the characters start in the baron's dungeon, you do have to design it—that's the site of your first adventure—but you don't have to worry about the names of all the baron's knights yet. Sketch out a simple map, think about the surrounding area, and consider whom the characters are most likely to interact with early in the campaign. Most important, visualize how this area fits into the theme and story you have in mind for your campaign. Then get to work on your first adventure!

## CHARACTER ORIGIN AND BACKGROUND

Once you've identified where you want to start your campaign, let the players help tell the story by deciding how their characters got there.

Some players might have trouble coming up with ideas—not everyone is equally inventive. You can help spur their creativity with a few simple questions about their characters.

✦ Are you a native, born and raised in the area? If so, who's your family? What's your current occupation?

✦ Are you a recent arrival? Where did you come from? Why did you come to this area?

✦ Are you a transplant who has been in the area for a year or more? Where are you from? Why did you come here, and what made you stay?

This step is one of your best opportunities to get the players doing some of the work of world design. Listen to their ideas, and say yes if you can. Even if you want all the characters to have grown up in the starting town, for example, consider allowing a recent arrival or a transplant if the player's story is convincing enough. You might suggest some alterations to a character's background so it better fits your world, or you might weave the first threads of your campaign story into her history.

## INFORMING YOUR PLAYERS

As you start to develop the ideas of your campaign, you'll need to fill in the players on the basics. The easiest way to do this is to compile essential information into a campaign handout. Typical material to include in the handout includes the following.

✦ Any restrictions or new options for character creation, such as new or prohibited races.

✦ Any information in the backstory of your campaign that the characters would know about. This gives the players an idea of the theme and story you have in mind.

✦ Basic information about the area where the characters are starting—the name of the town, important locations in and around it, prominent NPCs they'd know about, and perhaps some rumors that point to trouble brewing.

Keep this handout short, sweet, and to the point—two pages is a reasonable maximum. Even if you have a burst of creative energy that produces twenty pages of great background material, save it for your adventures. Let the characters uncover it gradually.

# STARTING AT HIGHER LEVEL

Sometimes you don't want to start characters at 1st level. A paragon- or epic-tier game might be more to your taste. Maybe you want to run a published adventure that requires higher-level characters, or you want to try a one-shot that pits 30th-level characters against Orcus. Whatever the reason, at some point you'll need to create higher-level characters. This process isn't much harder than making a 1st-level character.

The steps for creating a D&D character above 1st level are almost the same as those ones outlined in Chapter 2 of the *Player's Handbook* for a new character.

1. **Choose Race.** Remember that some racial traits improve at higher levels.

2. **Choose Class.** If your level is 11th or higher, choose a paragon path appropriate to your class. At 21st level or higher, you'll also need to choose an epic destiny.

3. **Determine Ability Scores.** Generate scores as for a 1st-level character, applying racial modifiers. Then increase those scores as shown on the Character Advancement table in the *Player's Handbook*, with increases at 4th level, 8th level, 11th, 14th, and so on. (You can also use the NPC Ability Scores table on page 187.)

4. **Choose Skills.** Make sure you meet skill prerequisites for a paragon path or epic destiny, if applicable.

5. **Select Feats.** You generally don't have to worry about the level at which you gained a particular feat, since retraining allows you to have the feats you want at any given level. Do watch out for paragon and epic feats, though. For example, a 14th-level character can't have more than seven paragon feats (those gained at 11th, 12th, and 14th level, as well as up to four retrained feats).

6. **Choose Powers.** You know two at-will powers from your class; remember to increase damage if your level is 21st or higher. The Powers by Class Level table summarizes the number and levels of powers you have in the other categories. These totals are not cumulative. The table assumes that you replace your lowest-level powers with those at higher levels, but you can keep lower-level ones if you wish.

7. **Choose Equipment and Magic Items.** Mundane equipment is much less important for higher-level characters than it is when you're starting out. Choose whatever standard adventuring gear you want from the tables in the *Player's Handbook*. For magic items, choose one item of your level + 1, one item of your level, and one item of your level − 1. In addition, you have gold pieces equal to the value of one magic item of your level − 1. You can spend this money on rituals, potions, or other magic items, or save it for later.

8. **Fill in the Numbers.** After noting the bonuses you gain from feats and magic items (as well as your increased level), calculate your hit points, Armor Class, defenses, initiative, base attack bonuses and damage bonuses, and skill modifiers. The Quick Hit Points table provides a formula for hit points by class.

9. **Roleplaying Character Details.** Flesh out your character, using the suggestions in Chapter 2 of the *Player's Handbook* or your own ideas.

## POWERS BY CLASS LEVEL

| Class Level | Encounter Powers | Daily Powers | Utility Powers |
|---|---|---|---|
| 1st | 1 | 1 | — |
| 2nd | 1 | 1 | 2 |
| 3rd | 3, 1 | 1 | 2 |
| 4th | 3, 1 | 1 | 2 |
| 5th | 3, 1 | 5, 1 | 2 |
| 6th | 3, 1 | 5, 1 | 6, 2 |
| 7th | 7, 3, 1 | 5, 1 | 6, 2 |
| 8th | 7, 3, 1 | 5, 1 | 6, 2 |
| 9th | 7, 3, 1 | 9, 5, 1 | 6, 2 |
| 10th | 7, 3, 1 | 9, 5, 1 | 10, 6, 2 |
| 11th | P, 7, 3, 1 | 9, 5, 1 | 10, 6, 2 |
| 12th | P, 7, 3, 1 | 9, 5, 1 | P, 10, 6, 2 |
| 13th | P, 13, 7, 3 | 9, 5, 1 | P, 10, 6, 2 |
| 14th | P, 13, 7, 3 | 9, 5, 1 | P, 10, 6, 2 |
| 15th | P, 13, 7, 3 | 15, 9, 5 | P, 10, 6, 2 |
| 16th | P, 13, 7, 3 | 15, 9, 5 | P, 16, 10, 6, 2 |
| 17th | P, 17, 13, 7 | 15, 9, 5 | P, 16, 10, 6, 2 |
| 18th | P, 17, 13, 7 | 15, 9, 5 | P, 16, 10, 6, 2 |
| 19th | P, 17, 13, 7 | 19, 15, 9 | P, 16, 10, 6, 2 |
| 20th | P, 17, 13, 7 | P, 19, 15, 9 | P, 16, 10, 6, 2 |
| 21st | P, 17, 13, 7 | P, 19, 15, 9 | P, 16, 10, 6, 2 |
| 22nd | P, 17, 13, 7 | P, 19, 15, 9 | P, 22, 16, 10, 6, 2 |
| 23rd | P, 23, 17, 13 | P, 19, 15, 9 | P, 22, 16, 10, 6, 2 |
| 24th | P, 23, 17, 13 | P, 19, 15, 9 | P, 22, 16, 10, 6, 2 |
| 25th | P, 23, 17, 13 | P, 25, 19, 15 | P, 22, 16, 10, 6, 2 |
| 26th | P, 23, 17, 13 | P, 25, 19, 15 | E, P, 22, 16, 10, 6, 2 |
| 27th | P, 27, 23, 17 | P, 25, 19, 15 | E, P, 22, 16, 10, 6, 2 |
| 28th | P, 27, 23, 17 | P, 25, 19, 15 | E, P, 22, 16, 10, 6, 2 |
| 29th | P, 27, 23, 17 | P, 29, 25, 19 | E, P, 22, 16, 10, 6, 2 |
| 30th | P, 27, 23, 17 | P, 29, 25, 19 | E, P, 22, 16, 10, 6, 2 |

**P:** Power from your paragon path.

**E:** Power from your epic destiny.

## QUICK HIT POINTS

| Class | Hit Points |
|---|---|
| Cleric | (level × 5) + 7 + Constitution score |
| Fighter | (level × 6) + 9 + Constitution score |
| Paladin | (level × 6) + 9 + Constitution score |
| Ranger | (level × 5) + 7 + Constitution score |
| Rogue | (level × 5) + 7 + Constitution score |
| Warlock | (level × 5) + 7 + Constitution score |
| Warlord | (level × 5) + 7 + Constitution score |
| Wizard | (level × 4) + 6 + Constitution score |

Running a campaign boils down to running a series of adventures. Chapter 6 provides plenty of advice for making adventures fun and compelling. Here you'll learn how to do the same for your campaign.

The secret of a good campaign lies in how you weave adventures together to form a larger story, including the little things that give the sense of a coherent, consistent world.

## LINKING ADVENTURES

Adventures that relate directly to your campaign's story trace its development over the characters' careers. A dungeon-of-the-week sort of campaign doesn't necessarily need any link between one adventure and the next, and even one with a tight theme can include occasional adventures that are completely unconnected to other events. But a campaign story that connects the adventures lets the players feel as though they're making real progress, not just racking up experience points.

A simple way to tie adventures together is to use common foes, related quests, and linked events that are related to the campaign's overall story. Each suite of adventures might contain enough encounters to advance the characters three or four levels, serving as a simple story arc. You need no more than that to take characters from 1st level all the way to 30th. The characters might spend most of their careers fighting the Nine Dread Scions, working their way through the nine dungeons where those villains reside, and then pursuing an epic quest to destroy their monstrous progenitor. Or they have to collect the pieces of the *Rod of Seven Parts* scattered in ruins across the world before confronting the primordial Queen of Chaos.

### STORY HOOKS

You can make a campaign feel like one story with many chapters by planting the seeds of the next adventure before the last one is finished. This technique naturally and smoothly moves the characters along. You don't have to do this all the time—it's all right for the party to have some downtime. But when you take the opportunity to introduce the right elements, you can hook the players and the characters effectively.

If you've set the hook properly, when the characters finish the current adventure, they'll naturally follow up on that "loose end." Perhaps a character drinks from a magic fountain in a dungeon and receives a mystifying vision that foreshadows the next episode. The party might find a cryptic map or bizarre relic that, once its meaning is puzzled out, points to the next quest. Perhaps an NPC warns the characters of impending danger or implores them for help.

Be careful, though, that you don't distract the characters from the adventure at hand. Designing an effective hook takes some experimentation. It should be compelling, but not so much that the characters stop caring about what they're doing right now. It should encourage them to finish the current adventure, preferably by requiring them to complete a related task. That way, they get interested early on, but they can't start the next adventure until they've successfully completed this one. They might have to assemble all the pieces of a map in a dungeon to learn where it leads. Alternatively, they find the map but can't decode it without the key, which they recover from the defeated villain.

The best way to keep players from straying is to save your hooks for the very end of your adventures. The villain wields a bizarre relic that leads the characters to learn more about its history, or the party discovers a letter demonstrating that the villain is working for someone else.

## HISTORY AND FORESHADOWING

You can make good use of the history behind your campaign by relating it to the unfolding story. Uncovering that history is a natural way to link adventures. For example, the ultimate villain might be some enormously powerful aberrant being that was imprisoned deep in the earth ages ago. Over the course of their adventures, the characters fight large numbers of aberrant creatures, slowly learning about this alien being. These hints foreshadow the climax of your unfolding story—the aberrant horror breaking free of its prison. Examples of such historical elements include the ruins of ancient temples devoted to the being, records of the destruction it caused during its rampages, copies of the rituals used to bind and imprison it, and hints to the location of its prison.

Foreshadowing doesn't need to have anything to do with history, though. If the party fights a lot of demons and undead over the course of adventures, your players will have a good idea that the campaign will end in a confrontation with Orcus. You can also use prophetic verses to hint at future events. Watch out for being heavy-handed or, conversely, too obscure. A well-designed prophecy is a kind of riddle that helps the characters recognize and deal with key events when they occur. (You'll find advice about constructing riddles on page 83.)

# KEEPING TRACK

Details matter. Your players will more easily imagine that their characters are living in a real world if it makes sense. If the characters frequent a particular tavern, the layout of the building, the staff, and even the decor shouldn't change dramatically from one visit to the next. Consistent details bring the world to life.

On the other hand, the world should definitely respond to the characters' actions. When the characters kill a monster, it stays dead; when they remove treasure from a room, it doesn't magically reappear the next time they enter. If they leave a door open, it should stay open–unless someone closes it. If you're meticulous about details, the players pay attention when things aren't as they expect.

No one's memory is infallible, so it pays to keep track of such details. A simple method is jotting notes directly on your adventure map to keep track of open doors, disarmed traps, and the like. Events beyond the scope of a single adventure are best recorded in a notebook dedicated to your campaign. Whether it's a literal book or some kind of electronic file, such a record is a great way to keep your notes organized.

Your notebook might contain any of the following entries.

✦ **Campaign Journal:** This is the place for notes about your campaign theme and story, including the plot outline for planning future adventures. Update that outline as the campaign develops, adding ideas as they come to you.

✦ **Campaign Handout:** Keep a copy of the handout you made for your players (page 25). You might want to revise it from time to time, summarizing the major events of the campaign to date and adding hints of things to come.

✦ **Adventure Log:** This briefly summarizes each adventure to help you keep track of the unfolding campaign story. You can give your players access to this log as well, or to an edited version stripped of your notes and secrets. The players might instead keep their own record of adventures, which you should also read and copy to your notebook.

✦ **Toolbox:** Here's where to keep notes whenever you create or significantly alter a monster, make up nonplayer characters, design unique traps, hazards, magic items, or artifacts, or generate random dungeons or encounters. (For more information, see Chapter 10.) That way, you don't repeat your work, and you'll be able to draw on this material later.

✦ **NPC Notes:** Record statistics and roleplaying notes for any nonplayer character the characters might interact with more than once. Here's where to identify the two bartenders with their different voices, as well as their names, the tavern where they work, the names of other staff members–maybe even what's on the menu. Keep notes on when and how the characters meet your NPCs, and keep track of the status of their relationships.

✦ **Character Notes:** Keep a running tally of the characters' classes and levels, their goals and backgrounds, any individual quests they're pursuing, the magic items they want, and any other details that might be significant to your planning. You might even maintain a copy of each character sheet, particularly if they're in electronic form. It's also a good ideas to make notes about the players–their motivations and play styles, what kinds of encounters they particularly enjoy, and what pizza toppings they prefer.

✦ **Campaign Calendar:** Your world feels more real to your players when the characters notice the passage of time. Here's where you note details such as the change of seasons and major holidays, and keep track of any important events that affect the larger story.

As characters grow in power, game play changes, and so will your campaign. At each level they gain access to new powers and extraordinary capabilities they didn't have before. At higher tiers, new powers and features from paragon paths and epic destinies can dramatically alter the feel of the game. Powerful rituals also come into play at the upper levels, sometimes drastically changing the way characters respond to situations outside combat.

As your campaign progresses, your story and the style of encounters need to take into account the different tiers of play.

## THE HEROIC TIER

Even 1st-level characters are heroes, set apart from the common people by natural characteristics, learned skills, and some hint of a greater destiny that lies before them.

At the start of their careers, characters rely on their own abilities and powers, and they wield mundane gear. They acquire magic items quickly, though, and might even fill their available item slots by 10th level. In combat, they can make mighty leaps or climb incredibly fast, but they're still basically earthbound and generally remain visible. Since they rely on healing surges to regain lost hit points, heroic tier characters are likely to take an extended rest when surges get dangerously low. However, toward the upper end of the tier, even death is a surmountable obstacle because of the Raise Dead ritual.

The fate of a village might hang on the success or failure of heroic tier adventurers, to say nothing of the characters' own lives. Heroic characters navigate dangerous terrain and explore haunted crypts, where they can expect to fight savage orcs, ferocious wolves, giant spiders, evil cultists, bloodthirsty ghouls, and shadar-kai assassins. If they face a dragon, it's a young one that might still be searching for a lair and has not yet found its place in the world—in other words, much like themselves.

## THE PARAGON TIER

By 11th level, characters are shining examples of courage and determination—true paragons in the world, set well apart from the masses.

Paragon tier adventurers are a lot more versatile than they were at lower levels, and they can find just the right tool for a given challenge. They can spend action points to gain additional effects, are able to use magic rings, and can sometimes regain limited powers they've expended. In combat, they exploit short-range flight and teleportation, making difficult terrain less important, and might be able to turn invisible or resist specific damage types. They also have ways to regain hit points beyond healing surges, including regeneration, so they can complete more encounters between extended rests. On the other hand, monsters at the paragon tier have more ways to thwart these new capabilities, including their own flight, damage resistance, and blindsight.

Rituals at the paragon tier begin to give characters magical ways to gather information and overcome obstacles. Divination rituals such as Consult Oracle grant access to knowledge they might otherwise not have, while View Object can make some kinds of mysteries obsolete. Exploration rituals such as Passwall and Shadow Walk let a party bypass solid barriers and quickly travel long distances.

The fate of a nation or even the world might depend on momentous quests that such characters undertake. Paragon-level adventurers explore uncharted regions and delve long-forgotten dungeons, where they confront savage giants, ferocious hydras, fearless golems, evil yuan-ti, bloodthirsty vampires, crafty mind flayers, and drow assassins. They might face a powerful adult dragon that has established a lair and a role in the world.

## THE EPIC TIER

By 21st level, characters have truly superheroic capabilities, and their deeds and adventures are the stuff of legend. Ordinary people can hardly dream of such heights of power.

Epic adventurers have even more ways to recover expended powers, more ways to heal damage without relying on healing surges, and more powers overall from magic items and epic destinies. In combat, flight and teleportation are routine, as well as extraordinary feats of climbing and jumping. Terrain in general is less important, unless it blocks extraordinary forms of travel. Invisibility is common. Such characters can last through many encounters before resting and can even return from death in the middle of a fight. Furthermore, epic destinies break the rules in dramatic ways.

At the epic tier, rituals include more and better kinds of divination, including the ability to spy on distant beings with Observe Creature. Epic characters can use True Portal to transport themselves instantly anywhere in the world.

Epic adventures have far-reaching consequences, possibly determining the fate of millions—in the natural world and even places beyond. Epic characters traverse otherworldly realms and explore never-before-seen caverns of wonder, where they fight savage balor demons, abominations such as the ferocious tarrasque, mind flayer masterminds, terrible archdevils, bloodthirsty lich archmages, and even the gods themselves. The dragons they encounter are ancient wyrms of truly earth-shaking power, whose sleep troubles kingdoms and whose waking threatens existence.

## IMMORTALITY

A character's epic destiny guides how he or she ultimately exits the world. That hero's story has to come to an end, though his or her actions leave existence indelibly changed. Each epic destiny presented in the *Player's Handbook* suggests a way for a character with that destiny to achieve immortality. It's up to you, in cooperation with your players, to determine how their characters get there.

The final quest of your campaign should be its dramatic climax. After the final encounter of that last adventure, the characters attain their destined immortality—the "happily ever after" to their careers. You might lift them to that state as soon as their enemy is defeated, or spend a little time wrapping up loose ends, letting the characters put their affairs in order and say their goodbyes.

If you don't have a clear endpoint in mind for your campaign, the characters' epic destinies can give you some direction for those last ten levels. Each individual quest takes on greater importance, so that the party achieves group immortality by completing each member's ultimate destiny.

Epic-level characters don't have to leave play. If you want to, you can prolong your campaign indefinitely with 30th-level adventurers, concocting new challenges to their godlike capabilities. At some point, though, your campaign will have to end—and it's better to do it with a thrilling final quest and a glorious victory than to let it fizzle out.

# ENDING A CAMPAIGN

Wind your campaign up with a bang. As with the ending of an adventure, a campaign's ending should tie up all the threads of its beginning and middle. Create an exciting and satisfying conclusion for the theme and story you've crafted.

If your campaign has an ultimate villain, the campaign's climax ought to feature a final confrontation. If some other threat has menaced the world, the characters should put an end to that threat—or if they cannot, take dramatic action to help the world weather the storm. A party on a mission should finally complete it, and an unfolding prophecy should be fulfilled one way or another. Even if your campaign is based on simple discovery, with the characters spending their entire careers exploring the world, it's not enough for them to simply draw in the last few lines on the map. They need a final adventure that gives some meaning to that long quest and makes that last pen stroke truly significant.

You don't have to take a campaign all the way to 30th level. Ending it at 10th or 20th level can be just as satisfying, Whenever your story reaches its natural conclusion is where you should wrap it up. If you see the end approaching, and the characters are getting close to 10th, 20th, or 30th level, consider stretching out the last adventure or two to help them reach that level by the climax.

Make sure you allow space and time near the end of your campaign for the characters to finish up any personal goals. Their own stories need to end in a satisfying way, just as the campaign story does. Ideally, try to link all the characters' individual goals to the ultimate goal of the final adventure. If you can't, though, give them a chance to finish those quests before the very end.

Once the campaign has ended, a new one can begin. If you'll be running a new campaign for the same group of players, you can really help them get invested in the new setting by using their previous characters' actions as the basis of legends. Let the new characters experience how the world has changed because of the old ones. In the end, though, the new campaign is a new story with new protagonists. They shouldn't have to share the spotlight with the heroes of days gone by.

---

### TIPS FROM THE PROS

Know where you are going with your campaign. Don't be afraid to end it when you get there.

—*Andrew Finch*

# CHAPTER 9

# THE WORLD

**YOU WON'T** find a world map in this or any of the core D&D rulebooks. "The world" in which the D&D game takes place doesn't have a map—not until you create one. And you shouldn't feel in any great hurry to create one. A map is important only when the characters seek out the places shown on it.

That said, these books do make some assumptions about the world in which your adventures take place. This chapter talks about those assumptions, and then discusses how you might change them. In the end, the setting of your campaign is *your* world—the details are yours to change or create from whole cloth. But these aren't details you have to worry about when you're starting out as a DM.

This chapter includes the following sections.

✦ **The D&D World:** The game is built around certain core assumptions, but you can fill in the details or alter those assumptions to make the world your own.

✦ **Civilization:** Civilized parts of the world are points of light in the darkness, and they can be exciting adventure sites as well as safe home bases. This section describes how to design settlements for various purposes in your campaign.

✦ **The Wild:** Most of the world is untamed wilderness, and its dangers include more than monsters and raiders. Weather and harsh environments add to the risks of adventuring far from civilization.

✦ **The Planes:** Beyond the natural world, the universe holds greater challenges and greater rewards for brave adventurers.

✦ **The Gods:** The *Player's Handbook* introduces the D&D pantheon. This section gives more information about the nature of these deities, as well as details about the evil gods whose servants can challenge the characters.

✦ **Artifacts:** Powerful magic items with agendas of their own, artifacts can be exciting additions to a campaign at any level.

✦ **Languages:** This section includes more information about the languages and scripts of the D&D world and how to use them in your game.

HOWARD LYON

The rules and story elements in the D&D game are built around a set of core assumptions about the world. Here are some of the most important.

**The World Is a Fantastic Place.** Magic works, servants of the gods wield divine power, and fire giants build strongholds in active volcanoes. The world might be based on reality, but it's a blend of real-world physics, cultures, and history with a heavy dose of fantasy. For the game's purposes, it doesn't matter what historical paladins were like; it cares about what paladins are like in the fantasy world.

**The World Is Ancient.** Empires rise and empires crumble, leaving few places that have not been touched by their grandeur. Ruin, time, and natural forces eventually claim all, leaving the D&D world rich with places of adventure and mystery. Ancient civilizations and their knowledge survive in legends, magic items, and the ruins they left behind, but chaos and darkness inevitably follow an empire's collapse. Each new realm must carve a place out of the world rather than build on the efforts of past civilizations.

**The World Is Mysterious.** Wild, uncontrolled regions abound and cover most of the world. City-states of various races dot the darkness, bastions in the wilderness built amid the ruins of the past. Some of these settlements are "points of light" where adventurers can expect peaceful interaction with the inhabitants, but many more are dangerous. No one race lords over the world, and vast kingdoms are rare. People know the area they live in well, and they've heard stories of other places from merchants and travelers, but few know what lies beyond the mountains or in the depth of the great forest unless they've been there personally.

**Monsters Are Everywhere.** Most monsters of the world are as natural as bears or horses are on Earth, and monsters inhabit civilized parts of the world and the wilderness alike. Griffon riders patrol the skies over dwarf cities, domesticated behemoths carry trade goods over long distances, a yuan-ti empire holds sway just a few hundred miles from a human kingdom, and a troop of ice archons from the Elemental Chaos might suddenly appear in the mountains near a major city.

**Adventurers Are Exceptional.** Player characters are the pioneers, explorers, trailblazers, thrill seekers, and heroes of the D&D world. Although nonplayer characters might have a class and gain power, they do not necessarily advance as PCs do, and they exist for a different purpose. Not everyone in the world gains levels as PCs do. An NPC might be a veteran of numerous battles and still not become a 3rd-level fighter; an army of elves is made up of soldiers, not fighters.

**The Civilized Races Band Together.** The character races in the *Player's Handbook* all drew closer together during the time of the last great empire (which was human-dominated). That's what makes them the civilized races—they're the ones found living together in the towns and cities of civilization. Goblins, orcs, gnolls, and kobolds—along with plenty of other races in the *Monster Manual*—were never part of that human empire. Some of them, such as the militaristic hobgoblins, have cities, organized societies, and kingdoms of their own. These are islands of civilization in the wilderness, but they are not "points of light."

**Magic Is Not Everyday, but it Is Natural.** No one is superstitious about magic, but neither is the use of magic trivial. Practitioners of magic are as rare as fighters. People might see evidence of magic every day, but it's usually minor—a fantastic monster, a visibly answered prayer, a wizard flying by on a griffon. Powerful and experienced practitioners of magic are far from commonplace.

**Gods and Primordials Shaped the World.** The primordials, elemental creatures of enormous power, shaped the world out of the Elemental Chaos. The gods gave it civility and permanence, and warred with the primordials for control of the new creation. The gods eventually triumphed, and primordials now slumber in remote parts of the Elemental Chaos, rage in hidden prisons, or float, lifeless, through the Astral Sea.

**Gods Are Distant.** Gods exist, though most of them maintain a distance and detachment from the everyday happenings of the world. Exarchs act in the world on behalf of their gods, and angels appear to undertake missions that promote the agendas of the gods they serve. Gods are extremely powerful, compared to mortals and monsters, but they aren't omniscient or omnipotent. They provide access to the divine power source for their clerics, paladins, and other prayer-using followers, and their followers pray to them in hopes that they or their exarchs will hear them and bless them.

# It's Your World

The preceding section sums up the basics of what the game assumes about the D&D world. Within those general parameters, though, there's a lot of room for you to fill in the details. Each published campaign setting describes a different world that adheres to some of those core assumptions, alters others, and then builds a world around them. You can do the same to create a world that's uniquely yours.

## The Details

Where the core D&D rulebooks talk about the world, they drop names that exemplify the core assumptions—such as the tiefling empire of Bael Turath and the *Invulnerable Coat of Arnd*. Just as you can alter names in published adventures to suit the flavor of your campaign, you can change the names of these assumed parts of the world. For example, you might decide that the tieflings of your world have a culture reminiscent of medieval Russia, and call their ancient empire Perevolochna. Or, to use the example from Chapter 6, a peasant hero named Al-Rashid might have worn the *Invulnerable Coat* in ancient days.

Aside from these changeable assumed details, most of the specifics of the world are left to your own invention. Even if you begin your campaign in the town of Fallcrest and lead the characters on to Winterhaven and Hammerfast, eventually the characters will move off the map in Chapter 11 and explore new lands of your own creation.

If you follow the core assumptions of the game, sketching out the world beyond your starting area is a simple matter. Great tracts of wilderness separate civilized areas. South of Fallcrest, the characters might travel through a forest on an old, overgrown road they've been told leads to the city-state of Iron-wood. You can throw adventures in their path along the way, then draw them into another grand dungeon adventure when they arrive in what turns out to be the gnoll-infested ruins of Ironwood.

You can draft a map of the whole continent at or near the beginning of your campaign. You don't have to, of course, but even if you do, it's a good idea to keep it sketchy. As the campaign progresses, you'll find that you want certain terrain features in specific places, or an element of the campaign story will lead you to fill in details of the map in ways you couldn't have anticipated at the start of the campaign. Just as when you prepare an adventure, don't overprepare your campaign. Even in a published campaign, the large-scale maps of regions and continents don't detail every square mile of land. You can and should feel free to add details where you need them—and alter them when your campaign suggests it.

## Altering Core Assumptions

One definition of speculative fiction (of which fantasy and science fiction are two branches) is that it starts with reality as we know it and asks, "What if some aspect of the world was different?" Most fantasy starts from the question, "What if magic was real?"

The assumptions sketched out on the previous page aren't graven in stone. They make for an exciting D&D world full of adventure, but they're not the only set of assumptions that do so. You can build an interesting campaign concept by altering one or more of those core assumptions. Ask yourself, "What if this wasn't true in my world?"

**The World Is a Fantastic Place.** What if it's not? What if your characters all use the martial power source, and magic is rare and dangerous? What if your campaign is set in a version of historical Europe?

**The World Is Ancient.** What if your world is brand-new, and the characters are the first heroes to walk the earth? What if there are no ancient artifacts and traditions, no crumbling ruins?

**The World Is Mysterious.** What if it's all charted and mapped, right down to the "Here there be dragons" notations? What if great empires cover huge stretches of countryside, with clearly defined borders between them?

**Monsters Are Everywhere.** What if monsters are rare and terrifying?

**Adventurers Are Exceptional.** What if the cities of the world are crowded with adventurers, buying and selling magic items in great markets?

**The Common Races Band Together.** What if, to use a fantasy cliché, dwarves and elves don't get along? What if hobgoblins live side by side with the other races?

**Magic Is Not Everyday.** What if every town is ruled by a powerful wizard? What if magic item shops are common?

**Gods and Primordials Shaped the World.** What if the primordials won, and hidden cults dedicated to a handful of surviving deities are scattered through a shattered world that echoes the Elemental Chaos?

**Gods Are Distant.** What if the gods regularly walk the earth? What if the characters can challenge them and seize their power? Or what if even exarchs and angels never sully themselves by contact with mortals?

The D&D world is a wide and wondrous place, filled with monsters and magic. However, most people live in relatively safe communities, and even bold adventurers need safe havens. Such areas are points of light in a dark world, and they share common traits. When you think about the civilized areas of your world, consider these questions:

**COMPONENTS OF A SETTLEMENT**
- ✦ What purpose does it serve in your game?
- ✦ How big is it? Who lives there?
- ✦ Who governs it? Who else holds power?
- ✦ What are its defenses?
- ✦ Where do characters go to find what they need?
- ✦ What temples are there? What other organizations?
- ✦ What fantastic elements distinguish it from the ordinary?

The guidelines in this section are just that. They're here to help you build the settlement you want for the purpose you have in mind. If you decide that you want a particular feature in a settlement you create, don't let anything in this section stop you.

# PURPOSE

A settlement's primary purpose is to facilitate the fun in your game. Creating a settlement should also be fun. Other than these two points, the actual purpose the settlement serves determines the amount of detail you need to put into it.

As always, don't do more work than you have to. Create only the features of a settlement that you know you'll need, along with notes on general features. Then allow the place to grow organically as the PCs interact with more and more of it, keeping notes on new places you invent and use in the game. Eventually, you'll have a living town that you can use again and again.

## HOME BASE

The primary reason to create a settlement is to give the characters a place to live, train, and recuperate between adventures. Such a settlement is the launching pad from which the characters go out into the wider world. An entire campaign can center on a particular town or city. Sometimes, however, a base is just a temporary stopover for one or more adventures before the characters move on.

If the characters start their careers in a particular locale, one that they all call home, that town can have a special place in their hearts and minds. What happens in and to that place takes on personal meaning. Characters might want to protect the town from destruction and corruption, or they could want to escape the memories and limitations the place holds.

A home base needs a moderate amount of detail, but that's work that the players can help you with. Ask the players to tell you a bit about mentors, family members, and other important people in their characters' lives. You can add to and modify what they give you, but you'll at least start with a solid foundation of the NPCs who are important to the characters. You might also have the players tell you where and how their characters spend their time—a favorite tavern, library, or temple, perhaps. Unless the home base is also an adventure site, you don't need more detail than that at the outset.

## ADVENTURE SITE

A settlement makes a great adventure site (see Chapter 6 for more about urban adventuring). The amount of preparation you need for such a settlement depends on the adventures you want to run there. You might detail adventure areas, such as battlements or towers (see "City Buildings" on page 111). For an event-based adventure, you need notes on the NPCs who play a part in the adventure. This work is adventure preparation as much as it is world building, but the cast of characters you develop for your adventure—including allies, patrons, enemies, and extras—can become recurring figures in your campaign.

## LOCAL COLOR

Often, a settlement is just a place where the characters stop in to rest and buy supplies. A settlement of this sort needs no more than a narrative description. Include the town's name, decide how big it is, add a dash of flavor ("The prominent temple to Avandra suggests that this town hasn't outgrown its pioneer roots"), and let the characters get down to business. The history of the inn where the characters spend the night, the mannerisms of the shopkeeper they buy supplies from—you can add this level of detail, but you don't have to. It's fine to toss in these bits if the characters return to the same town—at that point, it begins to feel a little more like a home base, if a temporary one. Let it grow as the need arises.

# SIZE

The size of a settlement is largely a matter of flavor, but it can also influence the goods and services available there. Since even small villages spring into being along trade routes, it's safe to assume that characters can find what they want or need to buy in practically any settlement, given enough time. Don't let a community's size get in the way of your characters' enjoyment of the game by forcing them to travel hundreds of miles out of their way to buy the magic items they want.

The vast majority of distinct settlements in the D&D world are villages clustered around a larger town or city. Farming villages help supply the town or city population with food, in exchange for the goods the farmers can't produce themselves. Towns and cities are the seats of the local nobles who govern the surrounding area, who also carry the responsibility for defending the villages from attack. Occasionally, the local lord lives in a keep or fortress with no nearby town or city.

# VILLAGE

Most settlements are agricultural villages, supporting themselves and nearby towns or cities with crops and meat. The citizens of a village are involved in food production in one way or another—if not tending the crops, then supporting those who do by shoeing horses, weaving clothes, milling grain, and the like. They maintain trade with nearby settlements.

Villages pop up within areas protected by the local rulers, or on land with a defensive geographic advantage such as a river. Some villages support and surround military fortresses and outposts, and others crop up as boomtowns when valuable resources are discovered. Villages can also become isolated over time, as kingdoms crumble.

A village's population is dispersed around a large area of land. Farmers live on their land, which spreads them widely around the village center. At the heart of the village, a standard set of structures cluster together: essential services, a marketplace, a temple or two, some kind of gathering place, and perhaps an inn for travelers.

## VILLAGE TRAITS

✦ **Population:** Up to about 1,000.
✦ **Government:** Noble ruler (usually not resident), with an appointed agent (a reeve) in residence to adjudicate disputes and collect taxes for the lord.
✦ **Defense:** The reeve might have a small force of soldiers; otherwise the village relies on a citizen militia.
✦ **Commerce:** Basic supplies are readily available, possibly an inn. Other goods available from traveling merchants.
✦ **Organizations:** One or two temples or shrines, farmer associations, few or no other organizations.

# TOWN

Towns are major trade centers, where important industries and reliable trade routes allowed the population to grow. As many as half of a town's citizens are part of a thriving middle class of artisans. Towns rely on commerce—the import of raw materials and food from surrounding villages, and the export of crafted items to those villages as well as other towns and cities.

Towns grow in places where roads intersect waterways, or at the meeting of major land trade routes. A town might also grow in a place with a strategic defensive location or near significant mines or similar natural resources.

A town's population is centralized in an area surrounded by defensible walls. Its population is more diverse than that of villages—during the time of the last human empire, merchants and artisans of all races mingled together in the towns and cities, whereas villages remained more homogeneous.

## TOWN TRAITS

✦ **Population:** Up to about 10,000.
✦ **Government:** Noble ruler in residence, with an appointed lord mayor to oversee administration and an elected town council representing the interests of the middle class.
✦ **Defense:** Sizable army of professional soldiers as well as the noble's personal soldiers.
✦ **Commerce:** Basic supplies are readily available, though exotic goods and services are harder to find. Inns and taverns support travelers.
✦ **Organizations:** Several temples might hold political as well as spiritual authority, merchant guilds, some other organizations.

# CITY

Cities are overgrown towns and function in the same way. Their larger populations require more support from both surrounding villages and trade routes, so they're rare. They typically appear in areas where large expanses of fertile, arable land surround a location that's friendly to trade, almost always on a navigable waterway.

Cities are walled like towns, and it's possible to identify the stages of a city's growth from the expansion of the walls beyond the central core. These internal walls naturally divide the city into wards, which have their own representatives on the city council and their own noble governors. In some cities, shrinking populations since the fall of the great empires have left wards abandoned and in ruin.

Cities with more than 25,000 people are extremely rare in the current age, but they stand as monuments of civilization and vital points of light in the D&D world.

## CITY TRAITS

✦ **Population:** Up to about 25,000.
✦ **Government:** Noble ruler in residence, with several other nobles sharing responsibility for surrounding areas and government functions. One such noble is the lord mayor, who oversees the city administration. An elected city council represents the middle class, and might hold more power than the lord mayor. Other groups serve as important power centers as well.
✦ **Defense:** Large army of professional soldiers, guards, and town watch. Each noble in residence has at least a small force of personal soldiers.
✦ **Commerce:** Almost any goods or services are readily available. Many inns and taverns support travelers.
✦ **Organizations:** Many temples, guilds, and other organizations, some of which hold significant power in city affairs.

# GOVERNMENT

In the absence of empires or large kingdoms, power and authority in the D&D world are concentrated in towns and cities. Here minor nobles cling to the titles their families carried under past empires–dukes, barons, earls, counts, the occasional prince, here and there a self-styled king. These nobles hold authority over the towns and cities where they live and the surrounding lands. They collect taxes from the populace, which they use for public building projects, to pay the soldiery, and support a comfortable lifestyle for themselves (although nobles also have considerable hereditary wealth). In exchange, they promise to protect their citizens from threats such as orc marauders, hobgoblin armies, and roving human bandits.

The noble lords appoint officers to act as their agents in villages, to supervise the collection of taxes and serve as judges in disputes and criminal trials. These reeves, sheriffs, or bailiffs are commoners native to the villages they govern, chosen for their position because they already claim the respect of their fellow citizens.

Within the towns and cities, the lords share authority (and administrative responsibility) with lesser nobles, usually their own relatives, and also with representatives of the middle class. A lord mayor of noble birth is appointed to head the town or city council, and to perform the same administrative functions that reeves do in villages. The council is made up of representatives elected by the middle class of traders and artisans. Only foolish nobles ignore the wishes of their town councils, since the economic power of the middle class is more important to the prosperity of a town or city than the hereditary authority of the nobility.

## MAPPING A SETTLEMENT

When you draw a map for a settlement in your game, don't worry about the placement of every building.

For a village, sketch out the roads, including trade routes leading beyond the village and local roads that connect outlying farms to the village center. Note the location of the village center and any important terrain features in the area. If the characters visit specific places in the village, you can mark those spots on your map.

For towns and cities, again, note major roads and waterways as well as surrounding terrain. Outline the walls, and mark the locations of features you know will be important—the lord's keep, significant temples, and the like. For cities, add internal walls and think about the personality of each ward. You might give the wards names reflecting their personalities, which also identify the kinds of trades that dominate the neighborhood (Tannery Square, Temple Row), a geographical characteristic (Hilltop, Riverside), or a dominant site (the Lords' Quarter).

The larger a settlement, the more likely it is that other individuals or organizations hold significant power there as well. Even in a village, a popular individual–a wise elder or a well-liked farmer–can wield more influence than the appointed reeve, and a wise reeve avoids making an enemy of such a person. In towns and cities, the same power might lie in the hands of a prominent temple, a guild independent of the council, or a single individual with magical power to back up her influence.

# DEFENSE

Soldiers–both professional and militia–serve double duty in most settlements. They carry the responsibility of defending the settlement from outside threats, including bandits and raiders. They also keep order within the settlement. The largest cities maintain separate forces for these two purposes (a guard and a watch). In many cities, the noble ruler also has a personal force of soldiers to maintain the security of the keep in addition to those responsible for defending the city walls. These soldiers come from noble families themselves.

The size of a professional soldiery depends on the type of settlement as well as its population. If a village has full-time soldiers at all, they number no more than perhaps twenty-five. A town or city might have as little as one soldier for every hundred residents, or as many as twice that in particularly dangerous or crime-ridden areas.

Except in the largest cities, the watch is more adept at handling disturbances than at investigating crime. Inquisitives who specialize in solving mysteries are rare. Instead, the watch commonly offers rewards for solving mysteries or bringing criminals to justice–fine opportunities for adventurers to prove themselves!

# COMMERCE

Even small villages give characters ready access to the gear they need to pursue their adventures. Provisions, tents and backpacks, and simple weapons are commonly available. Traveling merchants carry armor, military weapons, and more specialized gear. Most villages have inns that cater to travelers, where adventurers can get a hot meal and a bed, even if the quality leaves much to be desired. When characters stop in at a settlement to rest and restock their supplies, give them a bit of local flavor, such as the name of the inn where they spend the night, and move on with the adventure.

Even small villages rely heavily on trade with other settlements, including larger towns and cities. Merchants pass through regularly, selling necessities and luxuries to the villagers, and any good merchant has far-reaching contacts across the region. When characters have magic items to sell, a traveling merchant is in town—or will be soon—to take it off their hands. The same applies to exotic mundane goods as well: No one in the village makes silk rope or has much use for it, but merchants making their way between major cities carry it all the time.

Traveling merchants are also a great way to introduce adventure hooks to the characters as they conduct their business. Since they make their living traversing roads that are not as safe as they used to be, merchants hire competent guards to keep their goods safe. They also carry news from town to town, including reports of situations that cry out for adventurers to get involved.

These merchants can't provide specialized services, however. When the characters are in need of a library or a dedicated sage, a trainer who can handle the griffon eggs they've found, or an architect to design their castle, they're better off going to a large city than looking in a village. These services are less important in the economy of the game than magic items and other goods, so you shouldn't feel as though you have to compromise your common sense for the sake of game play.

Of course, it's natural for characters to travel far beyond their native villages as they pursue adventure. When they're in the City of Brass, they should be able to buy even the most expensive magic items readily. If it doesn't interfere with the flow of your game, it's fine to expect that characters will travel to larger cities to do business as they reach higher levels and deal with larger sums of money.

### THE MAGIC ITEM ECONOMY

Most of the time, characters find magic items on their adventures that are above their level. These are exciting items, and the characters have a strong incentive to keep these items and use them. As characters attain higher levels, the items they find might replace items they already have—the fighter finds a +3 *flaming sword* and no longer wants his +2 *magic sword*.

When this happens, the characters ordinarily sell those items—it's slightly more beneficial to do that than to use the Disenchant Magic Item ritual, because the characters don't have to pay the component cost. A merchant, agent, or fence buys items from the character at one-fifth the items' value, in the hope of selling them at significant profit (usually, above the items' value). Buyers are hard to find, but the profit to be made makes it worth the merchant's risk.

Characters can use the monetary treasure they find, as well as the gold from selling items, to acquire new magic items. They can't make items above their level, and can't often afford items more than a few levels above theirs. It's to their benefit to use the Enchant Magic Item ritual for items of their level or lower, rather than buying these items from merchants, agents, or fences, because of the 10-40 percent markup over items' value that these sellers charge.

When they want items above their levels, they have to go to merchants.

The game still works if you decide that magic items can't be bought and sold in your world. Characters can rely entirely on rituals to duplicate the economy of buying and selling without money changing hands. The *residuum* they collect from disenchanting items provides the expensive ritual components they need for the enchanting ritual. If you want characters to rely entirely on these rituals, remove the cost to perform the Disenchant Magic Item ritual, making it just as efficient as selling.

On the flip side, you can drive the characters to markets instead of rituals by altering the prices they pay for magic items. You can remove the random markup, or even alter it to allow the possibility of finding items for sale below normal price. For example, roll 1d6 as usual, but a 1 means the item is available for 10 percent below the base price, a 2 means it's available for the base price, and 3-6 means a 10 percent to 40 percent markup. Items are readily available, and sometimes characters can get a good deal.

## ORGANIZATIONS

Temples, guilds, secret societies, colleges, and orders are important forces in the social order of any settlement. Occasionally, their influence stretches across multiple cities, echoing the wide-ranging political authority that crumbled with the fall of empires. Organizations can also play an important part in the lives of player characters, acting as their patrons, allies, or enemies just as individual nonplayer characters do. When characters join these organizations, they become a part of something larger than themselves, which can give their adventures a context in the wider world.

### RELIGION

Temples and religious orders are among the most important and influential organizations in the world. They're likely to have direct influence on characters who use the divine power source, even though clerics and paladins operate as free agents, independent of these hierarchies.

Though the worship of the pantheon of gods is universal, there are no worldwide hierarchies devoted to these gods. A temple to Bahamut in one city is unconnected to Bahamut's temple in the next city, with each having different rites and differently nuanced interpretations of the god's commands.

Most temples are dedicated to more than one deity, and a temple where Bahamut's altar is next to Moradin's might paint a different picture of the Platinum Dragon than a temple where he's worshiped alongside Erathis. In the first, his protective aspects might be emphasized—he and Moradin stand together to shield the community. Beside Erathis, he might be more of a crusading god, conquering evil to help the spread of civilization.

In the Temple of the Celestial Mountain, for example, Bahamut, Moradin, and Kord share temple space as they're said to share a divine dominion. In village temples, Bahamut's altar stands alongside Moradin's and Pelor's, and the rites ask the gods' protection over both village and crops. The Temple of the Bright City is devoted to Pelor, Erathis, and Ioun, who all share a dominion and an interest in the various aspects of urban life and civilization. Wayside shrines built along trade routes, by contrast, celebrate the gods of the roads and wild places—Avandra, Melora, and Sehanine. The Temple of the Fates worships the three gods of destiny: the maiden Avandra, god of luck; the matron Ioun, god of prophecy; and the crone, the Raven Queen, who ultimately cuts the thread of each person's life. Eladrin temples (and some elven ones) feature altars to Corellon and Sehanine—and a few have bare altars where no sacrifice is offered, saving a place for Lolth when she is ultimately reconciled to the other gods of her family.

A temple in the D&D world doesn't hold scheduled worship services. Rather, the temple is always open and constantly busy. Priests perform the daily rites the gods require, each at a separate altar. Worshipers bring children, ailing family members, and livestock in for the priests' blessings, and they bring their own prayers and sacrifices to ask the gods' favor. Worshipers and petitioners stand or kneel in large open spaces. On holy days, crowds press in to fill every available space, sometimes for the entire length of the day. These are as much social events as religious ones, and the words of the rites can be drowned out in the hubbub of conversation.

Other organizations have a religious foundation, too. Knightly orders dedicated to Bahamut or Bane, colleges devoted to Ioun, civic organizations that honor Erathis, travelers' aid societies dedicated to Avandra, craft guilds that invoke Moradin's name, and secret societies of assassins dedicated to Zehir all wield influence in the cities and larger towns of the world.

## OTHER ORGANIZATIONS

Organizations don't always have religious underpinnings, of course. Knightly orders are formed with noble patronage. Like-minded scholars with interests in related subjects gather in colleges. Inns in different towns create informal networks and aid societies to help travelers. Merchants and artisans form guilds to protect their interests in city governments and supervise the training of apprentices. Criminal organizations of all kinds operate in the shadows and alleys of settlements.

Although people of the wizard class are not common, every large city has associations for practitioners of arcane rituals, mages who can manage simple spells, and scholars with an interest in magical subjects as well as true wizards. These organizations can be important resources for wizard and warlock characters, a place to find a mentor or purchase rituals. They represent specific magical traditions, which might be reflected in unique spells, rituals, feats, and paragon paths. The Spiral Tower is an example—a religious organization dedicated to Corellon that teaches a fey tradition of arcane magic and guides wizard characters into a specific paragon path (described in the *Player's Handbook*). The Order of the Golden Wyvern is a loose association of spellcasters who use their talents in military pursuits. Golden Wyvern wizards learn the battle mage paragon path and take feats such as Spell Accuracy.

Military organizations can support any character, particularly characters who use the martial power source—fighters, warlords, rangers, and rogues. These characters might be veterans of a city's guard or watch, a noble's personal retinue, or a mercenary company that travels from city to city as its services are needed. Knightly orders, too, charge their members to travel the countryside in pursuit of the orders' goals, which squares nicely with the adventuring life.

Criminal gangs, guilds, cults, and secret societies are prominent enemies, particularly in campaigns centered in urban areas. Characters might pursue a single villain and bring her to justice, only to find themselves the target of assassins from the villain's criminal guild. Suddenly, they're involved in a bigger adventure than they thought, dealing with a criminal underground that considers them deadly enemies.

## TELEPORTATION CIRCLES

A feature of major cities that helps cement their important place in the economy of the fantasy world is the presence of permanent teleportation circles. Rituals such as Linked Portal and Planar Portal rely on these circles, which are commonly found in temples (particularly those dedicated to Ioun, Avandra, or Erathis), universities, the headquarters of arcane organizations, and prominent civic locations. However, since every teleportation circle is a possible means of entry into a city, they're typically guarded by both military and magical protection.

As you design a fantasy city, think about what teleportation circles it might contain and which ones characters who learn Linked Portal are likely to know about. If characters commonly return to their home base city by means of a teleportation circle, you can use that circle as a hook for plot developments in your campaign. What do the characters do if they arrive in a teleportation circle and find all the familiar wards disabled and guards lying in pools of blood? What if their arrival interrupts an argument between two feuding priests at the Temple of the Bright City?

# FANTASTIC SETTLEMENTS

In the magical world of the D&D game, most settlements follow the patterns described above. But fantastic exceptions abound, cities where magic or monsters play a significant role in government, defense, commerce, or organizations. Different races might also have different settlements from those described above, and you can use these variations to inject a fantastic flavor into the settlements your players visit.

Rather than a noble lord who's nothing more than a titled aristocrat, a town or city might be ruled by a wizard, perhaps a retired adventurer, whose magical power makes a personal retinue of soldiers unnecessary. Such a settlement might feature easily accessible rituals and minor magic items—or the wizard might severely restrict magic that could challenge his authority.

A cleric, paladin, angel, or demigod might rule a city as a theocracy, where religious commandments hold the same status as laws. Depending on the ruler, a theocracy can be a very good or a very bad place to live or visit.

What happens when a dragon decides to take over a city? Or a mind flayer secretly controls the baron, steering the city toward its own mysterious purposes? What if the ruler is a lich or vampire who installs undead in positions of power?

As those examples suggest, not every settlement in the D&D world is a point of light in the darkness—some are part of the darkness. Hobgoblins and drow are just as civilized as humans, but their cities are nightmarish tyrannies where other races are enslaved. Even a mundane town can be a dark and dangerous place, when the ruler is a devotee of Asmodeus or even just an inflexible autocrat. A visit to these cities is an adventure in itself, and you might build a whole campaign that puts the characters in the role of criminals or rebels in such a place, freeing slaves and working to overthrow the tyrannical ruler.

Even in a fantastic settlement, there shouldn't be many nonplayer characters with classes from the *Player's Handbook*. The player characters are exceptional, in part because they have these classes and gain levels through their adventuring. Most citizens are 1st-level minions or other low-level examples of their races drawn from the *Monster Manual* or created using the design guidelines in Chapter 10. The priests in a temple are ordinary people who might have some mastery of rituals—and might not. A hedge wizard might be the human mage from the *Monster Manual*, with simple spells and rituals. Reserve classes for exceptional and important NPCs, particularly patrons and villains.

ROB ALEXANDER

Uncounted miles stretch between the civilized areas of the world, wild and dangerous. When characters leave the relative safety of towns and cities, they quickly enter a world of monsters and raiders, where the land can be actively hostile. Even if they're traversing only a few miles between a village and a nearby dungeon, the wilderness is a force to be reckoned with.

Wilderness areas fall into three broad categories. Formerly settled regions have been reclaimed by the forces of nature—overgrown with forest, swallowed into swamp, or worn into rubble by desert wind and scouring sand. Once-busy roadways are now nothing but fragments of brick littering the ground. Even in the peak of the great empires of the past, the lands between cities were wild, and only frequent patrols kept trade routes safe. Now those lands are full of monster-haunted ruins, including the crumbled remains of those ancient cities. Quests might lead adventurers to these ruins in search of lost libraries or artifacts, investigating a rumor of a surviving settlement buried in the wilderness, or looking for treasure.

Other regions have never been settled. These consist primarily of inhospitable terrain—deserts, mountains, and frozen tundra, expanses of jungle and wide swamps. These areas hold no ruins from the ancient empires of the world, except the occasional hint of a short-lived colony that failed to tame the wilderness around it. These regions hold more fantastic terrain—places where magic gathers in pools, or where parts of the Feywild, the Shadowfell, or the Elemental Chaos overlap with the world and alter nature with their proximity. Adventurers might find a foundry built by fire archons or a snow-capped mountain torn from its roots and suspended in the air. Their quests might lead them to seek a font of magical power on a forbidding peak or a city supposed to appear in the desert once every century.

Finally, even in these days of fallen empires, colonists and pioneers fight back the wilderness on the frontier, hoping to spread the light of civilization and found new kingdoms and empires. The world's largest city-states establish colonies at the edge of their sphere of influence, and brave and hardy souls build hardscrabble villages near sources of minerals or other resources. Devotees of Erathis seek to tame the wilderness, and followers of Avandra roam in search of new frontiers. These tiny outposts of civilization barely shed a glimmer of light into the surrounding wilderness, but they can be home bases for adventurers who have reason to venture into the wilds around them. A city-state might send characters on a quest to find or save a colony that has broken contact, or characters who serve Erathis might undertake a quest to found a colony of their own.

## WEATHER

As characters adventure in the wilderness, the weather can be one of the most significant threats they face. It might be as simple as drizzling rain that obscures their foes or gusting wind that hampers movement in combat. Blinding snow can complicate a climb through a mountain pass, or a living storm might attack at random as they scramble for cover. These examples show four ways you might use weather in a wilderness adventure.

Rain, fog, or falling snow creates obscured terrain (see page 61). It might also create difficult terrain on the ground. Use these weather features as you would other kinds of terrain when building encounters.

Gusting wind might be an obstacle hazard in an encounter (see page 86). In a narrow mountain pass, the wind might be a constant force that acts like a current in water. Or it might gust every few rounds (roll 1d4 each round, with a 4 indicating a gust).

Blinding snow in a treacherous mountain pass complicates a skill challenge encounter. It might force PCs to make Endurance checks every hour, or Acrobatics checks to avoid slipping and taking damage.

A living storm is a blaster trap, possibly a solo trap that constitutes an encounter. It attacks every round, with bolts of lightning, gusts of wind, or blasts of thunder. In open terrain, the PCs can't take cover—and they might find that the storm turns cover where it is available into an additional hazard, blasting tree branches or rock from an overhang down onto them where they hide. Countermeasures could include Nature checks to predict and avoid its attacks. Defenders can use the aid another action to shelter less hardy characters from the storm's effects, granting a bonus to those characters' defenses against the storm's attacks.

Weather can also just be a narrative detail you use to set the atmosphere of your adventure or an encounter. It's an important part of your description—your world feels more real if the weather changes and the seasons change. But the weather is what you want and need it to be at any given time, and it doesn't need to follow the rules of real-world meteorology.

## ENVIRONMENTAL DANGERS

Wilderness adventures pose another sort of risk: the environment itself. Polar adventurers risk frostbite and ex-posure, desert explorers face heat stroke, and mountaineers must contend with the perils of high altitudes.

In the D&D world, cataclysmic magical events can render entire regions hostile. The Lands of the Screaming Dead sap the life force of those who cross its borders, and the ash from the volcanic Mount

Skuldan, stoked by fire titans, can choke the last living breath from even a hardy adventurer.

The Endurance skill determines how well a character can withstand such dangers. Every eight hours within an area of environmental danger, the character must succeed on an Endurance check. Each time a character fails, he loses one healing surge. If a character has no healing surges left when he fails a check, he loses hit points equal to his level.

The adventure sets the DC for the Endurance check. Here are some useful benchmarks. When designing your own environmental dangers, rely on the Difficulty Class and Damage by Level table (page 42) and your common sense.

| Condition | Endurance DC |
|---|---|
| Severe weather | 20 |
| High altitude | 21 |
| Extreme altitude | 26 |
| Cold | 22 |
| Frigid cold | 26 |
| Heat | 22 |
| Stifling heat | 26 |
| Pervasive smoke or ash | 26 |
| Pervasive necromantic energy | 31 |

If a character takes an extended rest while in an area of environmental danger, he recovers healing surges lost in combat but not those lost from failed Endurance checks. During the six hours that include extended rest, the character gets a +2 bonus to Endurance checks because he's resting and not exerting himself.

If two or more environmental dangers apply at the same time (such as climbing a mountain in a snowstorm), characters make Endurance checks against each danger.

## Starvation, Thirst, and Suffocation

When deprived of food, water, or air, the rule of three applies. An adventurer can handle three weeks without food, three days without water, and three minutes without air outside of strenuous situations. After that, such deprivation is a significant test of a PCs' stamina.

At the end of the time period (three weeks, three days, or three minutes), the character must succeed on a DC 20 Endurance check. Success buys the character another day (if hungry or thirsty), or round (if unable to breathe). Then the check is repeated at DC 25, then at DC 30, and so on.

When a character fails the check, he loses one healing surge and must continue to make checks. A character without healing surges who fails a check takes damage equal to his level.

In strenuous situations, such as combat, going without air is much harder. A character holding his breath during underwater combat, for example, must make a DC 20 Endurance check at the end of his turn in a round where he takes damage.

As with environmental dangers, a character cannot regain healing surges lost to starvation, thirst, or suffocation until he eats a meal, drinks, or gains access to air again, respectively.

A character with 0 or fewer hit points who continues to suffer from one of these effects keeps taking damage as described above until he dies or is rescued.

# THE PLANES

The world occupies a special place at the center of the universe. It's the middle ground where the conflicts between gods and primordials, and among the gods themselves, play out through their servants both mortal and immortal. But other planes of existence surround the world, nearby dimensions where some power sources are said to originate and powerful creatures reside, including demons, devils, and the gods.

Before the world existed, the universe was divided into two parts: the Astral Sea and the Elemental Chaos. Some legends say that those two were once one realm, but even the gods can't know that for certain, for they had their origin in the Astral Sea.

## THE ASTRAL SEA

The Astral Sea floats above the world, an ocean of silvery liquid with the stars visible beneath the shallow sea. Sheets of shimmering starlight like gossamer veils part to reveal the dominions, the homes of the gods, like islands floating in the Astral Sea. Not all the gods live in dominions—the Raven Queen's palace of Letherna stands in the Shadowfell, and Lolth's home, the Demonweb Pits, is located in the Abyss. Avandra, Melora, and Torog wander the world, and both Sehanine and Vecna wander the whole cosmos.

Arvandor is a realm of natural beauty and arcane energy that echoes the Feywild. It's the home of Corellon and sometimes of Sehanine. Arvandor seems to be as much a part of the Feywild as of the Astral Sea, and travelers claim to have reached it through both planes.

The Bright City of Hestavar, as its title suggests, is a vast metropolis where Erathis, Ioun, and Pelor make their homes. Powerful residents of all the planes make their way to the Bright City to buy and sell exotic goods.

Tytherion, called the Endless Night, is the dark domain that Tiamat and Zehir share. No light can pierce its darkest depths, and both serpents and dragons haunt its otherworldly wilderness.

The Iron Fortress of Chernoggar is Bane's stronghold in the Astral Sea. As its name suggests, it's a mighty stronghold of rust-pitted iron, said to be impregnable to attack. Even so, Gruumsh makes his home on an eternal battlefield outside the fortress's walls, determined to raze it to the ground one day. Immortal warriors fight and die on both sides of this conflict, returning to life with every nightfall.

Celestia is the heavenly realm of Bahamut and Moradin. Kord also spends a good deal of time on its mountainous slopes because of an old friendship with the other gods, but his tempestuous nature keeps him from calling it home. Upon parting a veil to enter Celestia, a traveler arrives on the lower reaches of a great mountain. Behind him, the mountains disappear into silvery mist far below.

The Nine Hells is the home of Asmodeus and the devils. This plane is a dark, fiery world of continent-sized caverns ruled by warring princelings, though all are ultimately under the iron fist of Asmodeus.

## THE ELEMENTAL CHAOS AND THE ABYSS

At the foundation of the world, the Elemental Chaos churns like an ever-changing tempest of clashing elements—fire and lightning, earth and water, whirlwinds and living thunder. Just as the gods originated in the Astral Sea, the first inhabitants of the Elemental Chaos were the primordials, creatures of raw elemental power. They shaped the world from the raw material of the Elemental Chaos, and if they had their way, the world would be torn back down and returned to raw materials. The gods have given the world permanence utterly alien to the primordials' nature.

The Elemental Chaos approximates a level plane on which travelers can move, but the landscape is broken up by rivers of lightning, seas of fire, floating earth-bergs, ice mountains, and other formations of raw elemental forces. However, it is possible to make one's way slowly down into lower layers of the Elemental Chaos. At its bottom, it turns into a swirling maelstrom that grows darker and deadlier as it descends.

At the bottom of that maelstrom is the Abyss, the home of demons. Tharizdun, the Chained God, planted a shard of pure evil in the heart of the Elemental Chaos before the world was finished, and the gods imprisoned him for this act of blasphemy. (This story is told in more detail in the "Demon" entry of the *Monster Manual*.) The Abyss is as entropic as the Elemental Chaos where it was planted, but it is actively malevolent, where the rest of the Elemental Chaos is simply untamed.

## THE WORLD AND ITS ECHOES

The world has no proper name, but it bears a wide variety of prosaic and poetic names among those people who ever find need to call it anything but "the world." It's the creation, the middle world, the natural world, the created world, or even the First Work.

---

### SIGIL, THE CITY OF DOORS

Somewhere between the planes, neither adrift in the Astral Sea nor rooted in the Elemental Chaos, spins the City of Doors, the bustling metropolis of Sigil. Planar trade flows freely through its streets, facilitated by a bewildering number of portals leading to and from every known corner of the universe—and all the corners yet to be explored. The ruler of the City of Doors is the enigmatic Lady of Pain, whose nature is the subject of endless speculation.

The primordials formed the world from the raw materials of the Elemental Chaos. Looking down on this work from the Astral Sea, the gods were fascinated with the world. Creatures of thought and ideal, the gods saw endless room for improvement in the primordials' work, and their imaginings took form and substance from the abundance of creation-stuff still drifting in the cosmos. Life spread across the face of the world, the churning elements resolved into oceans and landmasses, diffuse light became a sun and moon and stars. The gods drew astral essence and mixed it with the tiniest bits of creation-stuff to create mortals to populate the world and worship them. Elves, dwarves, humans, and others appeared in this period of spontaneous creation. Resentful of the gods' meddling in their work, the primordials began a war that shook the universe, but the gods emerged victorious and the world remains as they have shaped it.

As the world took shape, the primordials found some pieces too vivid and bright, and hurled them away. They found other pieces too murky and dark, and flung them away as well. These discarded bits of creation clustered and merged, and formed together in echoes of the shaping of the world. As the gods joined in the act of creation, more ripples spread out into the Feywild and the Shadowfell, bringing creatures to life there as echoes of the world's mortals. Thus the world was born with two siblings: the bright Feywild and the dark Shadowfell.

The Shadowfell is a dark echo of the world. It touches the world in places of deep shadow, sometimes spilling out into the world, and other times drawing hapless travelers into its dark embrace. It is not wholly evil, but everything in the Shadowfell has its dark and sinister side. When mortal creatures die, their spirits travel first to the Shadowfell before moving on to their final fate.

The Feywild is an enchanted reflection of the world. Arcane energy flows through it like streams of crystal water. Its beauty and majesty is unparalleled in the world, and every creature of the wild is imbued with a measure of fantastic power.

## And Beyond

Scholars claim that the universe described here is not all there is—that something else exists beyond the Astral Sea and the Elemental Chaos. Evidence for this idea appears in the form of the most alien creatures known, aberrant monsters such as the aboleth and gibbering orb. These creatures don't seem to be a part of the world or any known realm, and where they live in the world, reality alters around them. This fact has led sages to postulate the existence of a place they call the Far Realm, a place where the laws of reality work differently than in the known universe.

In addition, the souls of the dead—though they travel first to the Shadowfell—pass beyond it after a time. Some souls are claimed by the gods and carried to the divine dominions, but others pass to another realm beyond the knowledge of any living being.

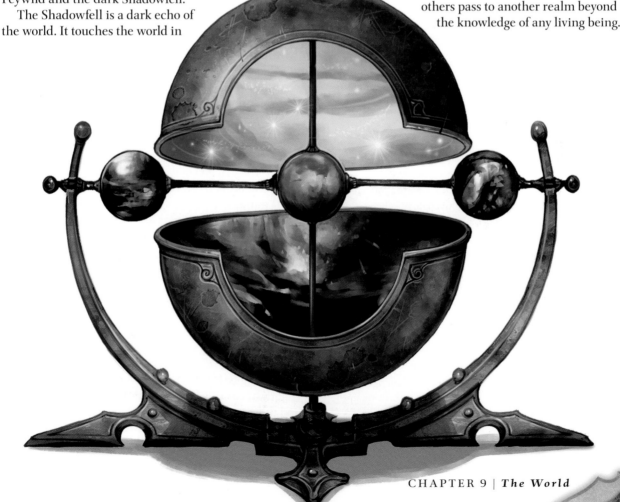

The deities of the D&D world are powerful but not omnipotent, knowledgeable but not omniscient, widely traveled but not omnipresent. They alone of all creatures in the universe consist only of astral essence. The gods are creatures of thought and ideal, not bound by the same limitations as beings of flesh.

Because of their astral nature, the gods can perform deeds that physical creatures can't. They can appear in the minds of other creatures, speaking to them in dreams or visions, without being present in physical form. They can appear in multiple places at once. They can listen to the prayers of their followers (but they don't always). But they can also make physical forms for themselves with a moment's effort, and they do when the need arises—when presumptuous epic-level mortal adventurers dare to challenge them in their own dominions, for example. In these forms, they can fight and be fought, and they can suffer terrible consequences as a result. However, to destroy a god requires more than merely striking its physical form down with spell or sword. Gods have killed other gods (Asmodeus being the first to do so), and the primordials killed many gods during their great war. For a mortal to accomplish this deed would require rituals of awesome power to bind a god to its physical form—and then a truly epic battle to defeat that form.

### THE DEITIES

| Deity | Alignment | Areas of Influence |
|---|---|---|
| Asmodeus | Evil | Power, domination, tyranny |
| Avandra | Good | Change, luck, trade, travel |
| Bahamut | Lawful good | Justice, honor, nobility, protection |
| Bane | Evil | War, conquest |
| Corellon | Unaligned | Arcane magic, spring, beauty, the arts |
| Erathis | Unaligned | Civilization, invention, laws |
| Gruumsh | Chaotic evil | Turmoil, destruction |
| Ioun | Unaligned | Knowledge, prophecy, skill |
| Kord | Unaligned | Storms, strength, battle |
| Lolth | Chaotic evil | Spiders, shadows, lies |
| Melora | Unaligned | Wilderness, sea |
| Moradin | Lawful good | Creation, artisans, family |
| Pelor | Good | Sun, summer, agriculture, time |
| Raven Queen | Unaligned | Death, fate, winter |
| Sehanine | Unaligned | Trickery, moon, love, autumn |
| Tharizdun | Chaotic evil | Annihilation, madness |
| Tiamat | Evil | Wealth, greed, vengeance |
| Torog | Evil | Underdark, imprisonment |
| Vecna | Evil | Undeath, secrets |
| Zehir | Evil | Darkness, poison, serpents |

The most powerful servants of the gods are their exarchs. Some exarchs are angels whose faithful service has earned them this exalted status. Others were once mortal servants who won the station through their mighty deeds. Asmodeus has devils as exarchs, and both Bahamut and Tiamat have granted that status to powerful dragons. Every exarch is a unique example of its kind, empowered with capabilities far beyond those of other angels, mortals, or monsters.

## MALIGN GODS

The good, lawful good, and unaligned gods are described in the *Player's Handbook*. The evil and chaotic evil gods aren't detailed there, because the game assumes that player characters view these gods and their servants as enemies. The villains in your campaign, though, can be servants of these malign gods.

## ASMODEUS

Asmodeus is the evil god of tyranny and domination. He rules the Nine Hells with an iron fist and a silver tongue. Aside from devils, evil creatures such as rakshasas pay him homage, and evil tieflings and warlocks are drawn to his dark cults. His rules are strict and his punishments harsh:

✦ Seek power over others, that you might rule with strength as the Lord of Hell does.

✦ Repay evil with evil. If others are kind to you, exploit their weakness for your own gain.

✦ Show neither pity nor mercy to those who are caught underfoot as you climb your way to power. The weak do not deserve compassion.

## BANE

Bane is the evil god of war and conquest. Militaristic nations of humans and goblins serve him and conquer in his name. Evil fighters and paladins serve him. He commands his worshipers to:

✦ Never allow your fear to gain mastery over you, but drive it into the hearts of your foes.

✦ Punish insubordination and disorder.

✦ Hone your combat skills to perfection, whether you are a mighty general or a lone mercenary.

## GRUUMSH

Gruumsh is the chaotic evil god of destruction, lord of marauding barbarian hordes. Where Bane commands conquest, Gruumsh exhorts his followers to slaughter and pillage. Orcs are his fervent followers, and they bear a particular hatred for elves and eladrin because

Corellon put out one of Gruumsh's eyes. The One-Eyed God gives simple orders to his followers:

✦ Conquer and destroy.

✦ Let your strength crush the weak.

✦ Do as you will, and let no one stop you.

## LOLTH

Lolth is the chaotic evil god of shadow, lies, and spiders. Scheming and treachery are her commands, and her priests are a constant force of disruption in the otherwise stable society of the evil drow. Though she is properly a god and not a demon, she is called Demon Queen of Spiders. She demands that her followers:

✦ Do whatever it takes to gain and hold power.

✦ Rely on stealth and slander in preference to outright confrontation.

✦ Seek the death of elves and eladrin at every opportunity.

## THARIZDUN

Tharizdun is the chaotic evil god who created the Abyss. He is not mentioned in the *Player's Handbook* or named in the *Monster Manual*, because the fact of his existence is not widely known. A few scattered cults of demented followers revere him, calling him the Chained God or the Elder Elemental Eye. Tharizdun doesn't speak to his followers, so his commands are unknown, but his cults teach their members to:

✦ Channel power to the Chained God, so he can break his chains.

✦ Retrieve lost relics and shrines to the Chained God.

✦ Pursue the obliteration of the world, in anticipation of the Chained God's liberation.

## TIAMAT

Tiamat is the evil god of wealth, greed, and envy. She is the patron of chromatic dragons and those whose lust for wealth overrides any other goal or concern. She commands her followers to:

✦ Hoard wealth, acquiring much and spending little. Wealth is its own reward.

✦ Forgive no slight and leave no wrong unpunished.

✦ Take what you desire from others. Those who lack the strength to defend their possessions are not worthy to own them.

## TOROG

Torog is the evil god of the Underdark, patron of jailers and torturers. Common superstition holds that if his name is spoken, the King that Crawls burrows up from below and drags the hapless speaker underground to an eternity of imprisonment and torture. Jailers and torturers pray to him in deep caves and cellars, and creatures of the Underdark revere him as well. He teaches his worshipers to:

✦ Seek out and revere the deep places beneath the earth.

✦ Delight in the giving of pain, and consider pain you receive as homage to Torog.

✦ Bind tightly what is in your charge, and restrain those who wander free.

## VECNA

Vecna is the evil god of undead, necromancy, and secrets. He rules that which is not meant to be known and that which people wish to keep secret. Evil spellcasters and conspirators pay him homage. He commands them to:

✦ Never reveal all you know.

✦ Find the seed of darkness in your heart and nourish it; find it in others and exploit it to your advantage.

✦ Oppose the followers of all other deities so that Vecna alone can rule the world.

## ZEHIR

Zehir is the evil god of darkness, poison, and assassins. Snakes are his favored creation, and the yuan-ti revere him above all other gods, offering sacrifice to him in pits full of writhing serpents. He urges his followers to:

✦ Hide under the cloak of night, that your deeds might be kept in secret.

✦ Kill in Zehir's name and offer each murder as a sacrifice.

✦ Delight in poison, and surround yourself with snakes.

## DIVINE EVIL

Evil and chaotic evil deities have clerics and paladins just as other gods do. However, the powers of those classes, as presented in the *Player's Handbook*, are strongly slanted toward good and lawful good characters. Players might find it jarring to fight a paladin of Zehir whose weapon erupts with radiant light.

You can alter the nature of powers without changing their basic effects, making them feel more appropriate for the servants of evil gods: changing the damage type of a prayer, for instance, so that evil clerics and paladins deal necrotic damage instead of radiant damage. When a prayer would blind its target with holy light, it might instead shroud a character's eyes with clinging darkness. Holy fire consuming a foe with ongoing fire damage might become a coating of acidic slime that eats away at the flesh, or a purple hellfire with identical effects.

9

# ARTIFACTS

Artifacts are unique, named magic items whose creation or existence can't be explained by the normal laws of magic. Unlike common magic items, artifacts are an essential part of the world's weave, a piece of the story of the universe.

Artifacts have a level but no price—they can't be bought or crafted, and their temporary nature ensures that they don't have a long-term impact on a character's total wealth. As with normal magic items, an artifact's level measures the potency of its properties and powers, but artifacts break the usual magic item rules.

An artifact can't be created, disenchanted, or destroyed by any of the normal means available for other magic items. In fact, the characters' access to artifacts (and even their retention of recovered artifacts) is entirely within your control. A character can quest after a particular artifact whose existence is known or suspected, but even then the character acquires an artifact only if the DM says so.

Similarly, a character can research a specific method to destroy a known artifact, if destroying it fits with your plans for the campaign. Destroying an artifact should require an extraordinary effort—artifacts are normally immune to all forms of damage or unwanted alterations to their form—and each artifact has a unique means of destroying it. For instance, you might decide that a character can destroy the *Eye of Vecna* by hurling himself (with the *Eye* implanted in his skull) into the Rift of Pyradon, a fiery chasm in the depths of the Elemental Chaos. The *Hand of Vecna*, though, might survive that fate, requiring instead that its owner sever it from his arm with the sword of the same dead god whose skull crowns the *Wand of Orcus*.

## ARTIFACT USE LIMITS

Artifacts do not count as magic items when it comes to using their daily powers. In other words, the use of an artifact's daily power does not cost you the use of a magic item's daily power and does not count toward that limit.

## ARTIFACT BEHAVIOR

Artifacts are sentient—although they're not necessarily communicative—and they have their own motivations. In many ways, they function like nonplayer characters. An artifact cooperates with its owner as long as doing so fits with the artifact's goals and nature.

Each artifact's description contains a list of its goals and roleplaying notes for its personality. Some artifacts are malevolent and seek to corrupt their wielders, whereas others push the wielder to great acts of heroism.

What's more, an artifact's powers change depending on its attitude or connection to its current owner.

When its wielder performs actions in concert with its goals, an artifact becomes more powerful, but when the wielder acts against the artifact's wishes, its power diminishes. The artifact's mindset is measured by a concordance score.

## CONCORDANCE

An artifact's concordance score measures the artifact's attitude toward its wielder. The scale ranges from 0 (angered) to 20 (pleased).

When a character takes possession of an artifact, it starts with a concordance of 5. (The owner's race, class, or other characteristics might adjust this starting concordance.) Various actions and events increase or decrease this score as long as the character possesses the artifact. When the artifact is pleased with its wielder's actions, its concordance goes up. When the wielder acts contrary to the artifact's desires, its concordance decreases.

The wielder knows of the factors that alter the concordance—it's in the artifact's best interests to communicate its desires and expectations. But keep the artifact's concordance score a secret, telling the player only if the artifact's powers or properties change. The player shouldn't ever know exactly how close the artifact is to changing its attitude.

### CONCORDANCE

| Score | Artifact's Attitude |
| --- | --- |
| 16-20 | Pleased |
| 12-15 | Satisfied |
| 5-11 | Normal |
| 1-4 | Unsatisfied |
| 0 or lower | Angered |

## MOVING ON

Whatever their nature, all artifacts share one behavioral trait in common: They move on. When a character acquires the *Axe of the Dwarvish Lords*, she instinctively realizes that, as with all the heroes and villains before her who have held the artifact, her ownership will be temporary.

Every artifact has unique goals. When a wielder has advanced the artifact's goals or proven to be a hopeless case, the artifact moves on. For a few levels, make the artifact's intentions part of your story line and the PCs' possible quest. Consider the artifact's probable exit points before you allow a character to gain possession of an artifact.

### ARTIFACTS AND THE RPGA

Artifacts are not legal for use in RPGA events unless the event grants the use of the artifact. If you gain the use of an artifact during an RPGA event, the artifact automatically "moves on" at the end of the adventure; you cannot keep it for a future event.

As a rule of thumb, plan for an artifact to remain in a character's possession for somewhere between one and three levels of play. You can make exceptions, of course, but this is about the right amount of time to allow a specific artifact to play a role in your campaign.

An artifact moves on when you decide it does. A particularly mighty quest might provide a great finale for the artifact's presence—perhaps it must be sacrificed to complete the quest, or the final act of slaying the evil champion drains the artifact of its power, or the artifact just decides that it has other places to be and other things to do. Of course, not all exit points are heroic—a villain might steal the artifact for his own use, or the artifact's evil might move the characters to seek its destruction.

When an artifact decides to leave, it moves on in whatever manner is appropriate to the artifact, its current attitude, and the story of your campaign. A benevolent artifact, such as the *Axe of the Dwarvish Lords*, typically chooses a quiet time to take its leave. If its attitude is positive, it waits until the next time its wielder gains a level, wishing the character a fond farewell and good fortune in future adventures. If its attitude is negative, it disappears at the end of the current encounter, communicating its disappointment in its wielder as it departs.

A malevolent artifact such as the *Eye of Vecna* has no compunctions about leaving its owner at the most inopportune moment (for instance, ripping itself from the character's eye socket during a battle).

# UNDERSTANDING AN ARTIFACT

More than any other magic item, an artifact is a part of the world—its story stretches into the history and legends of the ancient past and possibly into the distant future as well. This chapter describes four artifacts by way of example, and future supplements and campaign guides include more. To understand an artifact and its place in your world, consider the following.

**1: What is it and what does it want?** Every artifact has a personality and goals. You don't need to come up with an exhaustive history, especially if the players are unlikely to learn that history during the course of the game. But consider how the artifact communicates and what it says, treating it like a nonplayer character with all the quirks and breadth of possibility that your other NPCs possess.

**2: Concordance modifiers.** Every artifact has one to three positive modifiers and one to three negative modifiers that match the artifact's personality and goals. Every artifact's concordance increases by 1d10 when its wielder gains a level. Other positive modifiers might include performing a quest on behalf of a specific group or individual (a religion or other organization, the heir of a specific lineage, or the like), or

killing a specific kind of enemy. Negative modifiers can include any behavior the artifact disapproves of, refusing its commands, or introducing it to someone the artifact thinks would be a better wielder.

**3: Attach effects to each attitude.** Artifacts typically have properties and powers that function the same way no matter what its concordance with its wielder is. These are comparable with other magic items of the artifact's level—a similar enhancement bonus (in the case of an artifact weapon, armor, or amulet), and other powers and properties in line with the character's powers.

An artifact's greatest powers are granted only to a wielder the artifact trusts. As the concordance between an artifact and its owner improves, the artifact grows more powerful. Its greater powers can exceed even the character's most potent abilities, though its best power is rarely more than five levels above the character's level.

On the other hand, when an artifact's attitude worsens, it grows less powerful. Its powers or properties are reduced in potency, it applies penalties that encourage (or discourage) particular behaviors, or it actively seeks to harm to its wielder or his allies.

A wielder can always utilize the standard powers of an artifact (unless specifically told otherwise by the artifact's attitude). The powers granted by an artifact's attitude, however, are only available while the artifact possesses the appropriate concordance score or higher.

# THE AXE OF THE DWARVISH LORDS

The *Axe* is appropriate for epic-level characters.

## Axe of the Dwarvish Lords — Epic Level

*One of five tools given to the first dwarves by Moradin, the Axe of the Dwarvish Lords appears in times of great crisis—often in the hands of a champion destined to save the dwarf people.*

The *Axe of the Dwarvish Lords* is a +5 *thundering greataxe* with the following properties and powers.

**Enhancement:** Attack rolls and damage rolls

**Critical:** +5d6 damage, or +5d10 damage against creatures larger than Medium size

**Property:** This weapon deals an extra 2d10 damage against creatures larger than Medium size.

**Property:** You can throw the *Axe* as a heavy thrown weapon (range 5/10). It returns to your hand after being thrown as normal for a magic thrown weapon.

**Property:** You can speak and understand the Dwarven language and read the Davek script.

**Power (Daily ✦ Divine, Healing):** Standard Action. You can use *death ward* (paladin 16).

**Power (Daily):** Free Action. You can use this power when you hit an enemy with the *Axe*. The enemy is knocked prone. That enemy's space, and all squares within 2 squares of the enemy, crack and fracture into rubble and become difficult terrain until the end of the encounter. You and your allies can move through this terrain as if it were normal.

## Goals of the Axe of the Dwarvish Lords

✦ Help the dwarves flourish in keeping with their ancient traditions.
✦ Give goblins and (especially) giants the deaths they so richly deserve.
✦ Become an inspiration to honorable people everywhere.

## Roleplaying the Axe of the Dwarvish Lords

The *Axe of the Dwarvish Lords* is taciturn–even by the standards of sentient weapons from the mists of ancient history. It communicates in gruff commands only its bearer can hear. It urges its bearer to battle any giants encountered, becoming sullen when refused this honor.

### CONCORDANCE

| Starting score | 5 |
| --- | --- |
| Owner gains a level | +1d10 |
| Owner is a dwarf | +2 |
| Owner completes a quest on behalf of dwarf leaders | +1 |
| Owner kills a giant (maximum 1/day) | +1 |
| Owner or an ally attacks a dwarf (max. 1/encounter) | -2 |
| Owner disobeys a directive from dwarf leaders | -2 |

### Pleased (16–20)

*"A thousand dwarf ancestors guide the path of this blade. I'm just one in an unbroken line of champions."*

The *Axe* is clearly in tune with its wielder at this point, and together they're doing the will of the dwarves.

The *Axe*'s enhancement bonus increases to +6.
**Critical:** +6d6 damage, or +6d10 damage against creatures larger than Medium size
**Property:** This weapon deals an extra 3d10 damage against creatures larger than Medium size.
**Power (Daily):** Minor Action. You call forth an *aura of thunder* (aura 1) that lasts until the end of your next turn. Any enemy that starts its turn within the aura takes 15 thunder damage and is knocked prone.
**Special:** An exarch or angel in the service of Moradin might occasionally emerge from the *Axe* to give you prophetic guidance or send you on a quest. It won't fight for you.

### Satisfied (12–15)

*"Quail in fear, giants! This Axe has spilled the blood of your savage ancestors."*

The wielder has proved to be a worthy representative of the dwarves, and the *Axe* does its wielder's bidding as long as the bearer remains worthy of its trust.

**Power (Daily):** Minor Action. You can heal yourself, recovering hit points as if you spent a healing surge.

### Normal (5–11)

*"The Axe asks for my fealty to the dwarves."*

The *Axe* is reserved and cautious with a new wielder until the character proves his worth and dedication.

### Unsatisfied (1–4)

*"I'm disappointing the Axe–and the dwarves."*

The wielder is fighting dwarves or disobeying their legitimate leaders, and the *Axe* is not pleased. If the wielder doesn't change his ways, the *Axe* soon leaves.

**Special:** You take a -2 penalty to attack rolls and damage rolls against any creatures other than goblins or giants. This applies whether you are using or even holding the *Axe*.

### Angered (0 or lower)

*"I have failed it–the Axe is not pleased."*

The wielder is not meeting the *Axe*'s expectations, and it will not remain in his possession for long.

The *Axe*'s enhancement bonus drops to +4.
**Critical:** +4d6 damage, or +4d10 damage against creatures larger than Medium size
**Property:** This weapon deals an extra 2d10 damage against creatures larger than Medium size.
**Special:** You take a -5 penalty to attack rolls and damage rolls against any creatures other than goblins or giants. This applies regardless if you are using or even holding the *Axe*.

### Moving On

*"The Axe tells me it's needed elsewhere now."*

The *Axe* wants to go where it's most useful, and at some point it knows that it's more needed in other hands. When the character next gains a level, the *Axe* disappears, its sentience and other abilities traveling to another land for a new hero to discover. If the *Axe* is at least satisfied, it leaves behind a normal +6 *thundering greataxe* for its champion to wield in its stead.

## THE EYE OF VECNA

The *Eye* is appropriate for paragon-level characters.

The *Eye of Vecna* doesn't do anything unless installed permanently in an empty eye socket. Removing an eye to make room for the *Eye of Vecna* is a gory process that deals damage equal to three times the character's healing surge value. These hit points can't be restored until after the character has taken an extended rest. Once installed, the *Eye of Vecna* becomes part of its possessor's body, functioning just like a normal eye (though it retains its unusual appearance).

## The Eye of Vecna — Paragon Level

*One of two relics left behind by Vecna before he ascended to god-hood, the Eye of Vecna is a red, embalmed orb that pulses as if alive, but remains icy cold to the touch. It retains a remnant of Vecna's mortal power—a power with a singular devotion to evil.*

**Body Slot:** Head
**Property:** You gain a +1 item bonus to Arcana, Insight, and Perception checks.
**Property:** The *Eye* grants you darkvision.
**Property:** When using an attack power granted by the *Eye*, you can use your highest mental ability score (Intelligence, Wisdom, or Charisma) for the attack, regardless of the normal ability score noted for the power.
**Power (At-Will ✦ Arcane, Charm, Implement, Psychic):** Standard Action. You can use *eyebite* (warlock 1).
**Power (Encounter ✦ Arcane, Illusion, Implement, Psychic):** Standard Action. You can use *mire the mind* (warlock 7).
**Power (Daily ✦ Arcane):** Standard Action. You can use *eye of the warlock* (warlock 16).

## Goals of the Eye of Vecna

✦ Be reunited with the *Hand of Vecna*.
✦ Spread the worship of Vecna across the world.
✦ Wrest secrets from those who keep them, then use those secrets as weapons of betrayal.
✦ Be installed in a powerful living vessel, preferably a powerful wielder of arcane magic.

## Roleplaying the Eye of Vecna

The *Eye of Vecna* communicates silently with its possessor, delivering vivid hallucinatory visions about what it wants. These visions are subtle at first, but eventually they become grisly and more explicit.

The *Eye's* ability to communicate is limited when it's not installed in an eye socket. Those who handle the *Eye* in its unattached state receive only brief visions of power—whatever is compelling to that person. They also gain a clear idea of what they need to do to acquire the *Eye's* power.

## Concordance

Until its wielder implants the *Eye*, the artifact has no concordance and the wielder doesn't gain any of its properties or powers.

| Starting score | 5 |
|---|---|
| Owner gains a level | +1d10 |
| Owner can cast at least one arcane spell | +2 |
| Owner attaches the *Hand of Vecna* | +2 |
| Owner betrays a close friend in dire straits | +1 |
| Owner wrests an important secret from a captive | +1 |
| Owner or ally kills an undead creature (maximum 1/encounter) | -2 |
| Owner spends 8 hours in the presence of a higher-level arcane spellcaster (maximum 1/day) | -2 |

## Pleased (16–20)

*"The Eye and I are one."*

The *Eye of Vecna* is pleased with its host—for now. It concentrates on advancing Vecna's designs on the world, confident that it has found an effective vehicle for its ambitions.

**Property:** The *Eye's* item bonus to Arcana, Insight, and Perception checks increases to +5.
**Property:** You take a -5 penalty to Diplomacy checks.
**Power (Daily ✦ Arcane, Implement):** Minor Action. You call forth an *aura of clear sight* (aura 10) that lasts until the end of your next turn. While the aura is active, you gain a +10 bonus to all attack rolls, skill checks, and ability checks made against targets within the aura.

## Satisfied (12–15)

*"The Eye . . . it reveals so much to me."*

The *Eye of Vecna* is satisfied enough with its host, but it's still looking for a better one. It's content to serve its host, but it occasionally sends a frightening vision to remind the possessor who's really in charge.

**Property:** The *Eye's* item bonus to Arcana, Insight, and Perception checks increases to +2.
**Property:** You take a -2 penalty to Diplomacy checks.
**Power (Encounter ✦ Arcane, Implement, Necrotic):** Standard Action. You can fire a beam of necrotic energy from the *Eye*. The attack is made with your highest mental ability score vs. Fortitude. A hit deals 3d6 + 5 necrotic damage and ongoing 5 necrotic damage (save ends).

## Normal (5–11)

*"I can feel the Eye's power."*

When first implanted in a host, the *Eye* is communicative, trying to set the terms of the relationship and explain what activities the *Eye* favors or abhors.

## Unsatisfied (1–4)

*"The Eye is showing me things. Horrible things."*

The *Eye of Vecna* believes that the host is unlikely to satisfy its ambitions, so it's actively seeks a better wielder. But it's evil enough to toy with the current host first, even in dangerous situations.

**Property:** You take a -2 penalty to Diplomacy checks.
**Special:** Once per day at any time, the *Eye* can induce a horrifying vision in your mind. The *Eye* makes a special attack against your Will defense, rolling 1d20 + your level. If this attack hits, you are stunned (save ends).

The *Eye* typically induces a vision during a nonthreatening situation first, trying to force a more compliant attitude from its owner. But the *Eye* isn't shy about inducing a vision during a combat situation.

## Angered (0 or lower)

*"Tear it out! Don't let it see you!"*

At this point, the *Eye of Vecna* is at war with its possessor, and it wants to torture its host before moving on to a more acceptable wielder.

**Property:** You take a -5 penalty to Diplomacy checks.

**Special:** Once per encounter at any time, the *Eye* can induce a horrifying vision in your mind. The *Eye* makes a special attack against your Will defense, rolling 1d20 + your level. If this attack hits, you are blinded and stunned (save ends).

**Special:** Each time you make an initiative check at the start of an encounter, there is a 25% chance that the *Eye* uses *eyebite* against one of your allies within range of the spell (determined randomly by the DM).

**Special:** The *Eye* can speak through you whenever you are stunned or unconscious. It can use either your natural voice or a sinister, eerily loud whisper.

## MOVING ON

*"I am Vecna."*

The *Eye of Vecna* consumes its owner, body and mind. The character dies instantly, and his body crumbles to dust. Even if the character is raised from the dead, he forever carries an empty eye socket as a souvenir of having once possessed the *Eye*.

The *Eye* rejoins its divine namesake. Vecna immediately gains all the knowledge of the former wielder and savors the secrets so acquired. After a time, he sends the *Eye* back into the world to glean more secrets from other unwitting or greedy arcane characters.

If the *Eye*'s wielder also bears the *Hand of Vecna*, that artifact also returns to the god.

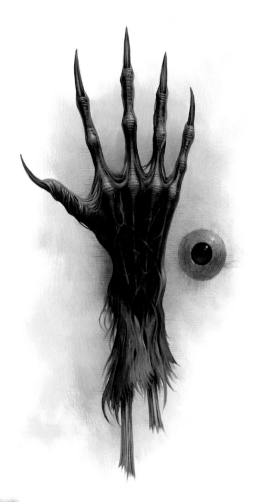

# THE HAND OF VECNA

The *Hand* is appropriate for characters in the middle of the paragon tier and upward.

The *Hand of Vecna* doesn't do anything unless attached to the stump of an arm where a hand once was. Removing a hand to make room for Vecna's Hand deals damage equal to one-half the character's maximum normal hit points. Once installed, the *Hand of Vecna* becomes part of its possessor's body. It retains its grisly appearance, though it functions just like as a normal hand.

| The Hand of Vecna | Paragon Level |
|---|---|

*One of two relics left behind by Vecna before he ascended to godhood, the Hand of Vecna is a blackened, mummified left hand, icy cold to the touch. It retains a remnant of Vecna's mortal power—a power with a singular devotion to evil.*

**Body Slot:** Hands

**Property:** You gain a +2 item bonus to Athletics checks.

**Property:** When using an attack power granted by the *Hand*, you can use your highest physical ability score (Strength, Constitution, or Dexterity) for the attack, regardless of the normal ability score noted for the power.

**Power (At-Will ✦ Arcane, Implement):** Standard Action. You can use *diabolic grasp* (warlock 1).

**Power (Encounter ✦ Arcane, Implement):** Standard Action. You can use *sign of ill omen* (warlock 7).

**Power (Encounter):** Move Action. You can use *spider climb* (warlock 6).

## GOALS OF THE HAND OF VECNA

✦ Be reunited with the *Eye of Vecna*.

✦ Spread worship of Vecna across the world.

✦ Wrest secrets from those who keep them, then use those secrets as weapons of betrayal.

✦ Be installed in a powerful living vessel, preferably a powerful wielder of arcane magic.

## ROLEPLAYING THE HAND OF VECNA

The *Hand of Vecna* can move independently of its owner's wishes to communicate, using a strange sign language that only a character who has attached the *Hand* can understand. Its ability to communicate is limited when it's not attached. When a humanoid character touches the *Hand*, it springs to life, scratching at the left hand of the creature that touched it. At the same time, the character feels a surge of power, accompanied by a sense that his greatest desires are within grasp.

## CONCORDANCE

Until its owner attaches the *Hand*, the artifact has no concordance and the owner doesn't gain any of its properties or powers.

| Starting score | 5 |
|---|---|
| Owner gains a level | +1d10 |
| Owner can cast at least one arcane spell | +2 |
| Owner implants the *Eye of Vecna* | +2 |
| Owner betrays a close friend in dire straits | +1 |
| Owner wrests an important secret from a captive | +1 |
| Owner or ally kills an undead creature (maximum 1/encounter) | -2 |
| Owner spends 8 hours in the presence of a higher-level arcane spellcaster (maximum 1/day) | -2 |

## Pleased (16–20)

*"I am Vecna's hand in the world."*

The *Hand of Vecna* is pleased with its host—for now. It concentrates on advancing Vecna's designs on the world, confident that it has found an effective vehicle for its ambitions.

**Property:** The *Hand*'s item bonus to Athletics checks increases to +5.

**Property:** You take a -5 penalty to Diplomacy checks.

**Power (Daily ✦ Arcane):** Minor Action. You call forth an *aura of death* (aura 10) that lasts until the end of your next turn. While the aura is active, enemies that enter the aura or start their turn in the aura take 10 necrotic damage. Each time an enemy takes damage in this manner, you heal 10 hit points.

## Satisfied (12–15)

*"All power is within the grasp of this Hand."*

The *Hand of Vecna* is satisfied enough with its host, but it's still looking for a better one. It's content to serve its host, but it occasionally acts on its own to remind the possessor who's really in charge. The wielder might wake in the middle of the night to find the *Hand* clenched around her throat, for example.

**Property:** The *Hand*'s item bonus to Athletics checks increases to +3.

**Property:** You take a -2 penalty to Diplomacy checks.

**Power (Encounter ✦ Arcane, Implement, Necrotic):** Standard Action. You can hurl a ball of necrotic energy from the *Hand*, (area burst 1 within 10 squares). The attack is made with your highest physical ability score vs. Reflex. A hit deals 2d10 + 5 necrotic damage and ongoing 5 necrotic damage (save ends) to all enemies in the burst.

## Normal (5–11)

*"I can feel the Hand's power."*

When first attached to a host, the *Hand* is communicative, trying to set the terms of the relationship and explain what activities the *Hand* favors or abhors.

## Unsatisfied (1–4)

*"The Hand doesn't do what I want, it does what it wants."*

The *Hand of Vecna* believes that the host is unlikely to satisfy its ambitions, so it actively seeks a better wielder. But it's evil enough to toy with the current host first, even in dangerous situations.

**Property:** You take a -2 penalty to Diplomacy checks.

**Special:** Once per day at any time, the *Hand* might choose to drop whatever it holds and attempt to choke you. The *Hand* makes a special attack against your Fortitude defense, rolling 1d20 + your level. If this attack hits, you are dazed (save ends). Until you make a saving throw, you also can't use the *Hand* to attack or manipulate objects or to use the *Hand*'s powers.

The *Hand* typically defies its host in a nonthreatening situation first, trying to demonstrate who's in charge. After that warning, any time becomes fair game.

## Angered (0 or lower)

*"Get it off me! Keep away from it!"*

At this point, the *Hand of Vecna* is at war with its possessor, and it wants to torture its host before moving on to a more acceptable wielder.

**Property:** You take a -5 penalty to Diplomacy checks.

**Special:** Once per encounter at any time, the *Hand* might choose to drop whatever it holds and attempt to choke you. The *Hand* makes a special attack against your Fortitude defense, rolling 1d20 + your level. If this attack hits, you are dazed (save ends). Until you succeed on a saving throw, you also can't use the *Hand* to attack or manipulate objects or to use the *Hand*'s powers.

**Special:** Each time you miss with an attack, there is a 25% chance that the *Hand* uses *diabolic grasp* against one of your allies within range of the spell (determined randomly by the DM).

## Moving On

*"I am Vecna."*

The *Hand of Vecna* consumes its owner, body and mind. The character dies instantly, and her body crumbles to dust. Even if the character is raised from the dead, she forever carries a handless stump as a souvenir of having once wielded the *Hand*.

The *Hand* rejoins its divine namesake. Vecna immediately gains all the knowledge of the former wielder and savors the secrets so acquired. After a time, he sends the *Hand* back into the world to glean more secrets from other unwitting or greedy arcane characters.

If the *Hand*'s wielder also bears the *Eye of Vecna*, that artifact also returns to the god.

9

# THE INVULNERABLE COAT OF ARND

The *Invulnerable Coat* is appropriate for characters in the middle of the heroic tier and upward.

| The Invulnerable Coat of Arnd | Heroic Level |
| --- | --- |

*This gleaming chain mail belonged to a poor cleric of Kord who fought to free his village from its tyrannical baron. Imbued with the cleric's fighting spirit and holy strength, the Invulnerable Coat of Arnd seeks to reclaim its ancient glory.*

The *Invulnerable Coat of Arnd* is a suit of +2 *chainmail*.
**Enhancement:** AC
**Property:** You gain resist 5 acid, resist 5 fire, and resist 5 lightning.
**Property:** You gain a +2 item bonus to saving throws.
**Power (At-Will ✦ Divine, Weapon):** Standard Action. You can use *valiant strike* (paladin 1).
**Power (At-Will):** Minor Action. Change one of the resistances granted by the armor to any of the following damage types: acid, cold, fire, force, lightning, necrotic, psychic, or radiant. That resistance remains changed until you use the power to change it again.
**Power (At-Will):** Minor Action. Change the Invulnerable Coat into plate armor, scale armor, or chainmail.
**Power (Encounter):** Minor Action. You can spend a healing surge.

## GOALS OF THE INVULNERABLE COAT OF ARND

✦ Attach itself to a hero who will be remembered in legend.
✦ Prove itself against ever greater threats and challenges.
✦ Overthrow tyrants.

## ROLEPLAYING THE INVULNERABLE COAT OF ARND

The *Invulnerable Coat* thrives on danger, so it urges its wearer to take on increasingly difficult risks. The *Invulnerable Coat*'s not happy unless the wearer is throwing himself into battle. Planning and strategy aren't high on the artifact's list of priorities. The *Invulnerable Coat* doesn't communicate with its wearer, but its emotional state does rub off, so the owner feels elated in battle and despairs at defeat.

### CONCORDANCE

| Starting score | 5 |
| --- | --- |
| Owner gains a level | +1d10 |
| Owner receives public acclaim for completing a major quest | +1 |
| Owner defeats an enemy three or more levels higher than he is (maximum 1/day) | +1 |
| Owner falls to 0 hit points in battle | -1 |
| Owner flees from combat | -1 |

## PLEASED (16–20)
*"There is no limit to the brave deeds we can accomplish."*

The *Invulnerable Coat of Arnd* is excited to have such a hero to protect. It starts to literally glow with pride, constantly shedding dim light in a 2-square radius.

**Property:** You gain resist 10 acid, resist 10 fire, and resist 10 lightning. This supersedes the normal resistances granted by the artifact.
**Property:** You gain a +5 bonus to Will defense against fear effects.
**Power (Daily):** Minor Action. You call forth an *aura of courage* (aura 2) that lasts until the end of your next turn. You and any ally within the aura gain a +5 bonus to attack rolls.

## SATISFIED (12–15)
*"We are destined for greatness."*

The *Invulnerable Coat of Arnd* is pleased with the wielder's bravery and drive, so it devotes more of its power to urging him on to greater glory.

**Property:** You gain a +2 bonus to Will defense against fear effects.
**Power (Daily):** Free Action. Gain 1 action point.

## NORMAL (5–11)
*"Glory waits for no one—we must seize it by the throat!"*

The *Coat* wants its wielder to put himself in harm's way, and it urges him toward acts of daring.

## UNSATISFIED (1–4)
*"All is not lost—I can still redeem myself!"*

**Special:** You take a -2 penalty to all defenses against creatures whose level is equal to or lower than yours.

## ANGERED (0 OR LOWER)
*"I'm not worthy of armor this fine."*

The *Coat* regards its wielder as a coward and urges him to find someone more worthy to wear it.

The artifact's enhancement bonus to AC drops to +1.
**Special:** You take a -5 penalty to all defenses against creatures whose level is equal to or lower than yours.

## MOVING ON
*"Our names shall live on in legend."*

The *Invulnerable Coat* recognizes that its wielder's bravery needs no further assistance.

When the wielder next gains a level, the *Invulnerable Coat* crumbles into *residuum* worth 5,000 gp. Its magic and sentience appear elsewhere in the world, encased in a new suit of armor.

Also, the wielder gains a permanent +1 bonus to Diplomacy checks and Intimidate checks. Even those who do not know of his bravery recognize an aura of greatness around him—a remnant of the *Coat*.

If the *Invulnerable Coat* moves on because it is unsatisfied with the wielder, then the wielder receives a permanent -1 penalty to Diplomacy and Intimidate checks, and the armor crumbles into worthless dust.

# LANGUAGES

The *Player's Handbook* introduces the ten languages spoken throughout the D&D world, along with the six scripts used to write them. The *Monster Manual* includes information on the languages creatures speak and understand, though of course individuals might vary from those standards.

A universe with ten languages might seem improbable, but it's explainable in the context of the D&D world and better for the play of the game.

The gods have their own language, Supernal, which they share with their angelic servants. When a god or angel speaks Supernal, listeners who don't speak Supernal understand the words as if the speaker used their own languages. The gods and angels can choose to disguise their speech, but in general Supernal is a universal language.

When the gods created the races of the world, each race heard the Supernal language in a different way, based on fundamental characteristics of their nature. From those distinct ways of hearing, the foundational languages of the world arose—Common for humans and halflings, Elven for elves and eladrin, Goblin for the goblin races, Dwarven for the dwarves, and Draconic for dragons.

The primordials had their own language with none of the special qualities of Supernal. The titans and giants adopted a debased version of this language for their own tongue, and Abyssal is a form of Primordial warped and twisted by the evil at the heart of the Abyss.

These foundational languages spread to other creatures of the world and the planes, with dialect variation but no more significant alteration.

Scripts follow a similar logic. Supernal and Primordial have their own scripts. The main civilized races developed different scripts to transcribe the foundational languages: Common, Davek runes for Dwarven, the Rellanic script for Elven, and Iokharic lettering for Draconic. Goblin is the only foundational language of the world that lacks its own script, owing to the brutal and barbaric nature of the goblin race. The Giant language uses the Davek runes of the dwarves, dating from the dwarves' long servitude to the giants.

The Deep Speech is a language related to the alien communication of the Far Realm, used by creatures influenced by the energy of that place beyond the world and the planes. It uses the Rellanic script because the drow were the first to transcribe it, since they share Underdark haunts with aberrant creatures.

## LANGUAGES IN THE GAME

Having only ten languages keeps the game moving. It's easy for a party of adventurers to master nearly every language, and intelligent creatures they encounter speak at least a little Common. Familiarity with languages lets adventuring parties read inscriptions and tomes they come across in their adventuring. The 1st-level ritual Comprehend Language covers the situations where they can't. Fundamentally, language never has to be an issue in the game—unless you want it to be.

Characters and their opponents can use languages as a kind of code, speaking among themselves in languages their enemies can't understand. An arrogant eladrin lord might refuse to speak in Common and ignore anyone who doesn't speak Elven. Barbaric goblins might not understand Common, forcing the characters to negotiate with them in Goblin for the release of captives. When you use languages in this way, make sure you don't leave players whose characters can't participate bored for too long.

Scripts are essentially independent of language. Just as different real-world languages use the same script to transcribe their different words, Common could be written in Davek or Rellenic as easily as in the Common script. Characters might run across old dwarf texts in Davek runes that use Common words—or the Abyssal language. Such a text would require familiarity with two languages to decipher.

The six basic scripts named in the *Player's Handbook* might not be the only scripts ever used in your world. You might decide that an ancient empire had its own script, one that none of the characters are familiar with. This would work just like a cryptogram puzzle (see page 83), forcing the players to figure out what runes or characters represent which letters in the "Common" script.

## WORDS OF POWER

The Supernal and Abyssal languages are both actual languages used to communicate, but they also include words of power—words whose syllables contain the raw magic of creation (in the case of Supernal) or primordial evil (Abyssal). Player characters can't know these languages initially. They might eventually learn the basics of communicating in these tongues, but without mastering these mighty sounds. Mortals who learn Supernal don't gain the ability to have their words universally understood. Texts containing these words in either language could unleash powerful effects—and these tomes or scrolls might be artifacts in their own right.

# THE DM'S TOOLBOX

As the Dungeon Master, you continually exercise your creative imagination to present new challenges to your players. You're not even limited by the encounter rules in this book or the selection of monsters in the *Monster Manual*—only your own imagination controls what you can do. This chapter is all about going beyond the basics and making the D&D game distinctly yours.

Customizing your campaign is a mix of art and science. Here is where you'll find plenty of "crunch"—new rules for creating and modifying monsters and other challenges. This chapter also offers plenty of advice on giving your imagination free rein without unbalancing your game. Above all, it's about having fun!

This chapter includes the following sections.

✦ **Customizing Monsters:** Tools to help you adjust abilities or add specialized roles or class levels to existing monsters.

✦ **Creating Monsters:** How to create your own monsters to supplement those in the *Monster Manual*.

✦ **Creating NPCs:** How to create nonplayer characters, who are important villains and allies. They work much as the players' characters do, using the same classes and the same basic rules.

✦ **Creating House Rules:** Advice on customizing your campaign with new rules of your own design.

✦ **Random Dungeons:** These rules let you create an adventure on the fly or provide starting points for a crafted dungeon.

✦ **Random Encounters:** A way to generate challenges on the spur of the moment—even without a Dungeon Master!

The *Monster Manual* provides hundreds of enemies for your adventures, but they aren't all that's available. You can customize existing monsters to increase their utility, making them stronger, weaker, or just different.

Whether you want to bump an ogre up a few levels or turn it into an elite berserker, this section gives you the tools you need to tinker with monsters. You'll also find rules for adding a class to a monster, mining the *Player's Handbook* for combat powers.

You can use several methods to adjust an existing monster: change its level, give it equipment, alter its appearance and behavior, and apply a template. Each of these approaches is discussed below.

## INCREASING OR DECREASING LEVEL

Boosting a monster's level is easy. Just increase its attack rolls, defenses, and AC by 1 for every level you add. For every two levels, increase the damage it deals with its attacks by 1. The monster also gains extra hit points at each level, based on its role (see the "Monster Statistics by Role" table on page 184).

Decreasing a monster's level works like increasing it, but in reverse. For each level down, reduce the creature's attack rolls, defenses, and AC by 1 and drop its hit points based on its role. For every two levels, also reduce its damage by 1.

This process works best for adjusting a monster's level up to five higher or lower. Beyond that, the monster changes so much that you'd do better to start with another creature of the desired role and level range.

## ADDING EQUIPMENT

You can add equipment to a monster to make it a little more challenging, or to put treasure into the characters' hands. Equipment shouldn't be random but should serve some purpose in the design of an encounter. Make sure to include any such items as part of the overall treasure you're giving out for the adventure (see "Treasure" on page 124).

**Armor:** When you add armor to a monster, you first need to determine if the armor is good enough to improve the monster's AC. Start with the monster's effective armor bonus—a measure of how much of the creature's AC comes from its armor or from its thick hide. This number is equal to its AC minus 10 minus the higher of its Dexterity or Intelligence ability modifiers. Do not include the Dexterity or Intelligence modifier if the creature wears heavy armor. Subtract the effective armor bonus from the creature's AC, and then add the bonus from its new armor. If the creature moved from

heavy to light armor, you can also add the higher of its Dexterity or Intelligence ability modifier to its AC.

If the creature's statistics block does not mention any worn armor, use the higher of its original AC or its new AC after adding armor. Most creatures have naturally thick hides that provide an armor bonus to AC. If the armor a creature wears is not as good as its natural armor, it uses the AC bonus provided by its natural armor. Worn armor, such as a suit of chainmail, and natural armor, such as an insect's carapace or a dragon's thick scales, do not stack.

For example, an ogre savage normally has an Armor Class of 19 (it's assumed to be wearing crude hide armor). Its effective armor bonus is +5 (19 - 10 - 4 [Dex]). Giving the ogre chainmail instead would improve its AC by 1 to 20, since the armor's +6 bonus is 1 higher than this number.

**Magic Items:** A monster equipped with magic items can use the powers those items grant.

*Enhancement Bonuses:* A monster benefits from an enhancement bonus to attack rolls, defenses, or AC only if that bonus is higher than its magic threshold, as shown on the table below.

A monster's magic threshold is an abstract representation of its equipment, power, and general effectiveness against characters of its level. If you give the monster a magic item that grants a bonus to attack rolls and damage rolls or to defenses, subtract the magic threshold from that bonus before you apply it. For example, if you give that 8th-level ogre savage a +2 *magic greatclub*, you add only a +1 bonus to its attack rolls and damage rolls, since its magic threshold is +1.

### MONSTER MAGIC THRESHOLD

| Monster Level | Magic Threshold |
| --- | --- |
| 1st–5th | +0 |
| 6th–10th | +1 |
| 11th–15th | +2 |
| 16th–20th | +3 |
| 21st–25th | +4 |
| 26th–30th | +5 |

Remember that a monster's game statistics are set to be appropriate for its level. Thus, altering a monster's attack, defense, or damage values is a lot like changing its level (see above). Avoid the temptation simply to give all your monsters better armor and weapons. Giving all your ogre savages plate armor and +3 *greatswords* may seem like a reasonable change, but now they have the attack, damage, and defense numbers of a higher-level monster—which makes them a tougher challenge than other 8th-level brutes.

If you want to give a monster equipment that changes its attack, defense, or damage values by more than a point or so, consider also making those alterations as part of changing its level. For example, those ogre savages in plate armor and wielding +3 *greatswords* have AC, attack rolls, and damage rolls three points higher than normal. That's pretty close to what a monster three levels higher would have (+3 to all defenses, +3 to attack rolls, and +1 damage), so you might as well make those ogre savages into 11th-level monsters and give them the extra hit points to go along with their other benefits.

# COSMETIC CHANGES

The characters are delving into the jungle-covered ruins of an ancient city now haunted by the yuan-ti. There they discover strange arboreal humanoids with long arms that swoop into battle on the backs of giant wasps. What are these mysterious beings?

This technique is useful for keeping players on their toes even when they know the *Monster Manual* backward and forward. Use the statistics of a given monster but completely alter its appearance when you describe it to the players. You can make minor changes to its powers as well, altering damage types or changing details of weapons (lashing tentacles become a whipping tail, for example).

# TEMPLATES

A template is like a recipe for changing a monster. Each template provides instructions for modifying hit points and defenses, and adds a number of powers and abilities. Simply pick a monster and a template, follow the directions, and you're ready to go.

This section provides more than a dozen templates for customizing monsters. **Functional templates** adapt a monster to a given purpose in an adventure. You can also add a functional template to a nonplayer character. See "Creating NPCs" on page 186 for more information. **Class templates** allow you to add features of a specific character class to a monster.

**Multiple Templates:** Each of these templates is intended for use by itself, making a monster into an elite opponent. However, you can turn a standard monster into a solo creature by adding two templates. Follow the process for adding each template, one at a time, but add just one template's hit point bonus (your choice which). Then double the creature's total hit points. Increase the monster's saving throw bonus to +5.

You can also advance an elite monster to a solo one by adding a template, then doubling its hit points and adjusting its saving throw as above.

This method is quick and easy, but it carries some risks. For example, the adjusted monster's hit points might be lower than those of a typical solo monster of its level and role. Once you've finished the process, be sure to "reality check" the monster by comparing its statistics and abilities to others of similar power.

| FUNCTIONAL TEMPLATES | CLASS TEMPLATES |
|---|---|
| Battle champion | Cleric |
| Bodyguard | Fighter |
| Death knight | Paladin |
| Death master | Ranger |
| Demagogue | Rogue |
| Demonic acolyte | Warlock |
| Devastator | Warlord |
| Feyborn | Wizard |
| Frost adept | |
| Lich | |
| Mummy lord | |
| Mummy champion | |
| Savage berserker | |
| Scion of flame | |
| Shadowborn stalker | |
| Vampire lord | |

# HOW TO READ A TEMPLATE

A template lists changes to a monster's statistics and grants it some new powers and abilities. In general, if a template does not alter a certain statistic, that entry does not appear in the list.

Each template notes any prerequisites for adding it to a monster. Some can be added to any creature, while others work only with particular types or at certain adventuring tiers.

The modified monster retains all its normal powers and abilities except those that overlap or conflict with those bestowed by the template.

Here's a sample template, the lich.

## LICH

**Prerequisite:** Level 11, Intelligence 13

| Lich | Elite Controller or Artillery |
|---|---|
| (undead) | XP Elite |

**Senses** Darkvision
**Defenses** +2 AC; +4 Fortitude; +4 Will
**Immune** disease, poison
**Resist** 5 + 1/2 level necrotic
**Saving Throws** +2
**Action Point** 1
**Hit Points** +8 per level (controller) or +6 per level (artillery)
**Regeneration** 10. If the lich takes radiant damage, its regeneration doesn't function on its next turn.
POWERS
**Spellmaster** (minor; recharge ⚄ ⚅)
   The lich regains the use of an expended encounter power.
**Necromantic Aura (Necrotic)** aura 5
   Any living creature that enters or starts its turn in the aura takes 5 necrotic damage.
**Necrotic Master**
   The lich can convert any attack power it has to necrotic. Change a power's energy keyword to necrotic, or add necrotic energy to an attack power that doesn't normally deal energy damage.

Every template begins with a brief descriptive passage that explains the essential nature of the template, followed by a paragraph that tells you what types of creatures or classes the template can be applied to.

**Prerequisite:** This entry appears if the monster must meet certain requirements to gain the template, such as a specific type or a minimum level.

The remaining information is presented in monster stat block form, for easy insertion into the monster's existing statistics.

**Role:** The monster's combat role appears in the upper right corner of the stat block header.

**Type and Keyword:** The left-hand entry of the second line of the stat block header states this information. If the template adds a keyword to the monster, such as undead, it is included here. The monster retains any previous keywords.

**Senses:** Add the given abilities to the monster's Senses entry.

**Defenses:** Adjust the monster's AC and other defenses as described in this entry.

**Immune/Resist/Vulnerable:** Add the stated entries and values. If the monster already has one or more of these abilities, use the more beneficial value.

**Saving Throws +2:** All elite monsters have a +2 bonus to saving throws.

**Action Point 1:** All elite monsters have 1 action point.

---

## DUPLICATE OR CONFLICTING MONSTER ABILITIES

When you a overlay a template on a monster, you simply add the template's abilities and powers to those the monster already has. Sometimes, though, these powers and abilities contradict or duplicate previously existing ones.

The basic rule in such situations is that numeric values of duplicate abilities are not cumulative. (See "Bonuses and Penalties" on page xx of the *Player's Handbook* for complete information.) The monster retains the value more favorable to it.

The following points deal with unusual situations.

✦ If a monster has vulnerability to a given damage type and then receives a template that grants resistance or immunity to the same damage type, it retains its vulnerability. For example, a creature that has vulnerable 10 necrotic and gains resist 10 necrotic from a template ends up taking no extra damage from a necrotic attack. However, if an effect strips it of its necrotic resistance, it is still vulnerable to necrotic damage.

✦ If a template grants a monster an encounter power it already had, the monster now has two uses of that power per encounter. Track the two abilities separately—the one conferred by the template might have a different recharge requirement, for example.

**Hit Points:** Add the stated number of hit points for the monster's new role, and then also add its Constitution score to the new hit point total.

**Powers:** Add the stated powers to the monster's stat block, calculating attack and damage numbers. The level of an attack power usually depends on the monster's level and is expressed as "Level + *n*," where "Level" is the monster's level and *n* is a number you add to that value. Damage is adjusted by the modifier for a given ability score, just as with characters' attack powers.

# FUNCTIONAL TEMPLATES

Functional templates adapt a monster or a nonplayer character to a given purpose in an adventure. Some reflect a classic villain archetype, such as the death master that commands armies of undead. Others help a monster fill a useful niche in an encounter, such as the bodyguard that holds back the party while its master fulfills her plans.

## BATTLE CHAMPION

The battle champion is a tougher-than-normal humanoid monster from a civilized tribe or nation, such as a goblin king, a drow duelist, or the commander of a garrison of dwarves. It is not only a skilled warrior, but also a rallying point for allies in combat.

"Battle champion" is a template you can apply to any humanoid monster. If you are modifying a nonplayer character, this template works best with the fighter, paladin, and warlord classes.

**Prerequisite:** Humanoid

| Battle Champion | Elite Soldier (Leader) |
|---|---|
| Humanoid | XP Elite |

**Defenses** +2 AC; +2 Fortitude
**Saving Throws** +2
**Action Point** 1
**Hit Points** +8 per level + Constitution score
**POWERS**

**Battle Lord Tactics**
    The battle champion and its allies deal an extra 1d6 damage against enemies that the battle champion flanks. Increase this extra damage to 2d6 at 11th level and to 3d6 at 21st level.

**Battle Talent**
    The battle champion can score critical hits on attack rolls of natural 19 and 20.

**Inspiring Assault**
    Whenever it scores a critical hit, the battle champion and all allies within 5 squares of it regain hit points equal to one-half the battle champion's level.

# BODYGUARD

Villains can always find guileless dupes to carry out their plans. Yet they still need capable, skilled assistants. The bodyguard is one of the most important followers a villain can have, a fanatic melee combatant who gladly gives its life to protect its master.

"Bodyguard" is a template you can apply to any humanoid creature. If you are modifying a nonplayer character, this template works best with the fighter, paladin, and ranger classes.

**Prerequisite:** Humanoid

| Bodyguard | Elite Soldier |
|---|---|
| Humanoid | XP Elite |

**Defenses** +2 AC; +2 Fortitude, +1 Reflex, +1 Will
**Saving Throws** +2
**Action Point** 1
**Hit Points** +8 per level + Constitution score
POWERS

**Indomitable Presence**
Every time a bodyguard attacks an enemy, whether the attack hits or misses, it marks that target. The mark lasts until the end of the bodyguard's next turn. When a target is marked, it takes a -2 penalty to attack rolls if the attack doesn't include the bodyguard as a target. A creature can be subject to only one mark at a time. A new mark supersedes a mark that was already in place.
In addition, whenever a marked enemy that is adjacent to the bodyguard shifts or makes an attack that does not include the bodyguard, the bodyguard can make a basic melee attack against that enemy as an immediate interrupt.

**Shieldbearer**
Allies adjacent to the bodyguard gain a +2 power bonus to AC.

# DEATH KNIGHT

Death knights were once powerful warriors who have been granted eternal undeath, whether as punishment for a grave betrayal or reward for a lifetime of servitude to a dark master. A death knight's soul is bound to the weapon it wields, adding necrotic power to its undiminished martial prowess. Death knights make good leaders for groups of undead creatures.

"Death knight" is a template that can be added to any monster. Most death knights begin as NPC defenders, such as fighters and paladins. However, monsters in the soldier role can make effective death knights, from fire giants to githyanki to yuan-ti abominations.

**Prerequisite:** Level 11

| Death Knight | Elite Soldier (Leader) |
|---|---|
| (undead) | XP Elite |

**Senses** Darkvision
**Defenses** +2 AC; +4 Fortitude; +2 Will
**Immune** disease, poison
**Resist** 10 necrotic at 11th level, 15 necrotic at 21st level
**Vulnerable** 10 radiant
**Saving Throws** +2
**Action Point** 1
**Hit Points** +8 per level + Constitution score
POWERS

**Marshal Undead**
Aura 10; lower-level undead allies in the aura gain a +2 bonus to their attack rolls.

**Soul Weapon ✦ Necrotic, Weapon**
When attacking with its melee weapon, the death knight deals an additional 5 necrotic damage to its target.

**⟵ Unholy Flames** (standard; recharge ⚅ ⚀) **✦ Fire, Necrotic**
Close burst 2; level +2 vs. Reflex; 6d8 + Constitution modifier necrotic and fire damage to living creatures; undead creatures within the burst (including the death knight) deal an extra 2d6 fire damage with melee attacks until the end of the death knight's next turn.

# DEATH MASTER

A death master is the epitome of necromantic power. It can call undead creatures from the grave to serve it and to smite its enemies with fell magic that drain life energy for its own use.

> ## SOUL WEAPON
>
> The process of becoming a death knight requires its caster to bind his immortal essence into the weapon used in the ritual. If this soul weapon is broken or destroyed, the death knight can restore it to perfect condition by touch as a minor action.
>
> A death knight is dazed and weakened while it doesn't have possession of its soul weapon. Any creature other than the death knight is dazed and weakened while carrying the soul weapon.
>
> The soul weapon loses its soul weapon properties when the death knight is destroyed.

"Death master" is a template you can apply to any humanoid, usually a cleric, wizard, or warlock. It represents a spellcaster who has delved into the secrets of necromantic lore and used them to create and control the undead.

A death master is always accompanied by four undead minions of the death master's level or lower.

**Prerequisite:** Humanoid

| Death Master | Elite Controller (Leader) |
|---|---|
| Humanoid (shadow) | XP Elite |

**Defenses** +2 AC; +2 Fortitude; +2 Will
**Resist** 5 necrotic at 1st level, 10 necrotic at 11th level, 15 necrotic at 21st level
**Saving Throws** +2
**Action Point** 1
**Hit Points** +8 per level + Constitution score
**Powers**
**Shroud of the Grave** (necrotic) aura 5
  All undead within 5 squares of the death master lose any vulnerability to radiant damage.
**Call of the Grave** (standard; encounter)
  Ranged 10; four undead minions of the death master's level or lower appear in any unoccupied space within range. These undead minions take their turns immediately after the death master.

## DEMAGOGUE

This template portrays a villain with overwhelming force of personality who desires to manipulate and use others. Its followers are utter fanatics dedicated to the cause, no matter the price—even death or worse.

"Demagogue" is a template you can apply to any humanoid or magical beast to represent the leader of an evil organization or group. Any NPC or monster that leads and uses others is a good fit for this template.

**Prerequisite:** Humanoid or magical beast

| Demagogue | Elite Controller (Leader) |
|---|---|
| Humanoid or magical beast | XP Elite |

**Defenses** +2 Fortitude; +4 Will; +4 to all defenses against charm and fear effects
**Saving Throws** +2
**Action Point** 1
**Hit Points** +8 per level + Constitution score
**Powers**
**Deathless Fanaticism** aura 5
  Lower-level allies (other than minions) in the aura remain alive when reduced to 0 hit points. An affected creature dies at the end of its next turn if it is still at 0 hit points or below.
**Mob Defense**
  The demagogue gains a +1 bonus to all defenses for each ally adjacent to it.
**Clever Escape** (move; recharge ⚅ ⚅)
  The demagogue moves up to twice its speed. It can move only into squares that take it farther away from its enemies. This movement does not provoke opportunity attacks.

## DEMONIC ACOLYTE

This template reflects grim priests of Orcus, raving cult lords of Demogorgon, sacred berserkers of Baphomet, and devotees of other demon lords. A demon lord must personally invest power in an acolyte, making such foes particularly dangerous.

"Demonic acolyte" is a template you can apply to any humanoid or magical beast to represent the priesthood of a demon's cult. If you are modifying a nonplayer character, this template works best with the cleric, warlock, and wizard classes. In particular, clerics who have turned away from the gods and sought power from demons are ideal candidates for such "blessings."

**Prerequisite:** Humanoid or magical beast

| Demonic Acolyte | Elite Controller (Leader) |
|---|---|
| Humanoid or magical beast (demon) | XP Elite |

**Defenses** +1 AC; +2 Fortitude; +2 Will
**Resist** 5 (choose one type) at 1st level, 10 (choose two types) at 11th level, 15 (choose three types) at 21st level
**Saving Throws** +2
**Action Point** 1
**Hit Points** +8 per level + Constitution score
**Powers**
**Shield of Abyssal Majesty** aura 5
  Allies in the aura gain the demonic acolyte's resistance(s).
**Abyssal Might**
  The demonic acolyte gains a +2 power bonus to damage rolls with all attacks. This bonus increases to +4 at 11th level and +6 at 21st level.
**Consume Soul** (immediate reaction, when an ally within 5 squares of the acolyte is reduced to 0 hit points)
  The demonic acolyte regains hit points equal to one-half its level.

## DEVASTATOR

The devastator is an expert at battle magic. It excels at laying down a continuous fire of destructive spells to blast enemies from the field.

"Devastator" is a template you can apply to any humanoid creature to represent a spellcaster trained for war. If you are modifying a nonplayer character, this template works best with the cleric, warlock, and wizard classes.

**Prerequisite:** Humanoid

| Devastator | Elite Artillery |
|---|---|
| Humanoid | XP Elite |

**Defenses** +2 AC; +2 Reflex
**Saving Throws** +2
**Action Point** 1
**Hit Points** +6 per level + Constitution score
**Powers**
**Spell Shaper**
  Whenever the devastator uses a close burst or an area attack power, it can choose up to two allies in the power's area of effect. Those allies are not targeted by the power.
**Endless Power** (minor; recharge ⚅)
  The devastator regains the use of an expended encounter power.

# FEYBORN

Feyborn creatures embody the Feywild. They have been subtly transformed by the plane's powerful, uncontrolled magic. Some underwent prolonged exposure to powerful fey magic. Others are favorites of fey lords, who granted them special boons in return for faithful service.

"Feyborn" is a template you can apply to any beast or humanoid creature, representing a being infused with the mystical power of the fey.

**Prerequisite:** Beast or humanoid

| Feyborn | Elite Skirmisher |
|---|---|
| Beast or humanoid (fey) | XP Elite |

**Defenses** +1 AC; +2 Reflex, +2 Will
**Saving Throws** +2
**Action Point** 1
**Hit Points** +8 per level + Constitution score
POWERS
**Step Through the Mists** (move; encounter)
  The feyborn creature teleports up to 3 squares.
✣ **Undeniable Beauty** (immediate interrupt, when feyborn creature is targeted by a melee attack; at will)
  Level + 2 vs. Will against the attacker; the attacker must target a different creature or end its attack.
✈ **Lure of the Wild** (standard; recharge ⚅)
  Ranged 10; level + 2 vs. Will. The target is pulled 5 squares and is dazed (save ends).

# FROST ADEPT

A frost adept is a champion of elemental cold, specially chosen for strict adherence to its master's power. Elemental beings grant the might of ice to especially faithful servants, such as an utterly devoted priest or a warrior of unmatched skill.

"Frost adept" is a template you can apply to any humanoid or magical beast to represent a monster blessed with the power of elemental cold. If you are modifying a nonplayer character, this template works best with the warlock and wizard classes.

**Prerequisite:** Humanoid or magical beast

| Frost Adept | Elite Controller |
|---|---|
| Humanoid or magical beast (elemental) | XP Elite |

**Defenses** +2 AC; +2 Fortitude
**Resist** 5 cold at 1st level, 10 cold at 11th level, 15 cold at 21st level
**Saving Throws** +2
**Action Point** 1
**Hit Points** +8 per level + Constitution score
POWERS
**Body of Ice**
  Any creature that hits the frost adept with a melee attack is slowed until the end of that creature's next turn.
**Ice Master**
  The frost adept can convert any attack power it has to cold. Change a power's energy keyword to cold, or add cold energy to an attack power that doesn't normally deal energy damage.

# LICH

Liches are evil arcane masterminds that pursue the path of undeath to achieve immortality. They are cold, scheming creatures who hunger for ever-greater power, long-forgotten knowledge, and the most terrible of arcane secrets.

Some liches know a ritual that sustains them beyond destruction by tying their essence to a phylactery. When a lich who has performed this ritual is reduced to 0 hit points, its body and possessions crumble into dust, but it is not destroyed. It reappears (along with its possessions) in 1d10 days within 1 square of its phylactery, unless the phylactery is also found and destroyed.

"Lich" is a template you can add to any intelligent creature of 11th level or higher. It best complements an arcane NPC, such as a wizard or warlock, or a monster with arcane powers, such as a beholder or oni. Other highly intelligent creatures might also become liches; for example, mind flayers, who draw on psionic power.

**Prerequisite:** Level 11, Intelligence 13

| Lich | Elite Controller or Artillery |
|---|---|
| (undead) | XP Elite |

**Senses** Darkvision
**Defenses** +2 AC; +4 Fortitude, +4 Will
**Immune** disease, poison
**Resist** 5 + 1/2 level necrotic
**Saving Throws** +2
**Action Point** 1
**Hit Points** +8 per level + Constitution score (controller) or +6 per level + Constitution score (artillery)
**Regeneration** 10. If the lich takes radiant damage, its regeneration doesn't function on its next turn.
POWERS
**Spellmaster** (minor; recharge ⚄ ⚅)
  The lich regains the use of an expended encounter power.
**Necromantic Aura** (Necrotic) aura 5
  Any living creature that enters or starts its turn in the aura takes 5 necrotic damage.
**Necrotic Master**
  The lich can convert any attack power it has to necrotic. Change a power's energy keyword to necrotic, or add necrotic energy to an attack power that doesn't normally deal energy damage.

# MUMMY CHAMPION

A mummy champion is created through a dark ritual intended to sustain a creature past its mortal life span, or revive it after death. Such rituals are typically reserved for important religious champions and warriors, but they could also curse an unfortunate soul to a prison of undeath.

"Mummy champion" is a template you can apply to any humanoid creature, especially one with the brute or leader role.

This monster has a strongly divine flavor, so NPCs with the template are usually clerics, paladins, or fighters in service to a god.

**Prerequisites:** Humanoid, level 11

| **Mummy Champion** | **Elite Brute (leader)** |
|---|---|
| Humanoid (undead) | XP Elite |

**Senses** Darkvision
**Defenses** +2 AC; +2 Fortitude, +4 Will
**Immune** disease, poison
**Resist** 10 necrotic at 11th level, 15 necrotic at 21st level
**Saving Throws** +2
**Action Point** 1
**Hit Points** +10 per level + Constitution score
**Regeneration** 10. If the mummy champion takes fire damage, its regeneration doesn't function on its next turn.
POWERS
**Despair (Fear) aura 5**
   Enemies within the aura receive a -2 penalty to attack rolls against a mummy champion.
(+) **Rotting Slam** (standard; at will) ✦ **Necrotic**
   Level + 5 vs. AC; 2d8 + Strength modifier necrotic damage, and the target contracts mummy rot (see page 49). Mummy rot's level is equal to the mummy champion's level.

## MUMMY LORD

A mummy lord is created through a dark ritual intended to sustain a creature past its mortal life span, or revive it after death. Such rituals are typically reserved for important religious leaders, but they could also curse an unfortunate soul to a prison of undeath.

"Mummy lord" is a template you can apply to any humanoid creature, especially one with the controller or leader role. This monster has a strongly divine flavor, so NPCs with the template are usually clerics. A drow priestess, foulspawn seer, kuo-toa whip, or yuanti malison disciple of Zehir are all good candidates for the mummy lord template.

**Prerequisites:** Humanoid, level 11

| **Mummy Lord** | **Elite Controller (leader)** |
|---|---|
| Humanoid (undead) | XP Elite |

**Senses** Darkvision
**Defenses** +2 AC; +2 Fortitude, +4 Will
**Immune** disease, poison
**Resist** 10 necrotic at 11th level, 15 necrotic at 21st level
**Saving Throws** +2
**Action Point** 1
**Hit Points** +8 per level + Constitution score
**Regeneration** 10. If the mummy lord takes fire damage, its regeneration doesn't function on its next turn.
POWERS
**Despair (Fear) aura 5**
   Enemies within the aura receive a -2 penalty to attack rolls against a mummy lord.
↩ **Mummy's Curse** (when reduced to 0 hp)
   Close burst 10; level +2 vs. Will; all enemies within burst contract the mummy rot disease (see page 49). Mummy rot's level is equal to the mummy lord's level.

## SAVAGE BERSERKER

A savage berserker is a brutal, vicious champion of battle. It doesn't need allies to succeed in combat but draws on its own toughness and brutal strength.

"Savage berserker" is a template you can apply to any humanoid creature. It's ideal for creating a villain based on an evil humanoid race, such as an orc war leader, a hill giant chieftain, or the champion of a lizardfolk tribe. If you are modifying a nonplayer character, this template works best with the fighter and paladin classes.

**Prerequisite:** Humanoid

| **Savage Berserker** | **Elite Brute (leader)** |
|---|---|
| Humanoid | XP Elite |

**Defenses** +4 Fortitude
**Saving Throws** +2
**Action Point** 1
**Hit Points** +10 per level + Constitution score
**Regeneration** 5 at 1st level, 10 at 11th level, 15 at 21st level
POWERS
**Murderous Frenzy**
   The savage berserker gains 1 action point the first time it reduces a foe to 0 hit points in an encounter.
**Savage Rebuke** (immediate reaction, when hit by a melee attack; at will)
   The savage berserker makes a basic melee attack.

## SCION OF FLAME

A scion of flame is a champion of elemental fire, specially chosen for its devotion to the all-consuming flame. Elemental beings grant the blessings of fire to especially faithful servants.

"Scion of flame" is a template you can apply to any humanoid or magical beast to represent a monster infused with the power of elemental fire. If you are modifying a nonplayer character, this template works best with the warlock and wizard classes.

**Prerequisite:** Humanoid or magical beast

| Scion of Flame | Elite Controller |
|---|---|
| Humanoid or magical beast (elemental) | XP Elite |

**Defenses** +1 AC; +2 Fortitude, +2 Reflex
**Resist** 5 fire at 1st level, 10 fire at 11th level, 15 fire at 21st level
**Saving Throws** +2
**Action Point** 1
**Hit Points** +8 per level + Constitution score
POWERS
**Body of Flame**
Any creature that hits the scion of flame with a melee attack takes fire damage equal to 2 + one-half the scion's level.
**Fire Master**
The scion of flame can convert any attack power it has to fire. Change a power's energy keyword to fire, or add fire energy to an attack power that doesn't normally deal energy damage.

## SHADOWBORN STALKER

The Shadowfell offers power to those willing to delve into forbidden lore and dark rituals. A shadowborn stalker draws the essence of the plane into its body and soul, causing a radical transformation in its abilities and appearance. It gains light gray skin, jet-black hair, and white, pupilless eyes. An aura of shadow plays about a shadowborn stalker, granting it a sinister cast.

"Shadowborn stalker" is a template you can apply to any humanoid creature to represent an assassin or thief who has struck a bargain with the powers of the Shadowfell. Goblins, drow, shadar-kai, and other beings that rely on stealth are good choices for this template. If you are modifying a nonplayer character, this template works best with the rogue and warlock classes.

**Prerequisite:** Humanoid

### MONSTERS, POWERS, AND ATTACK BONUSES

When you apply a class template to a monster, you can determine its attack bonus in one of two ways. Use whichever one yields the higher value, so that your villains have a reasonable chance to hit the characters.

The simplest method is to calculate attack bonus using the creature's level, equipment (if any), and ability scores as you would when making a character. However, this result might be lower than the expected attack bonus for the monster's role and level. In that case, calculate the value for role and level and use that value if it is higher. Use the role provided by the class template, not the monster's original role, when making this comparison.

Use your own judgment about what is an appropriate value, but keep in mind that a monster with a lower-than-expected attack bonus is unlikely to pose much of a threat.

| Shadowborn Stalker | Elite Lurker |
|---|---|
| Humanoid (shadow) | XP Elite |

**Senses** Darkvision
**Defenses** +2 AC; +2 Reflex, +2 Will
**Saving Throws** +2
**Action Point** 1
**Hit Points** +6 per level + Constitution score
POWERS
**Cloak of Shadows** (minor; encounter)
The shadowborn stalker is invisible until the end of its next turn.
✤ **Cloud of Darkness** (minor; encounter)
Close burst 1; this power creates a zone of darkness that remains in place until the end of the shadowborn stalker's next turn. The zone blocks line of sight for all creatures except the shadowborn stalker. Any creature entirely within the area (except the shadowborn stalker) is blinded.

## VAMPIRE LORD

Vampire lords are powerful and dangerous undead villains. Some are former spawn freed by their creators' deaths, others mortals chosen to receive the "gift" of vampiric immortality. They can create armies of dominated vampire spawn or pass on their powers to chosen mortals.

"Vampire lord" is a template you can apply to any humanoid creature of 11th level or higher. Vampire

LEE MOYER

lords retain their living appearance, although they are paler and their canines somewhat more pronounced, and they are wholly evil.

**Prerequisites:** Humanoid, level 11

| Vampire Lord | Elite Controller or Skirmisher |
|---|---|
| Humanoid (undead) | XP Elite |

**Senses** Darkvision
**Defenses** +2 AC; +2 Fortitude, +2 Reflex, +2 Will
**Immune** disease, poison
**Resist** 5 necrotic at 1st level, 10 necrotic at 11th level, 15 necrotic at 21st level
**Vulnerable** radiant 10
**Saving Throws** +2
**Action Point** 1
**Hit Points** +8 per level + Constitution score
**Regeneration** 10 (regeneration does not function while the vampire lord is exposed to direct sunlight)
**POWERS**
⚁ **Blood Drain** (standard, encounter; recharges when an adjacent creature becomes bloodied) ✦ **Healing**
Requires combat advantage. Level + 2 vs. Fortitude; 2d12 + Charisma modifier damage, and the target is weakened (save ends), and the vampire lord heals hit points equal to one-quarter of its normal total.
⚁ **Dominating Gaze** (minor, *recharge* ⚅) ✦ **Charm**
Ranged 5; Level + 2 vs. Will; the target is dominated (save ends, with a –2 penalty to the saving throw). Aftereffect: The target is dazed (save ends). The vampire lord can dominate only one creature at a time.
⚁ **Mist Form** (standard; encounter) ✦ **Polymorph**
The vampire lord becomes insubstantial and gains a fly speed of 12, but cannot make attacks. The vampire lord can remain in mist form for up to 1 hour or end the effect as a minor action.

# CLASS TEMPLATES

Class templates allow you to add features of a specific character class to a monster. The following eight templates represent all the classes in the *Player's Handbook*.

Adding a class to an existing monster is a simple matter of overlaying the appropriate template. If you want to advance the monster in a class, first increase its level as described on page 174, then add the relevant class template.

This method works best with existing monster statistics blocks. Use the rules for creating new monsters (page 184) if you are adding class levels to creatures of your own design.

If the effect of a class feature or power depends on level, such as the cleric's *healing word*, use the monster's level. As usual, the monster retains its own abilities and powers unless they contradict or duplicate those provided by the template.

# CHOOSING CLASS POWERS

The heart of applying a class template is choosing suitable powers for the monster. For a heroic-tier monster, select one power from that class's list for each category: at-will, encounter, and daily attack powers, and utility powers. For monsters at higher tiers, choose additional powers as summarized below.

- ✦ **At-Will Powers** Choose one.
- ✦ **Encounter Powers** Choose one of a level up to the monster's level. For a monster of 11th level or higher, choose one additional encounter power. The powers must be of different levels.
- ✦ **Daily Powers** Choose one of a level up to the monster's level. For a monster of 21st level or higher, choose one additional daily power. The powers must be of different levels.
- ✦ **Utility Powers** Choose one of a level up to the monster's level. For a monster of 11th level or higher, choose one additional utility power. For one of 21st level or higher, select a third utility power. The powers must all be of different levels.

# HOW TO READ A CLASS TEMPLATE

Class templates follow the same general format as functional templates. Categories of information that appear only in class templates are explained below.

**Power Source:** This information sometimes interacts with other game rules. See page 54 of the *Player's Handbook* for more information.

**Skills:** If the monster already has training in the a skill granted by the template, it cannot substitute another skill.

**Class Features:** Refer to the relevant entries in the *Player's Handbook* for descriptions of class features.

**Implement:** If a class template enables a creature to use one or more kinds of implements, that information is noted here.

**Weapon Proficiency/Armor Proficiency:** If the monster already uses the weapon or armor types granted by the template, it cannot substitute others.

# CLERIC
**Power Source:** Divine.

| Cleric | Elite Controller (Leader) |
|---|---|

**Defenses** +2 Will
**Saving Throws** +2
**Action Point** 1
**Hit Points** +8 per level + Constitution score
**Weapon Proficiency** Simple weapons
**Armor Proficiency** Cloth, leather, hide, chainmail
**Trained Skills** Religion, plus one other skill from the cleric class list
**Class Features** Channel Divinity, Healer's Lore, *healing word*
**Implement** Holy symbol

# FIGHTER

**Power Source:** Martial.

| Fighter | Elite Soldier |
|---|---|

**Defenses** +2 Fortitude
**Saving Throws** +2
**Action Point** 1
**Hit Points** +8 per level + Constitution score
**Weapon Proficiency** Simple melee, military melee, simple ranged, military ranged
**Armor Proficiency** Cloth, leather, hide, chainmail, scale; light shield, heavy shield
**Trained Skills** Two skills from the fighter class list
**Class Features** Combat Challenge, Combat Superiority, Weapon Talent

# PALADIN

**Power Source:** Divine.

| Paladin | Elite Soldier |
|---|---|

**Defenses** +1 Fortitude, +1 Reflex, +1 Will
**Saving Throws** +2
**Action Point** 1
**Hit Points** +8 per level + Constitution score
**Weapon Proficiency** Simple melee, military melee, simple ranged
**Armor Proficiency** Cloth, leather, hide, chainmail, scale, plate; light shield, heavy shield
**Trained Skills** Religion, plus one other skill from the paladin class list
**Class Features** Channel Divinity, Divine Challenge, *lay on hands*
**Implement** Holy symbol

# RANGER

**Power Source:** Martial.

| Ranger | Elite Skirmisher |
|---|---|

**Defenses** +1 Fortitude, +1 Reflex
**Saving Throws** +2
**Action Point** 1
**Hit Points** +8 per level + Constitution score
**Weapon Proficiency** Simple melee, military melee, simple ranged, military ranged
**Armor Proficiency** Cloth, leather, hide
**Trained Skills** Dungeoneering or Nature (your choice), plus one other skill from the ranger class list
**Class Features** Fighting Style, Hunter's Quarry, Prime Shot

# ROGUE

**Power Source:** Martial.

| Rogue | Elite Skirmisher |
|---|---|

**Defenses** +2 Reflex
**Saving Throws** +2
**Action Point** 1
**Hit Points** +8 per level + Constitution score
**Weapon Proficiency** Dagger, hand crossbow, shuriken, sling, short sword
**Armor Proficiency** Cloth, leather
**Trained Skills** Thievery plus one other skill from the rogue class list
**Class Features** First Strike, Rogue Tactics, Rogue Weapon Talent, Sneak Attack

# WARLOCK

**Power Source:** Arcane.

| Warlock | Elite Skirmisher |
|---|---|

**Defenses** +1 Reflex, +1 Will
**Saving Throws** +2
**Action Point** 1
**Hit Points** +8 per level + Constitution score
**Weapon Proficiency** Simple melee, simple ranged
**Armor Proficiency** Cloth, leather
**Trained Skills** Two skills from the warlock class list
**Class Features** *Eldritch blast*, Eldritch Pact, Prime Shot, Warlock's Curse
**Implements** Rods, wands

# WARLORD

**Power Source:** Martial.

| Warlord | Elite Soldier (leader) |
|---|---|

**Defenses** +1 Fortitude, +1 Will
**Saving Throws** +2
**Action Point** 1
**Hit Points** +8 per level + Constitution score
**Weapon Proficiency** Simple melee, military melee, simple ranged
**Armor Training** Cloth, leather, hide, chainmail, light shield
**Trained Skills** Two skills from the warlord class list
**Class Features** Combat Leader, Commanding Presence, *inspiring word*

# WIZARD

**Power Source:** Arcane.

| Wizard | Elite Artillery |
|---|---|

**Defenses** +2 Will
**Saving Throws** +2
**Action Point** 1
**Hit Points** +6 per level + Constitution score
**Weapon Proficiency** Dagger, quarterstaff
**Armor Proficiency** Cloth
**Trained Skills** Arcana plus one other skill from the wizard class list
**Class Features** Arcane Implement Mastery, cantrips, Ritual Caster, spellbook
**Implements** Orbs, staffs, wands

The information on customizing monsters (page 174) and the creatures provided in the *Monster Manual* and future volumes should handle most of your needs for monsters. When you really need to create something from scratch, the guidelines here will help you with the process.

## MONSTER DESIGN STEPS

Following these steps won't result in a fully designed and developed monster, but they'll provide a good approximation.

**1. Choose Level.** The level of the monster determines its key statistics, including defenses, attack bonuses, and hit points.

**2. Choose Role.** A monster's role suggests the kinds of powers it uses in combat. Chapter 4 describes monster roles more fully, and the Monster Statistics by Role table on this page shows how a monster's role influences the statistics and powers you give it.

**3. Determine Ability Scores.** It's helpful to think of ability scores in pairs, each pair corresponding to one of the three defenses (Fortitude, Reflex, and Will). Ability scores also help determine the monster's attack bonuses, ability and skill checks, and Armor Class.

On average, the highest ability score of a pair is equal to 13 + one-half the monster's level. For example, the target score for an 8th-level monster is 17 (13 + 4). However, set the ability that governs the monster's primary attacks to be 3 higher, or 16 + one-half the monster's level. An 8th-level monster that relies on melee attacks should have a Strength of 20.

**4. Determine Hit Points.** Level and role determine hit points. The monster gains a flat number of hit points at each level, just as characters do. Use the Monster Statistics by Role table to set hit points.

**5. Calculate Armor Class.** A monster's Armor Class is based on its level and role. Average AC is equal to 14 + the monster's level, but some roles alter this target number, as shown in the table.

**6. Calculate Other Defenses.** A monster's level determines its defenses. A given defense based on an average ability score is equal to 12 + the monster's level.

For every 2 points the ability score varies from the average, adjust the defense by +1 (if higher) or -1 (if lower).

**7. Choose Powers.** The most complex part of monster creation is creating powers for the monster. For inspiration, check the powers for creatures in the *Monster Manual*. That book has a list of monsters by level and role, so you can quickly look up other creatures that are similar to your new monster. Then either choose some powers that seem right, modifying them as needed, or create new ones of comparable effect.

A monster needs a basic attack, which can be melee or ranged and is usable at will; some kinds of monsters might have a second basic attack. Then add one encounter power or rechargeable power per tier (one at heroic, two at paragon, three at epic).

**8. Calculate Attack Bonus.** The monster's attack bonus is a function of its level and role. Powers that target AC typically have a higher attack bonus than those that target other defenses.

**9. Set Damage for Attacks:** Use the Damage by Level table to set damage for the monster's attacks. Most at-will attacks should use the medium normal damage shown on the table. For attacks against multiple targets, the melee attacks of artillery monsters, and controller attacks that also include significant control functions, use the low normal damage column. For attacks that have low accuracy (including brute attacks) and the high-damage attacks of lurker monsters, use the high normal damage column. Use the limited damage expressions for powers the monster can use only once or twice a fight—powers that have encounter recharge or recharge rolls.

**10. Additional Details.** Monster design doesn't stop once you've done all the math. Add flavor, appearance, and tactics to round out your creation.

## ELITE AND SOLO MONSTERS

Elite and solo monsters represent the toughest foes the characters can face; Chapter 4 has more about these role enhancements. They make great villains, stars of a campaign, or intimidating "boss" monsters at the climax of an adventure.

### MONSTER STATISTICS BY ROLE

| | Skirmisher | Brute | Soldier | Lurker | Controller | Artillery |
|---|---|---|---|---|---|---|
| **Initiative bonus** | +2 | — | +2 | +4 | — | — |
| **Hit points** | 8 + Con + (level × 8) | 10 + Con + (level × 10) | 8 + Con + (level × 8) | 6 + Con + (level × 6) | 8 + Con + (level × 8) | 6 + Con + (level × 6) |
| **AC** | Level + 14 | Level + 12 | Level + 16 | Level + 14 | Level + 14 | Level + 12 |
| **Other defenses** | Level + 12 | Level + 12 | Level + 12 | Level + 12 | Level + 12 | Level + 12 |
| **Attack vs. AC*** | Level + 5 | Level + 3 | Level + 7 | Level + 5 | Level + 5 | Level + 7 |
| **Attack vs. other defenses*** | Level +3 | Level + 1 | Level + 5 | Level + 3 | Level + 4 | Level + 5 |

*Reduce the attack bonus by 2 for powers that affect multiple creatures.

## DAMAGE BY LEVEL

| Level | Normal Damage Expressions | | |
| --- | --- | --- | --- |
| | Low | Medium | High |
| 1st-3rd | 1d6 + 3 | 1d10 + 3 | 2d6 + 3 |
| 4th-6th | 1d6 + 4 | 1d10 + 4 | 2d8 + 4 |
| 7th-9th | 1d8 + 5 | 2d6 + 5 | 2d8 + 5 |
| 10th-12th | 1d8 + 5 | 2d6 + 5 | 3d6 + 5 |
| 13th-15th | 1d10 + 6 | 2d8 + 6 | 3d6 + 6 |
| 16th-18th | 1d10 + 7 | 2d8 + 7 | 3d8 + 7 |
| 19th-21st | 2d6 + 7 | 3d6 + 8 | 3d8 + 7 |
| 22nd-24th | 2d6 + 8 | 3d6 + 8 | 4d6 + 8 |
| 25th-27th | 2d8 + 9 | 3d8 + 9 | 4d6 + 9 |
| 28th-30th | 2d8 + 10 | 3d8 + 10 | 4d8 + 10 |

| Level | Limited Damage Expressions | | |
| --- | --- | --- | --- |
| | Low | Medium | High |
| 1st-3rd | 3d6 + 3 | 2d10 + 3 | 3d8 + 3 |
| 4th-6th | 3d6 + 4 | 3d8 + 4 | 3d10 + 4 |
| 7th-9th | 3d8 + 5 | 3d10 + 5 | 4d8 + 5 |
| 10th-12th | 3d8 + 5 | 4d8 + 5 | 4d10 + 5 |
| 13th-15th | 3d10 + 6 | 4d8 + 6 | 4d10 + 6 |
| 16th-18th | 3d10 + 6 | 4d10 + 7 | 4d12 + 7 |
| 19th-21st | 4d8 + 7 | 4d10 + 7 | 4d12 + 7 |
| 22nd-24th | 4d8 + 8 | 4d12 + 8 | 5d10 + 8 |
| 25th-27th | 4d10 + 9 | 5d10 + 9 | 5d12 + 9 |
| 28th-30th | 4d10 + 9 | 5d10 + 9 | 5d12 + 9 |

Iconic D&D villains, such as the vampire Count Strahd von Zarovich or the demilich Acererak, are solo monsters. Such enemies are powerful enough by themselves to take on an entire party of adventurers. Elite monsters are tough enough to fight a lower-level party on their own, but normally they have a few allies on hand. Lareth the Beautiful, an evil cleric of Lolth, is a good example. Although powerful, he never enters battle without bandits, gnolls, or ghouls at his side.

## CREATING NEW ELITES

An easy way to create a memorable villain is to convert an existing monster into an elite version. In a goblin-infested dungeon, for example, an elite bugbear warrior makes a natural chieftain. Adding a template is an easy way to "upgrade" a monster, whether it's one in the *Monster Manual* or a new creation of your own.

You can also follow these guidelines to advance a monster to elite status.

**1. Adjust Role.** The monster's level and role remain the same, but it is now an elite version.

**2. Adjust Hit Points.** An elite monster has hit points equal to twice the hit points of the standard monster, plus twice its Constitution score.

**3. Adjust Defenses.** Increase up to three defenses, including AC, by 2. Focus on the creature's best defenses first. If your monster has a specific weak defense, don't increase it.

**4. Adjust Saving Throws:** All elite monsters have a +2 bonus to saving throws.

**5. Add 1 Action Point:** All elite monsters have 1 action point.

**6. Adjust Powers and Abilities:** Although your elite creature represents two monsters in combat, it still has only one set of actions each turn. In effect, you're trading two sets of actions for one. Thus, an elite monster needs additional opportunities to attack, hinder, or otherwise react to the characters.

*Recharge When First Bloodied:* As a rule, elite monsters are more dangerous when the chips are down. To reflect this, select one of the creature's encounter powers. It gains another use of this power when it becomes bloodied for the first time in an encounter.

*Immediate Actions:* An elite monster typically has some way to interfere with or respond to the characters' actions. Many of the templates described earlier in this chapter include powers that grant an immediate action, whether interrupt or reaction, to counter or respond to an opponent's attack or movement.

*Additional Attacks:* As an alternative to immediate actions, allow an elite creature to make an additional attack on its turn. This might be a special attack it can use as a minor action once during its turn, or simply a double attack using a standard action.

## CREATING NEW SOLOS

You can turn a basic creature into a terrifying solo monster as the high point of an adventure.

You can make a "quick and dirty" solo monster by applying two templates (or one, if the monster is already elite), as described in the "Templates" section. Alternatively, you can create a new solo from scratch.

**1. Adjust Role.** The monster's level and role remain the same, but it is now a solo version.

**2. Adjust Hit Points.** A solo has hit points equal to 8 times its level +1, plus its Constitution score. If the solo is level 10 or lower, multiply that result by 4 for its final hit points. If it is level 11 or higher, multiply that result by 5 for its final hit points.

**3. Adjust Defenses.** Increase up to three defenses, including AC, by 2.

**4. Adjust Saving Throws:** All solo monsters have a +5 bonus to saving throws.

**5. Add 1 Action Point:** All solo monsters have 2 action points.

**6. Adjust Powers and Abilities:** A solo creature represents five monsters in combat, so it needs a number of ways to take additional actions. It also needs more ways to use powers on its own turn and to interfere with the characters.

*More At-Will Powers:* Select one of the creature's encounter powers. It can now use that power at will.

*Additional Standard Action:* The easiest way to let a solo take on an entire party at once is to give it an additional standard action on each of its turns. Thus, it can always make at least two attacks on its turn, and can make a third when necessary by using an action point.

Nonplayer characters (NPCs) are the supporting cast in the drama that stars your players' characters. Creating NPCs helps to bring your adventures and your campaign to life, creating a world that seems real.

NPCs are typically humanoid beings with a clearly defined purpose in your campaign and distinctive personalities. One might be a paladin of the Raven Queen who stalks the land, a gloomy figure who could become enemy or ally. Another is the scheming cleric of Asmodeus who leads the god's hidden cult, the main antagonist of your adventure. A third is a brutal yet honorable orc champion, a powerful warlord and another ultimate adversary or ally. All have a strong flavor based on their class and their connections to other parts of the world.

That said, no NPC needs the depth of background, personality, and statistics that a well-crafted player character has. Many NPCs just need a name, a couple of skills, and a word or two about their place in the world and how it relates to the PCs. For example, the town priest Avarun worships Erathis and has a number of ritual scrolls that he can use: Cure Disease (4), Raise Dead (1), and Remove Affliction (2).

You can also compose seven sentences to summarize an NPC's essential elements so that he or she can interact with the player characters in a meaningful and memorable way.

**Occupation:** The first sentence introduces the NPC, describing the character's way of life.

**Physical Description:** This sentence provides a brief summary of the NPC's appearance. In addition to covering the basics (height and build, color of skin, hair, and eyes, and so forth), think about a distinctive quirk to help set the character apart in the players' minds. Roll or choose a quirk from the table, or come up with one of your own.

**Attributes and Skills:** Here is where you note whether any of the NPC's abilities are markedly above or below average—great strength or monumental stupidity, for example. You should also mention any special skills he or she has, even if they're not associated with the character's occupation. These notes will help you create appropriate statistics later.

**Values and Motivations:** Summarize the values that the NPC holds dear, and what spurs him or her to action. These factors can have an impact on the party's interaction with that person. These details also help you decide how the NPC reacts to the characters.

**Behavior:** This sentence describes how the NPC interacts with others—traits that will stand out in the players' minds. An NPC might be urbane, sarcastic, loud and obnoxious, soft-spoken, or condescending. If this behavior is applied differently depending on who you are, people than with strangers, note that here.

**Useful Knowledge:** Does the NPC know something that might benefit the PCs? This information might be purely for flavor, or it could be a key clue leading the PCs deeper into the adventure.

**Mannerism:** Describe a memorable characteristic of the NPC, something for the players to remember. They might forget a name, but they'll remember the blacksmith with the elaborate vocabulary. Roll or pick a mannerism from the table, or make up your own.

## NPC MANNERISMS

| d20 | Mannerism |
|-----|-----------|
| 1 | Is prone to singing, whistling, or humming quietly |
| 2 | Speaks in rhymes or meter |
| 3 | Has particularly low or high voice |
| 4 | Slurs words, lisps, or stutters |
| 5 | Enunciates very clearly |
| 6 | Speaks loudly |
| 7 | Whispers |
| 8 | Uses flowery speech or long words |
| 9 | Frequently uses the wrong word |
| 10 | Uses colorful oaths and exclamations |
| 11 | Constantly makes jokes or puns |
| 12 | Is prone to predictions of certain doom |
| 13 | Fiddles and fidgets nervously |
| 14 | Squints |
| 15 | Stares into distance |
| 16 | Chews something |
| 17 | Paces |
| 18 | Taps fingers |
| 19 | Bites fingernails |
| 20 | Twirls hair or tugs beard |

## NPC QUIRKS

| d20 | Quirk |
|-----|-------|
| 1 | Distinctive jewelry (earrings, necklace, bracelets) |
| 2 | Piercing |
| 3 | Flamboyant or outlandish clothes |
| 4 | Formal or very clean clothes |
| 5 | Ragged and very dirty clothes |
| 6 | Pronounced scar |
| 7 | Missing tooth |
| 8 | Missing finger |
| 9 | Unusual eye color (or two different colors) |
| 10 | Tattoo |
| 11 | Birthmark |
| 12 | Unusual skin color |
| 13 | Bald |
| 14 | Braided beard or hair |
| 15 | Unusual hair color |
| 16 | Nervous eye twitch |
| 17 | Distinctive nose |
| 18 | Distinctive posture—crooked or very rigid |
| 19 | Exceptionally beautiful |
| 20 | Exceptionally ugly |

# NPC Design Steps

When the *Monster Manual* doesn't have the exact entry you need, use these guidelines to craft an NPC. Remember that many NPCs simply need a name, a couple of sentences of background (as described on the previous page), a key skill or two, and maybe a ritual. Most don't have classes or even roles (in the monster sense). Only go to the trouble of adding game statistics if the NPC is going to serve as an opponent or an adventuring ally for the PCs. Otherwise, you're doing too much work.

Along the same lines, treat NPCs as you would monsters. That is, only give them the things you'll need to run them in an encounter or an adventure. Don't stat out an NPC as a player stats out a player character. That's just too much work for what you really need. Most NPCs, even opponents, only need as much detail as a monster. In the rare case where you want to build a campaign-long villain, then it might serve for you to fully stat out the NPC in PC fashion, but this should be the exception–the rare exception.

**1. Choose Level.** The level of the NPC determines key statistics, as well as its threat to the party.

**2. Choose Race and Class.** Decide which class most closely matches the NPC's role. Some classes work well for more than one role, depending on the powers you select. Use the NPC class blocks that follow.

**3. Determine Ability Scores.** Use the standard ability array. Assign the six numbers as appropriate to the NPC's class, applying any racial modifiers. Then adjust the scores to account for the NPC's level, just as you would for a player character. The table below summarizes the total ability score increases at specific levels. (These increases are not cumulative.)

## NPC ABILITY SCORES

**Standard Ability Array: 16, 14, 13, 12, 11, 10.**

| Level | Ability Score Increases |
|---|---|
| 4th | +1 to two |
| 8th | +2 to two |
| 11th | +3 to two, +1 to all others |
| 14th | +4 to two, +1 to all others |
| 18th | +5 to two, +1 to all others |
| 21st | +6 to two, +2 to all others |
| 24th | +7 to two, +2 to all others |
| 28th | +8 to two, +2 to all others |

**4. Determine Hit Points and Healing Surges.** An NPC's hit points are primarily determined by his class, role, and level, as described below. An NPC is, fundamentally, like a monster, and therefore the NPC's hit point total must be close to that of a monster.

NPCs can use healing surges. Like monsters, they have one healing surge per tier. So, a heroic tier NPC (1st–10th level) has one healing surge, and an epic tier NPC (21st level or higher) has three.

Like player characters, NPCs can use their second wind once per encounter as a standard action.

**5. Calculate Defenses.** Determine the scores for the NPC's Fortitude, Reflex, and Will defenses using the standard formula: 10 + 1/2 level + relevant ability modifier. Calculate the NPC's Armor Class as you would for a player character, including bonuses from armor.

After you have calculated these numbers, add any bonuses from class or race to all defenses. Then add the level bonus to represent improvements based on level advancement, as described in the "Level Bonus and Magic Threshold" sidebar.

If you gave the NPC a magic item that grants a bonus to defenses, you must also subtract the magic threshold from that bonus, as noted in the sidebar.

## NPC LEVEL BONUS AND MAGIC THRESHOLD

| Level | Level Bonus | Magic Threshold |
|---|---|---|
| 1st–5th | +1 | +0 |
| 6th–10th | +3 | +1 |
| 11th–15th | +5 | +2 |
| 16th–20th | +7 | +3 |
| 21st–25th | +9 | +4 |
| 26th–30th | +11 | +5 |

**6. Choose Powers.** As described below.

*At-Will Powers:* Choose one.

*Encounter Powers:* Choose one of the NPC's level. Add an additional power of a lower level if 11th level or higher.

*Daily Powers:* Choose one of the NPC's level. Add an additional power of a lower level if 21st level or higher.

*Utility Powers:* Choose one of the NPC's level. Add an additional power of a lower level if 11th level or higher, and another if 21st level or higher.

## LEVEL BONUS AND MAGIC THRESHOLD

As player characters gain levels, they choose feats and gain magic items that increase their attack bonuses and defenses. The level bonus, shown on the table below, is an abstraction that helps NPCs keep pace with characters. You can think of it as representing feats you're not bothering to choose, low-level magic items, or the NPC's intrinsic power.

Add this number to the NPC's Armor Class and other defenses, attack rolls, and damage rolls.

An NPC's magic threshold is related to the level bonus. If you give an NPC a magic item that grants a bonus to attack rolls and damage rolls or to defenses, subtract the magic threshold from that bonus before you apply it.

For example, if you give a 12th-level NPC a +4 *magic longsword*, add only a +2 bonus to his or her attack rolls and damage rolls, since the magic threshold at that level is +2.

**7. Choose Skills.** Pick a skill or two for the NPC to be trained in, using the information below.

**8. Choose Equipment.** Select weapons and armor from Chapter 7 of the *Player's Handbook*, taking into account class and race.

You can give the NPC a magic item of a suitable level, but if he or she is an antagonist, count the item as part of the treasure for the adventure. (See "Awarding Treasure," page 125, for more information.)

**9. Calculate Attack and Damage Bonuses.** Calculate the NPC's attack bonuses and damage bonuses as you would for a player character, then add the level bonus to each just as you did for defenses in step 5. The weapon you chose in step 8 determines the damage of weapon-based powers.

If you gave the NPC a magic item, remember to subtract the magic threshold, just as you did for defenses in step 5.

**10. Choose Rituals:** Giving your NPC certain ritual scrolls might be appropriate, especially if he or she is an ally of the characters. Ritual scrolls work well for NPCs that aren't ritual casters. Remember that villains can perform powerful rituals "off camera" to help drive your narrative.

## CLERIC NPC

**Power Source:** Divine.   **Role:** Controller (Leader)
   **Defenses** +2 Will
   **Hit Points** 8 per level + Constitution score
   **Weapon Proficiency** Simple weapons
   **Armor Proficiency** Cloth, leather, hide, chainmail
   **Trained Skills** Religion, plus one other skill from the cleric class list
   **Class Features** Channel Divinity (one power), *healing word*
   **Implement** Holy symbol

## FIGHTER NPC

**Power Source:** Martial.   **Role:** Soldier
   **Defenses** +2 Fortitude
   **Hit Points** 8 per level + Constitution score
   **Weapon Proficiency** Simple melee, military melee, simple ranged, military ranged
   **Armor Proficiency** Cloth, leather, hide, chainmail, scale; light shield, heavy shield
   **Trained Skills** Two skills from the fighter class list
   **Class Features** Combat Challenge

## PALADIN NPC

**Power Source:** Divine.   **Role:** Soldier
   **Defenses** +1 Fortitude, +1 Reflex, +1 Will
   **Hit Points** 8 per level + Constitution score
   **Weapon Proficiency** Simple melee, military melee, simple ranged
   **Armor Proficiency** Cloth, leather, hide, chainmail, scale, plate; light shield, heavy shield
   **Trained Skills** Religion, plus one other skill from the paladin class list
   **Class Features** Divine Challenge, *lay on hands*
   **Implement** Holy symbol

## RANGER NPC

**Power Source:** Martial.   **Role:** Skirmisher
   **Defenses** +1 Fortitude, +1 Reflex
   **Hit Points** 8 per level + Constitution score
   **Weapon Proficiency** Simple melee, military melee, simple ranged, military ranged
   **Armor Proficiency** Cloth, leather, hide
   **Trained Skills** Dungeoneering or Nature (your choice), plus one other skill from the ranger class list
   **Class Features** Fighting Style, Hunter's Quarry

## ROGUE NPC

**Power Source:** Martial.   **Role:** Skirmisher
   **Defenses** +2 Reflex
   **Hit Points** 8 per level + Constitution score
   **Weapon Proficiency** Dagger, hand crossbow, shuriken, sling, short sword
   **Armor Proficiency** Cloth, leather
   **Trained Skills** Thievery plus one other skill from the rogue class list
   **Class Features** First Strike, Rogue Weapon Mastery, Sneak Attack

## WARLOCK NPC

**Power Source:** Arcane.   **Role:** Skirmisher
   **Defenses** +1 Reflex, +1 Will
   **Hit Points** 8 per level + Constitution score
   **Weapon Proficiency** Simple melee, simple ranged
   **Armor Proficiency** Cloth, leather
   **Trained Skills** Two skills from the warlock class list
   **Class Features** *Eldritch blast*, Eldritch Pact, Warlock's Curse
   **Implements** Rods, wands

## WARLORD NPC

**Power Source:** Martial.   **Role:** Soldier (Leader)
   **Defenses** +1 Fortitude, +1 Will
   **Hit Points** 8 per level + Constitution score
   **Weapon Proficiency** Simple melee, military melee, military ranged
   **Armor Training** Cloth, leather, chainmail; light shield
   **Trained Skills** Two skills from the warlord class list
   **Class Features** Combat Leader, *inspiring word*

## WIZARD NPC

**Power Source:** Arcane.   **Role:** Artillery
   **Defenses** +2 Will
   **Hit Points** 6 per level + Constitution score
   **Weapon Proficiency** Dagger, quarterstaff
   **Armor Proficiency** Cloth
   **Trained Skills** Arcana plus one other skill from the wizard class list
   **Class Features** Arcane Implement Mastery, Ritual Caster, spellbook
   **Implements** Orbs, staffs, wands

# CREATING HOUSE RULES

As Dungeon Master, you wear several hats: storyteller, rules arbiter, actor, adventure designer, and writer. Some DMs like to add a sixth hat to that stack: rules designer. House rules are variants on the basic rules designed specifically for a particular DM's campaign. They add fun to your D&D game by making it unique, reflecting specific traits of your world.

A house rule also serves as a handy "patch" for a game feature that your group dislikes. The D&D rules cannot possibly account for the variety of campaigns and play styles of every group. If you disagree with how the rules handle something, changing them is within your rights.

This advice can't turn you into an expert game designer—we'd need more than a page for that. Instead, this is a basic introduction to the concepts behind rules design. Once you've become familiar with these ideas, the best way to learn more about game design is to play, see what's fun and what's not, and use your discoveries to guide your own work.

## RULES DESIGN 101

Before you begin designing a house rule, ask yourself how necessary it is. A new rule won't help your game if it keeps all the problems of the old one. Keep in mind:

✦ Why do I want to change or add this rule?
✦ What should the change accomplish?
✦ How should my new rule accomplish its goal?

Think carefully about the reason for changing or adding a rule. Are you reacting to a persistent problem in your campaign, or to one specific incident? Isolated problems might be better handled in other ways. More important, do the other players agree to the need for a change? You have the authority to do whatever you want with the game, but your efforts won't help if you have no group.

If a change still seems in order, consider what the new or revised rule should do. You need a clear grasp of the rule's function before you can begin design. Start by thinking about intent—don't worry about the mechanics yet. Imagine what you want to happen at the game table when the rule comes into play.

Once you have worked out the rule's intended function, write up how it works. This material doesn't need to be exhaustive or resemble a legal code. You can modify the rule or make judgment calls during play.

Playing with the new rule is the most important part of the design process. Keep a close eye on how the rule affects the game. Does it achieve the desired goal? Is your group enjoying the game more because of it? If not, try revising how it works—or even start over. A rule hardly ever works perfectly the first time.

## EXAMPLE HOUSE RULES

Here are a couple of sample house rules, followed by discussions on their intended purpose.

### FUMBLE
Whenever you make an attack roll of natural 1, your turn immediately ends, and you grant combat advantage to all attackers until the start of your next turn.

If the roll is part of a close or area attack, resolve all the other attack rolls before ending your turn.

A fumble, or "critical miss," is a failed attack that leaves the attacker in a bad position. A lot of DMs like the symmetry of having fumbles on natural 1s to balance the possibility of critical hits on natural 20s. This rule models the uncertainty of combat, when even a skilled warrior can take a bad step or misjudge an attack so badly as to be unable to respond to any counterstrike.

The exception for close and area attacks is something that you'd likely discover a need for in play. Such powers affect all targets at once, as opposed to those that let you blast one foe at a time, so it doesn't make sense to cancel the remaining attacks. This way, if a wizard fumbles a single attack roll with *fireball*, the spell still fries the other monsters in its area.

Characters using powers that give them multiple attack rolls will fumble more than other characters, because they're rolling more attacks (and thus getting more natural 1s). The wizard in the party might get frustrated from fumbling in every fight just because he's rolling three times as many attacks as the fighter.

A fumble rule adds a sense of uncertainty to every attack, so it works best with players who like a random element of danger. It's also a lot of fun to take advantage of a monster's critical miss.

### CRITICAL SUCCESS AND FAILURE
On a skill or ability check, a roll of natural 20 is a critical success and a roll of natural 1 is a critical failure.

On a critical success, the check automatically succeeds, and you gain a +5 bonus to checks with that skill until the end of your next turn. In a skill challenge, add one extra victory to the tally.

On a critical failure, the check automatically fails, and you take a -5 penalty to checks with that skill until the end of your next turn. In a skill challenge, add one extra defeat to the tally.

This house rule extends the symmetry of natural 20s and natural 1s to skill checks. Some DMs don't like the idea of skill checks that always succeed, or conversely, that have no chance in a desperate attempt.

This house rule adds an extra layer of uncertainty and tension to noncombat situations, especially in skill challenges (see page 72). Monsters and NPCs can gain the benefits (and take the risks) of this rule too, which might have unintended consequences in play.

Did the characters unexpectedly wander into the Great Labyrinth below the minotaur city? Perhaps you find yourself with less time to prepare than usual, or you just want a dungeon environment that's a little wacky. Whether you want to prepare something quick for tonight's adventure or have some fun on a rainy day, creating random dungeons is a simple way to fill a sheet of graph paper.

The tables provided in this section help you quickly create a dungeon environment. You can either draw the chambers and corridors yourself, using the examples provided here, or use pieces from any *D&D Dungeon Tiles* product to represent them. Dimensions are given in squares.

To start, copy one of the areas pictured in this section onto a sheet of graph paper or use photocopies of the battle grid on pages 222 and 223 of this book. If you're building a dungeon on the fly while your players are at the table, lay down tiles to create the starting area or draw it onto your battle grid. Then pick an exit—or let the players choose one—and roll a d20, consulting either the Corridors table or the Doors table below.

## HOW DOES IT END?

Following these instructions can lead to sprawling complexes that more than fill a single sheet of graph paper. If you want to constrain the dungeon somewhat, you can set some limits ahead of time to just how far it can grow.

**Don't Leave the Paper:** If a feature would exceed the boundaries of your sheet, cut it short or otherwise limit it. A corridor might turn or come to a dead end at the map edge. A chamber can become smaller, or be replaced by stairs or a dead-end corridor.

**One Level at a Time:** Once you've created eight to ten chambers, stop. The result is a dungeon section that should advance your characters one level and give them about a level's worth of treasure. You can either go back and erase doors and corridors on the map that you haven't filled out yet, or find ways to connect them up with each other.

## CORRIDORS

A dungeon can start with a corridor, or you can place a corridor as a separator between doors or chambers.

**Result of 1-19:** If the corridor ends in a door, a chamber, or stairs, refer to the appropriate section and roll again on the tables provided there.

If the passage divides at an intersection or has a side branch, choose a path and roll again on the Corridors table. If the corridor continues and also has a door or stairs, choose either the corridor or the door or stairs and roll on the appropriate table. You decide

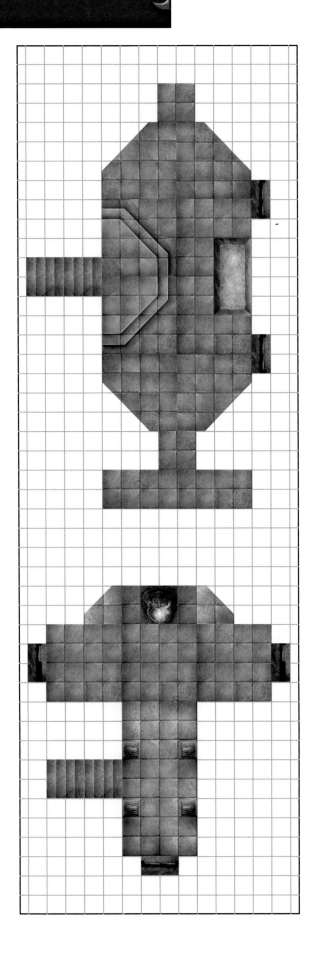

which square an opening, door, or stairway is in, either by drawing it on the map or aligning a dungeon tile the way you want.

If the corridor dead-ends, choose a different exit and roll on the indicated table.

**Result of 20:** A roll of 20 results in a random encounter of some sort, whether a trap or hazard, or one or more monsters. See the "Random Encounters" section starting on page 193 for help on working out what's there.

### CORRIDORS

| d20 | Corridor |
|---|---|
| 1 | Straight 4 squares |
| 2 | Straight 8 squares |
| 3-5 | Ends in door |
| 6 | Straight 4 squares, door on right |
| 7 | Straight 4 squares, door on left |
| 8 | Straight 4 squares, side passage on right |
| 9 | Straight 4 squares, side passage on left |
| 10 | Three-way intersection ("T") |
| 11 | Four-way intersection |
| 12 | 90-degree turn left |
| 13 | 90-degree turn right |
| 14-15 | Ends in chamber (no door) |
| 16 | Ends in stairs |
| 17 | Straight 4 squares, stairs on right |
| 18 | Straight 4 squares, stairs on left |
| 19 | Dead end |
| 20 | Random encounter |

# DOORS

The first step in creating random doors is deciding whether they're all easy to open or not. If you want doors of varying difficulty, consult the Door Types table first. The door's material determines how hard it is to open, with difficulty increasing by tier (roll on the applicable column). Refer to page xx in Chapter 4 for details of different sorts of doors and portcullises.

### DOOR TYPES

| | | Door Type | |
|---|---|---|---|
| d20 | Heroic | Paragon | Epic |
| 1-4 | Not stuck | Barred or locked | Stone |
| 5-8 | Wooden | Stone | Iron |
| 9-11 | Barred or locked | Iron | Wooden portcullis |
| 12-14 | Stone | Wooden portcullis | Adamantine |
| 15-17 | Iron | Adamantine | Iron portcullis |
| 18-20 | Wooden portcullis | Iron portcullis | Adamantine portcullis |

After deciding on the door's difficulty, roll another d20 and refer to the following table to see what lies beyond.

### BEYOND A DOOR

| d20 | Feature |
|---|---|
| 1-2 | Corridor left and right |
| 3-8 | Corridor straight ahead |
| 9-18 | Chamber |
| 19 | Stairs |
| 20 | False door plus trap |

**Result of 1-8:** If the die roll results in a corridor of some sort, refer to the "Corridors" section below and roll again on that table.

**Result of 9-18:** If the die roll results in a chamber, refer to the "Chambers" section below and roll again on the tables there.

**Result of 19:** If the die roll indicates stairs, refer to the "Stairs" section below and roll again on that table. If your dungeon has only one floor, reroll this result or substitute another kind of exit.

**Result of 20:** A roll of 20 results in a false door that triggers a trap. See "Traps and Hazards" in Chapter 5 to choose a suitable trap for your characters' level.

# CHAMBERS

Quite often, a door or corridor leads into a chamber of some kind. Although small rooms are possible, larger areas work better for combat since they allow more movement choices and varied terrain. The chambers provided in the following table are big enough to leave lots of space for the party and monsters or hazards.

First roll on the Chamber Size and Shape table, then refer to the Chamber Exits table to determine how many exits lead out (the way in doesn't count). You'll have to decide how many exits are in which walls, or you can choose a suitable dungeon tile with the right number. For each exit that isn't stairs, roll another d20 to see if it's a door or a corridor. If your dungeon has only one floor, reroll a result that includes stairs, or substitute another kind of exit.

### CHAMBER SIZE AND SHAPE

| d20 | Chamber |
|---|---|
| 1-2 | Square, 8 × 8 squares |
| 3-4 | Square, 10 × 10 squares |
| 5-6 | Rectangle, 6 × 8 squares |
| 7-8 | Rectangle, 8 × 10 squares |
| 9-10 | Rectangle, 10 × 16 squares |
| 11-12 | Octagon, 8 × 8 squares |
| 13-14 | Octagon, 8 × 12 squares |
| 15-16 | Octagon, 12 × 12 squares |
| 17-18 | Irregular, roughly 8 × 10 squares |
| 19-20 | Irregular, roughly 10 × 16 squares |

## CHAMBER EXITS

| d20 | Exits |
| --- | --- |
| 1-5 | None |
| 6-11 | One |
| 12-15 | Two |
| 16-17 | Three |
| 18 | Four |
| 19 | Stairs only |
| 20 | One exit plus stairs |
| For each exit other than stairs, roll 1d20: | |
| 1-10, exit is a door | |
| 11-20, exit is a corridor | |

Finally, roll on the following table for unusual features in the chamber, placing them as you wish. You can roll more than once if you want to, or have multiple squares contain the same feature, but watch out for crowding. The "Terrain Features" section of Chapter 4 has more advice about using terrain effectively.

## CHAMBER FEATURES

| d20 | Features |
| --- | --- |
| 1-3 | Rubble or other difficult terrain |
| 4-5 | Crevasse or chasm |
| 6-7 | Statue, obelisk, or similar object |
| 8-9 | Pit |
| 10-13 | Pool, fountain, or basin |
| 14-16 | Furniture |
| 17-18 | Altar, brazier, or arcane symbol on floor |
| 19 | Platform or dais |
| 20 | Sarcophagus |

# STAIRS

The existence of stairs presumes a dungeon with more than one floor. If you want to keep your dungeon simple, reroll stairs results from other tables or replace them with other kinds of features.

For the purpose of this entry, "stairs" includes other means of going up and down, such as chimneys, shafts (with or without elevators), and ladders. The distance between the floors of your dungeon is up to you; 30 feet is a good starting number.

## STAIRS

| d20 | Stairs |
| --- | --- |
| 1 | Up to dead end |
| 2 | Down to dead end |
| 3-9 | Down one floor |
| 10-14 | Up one floor |
| 15-17 | Trapdoor plus ladder up one floor |
| 18-19 | Trapdoor plus ladder down one floor |
| 20 | Shaft up and down, one floor each way |

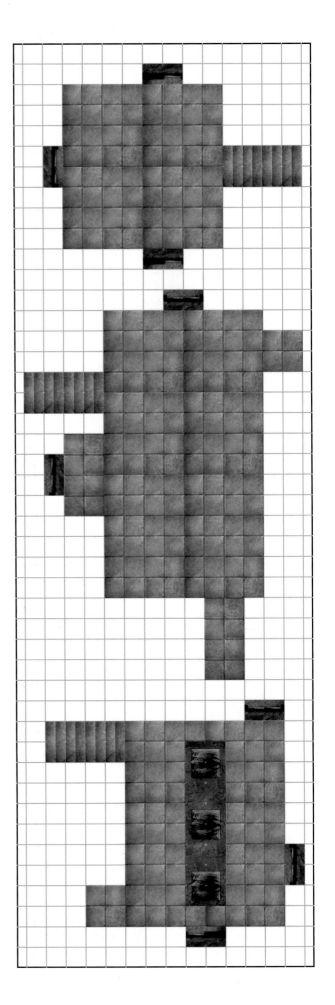

# RANDOM ENCOUNTERS

Sometimes you need a group of monsters to challenge your characters on the spur of the moment. This section shows you how to populate those random dungeons with challenging encounters. This is also where we at last reveal the secret of how to play D&D without a Dungeon Master!

A random encounter is usually less complex than one you craft yourself, but it doesn't have to be any less fun. You can create interesting tactical challenges with a few die rolls.

## Encounter Basics

Before you create your random encounter, you need to establish its difficulty and basic nature.

To determine the difficulty of the encounter, roll a d20 and consult the following table.

### ENCOUNTER DIFFICULTY

| d20 | Difficulty |
| --- | --- |
| 1-4 | Easy |
| 5-16 | Moderate |
| 17-20 | Hard |

Now, roll d10 on the Encounter Template table below to determine the sort of encounter. Encounter templates are described in Chapter 4.

### ENCOUNTER TEMPLATE

| d10 | Template |
| --- | --- |
| 1-2 | Commander and troops |
| 3-4 | Wolf pack |
| 5-6 | Dragon's den |
| 7-8 | Battlefield control |
| 9-10 | Double line |

If you want more variety, and an opportunity to work traps and hazards (see Chapter 5) into the process, roll d10 again and consult the Encounter Extra Feature table below.

### ENCOUNTER EXTRA FEATURE

| d10 | Extra Feature |
| --- | --- |
| 1-4 | No extra feature |
| 5 | Replace one monster with trap |
| 6 | Replace one monster with hazard |
| 7 | Replace one monster with lurker |
| 8 | As template from above, but add a trap |
| 9 | As template from above, but add a hazard |
| 10 | As template from above, but add a lurker |

Each encounter template in Chapter 4 suggests a composition for various difficulty levels. If the template offers multiple options for a given difficulty (such as

the wolf pack), you can either choose one or randomly select it.

Then comes the tricky part: choosing specific monsters (or traps and hazards) to build the encounter. For traps and hazards, choose an example in Chapter 5 that's closest to the level you want. For monsters, your best bet is to use the *Monster Manual*'s list of monsters by role and level. You can either choose the creatures you want from the list or roll them randomly. Let's say you're creating a commander and troops encounter for a 4th-level party, and you need 4th-level soldiers or brutes to fill it out. The *Monster Manual* includes four 4th-level brutes and three 4th-level soldiers. To choose randomly from the seven available monsters, roll a d8. If you get a result of 8, choose a 5th-level monster instead.

# THE ENCOUNTER DECK

You can generate random encounters by assembling a deck of cards that represent monsters, traps, and hazards. The stat cards included with *D&D Miniatures Game* products are ideal for this purpose, since they present brief monster statistics for easy reference. This approach requires some preparation but gives fun and flexible results.

Before the game, you need to assemble an encounter deck. For an adventure containing eight to ten encounters, aim for about fifty cards. You probably won't use them all, but this mix allows a nice variety. Create a mix of roles close to the following list.

## MONSTER MIX
- ✦ 18 soldiers or brutes
- ✦ 14 skirmishers
- ✦ 5 minions
- ✦ 5 artillery
- ✦ 5 controllers
- ✦ 2 lurkers
- ✦ 1 solo

Within this selection of monsters, put together a range of challenges along the following lines. In each case, "Level" refers to the level of the characters.

## MONSTER LEVEL
- ✦ 7 of Level - 2
- ✦ 30 within Level - 1 to Level + 1
- ✦ 8 of Level + 2 or Level + 3
- ✦ 5 of Level + 4 or Level + 5

You can choose monsters at random, but you can create more interesting and flavorful encounters by working with a theme, such as aberrant monsters or evil cultists. Mixing themes works well–along with the aberrant creatures, for example, you could have a strong contingent of demons and demon-worshipers. Multiple cards might well represent the same monster.

## GENERATING ENCOUNTERS

When it's time to generate an encounter, draw one card from the deck for each character in the party Each card stands for one monster of that role, with two exceptions. A card that indicates a soldier or brute represents two of the same monster, while each minion card represents four creatures.

Once you've drawn all your cards, assemble an encounter using the following principles. Shuffle any cards you don't use back into the deck for the next encounter.

+ Each encounter should contain two brutes or soldiers plus two or three monsters of other roles. If your group has more than five players, add a monster for each additional character.

+ If you draw a lurker, set it aside and draw another card. Build an encounter from the rest of the cards and the new one, then add the lurker to the mix.

+ A solo monster is the only creature in the encounter. Return all the others to the deck.

If certain monsters seem to naturally fit together in a certain situation, simply choose them from the deck instead of drawing randomly.

## TWISTS

You can add special characteristics to some of the cards in your deck to liven up your encounters and make them feel more like an adventure.

**Boss:** Add a card for a powerful monster (six or seven levels above that of the characters) and designate it as the "boss," the main villain of the adventure. The party's goal is to defeat that monster. The first time you draw the card, don't add it to the encounter—draw a replacement and shuffle the first back into the deck. Doing this give the characters their first tantalizing glimpse, setting up the later showdown with that enemy. The boss might be seen slipping out a door behind the other creatures, or standing at a safe vantage point to watch the progress of the battle. (This is a fine opportunity for it to utter a taunt such as "You've fallen into my trap, foolish adventurers!" and then laugh maniacally before getting away.) A really tricky boss might escape twice before finally confronting the adventurers.

Another way to handle a boss monster is to leave its card out of the deck at the beginning of the adventure. After the PCs have defeated one or two monsters you've designated as key, shuffle the card into the deck. For example, you might decide that the boss will arrive after the party encounters your solo monster.

**Evolving Deck:** To create a sense of progress, you can have your dungeon change over time. To do so, start with one encounter deck. As the characters advance through the dungeon, add in cards from a second deck of more difficult encounters.

To use this option, you'll need to create two encounter decks, with the creatures in the second of higher level than those in the first. Whenever the party defeats monsters, springs traps, or overcomes hazards in the first deck, replace those cards with an equal number of random cards from the second deck. As the adventure continues, the encounters become tougher and tougher.

You can combine this option with a boss monster. In this situation, leave out the boss's card until the characters defeat one or more creatures from the second deck. Then shuffle its card into the second deck.

For an interesting variant, try giving the two decks different themes. The first deck might contain mostly vermin and beasts, while the second is made up of evil clerics, their undead creatures, and their humanoid guards. In this example, the characters are out to locate and destroy an evil temple. They start out encountering miscellaneous dungeon denizens but then run into members of the temple, leading to the final battle.

**Traps and Hazards:** You can add traps, hazards, and interesting terrain features to your random encounters. To do this, include cards representing them, in addition to your fifty monster cards. Each time one of these cards comes up, add it to the encounter and draw another card from the encounter deck.

## PLAYING WITHOUT A DM

This might seem to be strange advice for a *Dungeon Master's Guide*, but it's entirely possible to play D&D without a Dungeon Master. If all you're looking for is fun and exciting combat, with no more than the barest hint of plot or purpose, a random dungeon with a random encounter deck is all you need. Someone needs to prepare the deck, and someone needs to run the monsters during the game. They doesn't need to be the same person. All the players can decide together what the monsters do, and let the player who's the target of an attack make that attack roll (or have the person to the left roll for the monsters).

A random dungeon with no DM makes for a good way to spend a game session when your regular DM can't play. It's also a fun activity over a lunch hour, as long as your school or office is forgiving of a group of people rolling dice and shouting battle cries!

# FALLCREST

RALPH HORSLEY

**W**HERE DO the player characters go when they're not battling through dismal dungeons or exploring ancient ruins? Where do they go to spend the treasure they win and rest up for the next adventure? The answer is simple: a base town.

A base town is a haven where the heroes can interact with patrons, listen for rumors, sell art objects or magic items, and buy new gear. It might be an elven tree-village that happens to be located near a dungeon the heroes are exploring, a prosperous human trade-town that interesting people pass through, an isolated dwarf stronghold in the borderlands, or a true city inhabited by thousands of people. Whatever the nature of the base town, it's the place your player characters return to between adventures, and the place where new adventures begin.

This chapter introduces a town called Fallcrest, which you can use as a base town for your first D&D game.

✦ **The Town of Fallcrest:** This section is a brief description of the town's story, important characters, and noteworthy locales. Fallcrest provides adventurers with inns to sleep in, taverns to frequent, merchants to barter with, and contacts or patrons who can point them at the next adventure.

✦ **The Nentir Vale:** The region surrounding Fallcrest is a thinly settled frontier dotted with ruins and monster lairs. This section is an overview of the lands around Fallcrest.

✦ **Involving the Players:** In this section we provide suggestions for giving your player characters story connections to Fallcrest and its people.

✦ **Kobold Hall:** The chapter concludes with a ready-to-play beginning adventure: Kobold Hall. If you're looking for a chance to start being a Dungeon Master, this adventure is for you.

Fallcrest stands amid the Moon Hills at the falls of the Nentir River. Here travelers and traders using the old King's Road that runs north and south, the dwarven Trade Road from the east, and the river all meet. The surrounding ridges shelter several small valleys where farmers and woodsfolk live; few are more than six or seven miles from the town. In general the people outside Fallcrest's walls earn their living by farming or keeping livestock, and the people inside the walls are artisans, laborers, or merchants. People with no other prospects can make a hard living as porters, carrying cargo from the Lower Quays to the Upper Quays (or vice versa).

Fallcrest imports finished goods from the larger cities downriver and ironwork from the dwarf town of Hammerfast, and exports timber, leather, fruit, and grain. It also trades with the nearby town of Winterhaven. The surrounding hills hold several marble quarries that once produced a good deal of stone, but the area has little demand for ornamental stone these days, and only a few stonecutters still practice their trade.

### FALLCREST

A small town built from the ruins of a larger city, Fallcrest is the crossroads of the Nentir Vale.

**Population:** 1,350; another 900 or so live in the countryside within a few miles of the town. The people of Fallcrest are mostly humans, halflings, and dwarves. No dragonborn or eladrin are permanent residents, but travelers of all races pass through on occasion.

**Government:** The human noble Faren Markelhay is the Lord Warden (hereditary lord) of the town. He is in charge of the town's justice, defense, and laws. The Lord Warden appoints a town council to look after routine commerce and public projects.

**Defense:** The Fallcrest Guard numbers sixty warriors (see the accompanying statistics block), who also serve as constables. Moonstone Keep is their barracks. The Lord Warden can call up 350 militia at need.

**Inns:** Nentir Inn; Silver Unicorn. The Silver Unicorn is pricier and offers better service; the Nentir Inn sees a more interesting clientele.

**Taverns:** Blue Moon Alehouse; Lucky Gnome Taphouse; Nentir Inn taproom.

**Supplies:** Halfmoon Trading House; Sandercot Provisioners.

**Temples:** Temple of Erathis; Moonsong Temple (Sehanine); House of the Sun (Pelor).

## FALLCREST'S STORY

Up until four centuries or so ago, the Moon Hills and the surrounding Nentir Vale were thinly settled borderlands, home to quarrelsome human hill-chieftains and remote realms of nonhumans such as dwarves and elves. Giants, minotaurs, orcs, ogres, and goblins plagued the area. Ruins such as those on the Gray Downs or the ring-forts atop the Old Hills date back

to these days, as do stories of the hero Vendar and the dragon of the Nentir.

With the rise of the empire of Nerath to the south, human settlers began to move up the Nentir, establishing towns such as Fastormel, Harkenwold, and Winterhaven. A Nerathan hero named Aranda Markelhay obtained a charter to build a keep at the portage of the Nentir Falls. She raised a simple tower at the site of Moonstone Keep three hundred ten years ago, and under its protection the town of Fallcrest began to grow.

Over the next two centuries, Fallcrest grew into a small and prosperous city. It was a natural crossroads for trade, and the Markelhays ruled it well. When the empire of Nerath began to crumble about a century ago, Fallcrest continued to flourish—for a time. Ninety years ago, a fierce horde of orcs known as the Bloodspears descended from the Stonemarch and swept over the vale. Fallcrest's army was defeated in a rash attempt to halt the Bloodspears out on Gardbury Downs. The Bloodspears burned and pillaged Fallcrest and went on to wreak havoc all across the Nentir Vale.

In the decades since the Bloodspear War, Fallcrest has struggled to reestablish itself. The town is a shadow of the former city; little trade passes up and down the river these days. The countryside for scores of miles around is dotted with abandoned homesteads and manors from the days of Nerath. Once again the Nentir Vale is a thinly settled borderland where few folk live. This is a place in need of a few heroes.

## KEY LOCATIONS

Fallcrest is divided into two districts by a steep bluff that cuts across the town. The area north of the bluff is known locally as Hightown. This district survived the city's fall in relatively good shape, and it was the first area resettled. To the south of the bluff lies Lowtown, which tends to be newer and poorer. In the event of a serious threat, people retreat up to Hightown—the bluff and the town walls completely ring this part of Fallcrest, making it highly defensible.

The map on the facing page depicts all the numbered locations discussed in this section. Four of the locations include statistics for nonplayer characters who might come into conflict with the PCs.

### 1. TOWER OF WAITING

This old fortification was built on a small island in the Nentir to guard the city from any waterborne attack from the north. It fell into ruin even before the sack of the old city, and now is little more than an empty shell overrun by mice and birds.

MIKE SCHLEY

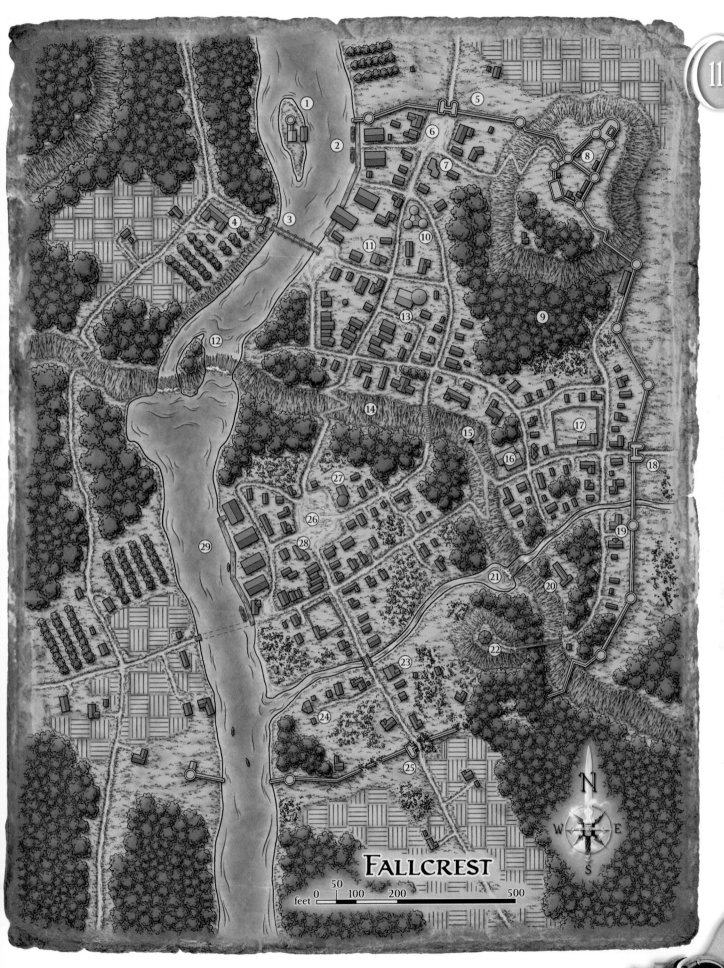

Fallcrest

**DM Tip:** According to local legend, the tower was once a prison for nobles who were too well connected to be killed out of hand or mistreated. The ghost of an evil princess who dabbled in demon worship haunts the tower. You can build your own small dungeon beneath the ruins, featuring a wrathful specter and minor demons.

## 2. UPPER QUAYS

Boats proceeding down the Nentir must stop here and offload their cargo, which is then portaged through the town to the Lower Quays and loaded onto boats below the falls. Likewise, cargo heading in the other direction is carried up to these quays and loaded aboard boats bound upstream.

A surly dwarf pugilist named Barstomun Strongbeard runs the porters' guild, and he takes a cut of any wages paid to laborers carrying cargo up or down around the falls. Barstomun and his thugs are trying to extend their reach by intimidating merchants who send their goods overland and forcing them to hire guild porters for any cargo handling in town.

| Barstomun Strongbeard | Level 4 Brute |
|---|---|
| Medium natural humanoid, dwarf | XP 175 |

**Initiative** +3 **Senses** Perception +4; low-light vision
**HP** 67; **Bloodied** 33
**AC** 16; **Fortitude** 18, **Reflex** 15, **Will** 15
**Saving Throws** +5 against poison effects
**Speed** 5
⊕ **Fist Pummel** (standard; at-will)
  +7 vs. AC; 1d6 + 4 damage.
✦ **Quick Punch** (minor; at-will)
  +7 vs. AC; 1d6 + 4 damage.
**Dodge and Throw** (immediate reaction; encounter; after an enemy misses with a melee attack)
  +7 vs Fortitude; slide target 1, and target is knocked prone.
**Stand Your Ground**
  When an effect forces Barstomun to move—through a push, a pull, or a slide—he moves 1 square less than the effect specifies. When an attack would knock Barstomun prone, he can immediately make a saving throw to avoid falling prone.
**Alignment** Unaligned **Languages** Common, Dwarven
**Skills** Endurance +7
**Str** 18 (+6) **Dex** 13 (+3) **Wis** 13 (+3)
**Con** 17 (+5) **Int** 11 (+2) **Cha** 8 (+1)

## 3. FIVE-ARCH BRIDGE

Dwarf artisans from the citadel of Hammerfast built a fine stone bridge over the Nentir two hundred years ago. Although the bridge was destroyed when Fallcrest fell, the great stone piers supporting it remained intact, so a few years back the people of the town laid a new timber trestle over the old stone footings.

A small toll house guards the western side of the bridge. Five Fallcrest guards under the command of Sergeant Thurmina watch this post. They collect a toll of 1 cp per head (and 1 sp per mount) making use of the bridge in either direction. Thurmina is a gruff woman who has been known to turn a blind eye to odd cargo moving over the bridge when paid to do so.

The river current begins to pick up on the south side of the bridge. Boats (or swimmers) venturing far from the banks are in danger of being carried over the falls.

## 4. NENTIR INN

A fine new building constructed of fieldstone and strong timber, the Nentir Inn stands on the west bank of the river. Merchants from Winterhaven or Hammerfast make up the clientele, along with travelers who happen to be passing through. A good room with two single beds goes for 5 sp per night. The Nentir Inn also boasts a lively taproom, which is popular with the folk who live in the vales on the west bank of the river.

The proprietor is a charming half-elf named Erandil Zemoar who showed up in Fallcrest one day about two years ago, bought land, and built an inn. The money that Erandil used to set up the Nentir isn't his; he charmed an aging noblewoman in the far south out of her fortune, and fled one step ahead of the authorities.

One of the Nentir Inn's current guests is an expatriate noble from the south named Serim Selduzar, who harbors ambitions against Fallcrest. This tiefling is clever and feigns good humor about his "present unfortunate circumstances," and he has a wickedly sarcastic streak to his wit. Serim claims to be the third son of a southern noble with little prospect to inherit. He tells inquirers that he is thinking of establishing a small manor somewhere nearby, but in truth he has set his sights on arranging the downfall of the Markelhay family and installing himself as the new Lord Warden. The tiefling is looking for capable associates to help him, and a band of enthusiastic adventurers would suit his purposes admirably. Given the chance, Serim befriends the player characters in the hope that he might dupe them into overthrowing the Markelhays for him.

## 5. KNIGHT'S GATE

Fallcrest's northern city gate is known as Knight's Gate, because the Lord Warden's riders normally come and go from the city by this road. The gate consists of strong outer doors of iron-reinforced timber and an inner portcullis between a pair of small stone towers. The portcullis is normally lowered at sunset, and the gates close only in times of danger.

The gatehouse barracks accommodates five Fallcrest guards plus Sergeant Nereth, who commands this gate. He is a stiff-necked fussbudget who rigorously enforces all rules; the guards stationed here can't stand their sergeant.

### THE TOWN WALLS

Fallcrest's Hightown is guarded on two sides by a wall (the river and the bluffs protect the other two sides). It consists of two parallel barriers of stone block with a few feet of fill between them, and stands about 20 feet tall. Every hundred yards or so, a small tower strengthens the wall. Two pairs of sentries (Fallcrest guards from the castle) walk the wall tops at night, but unless danger is imminent, the towers are left locked and aren't manned. The gatehouses are permanently garrisoned.

## 6. Silver Unicorn Inn

For many years, the Silver Unicorn has billed itself as "the Pride of Fallcrest," charging high rates for its attentive service and well-appointed rooms. The recent opening of the Nentir Inn put a big dent in the Silver Unicorn's business, and the owner, a stern halfling matriarch named Wisara Osterman, strongly disapproves. She's certain that there is something shifty about Erandil Zemoar, but can't put her finger on it.

A room in the Silver Unicorn costs 2 gp per night.

## 7. Halfmoon Trading House

The Halfmoon family is a large, far-flung clan of halflings who keep small trading posts in several settlements throughout the Nentir Vale. This is the largest and most important of those establishments. It's under the care of Selarund Halfmoon, a friendly halfling who dispenses a never-ending stream of advice to his customers, such as, "It never rains but as someone gets wet!" or "A nail ain't afraid of a hammer with no handle!" No one knows what he's talking about most of the time, but Selarund is more sly than he lets on and keeps a close eye on events all around the town.

The Halfmoon Trading House is an excellent place to buy any of the mundane tools, gear, supplies, or clothing mentioned in the *Player's Handbook*.

## 8. Moonstone Keep

The seat of Lord Warden Faren Markelhay, Moonstone Keep is an old castle that sits atop a steep-sided hill overlooking the town. The outer bailey includes barracks housing up to sixty Fallcrest guards. At any given time about twenty or so are off-duty. Other buildings in the courtyard include a stable, an armory, a chapel, a smithy, and several storehouses. The keep is the large D-shaped building at the north end of the castle.

Faren Markelhay is a balding, middle-aged human with a keen mind and a dry wit. He is a busy man and sees to local matters personally, so adventurers calling on him are likely to wait a long time for a short interview. However, he is eager for news of other towns in the Vale (and farther lands as well) and never turns away someone who brings him news or waits to see him.

**DM Tip:** The Lord Warden is always on the lookout for traveling sellswords or adventurers who might take on a contract to clear out a nest of bandits, drive off a dangerous beast, or escort a valuable cargo to its destination. The kobolds of Kobold Hall have been causing trouble on the King's Road lately, and they're at the top of his list; if the player characters are looking for work, Lord Markelhay points them toward Kobold Hall first (see the adventure later in this chapter). He also has word of trouble in the town of Winterhaven, and he encourages player characters to consider helping the Lord Mayor of that town.

Lord Markelhay's wife is Lady Allande Markelhay (female human wizard 4). She is a cool and reserved woman ten years younger than her husband. A student of the arcane arts, she uses her powers to advise her husband. They have four children; the eldest, Ernesto, is currently away in the south, living in the court of another ruler.

## 9. The Tombwood

Along the southern slopes of Moonstone Hill grows a large thicket that has never been entirely cleared. Within its tangled paths lies the old castle cemetery (now heavily overgrown), as well as a battle-mound dating back centuries.

**DM Tip:** These old crypts are linked by secret passages to dangerous, sealed-off parts of the Moonstone Caverns beneath the town. You can create your own dungeon here.

## 10. House of the Sun

When Fallcrest was a larger city, it supported several good-sized temples located in the Hightown districts. With the town's depopulation, several of these were abandoned, including the House of the Sun, a temple dedicated to Pelor. The place also includes shrines to Kord and Bahamut. Recently, a zealous dwarf priest of Pelor named Grundelmar came to Fallcrest from Hammerfast and reestablished this old temple. Grundelmar is loud and opinionated, a real fire-breather who goes on and on about smiting evil wherever it might lurk.

**DM Tip:** Grundelmar is worried about conditions on the Trade Road, and he strongly encourages any would-be heroes to search out the bandit lair of Raven Roost and deal with the outlaws. This lair is a good opportunity to build your own dungeon.

## 11. House Azaer

A small, well-off trading company, House Azaer is owned by the tieflings of the Azaer family. They import goods (including arms and armor) from Hammerfast, Harkenwold, and the lands to the south, and organize caravans up to Winterhaven several times a year. House Azaer is an excellent place to purchase nearly any mundane equipment from the *Player's Handbook*, although its prices are a little on the high side.

Amara Azaer is in charge of the house business in Fallcrest, and spends her time on the premises. Though young, the tiefling is quite sharp and doesn't miss an opportunity for profit in running the Azaer business.

## 12. The Nentir Falls

Here the Nentir River descends nearly 200 feet in three striking shelflike drops. On the small island in the middle of the falls stands the statue of an ancient human hero named Vendar, holding up his hand as if to challenge enemies approaching from downriver. Local legend tells that Vendar slew a dragon whose lair was hidden in caverns beneath the falls.

## 13. Temple of Erathis

This large, impressive stone temple is finished with Fallcrest's native marble. Its chapel is a large rotunda with a 30-foot-tall dome. The temple of Erathis is the largest and most influential temple in town. The place also includes shrines to Ioun and Moradin.

High Priest Dirina Mornbrow oversees two lesser priests and several acolytes—townsfolk who spend part of their day tending the temple. Dirina is a woman of about sixty who is convinced of the superiority of Erathis's dogma, and disappointed that more people in Fallcrest don't pay proper reverence to "our city's patron god." She is familiar with several divination and restoration rituals and can aid adventurers with ritual magic at need—for an appropriate gift to Erathis, of course. She has limited access to the following ritual scrolls: Hand of Fate (1), Cure Disease (4), Raise Dead (1), Remove Affliction (2).

## 14. The Bluffs

Fallcrest is divided in half by a great cliff snaking northwest to southeast across the town. The bluffs average 150 to 250 feet in height. They are not strictly vertical, but are too tall and steep to be easily climbed. Someone leaping (or pushed) off the upper edge would fall and roll about 2d6 [ts] 10 feet before sliding to a stop, likely on a precarious ledge.

## 15. The Catacombs

The limestone bluffs between Hightown and Lowtown hold a number of caves, which the folk of Fallcrest have used as burial crypts for centuries. As caves fill up, they are walled off and forgotten about. Naturally, stories abound in town about treasure hoards hidden away in the crypts, and the restless undead that guard them.

**DM Tip:** The stories are in part true; portions of the catacombs now in use are safe enough, but explorers forcing their way into older portions might stumble into deadly traps, ancient curses, evil shrines, and more than a few malevolent undead.

## 16. Moonsong Temple

The third of Fallcrest's temples is devoted to Sehanine. It also includes shrines to Corellon, Melora, and Avandra. The Markelhays regard Sehanine as their special patron, and over the years they have given generously to the temple. The temple occupies a commanding position atop the bluffs, and its white minarets can be seen from any corner of Lowtown.

The leader of the temple is High Priest Ressilmae Starlight, a wise and compassionate elf who finished adventuring decades ago and retired to a contemplative life. He is a musician of great skill who happily tutors the local children, even those who are poor and can't afford to pay for their lessons. He has limited access to the following ritual scrolls: Cure Disease (2), Raise Dead (1), Remove Affliction (1).

## 17. Fallcrest Stables

Lannar Thistleton owns this business, providing travelers with tack, harness, stabling, shoeing, wagons, and just about anything dealing with horses, mules, or ponies. He keeps a larger corral about a mile outside of town, and at any given time Lannar has several riding horses, draft horses, or mules in his paddock near Wizard's Gate. The halfling is an excellent source of rumors, since he sees the travelers coming or going by the roads. He is a friendly fellow of about forty, with a large brood of children at his home out in the countryside.

## 18. Wizard's Gate

Fallcrest's eastern city gate is known as Wizard's Gate, because it's the gate most convenient to the Septarch's Tower. The road to the east travels a few miles into the surrounding hills, linking a number of outlying farms and homesteads with the town.

The gate resembles Knight's Gate in construction, and is similarly watched by a detachment of five guards and a sergeant. The leader of this detachment is Sergeant Murgeddin, a dwarf veteran who fought in the Bloodspear War and was present at the Battle of Gardbury, where Fallcrest's army was defeated. A friendly drink goes a long way toward loosening Murgeddin's tongue about that long-ago war.

**DM Tip:** During the battle, Murgeddin saw the old Lord Markelhay flee into the catacombs under the Gardmore Abbey and never come out. The dwarf suspects that the ancestral sword of the Markelhays—Aranda Markelhay's magic longsword *Moonbane*—lies somewhere below the abbey. You can create your own dungeon in the ruins of the abbey.

## 19. Naerumar's Imports

Considered the finest of Fallcrest's retail establishments, Naerumar's Imports deals in gemstones, jewelry, art, and magic trinkets. The owner is Orest Naerumar, a tiefling who displays impeccable manners and discretion. Orest corresponds with relatives and colleagues in several towns and cities outside the Nentir Vale; given a few weeks, he can order in low-level magic items or other items of unusual value. Similarly, Orest purchases interesting items such as these, since other dealers in distant towns or cities might be looking for them.

Orest doesn't ask questions about where characters in his store found the goods they're selling to him, but he is not a fence—if he knows that something was obtained illegally, he declines to purchase it.

**DM Tip:** Orest normally arranges for halflings of the Swiftwater clan to transport special orders—jewelry, gems, or magic items of value. However, he sometimes makes other arrangements for items that seem especially valuable or dangerous. If the player characters are looking for something to do, Orest can hire them to carry or guard exceptionally valuable goods he's sending to a merchant in another town.

| Orest Naerumar | Level 8 Skirmisher |
|---|---|
| Medium natural humanoid, tiefling rogue | XP 350 |

**Initiative** +8      **Senses** Perception +5; low-light vision
**HP** 79; **Bloodied** 39
**AC** 21; **Fortitude** 19, **Reflex** 23, **Will** 22
**Resist** fire 9
**Speed** 6

⚔ **Dagger** +1 (standard; at-will) ✦ **Weapon**
+11 vs. AC; 1d4 + 1 damage.

↟ **Sly Flourish** (standard; at-will) ✦ **Martial, Weapon**
+14 vs. AC; 1d4 + 9 damage.

↟ **Dazing Strike** (standard; encounter) ✦ **Martial, Weapon**
+14 vs. AC; 1d4 + 4 damage and target dazed until the end of Orest's next turn.

**Infernal Wrath** (minor; encounter)
Orest gains a +1 power bonus to his next attack roll against an enemy that hit him since his last turn. If the attack hits and deals damage, Orest deals an extra 5 damage.

**First Strike**
At the start of an encounter, Orest has combat advantage against any creatures that have not yet acted.

**Sneak Attack**
Once per round, Orest gains +2d6 damage when he has combat advantage.

**Bloodhunt**
Orest gains a +1 racial bonus to attack rolls against bloodied foes.

**Alignment** Unaligned     **Languages** Common, Dwarven
**Skills** Bluff +13, Diplomacy +14, Insight +11, Stealth +10
**Str** 13 (+5)     **Dex** 19 (+8)     **Wis** 14 (+6)
**Con** 15 (+6)     **Int** 15 (+6)     **Cha** 20 (+9)
**Equipment** usually unarmored, might carry a level 6 through 8 magic dagger

## 20. Kamroth Estate

This is the home of the self-styled "lord" Armos Kamroth, a wealthy landowner who collects rents from scores of farmers and herders living in the countryside nearby. Armos is a brusque, balding man of about fifty who makes a show of loaning money in good faith and exacting only what the law allows—but somehow he has quietly bought up dozens of free farms over the years and turned their owners into his tenants.

Armos is a miser of the worst kind and is secretly a devotee of Tiamat. He leads a small circle of like-minded folk who meet secretly in hidden vaults beneath his comfortable estate. Any news of treasure discovered by itinerant heroes inflames his avarice and leads him to begin scheming for ways to part the adventurers from their wealth.

| Armos Kamroth | Level 5 Controller (leader) |
|---|---|
| Medium natural humanoid, human cleric | XP 200 |

**Initiative** +3     **Senses** Perception +6
**HP** 54; **Bloodied** 27
**AC** 18; **Fortitude** 16, **Reflex** 15, **Will** 20
**Speed** 5

(†) **Mace** (standard; at-will) ✦ **Weapon**
  +7 vs. AC; 1d8 + 3 damage.

⌁ **Lance of Faith** (standard; at-will ) ✦ **Divine, Implement**
  Ranged 5; +7 vs. Reflex; 1d8 + 5 damage, and one ally gains a +2 power bonus to his next attack against the target.

⌁ **Cause Fear** (standard; encounter) ✦ **Divine, Implement**
  Ranged 10; +7 vs. Will; the target moves its speed + 1 away from Armos. The fleeing target avoids unsafe squares and difficult terrain if it can. This movement provokes opportunity attacks.

**Divine Fortune** (free; encounter ) ✦ **Divine**
  Armos gains a +1 bonus to his next attack roll or saving throw before the end of his next turn.

**Healing Word** (minor; 2/encounter ) ✦ **Divine, Healing**
  Close burst 5; you or one ally can spend a healing surge and regain an additional 1d6 hit points.

| **Alignment** Evil | **Languages** Common, Draconic |
|---|---|
| **Skills** Diplomacy +8, Religion +7 | |

| **Str** 14 (+4) | **Dex** 12 (+3) | **Wis** 18 (+6) |
|---|---|---|
| **Con** 14 (+4) | **Int** 11 (+2) | **Cha** 12 (+3) |

**Equipment** chainmail, mace, symbol of Tiamat worn under shirt

## 21. Moonwash Falls

A small, swift stream known as the Moonwash flows through Fallcrest to meet the Nentir River. The stream is rarely more than 20 feet wide or 5 feet deep. The town's children love to play in the pool at the base of the falls in the summertime.

## 22. Septarch's Tower

This lonely structure is a tall, seven-sided spire of pale green stone that doesn't match anything else in the town. In the days before the Bloodspear War, this was the seat of Fallcrest's mages' guild—an order of a dozen or so wizards and arcane scholars. Defensive enchantments prevented the orcs from sacking the tower, but the guild's members died fighting for the city or fled to safer lands.

The tower is now the property of Nimozaran the Green, an elderly wizard who was once apprenticed to the last of the old guild mages. Nimozaran considers himself the "High Septarch of Fallcrest" and master of the guild, whose membership now includes only himself and a rather unpromising male halfling apprentice named Tobolar Quickfoot. Nimozaran expects any potential new guild members to pay a hefty initiation fee, and so far none of the few other arcanists living in or passing through Fallcrest have seen reason to join. He can teach a limited number of rituals, including Comprehend Language, Eye of Alarm, and Enchant Magic Item.

The topmost level of the tower is a room that includes a permanent teleportation circle. Characters using travel rituals can set this circle as their destination (although they'll certainly startle old Nimozaran if they do).

## 23. Blue Moon Alehouse

This brewhouse on the banks of the Moonwash Stream is the best tavern in Fallcrest. The owner is a nervous, easily flustered fellow of fifty or so named Par Winnomer. The true genius behind the Blue Moon is the halfling brewmaster Kemara Brownbottle. She is happy to let Par fret about running the taphouse, while she spends her time perfecting her selection of ales and beers.

The Blue Moon is popular with halfling traders whose boats tie up along the Lower Quay, well-off town merchants, and the farmers who live in the countryside south of Fallcrest. The old dwarves Teldorthan (area 24) and Sergeant Murgeddin (area 18) hoist a tankard or two here on frequent occasion, and both can provide beginning adventurers with good leads on potential adventures.

## 24. Teldorthan's Arms

The dwarf Teldorthan Ironhews is the town's weapon-smith and armorer. He is a garrulous old fellow who spends his time trading stories with his customers with a pipe clenched in his teeth, while his apprentices (two of whom are his sons) do the work. Make no mistake—Teldorthan is a master armorer, and under his supervision his apprentices turn out work of exceptional quality.

Teldorthan has in stock (or can soon manufacture) just about any mundane weapon or armor found in the *Player's Handbook*, although he advises beginners to try a hammer: "If you can drive a nail, you can kill an orc! You can drive a nail, can't you?"

**DM Tip:** Teldorthan recently lost a valuable strip of dragon hide he intended to make into scale armor. A trade caravan had sent it down from Winterhaven, but kobolds raided the caravan near the Cloak Wood and stole the wagon's goods. The dwarf strongly suspects that the kobolds are hiding out in the ruined manor called Kobold Hall, and he wants someone to recover his property. He is willing to pay the player characters to make the attempt. This offer leads characters into the sample adventure later in this chapter.

## 25. King's Gate

Fallcrest's southern gate was destroyed in the attack that devastated the city long ago, and it still has not been entirely rebuilt. One of the two paired towers is nothing but rubble, and several large gaps remain in the town walls south of the bluffs through which anyone could enter the city.

Despite its lack of functionality, the King's Gate is still used as a guardpost by the Fallcrest guards. Sergeant Gerdrand is in charge here; he is a tall, lanky man who doesn't say much, answering questions with a grunt or a shake of the head.

## 26. The Market Green

The majority of Fallcrest's folk live above the bluffs in Hightown and walk down to do business on the streets of Lowtown, which bustle with commerce. This wide square is an open, grassy meadow where Fallcrest's merchants and visiting traders do business in good weather. The town's children gather here for games of tag or kick-stones.

## 27. Sandercot Provisioners

The largest general store in Fallcrest, Sandercot's deals in just about anything–food, clothing, stores, rope, tools, gear, leather goods, and more. Compared to the Halfmoon Trading House, Sandercot's has slightly cheaper prices but goods of somewhat lower quality.

The owner is Nimena Sandercot, the widow of the late and unlamented Marken Sandercot. Marken associated with brigands and ne'er-do-wells, making a tidy sum by buying up goods stolen from his neighbors. His widow has continued the practice. Nimena puts on an air of rustic charm, but when it's time to talk "backroom business" she is ruthless, grasping, and greedy. She has three young sons, all of whom are quickly learning the family business.

Nimena is a willing fence for anything someone cares to sell, but she won't pay a copper more than she has to.

## 28. Lucky Gnome Taphouse

The Lucky Gnome is widely regarded as the cheapest and coarsest of Fallcrest's drinking establishments. It caters to the porters and laborers who work the nearby docks, and fistfights are a nightly occurrence.

The owner of the Lucky Gnome is an unsavory character named Kelson. Kelson runs the River Rats, a small street gang that plagues Lowtown, from the back room of his tavern.

| Kelson | Level 5 Skirmisher |
|---|---|
| Medium natural humanoid, human rogue | XP 200 |

**Initiative** +5      **Senses** Perception +6
**HP** 52; **Bloodied** 26
**AC** 20; **Fortitude** 16, **Reflex** 21, **Will** 16
**Speed** 6

⚔ **Dagger** (standard; at-will) ✦ **Weapon**
  +8 vs. AC; 1d4 + 3 damage.

✦ **Deft Strike** (standard; at-will ) ✦ **Martial, Weapon**
  Kelson can move 2 squares before the attack. +11 vs. AC; 1d4 + 6 damage.

✦ **King's Castle** (standard; encounter) ✦ **Martial, Weapon**
  +11 vs Reflex; 2d4 + 6 damage; Kelson can also switch places with a willing adjacent ally.

**First Strike**
  At the start of an encounter, Kelson has combat advantage against any creatures that have not yet acted.

**Nimble Reaction**
  Kelson gains a +2 racial bonus to AC against opportunity attacks.

**Second Chance** (immediate interrupt; encounter)
  When an attack hits Kelson, he forces the enemy to roll the attack again. The enemy must use the second roll.

**Sneak Attack**
  Once per round, Kelson gains +2d6 damage when he has combat advantage.

| **Alignment** Evil | **Languages** Common |
|---|---|

**Skills** Bluff +9, Diplomacy +9, Streetwise +7, Stealth +12

| **Str** 14 (+4) | **Dex** 20 (+7) | **Wis** 11 (+2) |
|---|---|---|
| **Con** 12 (+3) | **Int** 10 (+2) | **Cha** 15 (+4) |

**Equipment** leather armor, dagger, one level 4 through 6 magic item

## 29. Lower Quays

Keelboats and similar craft put in here to unload their cargo and portage it up to other boats above the falls. As described above for the Upper Quays, the porters' guild jealously defends its monopoly on moving cargo around the falls, and it frequently attempts to intimidate local merchants into paying for portage services–whether needed or not. In addition to the porters' guild, another gang of troublemakers lurks around the Lower Quays: the River Rats. These street toughs and thieves look out for the chance to pilfer from the warehouses or roll a drunk in a dark alleyway.

Boats belonging to a number of different travelers tie up here, the most common of which are the keelboats of the halfling Swiftwater Clan. The Swiftwaters carry cargo all the way down to the Nentir's mouth, hundreds of miles downriver. They're more than willing to take passengers for a small fee. Irena Swiftwater is the matriarch of the clan. She is a sharp merchant who passes herself off as an absent-minded reader of fortunes and maker of minor charms.

Fallcrest lies near the middle of the broad border-land region known as the Nentir Vale. The vale is now mostly empty, with a handful of living villages and towns scattered over this wide area. Abandoned farmsteads, ruined manors, and broken keeps litter the countryside. Bandits, wild animals, and monsters roam freely throughout the vale, threatening anyone who fares more than few miles away from one of the surviving settlements. Travel along the roads or river is usually safe—usually. But every now and then, travelers come to bad ends between towns.

The Nentir Vale is a northern land, but it sees relatively little snow—winters are windy and bitterly cold. The Nentir River is too big to freeze except for a few weeks in the coldest part of the year. Summers are cool and mild.

The "clear" parts of the map are covered in mixed terrain—large stretches of open meadowland, copses of light forest, gently rolling hills, and the occasional thicket of dense woodland and heavy undergrowth. The downs marked on the map are hilly grassland, with little tree cover. The hills are steeper and more rugged, and include light forest in the valleys and saddles between the hilltops.

Interesting locales in the Nentir Vale are described below.

## FIVELEAGUE HOUSE

Fiveleague House is more properly known as the Five-league Inn. It's a strongly built innhouse surrounded by a wooden palisade. Fiveleague House caters to travelers and merchants coming or going from Hammerfast, a day's journey (five leagues) farther east. The proprietor is a big, bearlike human named Barton. Barton makes a good show of joviality, but he's secretly allied with the bandits of Raven Roost and sends them word of travelers worth robbing who will be continuing west toward Fallcrest.

## GARDMORE ABBEY

The Gardbury Downs take their name from this striking ruin, a large monastery that has lain in ruins for almost one hundred fifty years. The abbey was dedicated to Bahamut and served as the base of a militant order of paladins who won great fame fighting in Nerath's distant crusades. As the story goes, the paladins brought a dark artifact back from a far crusade for safekeeping, and evil forces gathered to assault the abbey and take it back. Extensive dungeons lie beneath the ruins, which might still conceal the hoarded wealth of the old crusading paladins.

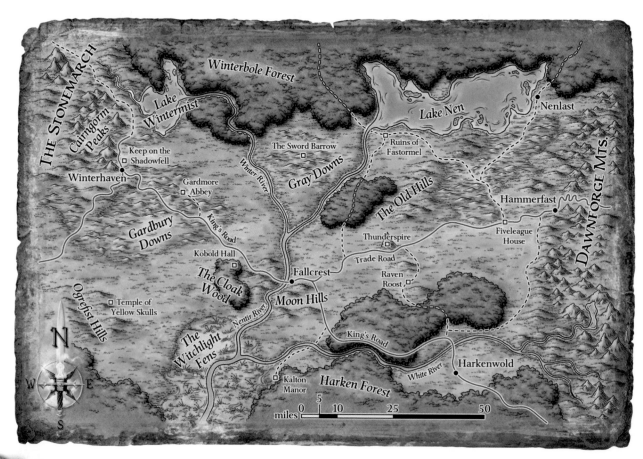

MIKE SCHLEY

# THE SWORD BARROW

This large burial mound stands near the middle of the Gray Downs, a desolate region. The old human hill-clans who lived in the Vale raised the barrow centuries before civilized folk settled in Fallcrest. The hill-folk are long gone, but their grim barrows remain. The Sword Barrow gained its name because scores of rusted blades of ancient design are buried around its edges, blades pointing inward; a visitor can turn up several in a few minutes of looking around. The blades seem completely ordinary, not hinting at the old warding magic that surrounds the place.

# HAMMERFAST

A dwarven hold cut from the rock of a deep vale in the Dawnforge Mountains, Hammerfast is the largest and wealthiest town in the region. The Trade Road runs through the citadel gates and continues eastward beyond the Dawnforge Mountains. Hammerfast is governed by a council of masters, each the leaders of one of the town's powerful guilds. The current High Master is the leader of the merchant guild, a dwarf named Marsinda Goldspinner. The dwarves of Hammerfast look to their own first and don't give away anything for free, but they are honest and industrious.

# HARKEN FOREST

This large woodland stretches from the Nentir River to the mountains and extends for miles to the south. It separates the Nentir Vale from the more populous coastal towns of the south. A strong goblin keep called Daggerburg lies somewhere in the southwest reaches, not too far from Kalton Manor; the goblins sometimes raid the river-traffic moving along the Nentir, or send small parties of marauders to Harkenwold's borders.

An elf tribe known as the Woodsinger Clan roams the eastern portions of the forest. They occasionally trade with the humans of Harkenwold and keep an eye on travelers along the old King's Road. They have a long-standing feud with the Daggerburg goblins, and the goblins keep to the western parts of the forest to avoid swift and deadly elven arrows. However, the goblins are growing more numerous and have become bolder in recent months.

# HARKENWOLD

Half a dozen small villages lie along the upper vales of the White River. Together, they make up the Barony of Harkenwold—a tiny realm whose total population is not much greater than Fallcrest's. The people of Harkenwold are farmers, woodcutters, and woodworkers; little trade comes up or down the old King's Road.

The ruler of Harkenwold is Baron Stockmer, an elderly man who was known for his strong sword arm in his youth. He is a just and compassionate ruler.

# KALTON MANOR

Back in the days when Nerath was settling the Nentir Vale, minor lords in search of land to call their own established manors and holds throughout the area. Kalton Manor was one of these, a small keep raised by Lord Arrol Kalton about two hundred years ago. Lord Arrol intended to settle the lower vale of the White River, but it was not to be—monsters from the Witchlight Fens drove off the tenants Arrol had brought with him. At the end, Arrol and a handful of his servants and family lived alone in a half-finished keep slowly falling into ruin until they disappeared as well. Stories tell of hidden treasure—the old Kalton fortune—hidden in secret chambers beneath the ruined keep.

# KEEP ON THE SHADOWFELL

Long ago, soldiers from Nerath built a strong fortress over the Shadowfell rift to protect it. The old keep lies in ruins now, and a new generation of cultists has secretly taken up residence here. They seek to undo the magical wards sealing the Shadowfell rift and open the way for undead horrors.

The keep is described in detail in the adventure *H1: Keep on the Shadowfell.*

# KOBOLD HALL

Like Kalton Manor, the wreck now known locally as Kobold Hall was the estate of a minor lord who came to Nentir Vale to establish his own demesnes. Ruined during the Bloodspear War, the old castle has been abandoned for almost a century. Kobold tribes from the Cloak Wood now lurk in its depths.

The short adventure at the end of this chapter is set in Kobold Hall.

# NENLAST

This tiny human village lies at the east end of Lake Nen. The folk here make a meager living by trading smoked fish to the dwarves of Hammerfast. They also deal with the Tigerclaw barbarians of the Winterbole Forest. When the wild folk choose to trade, they come to Nenlast to barter their pelts and amber for good dwarven metalwork.

# RAVEN ROOST

This small keep stands at the southern end of the Old Hills. Once it was the seat of a small manor, but it fell into ruin long ago and has recently been taken over by a gang of bandits. The leaders of the bandits are a trio of shadar-kai named Samminel, Erzoun, and Geriesh. They secretly deal with Barton, the proprietor of Fiveleague House, giving him a cut of the take when he tips them off about wealthy travelers on the Trade Road.

# RUINS OF FASTORMEL

Once a prosperous town on the shores of Lake Nen, Fastormel was destroyed by the Bloodspear orcs and has never been resettled. The town was ruled by a Lord Mage (the most powerful wizard in town claimed the ruler's scepter), and the Mistborn Tower of the last Lord Mage still stands amid the ruins of the town. The tower is shrouded in a strange silver mist that never dissipates, no matter what the weather would otherwise dictate.

# THE STONEMARCH

A rugged land of stony hills and deep gorges cut by white-rushing rivers, the Stonemarch is home to tribes of dangerous humanoids and giants. Orcs, ogres, giants, and trolls haunt the farther reaches of these barren lands. Fortunately for the residents of the vale, the monsters rarely come east over the Cairngorm Peaks. A great orc-warren known as the Fanged Jaws of Kulkoszar lies in the northern part of the wasteland; here the chief of the Bloodspear tribe rules over hundreds of the fierce warriors.

# TEMPLE OF YELLOW SKULLS

The ruins of an evil shrine stand in the middle of these desolate hills. Legend tells that a rakshasa prince summoned demons to this place and bound them to his service by imprisoning their vital essences in gold-plated human skulls. None of these have yet been recovered from the ruins, but the story persists. Deep caverns beneath the ruins lead all the way down to the Underdark, and from time to time dangerous monsters of the deep places emerge here and prowl the nearby lands.

# THUNDERSPIRE

This striking peak is the largest of the Old Hills. Beneath Thunderspire lies the ancient minotaur city of Saruun Khel. The minotaur kingdom fell almost a hundred years before Fallcrest was established, when a struggle for succession led to a vicious civil war. In the upper halls of the minotaur city the mysterious order of wizards known as the Mages of Saruun have established a secretive stronghold; merchants passing along the Trade Road sometimes take shelter here.

The labyrinth of Saruun Khel is the setting for adventure *H2: Thunderspire Labyrinth*.

# WINTERHAVEN

Hard under the Cairngorms at the west end of the Nentir Vale lies the remote town of Winterhaven. Like Fallcrest, Winterhaven is a small town surrounded by a few miles of farmland and pastures. Winterhaven serves as the characters' base of operations during the adventure *H1: Keep on the Shadowfell*.

# INVOLVING THE PLAYERS

When you begin a new DUNGEONS & DRAGONS campaign, it's a good idea to encourage the players to create characters grounded in your setting. Before your first game session, ask the players what sort of characters they would like to play. Armed with this information, you can build ties between the characters and the town of Fallcrest. The players will care a lot more about what's going on in and around the town if they see reasons why their characters would care.

If you don't like the ideas offered here, no problem—you're free to make up your own connections for the player characters, or have no connections at all. It's often fun for a player to roleplay being "the outsider."

## RACES

**Dragonborn:** No dragonborn are native to Fallcrest, but travelers occasionally pass through and take up work for a time, especially as bodyguards or caravan guards. The Halfmoon halflings, House Azaer, and the importer Naerumar have work available for a capable adventurer.

**Dwarf:** A fair number of dwarves live in Fallcrest, so a dwarf character could easily be a native of the city—perhaps a relative of Teldorthan Irontooth. If not, the nearest dwarven homeland is Hammerfast, a week's travel distant. Merchants and crafters from Hammerfast travel to Fallcrest to trade or work, lodging in one of the local inns for a few weeks.

**Eladrin:** Eladrin are not often seen in Fallcrest. Some of the old manors in the Moon Hills and the nearby parts of the Vale were once the homes of well-off eladrin families; a player character eladrin might hold the title to an abandoned estate a mile or two out of town, which provides a good reason to call on Lord Markelhay (and earns the enmity of Armos Kamroth, who wants the land for his own).

**Elf:** Elves are also scarce in Fallcrest, but a small number reside in and around the town. Ressilmae Starlight of the temple of Sehanine might be a relative or an old friend of an elf character. Elves from outside Fallcrest might belong to the Woodsinger clan from the Harkenwold Forest.

**Half-Elf:** A small number of half-elves reside in Fallcrest or the vicinity. Most are well-off farmers or herders living in the Moon Hills near the town; the rest are expert artisans—jewelers, tailors, or woodworkers—in the town. A half-elf player character can be the child or relative of a Fallcrest family.

**Halfling:** Halflings are the most numerous people in Fallcrest aside from humans, and they come from any walk of life. A Fallcrest native might be related to the Halfmoon family, the Ostermans of the Silver Unicorn, or the Thistletons of Fallcrest

Stables. Halflings descended from the traders who pass through Fallcrest can be members of the Swiftwater clan.

**Human:** Most of Fallcrest's people are human. Characters with rural backgrounds likely grew up on the farms in the nearby Moon Hills. Characters with an urban upbringing might be the children of well-off landowners such as the Kamroths, or ruffians and sellswords who had a hard childhood in Lowtown.

**Tiefling:** Two tiefling families and a few individuals live and thrive in Fallcrest, including the Azaers and the Naerumars.

# CLASSES

**Cleric:** Since there are temples of Erathis, Pelor, and Sehanine in town, a player character cleric devoted to one of these deities would naturally have allies and colleagues here.

**Fighter:** Fallcrest is a trading town, and merchants need bodyguards or caravan guards when they set out for distant towns. The Halfmoons or House Azaer might employ a fighter. Fighters from better-off families might be retainers in the service of the Markelhays—young "court blades" who are a cut above the typical garrison guard.

**Paladin:** As with clerics, paladins devoted to Erathis, Pelor, or Sehanine have natural allies in the temples of Fallcrest. In addition, paladin characters might also be aspiring knights sworn to the service of the Markelhay family.

**Ranger:** Many of the countryside folk living around Fallcrest are foresters and hunters; a ranger character could easily belong to one of these families. Rangers who aren't natives might hail from the Barony of Harkenwold or the remote village of Nenlast to the northeast.

**Rogue:** Members of groups such as the porters' guild or the River Rats are natural associates of a player character rogue. Capable people are in high demand anywhere, and a rogue might also fit in as an agent of a merchant house such as the Halfmoons or the Azaers.

**Warlock:** The folk of Fallcrest regard warlocks as they do wizards—mysterious figures to be treated cautiously. Well-off merchants or nobles often retain a "house mage" to advise them in magical matters, so a warlock could easily work for the Markelhays, Amros Kamroth, or other wealthy individual.

**Warlord:** Like fighters or paladins, warlords might be attached to the Markelhay household. Those of lower stature can serve as sellswords or agents of merchant companies such as House Azaer.

**Wizard:** A player character wizard might be an apprentice to Nimozaran, of the Septarch's Tower. Lady Markelhay is also a skilled mage and might take a wizard character into her confidence.

The ruined manor now known as Kobold Hall was once a minor lord's proud holding, a walled keep overlooking the old King's Road. That was years ago, and the lord's name and the glories he earned are long forgotten. Today, the place is called Kobold Hall after the malicious humanoids that infest the place. The Cloak Wood has overrun the grounds, with trees growing in the midst of abandoned gardens and courtyards.

Several kobold tribes dwell within the ruins, hiding in the multitude of tunnels, ruins, and cellars found here. The tribes squabble with each other, raid surrounding settlements, and attack caravans on the old King's Road. Lately, the kobolds have become more aggressive. The Skull Kicker tribe has taken over or driven off the rival tribes. Emboldened, the Skull Kickers stole a wagon loaded with valuable cargo from a caravan on the King's Road. As the adventure begins, the characters find themselves in the small town of Fallcrest. Explain to the players that their characters know each other and are looking for adventure.

Use one of the hooks below to set up the backstory for the adventurers, or create your own. You don't need a lot of details; you just need enough to explain why the PCs are together and why they are heading out to investigate Kobold Hall.

If you use one of these hooks, the PCs might also gain experience points for completing a quest. When the party finishes a quest, divide the XP award among all the characters who participated in the quest.

## HOOK: DRAGON HIDE

The player characters are hired by Teldorthan Goldcap, the dwarf armorer. Among the cargo in the stolen wagon was a cured green dragon hide destined for Teldorthan's shop. The dwarf intends to turn the hide into a fine suit of scale armor. Teldorthan hires the adventurers to enter the kobold lair and get back his dragon hide. If they succeed, he gives them 200 gp.

**Alternative:** The PCs hear about the loss of the wagon and the dragon hide and approach Teldorthan to see if there's a reward for its return.

**Quest XP:** 500 XP for recovering the dragon hide and returning it to Teldorthan Goldcap.

## HOOK: KOBOLD BOUNTY

The Lord Warden of Fallcrest has had enough of kobold raids along the old King's Road. If the PCs approach him looking for work, he readily offers them a bounty for clearing out Kobold Hall. The Lord Warden promises a bounty of 10 gp for each dispatched kobold and an additional 100 gp if the PCs bring proof that the ruins have been cleared out, such as the bone mask worn by the kobold leader.

**Alternative:** The Lord Warden specifically seeks out the PCs to ask them to undertake this mission.

**Quest XP:** 750 XP for bringing the wyrmpriest's bone mask to the Lord Warden as proof of the demise of the kobold threat.

## HOOK: TERRIBLE SECRET

Nimozaran the Green, High Septarch of Fallcrest, believes that something more terrible and dangerous is behind the kobold attacks. They seem too organized and too aggressive, compared to other kobolds the old wizard has dealt with in the past. He asks the PCs if they are willing to enter the creatures' lair to discover the secret of Kobold Hall. He offers them the use of his tower's teleportation circle if they accept the quest.

**Alternative:** The PCs approach the old wizard to offer him their services in exchange for his good will and any magical aid he might be willing to offer.

**Quest XP:** 500 XP for bringing back news of the presence of a white dragon in the ruins to Nimozaran.

## PLAYERS' INTRODUCTION

When the PCs decide to explore Kobold Hall, read or paraphrase the following to the players:

*You travel 15 miles from Fallcrest into the wilderness to find the once-sprawling manor now known as the ruins of Kobold Hall. Inside the keep, you find a trapdoor at the base of an old guard tower. It must lead beneath the ruins.*

## DM'S INTRODUCTION

"Kobold Hall" is a simple D&D adventure for five 1st-level player characters. It is short on plot and decision points; it's simply five combat encounters in a row. The adventure is intended to give you something easy to run the first time you try your hand as the Dungeon Master, while allowing the other players at the table to explore their characters' abilities and learn the game.

Try to bring the kobolds and the environment to life. The first encounter is a simple fight, but the next four use interactive environments and traps to show off elements of the D&D game.

Be sure to read each encounter thoroughly before running the adventure, particularly paying attention to the traps and terrain. You should also closely examine the monster statistics blocks. They've got some nasty tricks up their sleeves for the player characters!

## ALTERING TREASURE

As with any published adventure, it is possible that the treasures found here aren't optimal for your party. It's a good idea to replace such items with goods that appeal to the party. The levels of the two items found as treasure in this adventure are given to make it easier to find replacements.

KOBOLD HALL

One square = 5 feet

## Encounter Level 1 (500 XP)

## SETUP

This area serves as a guardroom for the kobolds. A pit filled with sludge provides an obstacle for intruders. When the PCs arrive, they see one kobold. The others stay hidden until the PCs move deeper into the area.

This encounter includes the following creatures.
**2 kobold slingers** (S)
**3 kobold skirmishers** (K)

**As the adventurers enter this chamber, read:**
*Dominating the room ahead is a long trench filled with a glowing green substance. Beyond the trench, a small, reptilian humanoid stands in a shadowy chamber, gaping at you. It carries a sling, and quickly reaches into a pouch at its belt for a stone. It hisses and shouts, "Intrudersss! Intrudersss!"*

| 3 Kobold Skirmishers (K) | Level 1 Skirmisher |
|---|---|
| Small natural humanoid | XP 100 each |

**Initiative** +5 — **Senses** Perception +0; darkvision
**HP** 27; **Bloodied** 13
**AC** 15; **Fortitude** 11, **Reflex** 14, **Will** 13; see also *trap sense*
**Speed** 6
(✦) **Spear** (standard; at-will) ✦ **Weapon**
  +6 vs. AC; 1d8 damage; see also *mob attack*.
**Combat Advantage**
  +1d6 damage on melee attacks and ranged attacks against target the skirmisher has combat advantage against.
**Mob Attack**
  +1 bonus to attack rolls per kobold ally adjacent to the target.
**Shifty** (minor; at-will)
  Shift 1 square as a minor action.
**Trap Sense**
  +2 bonus to all defenses against traps.
**Alignment** Evil — **Languages** Common, Draconic
**Skills** Acrobatics +8, Stealth +10, Thievery +10
**Str** 8 (-1) — **Dex** 16 (+3) — **Wis** 10 (+0)
**Con** 11 (+0) — **Int** 6 (-2) — **Cha** 15 (+2)
**Equipment** hide armor, light shield, spear

## FEATURES OF THE AREA

**Pit:** The pit is 10 feet deep, filled up to 4 feet with a thick, green sludge. Any PC who falls into the pit is immobilized. A DC 13 Strength check allows a PC to break free. The sludge is difficult terrain. Creatures can walk in it, but a creature that ends its move in the sludge is immobilized as described above.

Climbing out of the pit requires a DC 10 Athletics check. A creature that falls in takes 1d10-2 damage, since the sludge provides cushion against a fall.

**Portcullis:** The passage to the east has a portcullis designed to bar larger creatures. Small creatures ignore it, but it stops larger folk. Forcing the portcullis up requires a DC 15 Strength check. The lever to open it is down the hall from the portcullis.

| 2 Kobold Slingers (S) | Level 1 Artillery |
|---|---|
| Small natural humanoid | XP 100 each |

**Initiative** +3 — **Senses** Perception +1; darkvision
**HP** 24; **Bloodied** 12
**AC** 13; **Fortitude** 12, **Reflex** 14, **Will** 12; see also *trap sense*
**Speed** 6
(✦) **Dagger** (standard; at-will) ✦ **Weapon**
  +5 vs. AC; 1d4 + 3 damage.
(✦) **Sling** (standard; at-will) ✦ **Weapon**
  Ranged 10/20; +6 vs. AC; 1d6 + 3 damage; see also *glue shot*.
**Glue Shot** (standard; at-will)
  Ranged 10/20; +6 vs. Reflex; the target is immobilized (save ends).
**Shifty** (minor; at-will)
  Shift 1 square.
**Trap Sense**
  +2 bonus to all defenses against traps.
**Alignment** Evil — **Languages** Common, Draconic
**Skills** Acrobatics +8, Stealth +10, Thievery +10
**Str** 9 (-1) — **Dex** 17 (+3) — **Wis** 12 (+1)
**Con** 12 (+1) — **Int** 9 (-1) — **Cha** 10 (+0)
**Equipment** leather armor, dagger, sling with 20 bullets and 3 glue shot sling bullets (see above)

## TACTICS

The kobold slinger attempts to lure the PCs into the room, where the others hide. The slinger fires at the PCs, while the two skirmishers split up to circle around the pit and attack.

Meanwhile, the kobolds behind the portcullis wait until the PCs are in sight of their position. Once the PCs have moved up, they attack.

The kobolds are alert to area attacks. They never cluster together unless they can gain flanking attacks.

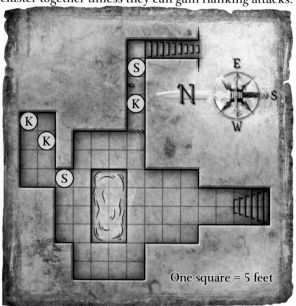

One square = 5 feet

# AREA 2. THE TOMB

## Encounter Level 1 (550 XP)

### SETUP

This chamber was once a tomb. The kobolds use the traps here to defend their lair.

This encounter includes the following creatures and traps.

**3 kobold skirmishers** (K)
**2 dart traps** (1 and 2)

**As the adventurers enter this chamber, read:**
*The room ahead has four stone coffins, all of which show signs of vandalism and abuse. To the left is a series of six niches, set apart into two groups of three. Two more niches along the walls each hold a suit of armor.*

*On the opposite end of the room is a raised section of floor with a makeshift altar to Tiamat set atop it. Three kobolds carrying spears stand in front of the altar.*

| 3 Kobold Skirmishers (K) | Level 1 Skirmisher |
|---|---|
| Small natural humanoid | XP 100 each |
| See page 212. | |

| Dart Trap | Level 1 Blaster |
|---|---|
| Trap | XP 100 |

*Darts fire from the suit of armor, filling the chamber with danger.*

**Trap:** When one of the traps is triggered, a dart flies from the suit of armor's visor.

**Perception**
✦ DC 20: The character notices the firing mechanisms in the .
✦ DC 25: The character notices a trigger stone.

**Trigger**
If a character enters a trigger square or starts its turn in a trigger square, the dart trap attacks.

**Attack**
**Immediate Interrupt   Ranged** 10
**Target:** Character who enters or starts its turn in a trigger square
**Attack:** +8 vs. AC
**Hit:** 1d6 + 2 damage, and target is Immobilized until the end of target's next turn.

**Countermeasures**
✦ An adjacent character can disable a trigger stone with a DC 20 Thievery check.
✦ An adjacent character can disable a firing mechanism with a DC 25 Thievery check.
✦ A suit of armor can be destroyed. Each has AC 12, 30 hp, and resist 5 to all damage.

### TACTICS

The kobolds attempt to use the traps to their advantage. They try to lure characters into chasing them across the room, taking advantage of the fact that creatures of Small size are too light to trigger the trap.

### FEATURES OF THE AREA

**Coffins:** The stone coffins are difficult terrain that provide cover.

**Armor:** These two suits of plate armor stand at attention. When the dart traps activate, their helmet visors swing open to reveal a dart-firing mechanism.

**Trigger Points:** Several squares on the map are marked with the number 1 or 2. The 1s correspond to squares that trigger dart trap 1. The same applies to trap 2. The two suits of armor are likewise marked 1 and 2 to indicate the location of each trap's firing mechanism.

**Altar:** The kobolds have lovingly crafted this crude altar to the evil dragon god. A small bag on the altar holds 60 gp, an offering to Tiamat.

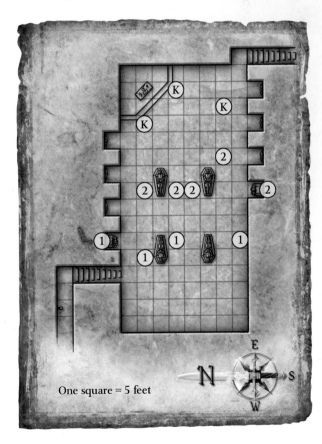

One square = 5 feet

MIKE SCHLEY (2)

**Encounter Level 2 (675 XP)**

## SETUP

This chamber has been turned into an arena for games of skull-skull, the sport of Kobold Hall. The player characters enter the chamber while a game is in progress and find that the game is an exercise in mindless violence, as befits kobolds.

This encounter includes the following creatures.

2 kobold slingers (S)
2 guard drakes (D)
4 kobold minions (M)

**As the adventurers enter this chamber, read:**

*This chamber looks like it was once a tomb, but the kobolds have transformed it into what you might almost call a playground.*

*Four stone coffins lie here, with a sludge-filled pit between them. On the opposite end of the room is a pair of wooden double doors. Flanking the double doors are two raised platforms, both 10 feet above the floor. Two kobolds stand on each platform.*

*Arrayed on the coffins are several animal skulls, all of them arranged in small piles. One kobold holds a sludge-drenched stone tied to a long rope that is secured in the ceiling.*

| **2 Guard Drakes (D)** | | **Level 2 Brute** |
|---|---|---|
| Small natural beast (reptile) | | XP 125 each |

**Initiative** +3     **Senses** Perception +7
**HP** 48; **Bloodied** 24
**AC** 15; **Fortitude** 15, **Reflex** 13, **Will** 12
**Immune** fear (while within 2 squares of an ally)
**Speed** 6
( ) **Bite** (standard; at-will)
    +6 vs. AC; 1d10 + 3 damage, or 1d10 + 9 damage while within 2 squares of an ally.
**Alignment** Unaligned     **Languages** –
**Str** 16 (+4)    **Dex** 15 (+3)    **Wis** 12 (+2)
**Con** 18 (+5)    **Int** 3 (-3)    **Cha** 12 (+2)

| **4 Kobold Minions (M)** | **Level 1 Minion** |
|---|---|
| Small natural humanoid | XP 25 each |

**Initiative** +3     **Senses** Perception +1; darkvision
**HP** 1; a missed attack never damages a minion.
**AC** 15; **Fortitude** 11, **Reflex** 13, **Will** 11; see also *trap sense*
**Speed** 6
( ) **Spear** (standard; at-will) ✦ **Weapon**
    +5 vs. AC; 2 damage.
( ) **Javelin** (standard; at-will) ✦ **Weapon**
    Ranged 10/20; +5 vs. AC; 2 damage.
**Shifty** (minor; at-will)
    Shift 1 square.
**Trap Sense**
    +2 bonus to all defenses against traps.
**Alignment** Evil     **Languages** Common, Draconic
**Skills** Stealth +5, Thievery +5
**Str** 8 (-1)    **Dex** 16 (+3)    **Wis** 12 (+1)
**Con** 12 (+1)    **Int** 9 (-1)    **Cha** 10 (+0)
**Equipment** hide armor, light shield, 3 javelins, 1 spear

| **2 Kobold Slingers (S)** | **Level 1 Artillery** |
|---|---|
| Small natural humanoid | XP 100 each |

**Initiative** +3     **Senses** Perception +1; darkvision
**HP** 24; **Bloodied** 12
**AC** 13; **Fortitude** 12, **Reflex** 14, **Will** 12; see also *trap sense*
**Speed** 6
( ) **Dagger** (standard; at-will) ✦ **Weapon**
    +5 vs. AC; 1d4 + 3 damage.
( ) **Sling** (standard; at-will) ✦ **Weapon**
    Ranged 10/20; +6 vs. AC; 1d6 + 3 damage; see also *glue shot*.
**Glue Shot** (standard; at-will)
    Ranged 10/20; +6 vs. Reflex; the target is immobilized (save ends).
**Shifty** (minor; at-will)
    Shift 1 square.
**Trap Sense**
    The kobold gains a +2 bonus to all defenses against traps.
**Alignment** Evil     **Languages** Common, Draconic
**Skills** Acrobatics +8, Stealth +10, Thievery +10
**Str** 9 (-1)    **Dex** 17 (+3)    **Wis** 12 (+1)
**Con** 12 (+1)    **Int** 9 (-1)    **Cha** 10 (+0)
**Equipment** leather armor, dagger, sling with 20 bullets and 3 rounds of glue shot (see above)

| Skull-Skull Stone | Level 1 Blaster |
|---|---|
| Trap | XP 100 |

*This sludge-covered stone is tied to a long rope that hangs from a hook in the ceiling.*

**Trap:** When a kobold throws the stone, it attacks a target and then returns to the kobold on the opposite platform.

**Trigger**

A kobold uses a standard action to attack with the skull-skull stone. It can be used by two different kobolds in each round.

**Attack**

**Standard Action   Melee**

**Target:** One character in the marked area on the map.

**Attack:** +8 vs. AC

**Hit:** 1d8+2 damage and push 2 squares.

**Countermeasures**

✦ A character in the marked area can ready an action to attack the rope (AC 14, 10 hp, and resist 5 to all damage).

✦ A character can make ranged attacks against the rope.

## TACTICS

The kobolds try to batter the PCs into submission while avoiding melee.

The kobold minions split up, two on each platform. Two take turns activating the skull-skull trap, one throwing a spear on a turn when it isn't activating the trap. The other two minions remain on the stairs, out of sight, ready to replace a fallen comrade and keep the trap operating.

The slingers fire at the PCs, hoping to use their special shots to harass characters and make them easier targets for the rock.

The kobolds' pet guard drakes remain on the other side of the door. They rush up the stairs to attack a PC who climbs up to the platforms. Otherwise, they attack anyone who breaches the door.

## FEATURES OF THE AREA

**Pit:** The pit is 10 feet deep, filled up to a depth of 4 feet with a thick green sludge. The sludge has two important traits.

First, it is sticky. Any character who falls into the pit is immobilized. A DC 13 Strength check allows a PC to break free.

The sludge is difficult terrain. Creatures can walk in it, but a creature that ends its move in the sludge is immobilized as described above.

Climbing out of the pit requires a DC 10 Athletics check. A creature that falls in takes 1d10-2 damage, since the sludge provides cushion against a fall.

**Door:** The door has 20 hit points. Bashing it down requires a DC 16 Strength check.

**Skull-Skull Stone:** This weird device counts as a trap. The kobolds normally swing it down to hit a skull on the coffins below. The object of the game is to get a skull to stick to the rock, and then grab the skull as it comes back to the thrower. When the PCs arrive on the scene, the kobolds are happy to use the rock against them.

**Platforms:** There are no railings for the raised platforms. Climbing the wall up to the platform from the floor requires a DC 15 Athletics check. Scattered on the floor in a small pile in the northern platform are 100 gp in coins, a ruby worth 50 gp, and two garnets worth 25 gp each.

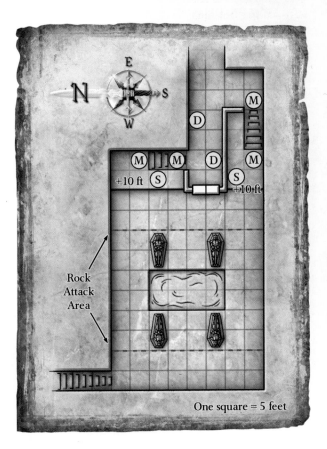

One square = 5 feet

## Encounter Level 4 (850 XP)

## SETUP

The kobold chieftain rules from this chamber. Paranoid at the thought of intruders, the chieftain and his minions erected an elaborate, crushing boulder trap in this room. When the PCs enter, the chieftain activates the boulder and hides in his lair. Meanwhile, kobolds pour forth to attack the PCs.

This encounter includes the following creatures and trap.

> 2 kobold slingers (S)
> 1 kobold wyrmpriest (W)
> 2 kobold dragonshields (K)
> 1 spiretop drake (D)
> 1 rolling boulder (T)

**As the adventurers enter this chamber, read:**
*You arrive at a chamber with a 20-foot-tall ceiling. Before you is a 10-foot tall wall that leaves passages open to both the right and left. Suddenly, the sound of cracking timbers echoes through the hall. The floor shakes, dust cascades down from the ceiling, and something big and heavy hurtles toward you!*

| Kobold Wyrmpriest (W) | Level 3 Artillery (Leader) |
|---|---|
| Small natural humanoid | XP 150 |

**Initiative** +4    **Senses** Perception +4; darkvision
**HP** 36; **Bloodied** 18
**AC** 17; **Fortitude** 13, **Reflex** 15, **Will** 15; see also *trap sense*
**Speed** 6
⚔ **Spear** (standard; at-will) ✦ **Weapon**
  +7 vs. AC; 1d8 damage.
➶ **Energy Orb** (standard; at-will) • see text
  Ranged 10; +6 vs. Reflex; 1d10 + 3 cold damage.
⬟ **Incite Faith** (minor; encounter)
  Close burst 10; kobold allies in the burst gain 5 temporary hit points and shift 1 square.
⬟ **Dragon Breath** (standard; encounter)
  Close blast 3; +6 vs. Fortitude; 1d10 + 3 cold damage. *Miss:* Half damage.
**Shifty** (minor; at-will)
  Shift 1 square.
**Trap Sense**
  +2 bonus to all defenses against traps.
**Alignment** Evil    **Languages** Common, Draconic
**Skills** Stealth +11, Thievery +11
| **Str** 9 (+0) | **Dex** 16 (+4) | **Wis** 17 (+4) |
| **Con** 12 (+2) | **Int** 9 (+0) | **Cha** 12 (+2) |

**Equipment** hide armor, spear, bone mask, *+1 staff of the war mage*

| 2 Kobold Dragonshields (K) | Level 2 Soldier |
|---|---|
| Small natural humanoid | XP 125 each |

**Initiative** +4    **Senses** Perception +2; darkvision
**HP** 30; **Bloodied** 15
**AC** 18; **Fortitude** 14, **Reflex** 13, **Will** 13; see also *trap sense*
**Resist** 5 cold
**Speed** 6
⚔ **Short Sword** (standard; at-will) ✦ **Weapon**
  +7 vs. AC; 1d6 + 3 damage, and the target is marked until the end of the kobold dragonshield's next turn.
**Dragonshield Tactics** (immediate reaction, when an adjacent enemy shifts away or an enemy moves adjacent; at-will)
  The kobold dragonshield shifts 1 square.
**Mob Attack**
  The kobold dragonshield gains a +1 bonus to attack rolls per kobold ally adjacent to the target.
**Shifty** (minor; at-will)
  Shift 1 square.
**Trap Sense**
  +2 bonus to all defenses against traps.
**Alignment** Evil    **Languages** Common, Draconic
**Skills** Acrobatics +7, Stealth +9, Thievery +9
| **Str** 14 (+3) | **Dex** 13 (+2) | **Wis** 12 (+2) |
| **Con** 12 (+2) | **Int** 9 (+0) | **Cha** 10 (+1) |

**Equipment** scale armor, heavy shield, short sword

| Spiretop Drake (D) | Level 1 Skirmisher |
|---|---|
| Small natural beast (reptile) | XP 100 |

**Initiative** +6    **Senses** Perception +3
**HP** 29; **Bloodied** 14
**AC** 16; **Fortitude** 11, **Reflex** 14, **Will** 13
**Speed** 4, fly 8 (hover); see also *flyby attack*
⚔ **Bite** (standard; at-will)
  +6 vs. AC; 1d6 + 4 damage.
⚔ **Snatch** (standard; at-will)
  +4 vs. Reflex; 1 damage, and the spiretop drake steals a small object from the target, such as a vial, scroll, or coin.
⬧ **Flyby Attack** (standard; at-will)
  The spiretop drake flies up to 8 squares and makes one melee basic attack at any point during that movement. The drake doesn't provoke opportunity attacks when moving away from the target of the attack.
**Alignment** Unaligned    **Languages** –
| **Str** 11 (+0) | **Dex** 18 (+4) | **Wis** 16 (+3) |
| **Con** 13 (+1) | **Int** 3 (-4) | **Cha** 11 (+0) |

| 2 Kobold Slingers (S) | Level 1 Artillery |
|---|---|
| Small natural humanoid | XP 100 each |

**Initiative** +3     **Senses** Perception +1; darkvision
**HP** 24; **Bloodied** 12
**AC** 13; **Fortitude** 12, **Reflex** 14, **Will** 12; see also *trap sense*
**Speed** 6

⚔ **Dagger** (standard; at-will) ✦ **Weapon**
    +5 vs. AC; 1d4 + 3 damage.
⤢ **Sling** (standard; at-will) ✦ **Weapon**
    Ranged 10/20; +6 vs. AC; 1d6 + 3 damage; see also *glue shot*.
**Glue Shot** (standard; at-will)
    Ranged 10/20; +6 vs. Reflex; the target is immobilized (save ends).
**Shifty** (minor; at-will)
    Shift 1 square.
**Trap Sense**
    +2 bonus to all defenses against traps.

**Alignment** Evil     **Languages** Common, Draconic
**Skills** Acrobatics +8, Stealth +10, Thievery +10

| **Str** 9 (-1) | **Dex** 17 (+3) | **Wis** 12 (+1) |
|---|---|---|
| **Con** 12 (+1) | **Int** 9 (-1) | **Cha** 10 (+0) |

**Equipment** leather armor, dagger, sling with 20 bullets and 3 glue shot sling bullets (see above)

| Rolling Boulder | Level 3 Blaster |
|---|---|
| Trap | XP 150 |

*A giant boulder rolls through the chamber.*

**Trap:** The boulder rolls over everything in its path.
**Perception**
✦ DC 10: The character notices the approaching boulder.
**Initiative** +5     **Speed** 8
**Trigger**
    As soon as the encounter begins, the trap rolls initiative.
**Attack**
**Opportunity Action**     Melee
**Target:** Attacks any character in a space it enters
**Attack:** +7 vs. Reflex
**Hit:** 2d6 damage and knock prone.
**Special:** If the boulder ends its turn in a space with a character, it makes a second attack. The character then moves to any open adjacent space (character's choice).
**Countermeasure**
    ✦ A character can attempts a DC 20 Athletics check as an immediate reaction to leap over the rolling boulder.

## Tactics

The kobolds prefer to let their boulder crush the PCs. They keep to the sides of the chamber, firing at the characters. The slingers climb ladders in the interior chamber to stand atop the interior walls and fire.

The chieftain (the wyrmpriest) and the two dragonshields remain on the platform. If a PC comes close to the platform, the dragonshields rush forward to attack. The chieftain uses his *+1 staff of the war mage* to increase the area of his dragon breath attack.

The spiretop drake is the chieftain's pet. It darts out to peck at the characters. If it can steal a potion from a PC, it does so and brings the trinket to its master.

## Features of the Area

**Central Room:** The wall here is 10 feet tall, and the ceiling in this chamber is 20 feet above the floor. PCs and kobolds can climb over the wall to reach the central chamber. Climbing requires a DC 10 Athletics check.

The wall is wide enough to allow a creature to stand on top of it.

**Door:** The door to the central room has 20 hit points. Bashing it down requires a DC 16 Strength check.

**Boulder:** Full stats for the trap are given above. It starts at the point marked on the map and follows the path.

**Platform:** There are no railings on the raised platforms. Climbing up the side of the platform requires a DC 15 Athletics check. The platform is 10 feet up.

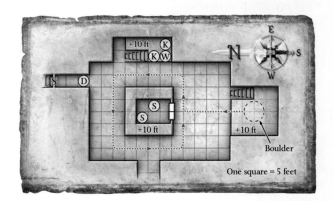

One square = 5 feet

## Ending the Encounter

When the characters defeat the kobolds, they find a small silver key in the chief's belt pouch, along with a piece of parchment that describes the location of a secret door in the alcove to the north. The key opens the door, revealing a secret set of stairs leading down to the final encounter area.

The kobold chieftain carries a *+1 staff of the war mage* (level 3 item).

**+1 Staff of the War Mage:** This staff provides its user with a +1 enhancement bonus to attack rolls and damage rolls. On a critical hit, it deals an extra 1d8 + 1 damage. In addition, once per day as a free action, the user can increase the size of a blast or a burst by 1.

## Encounter Level 3 (750 XP)

## SETUP

This chamber is the lair of the young white dragon Szartharrax. Although he is still small by the standards of his kind, Szartharrax is far and away the most dangerous monster in Kobold Hall. He is the reason the Skull Kickers managed to assert themselves over the other kobold gangs in the area; Szartharrax decided to back them and ate the rival chieftains, which persuaded the rest of the scaly little monsters to swear allegiance to the Skull Kickers. Szartharrax has an appetite for gold, and the white dragon has been demanding tribute from his loyal servants. Fear of the dragon's anger is driving the kobolds to attack caravans and launch raids against the nearby settlements.

Szartharrax is a tough opponent; the adventurers will have to fight well to survive.

This encounter includes the following creature.

**1 young white dragon** (D)

**As the adventurers enter this chamber, read:**
*You follow a long, winding passage from the kobold chieftain's throne room down and down into the earth. Eventually, the finely worked stone tunnels give way to natural passages. Finally, you come upon a large cavern. The air is unnaturally cold in here. In the center of the room is a large pool of frozen dark water. The cavern is quiet.*

## TACTICS

The dragon begins the encounter hiding in the area marked on the map. Since he is hidden behind the large pillar, make a Stealth check for the dragon, and then have the players make Perception checks for their characters. Player characters whose Perception checks are lower than the dragon's Stealth check are surprised. Roll initiative and begin the combat.

The dragon starts by flying to a spot just in front of the party and using his icy breath against as many player characters as he can catch in the area at one time. He then immediately spends 1 action point to use his Frightful Presence ability. In subsequent

| Young White Dragon (D) | Level 3 Solo Brute |
|---|---|
| Large natural magical beast (dragon) | XP 750 |

**Initiative** +1      **Senses** Perception +7; darkvision
**HP** 232; **Bloodied** 116; see also *bloodied breath*
**AC** 18; **Fortitude** 20, **Reflex** 18, **Will** 17
**Resist** 15 cold
**Saving Throws** +5
**Speed** 6 (ice walk), fly 6 (hover), overland flight 10
**Action Points** 2

⊕ **Bite** (standard; at-will) ✦ **Cold**
     Reach 2; +6 vs. AC; 1d8 + 4 plus 1d6 cold damage (plus an extra 1d6 cold damage on a successful opportunity attack).

⊕ **Claw** (standard; at-will)
     Reach 2; +6 vs. AC; 1d8 + 4 damage.

† **Dragon's Fury** (standard; at-will)
     The dragon makes two claw attacks. If the dragon hits a single target with both claws, it makes a bite attack against the same target.

↢ **Breath Weapon** (standard; recharge ⚄⚅) ✦ **Cold**
     Close blast 5; +4 vs. Reflex; 3d6 + 4 cold damage, and the target is slowed and weakened (save ends both).

↢ **Bloodied Breath** (free, when first bloodied; encounter) ✦ **Cold**
     The dragon's breath weapon recharges, and the dragon uses it immediately.

↢ **Frightful Presence** (standard; encounter) ✦ **Fear**
     Close burst 5; targets enemies; +4 vs. Will; the target is stunned until the end of the dragon's next turn. *Aftereffect:* The target takes a -2 penalty to attack rolls (save ends).

**Alignment** Evil      **Languages** Draconic
**Skills** Athletics +15
**Str** 18 (+5)      **Dex** 10 (+1)      **Wis** 12 (+2)
**Con** 18 (+5)      **Int** 10 (+1)      **Cha** 8 (+0)

rounds, the dragon tears the adventurers apart with his Dragon's Fury attack. If Szartharrax gets the chance to make any opportunity attacks, he uses his bite instead.

Szartharrax avoids heavily armored characters, preferring instead to pick off lightly armored foes. If the dragon becomes bloodied, he goes into a rage. He attacks the nearest PC, ignoring any intelligent tactics in favor of brute force.

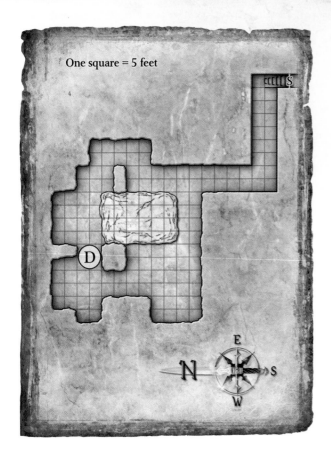

One square = 5 feet

## FEATURES OF THE AREA

**Pool:** The pool of water is 2 feet deep and frozen solid. The ice is difficult terrain, but the dragon ignores it if it walks through it (thanks to its ice walk ability).

## CONCLUSION

If the PCs manage to slay the dragon, they find a small cave up ahead that has a locked treasure chest (DC 20 Thievery check to open). The chest contains the piece of dragon hide that Teldorthan wanted recovered, 100 gold pieces, a pearl worth 20 gp in a small felt bag, and a *+1 lifedrinker longsword* (level 5 item).

**+1 Lifedrinker Longsword:** This longsword provides its user with a +1 enhancement bonus to attack rolls and damage rolls. On a critical hit, it deals an extra 1d6 necrotic damage. In addition, when the user drops an enemy to 0 hit points with a melee attack with this weapon, the user gains 5 temporary hit points.

## FURTHER ADVENTURES

The party slew the dragon and defeated the kobolds, but the PCs have only just begun their adventuring careers.

Slaying a dragon is no easy feat, and Szartharrax might have powerful allies who want revenge. Perhaps his mother or sibling hunts down the characters and their friends.

This adventure might also point to bigger things. The characters find a letter in Szartharrax's treasure chest. Written in Draconic, it is an offer of alliance from a goblin warlord who wishes to unite the monsters in the area against the people of Fallcrest. If you plan to run the *H1: Keep on the Shadowfell* adventure, that goblin could be Irontooth. The letter sends the PCs off on their next adventure.

Finally, there is nothing like a good, old-fashioned dungeon crawl. Having defeated the kobolds, the characters can explore Szartharrax's caves to uncover auxiliary passages leading deeper into the earth. Use the random dungeon generator or create an adventure of your own that involves the rest of the dragon's minions. Perhaps a kobold cleric and his undead minions uncovered a shrine to Tiamat, and Szartharrax needed Teldorthan's hide to finish a terrible rite to the dragon god. Using the encounters in this chapter as a guide, there's no better time than now to start creating your own adventures. Recruit some vicious monsters, draw some encounter maps, create a story to lead the PCs to the adventure, and keep playing!

MIKE SCHLEY

## PC COMBAT CARD

Init Result

Character Name

### Start of Turn: Apply Ongoing Damage

| Condition/End state | Condition/End state |
| --- | --- |
| Condition/End state | Condition/End state |
| Condition/End state | Condition/End state |
| Condition/End state | Condition/End state |

Second Wind used: ☐    Action Points used: ☐☐☐    Bloodied: ☐

Healing Surges used: ☐☐☐☐☐  ☐☐☐☐☐  ☐☐☐☐☐

Damage Taken

### End of Turn: Attempt Saving Throws, End Duration Effects

Notes

Conditions: Asleep, Blinded, Dazed, Deafened, Dominated, Dying, Helpless, Immobilized, Marked (put marking creature's name in parens), Ongoing damage, Petrified, Prone, Restrained, Slowed, Stunned, Surprised, Unconscious, Weakened.
End State Abbreviations: EoT = end of turn; SoT = start of turn; Sv = until saving throw; EoE = end of encounter. Indicate whose turn; for example "Dazed/Tordek EoT." Cross out the condition when it ends.

© 2008 Wizards

---

## MONSTER COMBAT CARD

Init Result

Monster Name

### Start of Turn: Check for Recharge, Apply Ongoing Damage

| Condition/End state | Condition/End state |
| --- | --- |
| Condition/End state | Condition/End state |
| Condition/End state | Condition/End state |
| Condition/End state | Condition/End state |

daily/encounter power used: ☐☐☐

daily/encounter power used: ☐☐☐    daily/encounter power used: ☐☐☐

Action points used (if elite or solo): ☐    Bloodied: ☐

Damage Taken

### End of Turn: Attempt Saving Throws, End Duration Effects

Notes

Conditions: Asleep, Blinded, Dazed, Deafened, Dominated, Dying, Helpless, Immobilized, Marked (put marking creature's name in parens), Ongoing damage, Petrified, Prone, Restrained, Slowed, Stunned, Surprised, Unconscious, Weakened.
End State Abbreviations: EoT = end of turn; SoT = start of turn; Sv = until saving throw; EoE = end of encounter. Indicate whose turn; for example "Dazed/Tordek EoT." Cross out the condition when it ends.

© 2008 Wizards

---

## PC COMBAT CARD

Init Result

Character Name

### Start of Turn: Apply Ongoing Damage

| Condition/End state | Condition/End state |
| --- | --- |
| Condition/End state | Condition/End state |
| Condition/End state | Condition/End state |
| Condition/End state | Condition/End state |

Second Wind used: ☐    Action Points used: ☐☐☐    Bloodied: ☐

Healing Surges used: ☐☐☐☐☐  ☐☐☐☐☐  ☐☐☐☐☐

Damage Taken

### End of Turn: Attempt Saving Throws, End Duration Effects

Notes

Conditions: Asleep, Blinded, Dazed, Deafened, Dominated, Dying, Helpless, Immobilized, Marked (put marking creature's name in parens), Ongoing damage, Petrified, Prone, Restrained, Slowed, Stunned, Surprised, Unconscious, Weakened.
End State Abbreviations: EoT = end of turn; SoT = start of turn; Sv = until saving throw; EoE = end of encounter. Indicate whose turn; for example "Dazed/Tordek EoT." Cross out the condition when it ends.

© 2008 Wizards

---

## MONSTER COMBAT CARD

Init Result

Monster Name

### Start of Turn: Check for Recharge, Apply Ongoing Damage

| Condition/End state | Condition/End state |
| --- | --- |
| Condition/End state | Condition/End state |
| Condition/End state | Condition/End state |
| Condition/End state | Condition/End state |

daily/encounter power used: ☐☐☐

daily/encounter power used: ☐☐☐    daily/encounter power used: ☐☐☐

Action points used (if elite or solo): ☐    Bloodied: ☐

Damage Taken

### End of Turn: Attempt Saving Throws, End Duration Effects

Notes

Conditions: Asleep, Blinded, Dazed, Deafened, Dominated, Dying, Helpless, Immobilized, Marked (put marking creature's name in parens), Ongoing damage, Petrified, Prone, Restrained, Slowed, Stunned, Surprised, Unconscious, Weakened.
End State Abbreviations: EoT = end of turn; SoT = start of turn; Sv = until saving throw; EoE = end of encounter. Indicate whose turn; for example "Dazed/Tordek EoT." Cross out the condition when it ends.

© 2008 Wizards

# INDEX